# BEFORE ENVIRONMENTAL LAW

This open access book unveils the history of defending Australia's natural environment and examines the subject's legal and political contexts from the birth of the nation in 1901 until the advent of the so-called modern era of environmental regulation in the late 1960s. Across nature conservation, pollution control, natural resources governance and other domains, this book reveals how many of today's environmental laws emerged from precedents or events much earlier in the 20th century.

The history is told through analysis of lawmakers' far greater efficacy to exploit rather than protect the environment, a discrepancy that grew as nature's backlash intensified in a rapidly degrading continent colonised to build the Australian nation. In exploring these dynamics, the book offers a rich tapestry of case studies illustrated with historic photographs that show the origins of Australia's environmental laws and how they borrowed from international precedents or furnished lessons for other nations to consider.

Through its multi-disciplinary enquiry, the book offers scholars and students of environmental law, legal history and the environmental humanities a unique story about the failures and successes in the making of environmental law.

# Before Environmental Law

## *A History of a Vanishing Continent*

Benjamin J Richardson

•HART•
OXFORD • LONDON • NEW YORK • NEW DELHI • SYDNEY

HART PUBLISHING

Bloomsbury Publishing Plc

Kemp House, Chawley Park, Cumnor Hill, Oxford, OX2 9PH, UK

1385 Broadway, New York, NY 10018, USA

Bloomsbury Publishing Ireland Limited, 29 Earlsfort Terrace, Dublin 2, D02 AY28, Ireland

HART PUBLISHING, the Hart/Stag logo, BLOOMSBURY and the Diana logo are trademarks of Bloomsbury Publishing Plc

First published in Great Britain 2023



A catalogue record for this book is available from the British Library.

A catalogue record for this book is available from the Library of Congress.

Library of Congress Control Number: 2023938423

ISBN: HB: 978-1-50996-902-9
ePDF: 978-1-50996-904-3
ePub: 978-1-50996-903-6

Typeset by Compuscript Ltd, Shannon

For product safety related questions contact productsafety@bloomsbury.com

To find out more about our authors and books visit www.hartpublishing.co.uk. Here you will find extracts, author information, details of forthcoming events and the option to sign up for our newsletters.

*For my mother, Margaret, a child of Orchardfield,*
*and to Vanisha, my samesie*

# ACKNOWLEDGEMENTS

Like many history books, *Before Environmental Law* had a long history of its own. It began decades ago when I enquired about my mother's ancestral farm, Orchardfield, established by her great grandfather Franklin Jackes in the 1860s near Armidale. My mother died before I could document all its environmental history but fortunately, I was assisted by my maternal uncle and aunt, Edward and Mary Jackes. Thank you also to cousin Warrick for some of the vintage photographs. Orchardfield inspired my larger journey to understand the environmental upheavals unleashed by the colonisation of the Australian continent and the failures or successes to govern them.

For the scholarly stage of this project, I'm indebted to a number of kind friends and academic colleagues in Australia and abroad. To Dr Vanisha Sukdeo, many thanks for your patience and perspicacious feedback on some of my ideas, and being a great role model in your own prodigious scholarly writing. Maria Riedl, a tenacious environmental activist, was a wonderful conveyor of environmental literature from her huge personal library. Dr Lisa-ann Gershwin, a world-famous jellyfish scientist, was a source of ebullient counsel, and an inspiration in her own prolific book authoring. Others who intellectually, spiritually or emotionally nourished my journey at various stages include Austra Maddox, Iona Flett, Paul Costin, Tabatha Badger, Liz Downes, Gary Burke, Claire Burgess, Neil Davidson and Ellen Lund Jensen. And Tui deserves a pat in appreciation of his patience. I'm also very grateful to my academic colleagues and friends closest to the book's subject, including Professor Afshin Akhtar-Khavari, Dr Phil McCormack, Dr Anja Hilkemeijer, and Dr Susan Bartie. From them I gained deeper insights into legal history and some of the subject's niches, although I remain accountable for any deficiencies in the text.

I'm fortunate that excellent museums and libraries were available to assist my research, especially Australia's National Library and National Archives, from where I sourced many of the book's photographs and newspaper archives. I also benefitted from the excellent advice of the anonymous peer reviewers of my draft manuscript. Finally, I'm thankful to the editorial staff of Hart Publishing for preparing the publication with scrupulous care and courtesy.

# TABLE OF CONTENTS

*Acknowledgements* ........ *vii*
*List of Abbreviations and Acronyms* ........ *xiii*
*List of Figures* ........ *xv*

PART I
GOVERNING 1901 TO 1967

**1. Young Nation, Ancient Continent ........ 3**
I. Coloniality and the Environment ........ 3
II. Tendrils of Governance ........ 7
III. 1901 to 1967 ........ 17
IV. Orchardfield: Fragment of a Vanishing Continent ........ 20
V. The Big Picture ........ 28
VI. The Book's Synopsis and Sources ........ 32

**2. 1901: Nature for Nation ........ 35**
I. Governing a Federation ........ 35
II. The States ........ 43
III. The Penumbra of English Law ........ 47
IV. Curating Nationalism ........ 50
V. Celebrating Nature ........ 57

**3. 1967: Nature for Nature ........ 64**
I. Protesting for Better Environmental Laws ........ 64
II. The City: Kelly's Bush ........ 68
III. Hydropower: Lake Pedder ........ 71
IV. Mining: Colong Caves ........ 74
V. Agriculture: Little Desert ........ 76
VI. Mining: Great Barrier Reef ........ 79
VII. Recognising Aboriginal People ........ 81

PART II
TRANSFORMING A CONTINENT

**4. Taming the Bush ........ 89**
I. Remaking the Land ........ 89
II. Property Tenure ........ 93

III. Bush Settlement Schemes ....98
IV. Land Clearing ....103
V. Nature Bites Back ....107

**5. Prickly Pears to Toxic Toads ....112**
I. Invasive Species ....112
II. Prickly Pear ....116
III. Cane Toads ....120
IV. Rabbits ....125
V. Vermin Wars ....129
VI. Science, Law and Nature's Backlash ....133

**6. Engineered Landscapes ....136**
I. Environmental Engineering Mania ....136
II. Planning the Snowy Mountains Scheme ....141
III. Environmental Issues in the Snowy Mountains Scheme ....143
IV. Powering the Tasmanian Economy ....149

**7. Testing Times Over the Outback ....155**
I. The Outback ....155
II. Bombs Away ....159
III. Safety and Environmental Issues ....164
IV. The Clean-up ....168
V. Aftermath ....170

PART III
DEFENDING A CONTINENT

**8. The Furry and Feathered ....175**
I. Valuing Wildlife ....175
II. Nature Museums, Zoos and Gardens ....177
III. Tentative Law Reforms ....182
IV. The Commonwealth Gets Involved ....186
V. Wildlife Conservation: From the Exception to the Ordinary ....189
VI. The Long and Short Arm of the Law ....192
VII. Threatened Fauna: Translocation and Acclimatisation ....194

**9. Scenic and Primitive Areas ....197**
I. Wilderness ....197
II. National Parks ....201
III. Saving the Blue Gum Forest ....207
IV. Logging Tasmania's Mount Field ....211
V. Perth's Kings Park ....214
VI. Reflections ....217

**10. Town Planning and the Bush Capital** .......... **219**
I. Modernist Planning .......... 219
II. Post-War Planning Shifts .......... 224
III. Siting the National Capital .......... 229
IV. Designing Canberra .......... 231
V. Building Canberra .......... 234
VI. Greening Canberra .......... 239
VII. The Griffins' Final Ventures and Legacies .......... 243

**11. Resource Users and Polluters** .......... **246**
I. Forestry Governance .......... 246
II. Soil Conservation .......... 254
III. Mining Regulation .......... 260
IV. Pollution Control .......... 266

**12. Looking South: Icy Lands and Stormy Seas** .......... **273**
I. Australia's Final Frontier .......... 273
II. Rise and Fall of Whaling .......... 276
III. Scramble for Antarctica .......... 278
IV. Antarctic Treaty .......... 281
V. Australia in Antarctica: Governance at a Distance .......... 284
VI. Environmental Governance in Antarctica .......... 287
VII. Australia's Subantarctic Islands .......... 291

PART IV
THE FUTURE'S PAST

**13. Restoring a Continent** .......... **297**
I. A New Agenda .......... 297
II. Orchardfield and the Vanishing Continent: Epilogue .......... 300
III. Environmental Restoration .......... 305
IV. Existing and Proposed Restorations .......... 308
V. Revisiting the 'Before' Environmental Law Mythology .......... 314

*Index* .......... *317*

# LIST OF ABBREVIATIONS AND ACRONYMS

| | |
|---|---|
| AAPA | Australian Aboriginal Progressive Association |
| AAD | Australian Antarctic Division |
| AAT | Australian Antarctic Territory |
| ACF | Australian Conservation Foundation |
| ACT | Australian Capital Territory |
| AGM | Annual general meeting |
| ALP | Australian Labor Party |
| AOFGS | Australian Organic Farming and Gardening Society |
| APCMA | Associated Portland Cement Manufacturers Australia |
| AWTSC | Atomic Weapons Tests Safety Committee |
| BANZARE | British Australian and New Zealand Antarctic Expedition |
| BLF | Builders Labourers Federation |
| BSES | Bureau of Sugar Experiment Stations |
| CPPB | Commonwealth Prickly Pear Board |
| CSIR | Council for Scientific and Industrial Research |
| CSIRO | Commonwealth Scientific and Industrial Research Organisation |
| CSR | Corporate social responsibility |
| EEZ | Exclusive Economic Zone |
| HEC | Hydro-Electric Commission (Tasmania) |
| IGY | International Geophysical Year |
| IUCN | International Union for Conservation of Nature |
| IWC | International Whaling Commission |

| | |
|---|---|
| NSW | New South Wales |
| SCAR | Scientific Committee on Antarctic Research |
| SMS | Snowy Mountains Scheme |
| UK | United Kingdom |
| UNESCO | United Nations Educational, Scientific and Cultural Organization |
| UNLCOS | United Nations Convention on the Law of the Sea |
| US | United States of America |

# LIST OF FIGURES


Figure 1.1 Antinomies of Australian environmental governance ........ 8

Figure 1.2 Lyre-bird stamp, 1932, a species the Commonwealth helped protect by banning international trade in its plumage; Australia Post ........ 18

Figure 1.3 Franklin Jackes (1830–84); author's family collection ........ 21

Figure 1.4 Spraying a cherry orchard, Orchardfield, 1947; author's family collection, and NSW State Archives and Library ........ 23

Figure 1.5 Pet kangaroo and my mother and her brother at Orchardfield, 1941; author's family collection ........ 24

Figure 1.6 Kangaroo mascot with Australian diggers, World War I: Australian War Memorial ........ 30

Figure 2.1 Opening of First Parliament of the Commonwealth of Australia, 9 May 1901, oil on canvas, Tom Roberts, 1901–03; National Library of Australia ........ 37

Figure 2.2 Commonwealth coat of arms; Melbourne Museum; photograph by author ........ 51

Figure 2.3 Wattle Day celebrations, South Australia, 1914; State Library of South Australia ........ 53

Figure 2.4 Australian animal furs at the British Empire Exhibition 1924; State Library of Queensland ........ 55

Figure 3.1 Sign at Kelly's Bush introducing bushwalkers to its history, 2022; photograph by author ........ 69

Figure 3.2 Lake Pedder and environs, c. 1971; photograph by Stefan Karpiniec; CC BY 2.0 licence ........ 73

Figure 3.3 Clearing mallee, Murrayville district, 1925; National Library of Australia ........ 77

Figure 3.4 Australian Aboriginal Progressive Association logo, 1924 ........ 83

Figure 4.1 Edwin James Brady, c. 1909, a leading advocate of settling Australia's interior; National Library of Australia ........ 91

Figure 4.2 Victorian Government poster promoting soldier settlement, 1920s; Public Record Office Victoria ....101

Figure 4.3 Youth taught how to ring-bark a tree, Riverview, Queensland, 1927; National Archives of Australia ....104

Figure 4.4 Receding river with dead livestock, Woolamit, Queensland, 1900; State Library of Queensland ....109

Figure 5.1 Caring for Orchardfield's English-style gardens, 1935; author's family collection ....115

Figure 5.2 Four men standing on a road between prickly pears, NSW, 1930s; National Library of Australia ....118

Figure 5.3 My brother inspecting a cane toad, Northern Territory, 2005; author's family collection ....121

Figure 5.4 Snake hunt on the Murray River, early 1900s; National Library of Australia ....130

Figure 5.5 Vermin inspectors, Hopetoun, Victoria, 1917; State Library Victoria ....131

Figure 6.1 Engineer John JC Bradfield, 1934; National Library of Australia ....138

Figure 6.2 Governor-General William McKell pushes the button to denote the first blast of dynamite, Snowy Mountains Scheme, 1949; National Archives of Australia ....142

Figure 6.3 Tasmanian Hydro-Electric Commission, advertisement, 1932; University of Tasmania ....150

Figure 6.4 Turbines of Waddamana power station, 2021; photograph by author ....151

Figure 7.1 Hans Heysen working in his garden, 1954; State Library of South Australia ....157

Figure 7.2 Desert rat-kangaroos; lithograph by Henry Richter and John Gould, 1845; Australian Museum ....158

Figure 7.3 Operation Hurricane, first nuclear bomb test in Australia, at Monte Bello Islands, 3 October 1952; Australian War Memorial ....160

Figure 8.1 Joyce Allan arranging bugs for the Australian Museum, 1933; National Library of Australia ....179

Figure 8.2 Entrance to Hobart's former Beaumaris zoo, 2021, photograph by author ....181

Figure 8.3 3,600 koala skins, Claremont, Queensland, 1927; State Library of Queensland ....188

Figure 9.1 Mystery bush hike organised by railway service, 1932; Powerhouse Museum ....199

Figure 9.2 Cradle Mountain, Lake Lilla, Gustav Weindorfer and his dog, 1922; National Library of Australia ....205

Figure 9.3 'In the Valley of the Grose', oil on canvas, William Piguenit 1880; State Library of NSW ....208

Figure 9.4 Blue Gum Forest, 1952, photograph by Max Dupain; State Library of NSW ....209

Figure 9.5 War Memorial, Kings Park, Perth, 1930; National Library of Australia ....215

Figure 10.1 Slums, Ultimo (Sydney), 1933; State Library of NSW ....222

Figure 10.2 Empress Towers, eye-sore erected in 1967 in historic Battery Point, Hobart; photograph by author ....227

Figure 10.3 Walter Burley Griffin's Plan of Canberra as finally revised and accepted, 1913, National Library of Australia ....235

Figure 10.4 Walter Burley Griffin and Marion Mahony Griffin, Castlecrag, 27 July 1930; National Library of Australia ....238

Figure 10.5 Planting trees near the first Parliament House, late 1920s; National Archives of Australia ....241

Figure 11.1 Parade passing big fig tree in Abbott Street, Cairns, which Dr Hugo Flecker sought to save, 1940s, Cairns Libraries and State Library of Queensland ....249

Figure 11.2 Edward HF Swain, 1902; State Library of Queensland ....251

Figure 11.3 Broken Hill dust storm, c. 1907; State Library of South Australia .... 255

Figure 11.4 Scarred landscape of Mt Lyell mine; Tasmania; 2022; photograph by author ....261

Figure 11.5 Smoke from New Farm Power House, 1952; State Library of Queensland ....267

Figure 12.1 Whale skeleton, Albany Whaling Station, Western Australia, 2022 photograph by author ....277

Figure 12.2 Antarctica and Australia's territory, Commonwealth Department of the Interior, 1939; National Library of Australia ....280

Figure 12.3 British Australian and New Zealand Antarctic Expedition (BANZARE) 1929–31, Proclamation ceremony on Proclamation Island: photographer Frank Hurley; National Archives of Australia ........ 286

Figure 12.4 Australian Antarctic Territory stamp, 1959; Australia Post ........ 286

Figure 12.5 World's subantarctic islands; Australian Antarctic Data Centre ........ 292

Figure 13.1 Environmental protest calling for radical change, Hobart, Tasmania, October 2020; photo by author ........ 299

Figure 13.2 Orchardfield environs in 1943; already extensively cleared, and showing location of Armidale airport today; photograph from author's family archives ........ 301

Figure 13.3 Artworks serving as bird nest sites, Tasmanian Midlands project, 2021; photograph by author ........ 311

# PART I

# Governing 1901 to 1967

# 1

# Young Nation, Ancient Continent

## I. Coloniality and the Environment

Concern for the environment isn't recent. Yet, conventional wisdom suggests environmental law dates from the late 1960s, give or take a few years, and that its forerunners were insignificant. A leading Australian textbook on the subject opens: 'the development of environmental law in Australia has been concentrated effectively into the last 50 years'.[1] Another declares, 'Most of what we would today identify as environmental law … had its origins in legislation introduced in the late 1960s and early 1970s'.[2] This view pervades other jurisdictions; American academic Richard Lazarus declared, 'prior to 1970 environmental protection law in the United States was essentially nonexistent'.[3] The shift, explains his compatriot Zygmunt Plater, unleashed 'a massive upwelling of layer upon layer of substantial public and private law doctrines, almost volcanic in the power and mass of its eruption'.[4] In so-called 'developing countries' the shift evidently occurred a bit later, such as in China promulgating its lodestar environmental statute in 1979.[5] Likewise in international law, one leading commentator observed 'there was little … environmental law before 1972' but in the following 'forty years … [it] evolved rapidly'.[6] A more liberal political climate coupled with economic prosperity and better scientific understanding of ecological impacts are among the factors scholars identify as nourishing these changes.[7]

[1] G Bates, *Environmental Law in Australia* (LexisNexis Butterworths, 2019) 1.

[2] L Godden and J Peel, *Environment Law* (Oxford University Press, 2010) 126.

[3] RJ Lazarus, 'The Greening of America and the Graying of United States Environmental Law: Reflections on Environmental Law's First Three Decades in the United States' (2001) 20 *Virginia Environmental Law Journal* 75, 76.

[4] Z Plater, 'From the Beginning, a Fundamental Shift of Paradigms: A Theory and Short History of Environmental Law' (1994) 27(3) *Loyola of Los Angeles Law Review* 981, 1003.

[5] B Zhang et al, 'A New Environmental Protection Law, Many Old Problems? Challenges to Environmental Governance in China' (2016) 28 *Journal of Environmental Law* 325.

[6] E Brown Weiss, 'The Evolution of International Environmental Law' (2011) 54 *Japanese Yearbook of International Law* 1, 1, 26.

[7] See also J Dryzek et al, *Green States and Social Movements: Environmentalism in the United States, United Kingdom, Germany and Norway* (Oxford University Press, 2003).

Like the few pioneers such as Tim Bonyhady, Ben Pontin and David Schorr unveiling environmental law's neglected history in other times or places,[8] my book does so in one country's era not yet closely examined – Australia in the first two-thirds of the twentieth century, from the nation's inauguration in 1901 until 1967. My aims are: to ascertain the various laws of relevance to environmental decision-making; to evaluate their changes over time; and thirdly, to assess their efficacy. I will argue that it's implausible to claim that prior to the late 1960s Australia lacked laws dealing with its environmental problems and challenges, but I show that their application was nested within broader modes of governance, which I call scientific expertise, enlightened despotism, polyarchy and markets, and via these modes there was a significant disparity in outcomes whereby Australians were far more effective at exploiting rather than conserving nature. Environmental law helped lessen the losses but much of the continent still vanished.

Australia is the world's only nation that governs an entire continent, a geologically ancient landmass whose animals and plants evolved from eons of continental drift, isolated from most of the world. Species endemism is high, with 87 per cent of its mammals, 45 per cent of its birds, 93 per cent of its reptiles and 92 per cent of its vascular plants unique to Australia.[9] The continent's biota co-existed with Aboriginal people for at least 60,000 years, the world's oldest continuous culture. The island continent has over 25,000 kms of coastline, encircled by the third largest maritime waters of any nation,[10] at 8.2 million $km^2$, larger than its landmass (7.69 million $km^2$). These and other distinct qualities of the ancient continent have helped make its landscapes and ecologies intensely significant to the nation, and their losses all the more jarring, as Australia has lost more mammal species to extinction than any other country.

Australia's history also owes much to factors beyond its shores, including the British Empire, immigrants and global trade. Especially in its early years, the young nation identified more with these exogenous influences than its ancient past. National identity was born out of European colonisation that disregarded Aboriginal traditions in search of the myth of a peacefully 'settled' continent. Australia's role in the Empire – notably the Gallipoli landings in 1915, a battle on foreign soil under British command[11] – acquired greater significance in national folklore than anything endogenous. A collateral national mythology as a 'big country', and an 'empty country', with abundant space and resources available to be exploited, fuelled violence against the ancient land and its Indigenous people.[12]

[8] DB Schorr, 'Historical Analysis in Environmental Law' in MD Dubber and C Tomlins (eds), *The Oxford Handbook of Legal History* (Oxford University Press, 2018) 1001; T Bonyhady, *The Colonial Earth* (Miegunyah Press, 2000); B Pontin, 'Nuisance Law and the Industrial Revolution: A Reinterpretation of Doctrine and Institutional Competence' (2012) 75 *Modern Law Review* 1010.

[9] AD Chapman, *Numbers of Living Species in Australia and the World* (Australia, Department of the Environment, Water, Heritage and the Art, 2009) 7.

[10] Defined as 'Exclusive Economic Zone' under international law.

[11] C Holbrook, *ANZAC, the Unauthorised Biography* (NewSouth, 2014).

[12] JM Powell, *An Historical Geography of Modern Australia: The Restive Fringe* (Cambridge University Press, 1988).

Narratives about 'man against nature', as the big country was tamed, complemented settlers' belief in Australia as a 'child of Mother England'.

The confluence between these endogenous and exogenous influences are key to understanding this book's history. Law is crucial for every nation's adaptive capacity, influencing how it understands and adapts to its environmental challenges.[13] Australia's environmental laws evolved within a legal system maladapted to the continent's geography, in which the nation's birth and official decolonisation in 1901 didn't entail any complementary commitment to decolonise how it governed its lands and Aboriginal people. In a society intent on creating what Ross Johnston calls a 'neo-Europe in the antipodes',[14] shaped by the legal traditions of the Mother Country, there was no radical paradigm shift to make Australia more attuned to the continent's geographical varieties and constraints. Nationhood intensified the colonial paradigm, levying an onerous environmental burden from expanded settlements and economic activity, along with consolidating the ongoing dispossession of the continent's First Nations.

With the nation's Constitution leaving largely undisturbed the former colonies' (now states) dominion over natural resources, an English property tenure system lacking norms of environmental stewardship, and bureaucratic regimes that stifled innovation, it would be difficult to interpolate environmental laws to leverage adaptive change. Such laws at federal and subnational levels nonetheless arose where they dovetailed with nationalism and economic success. Environmental lawmaking in Australia didn't begin with the nation's independence, as regulations governing some of these subjects were already enacted by the colonies or transplanted from Britain.[15] Though no empire of environmental law ensued, there were diverse achievements including the replacement or supplementation of the common law with statutory regimes (eg in water allocation), some centralisation of governance (eg for transboundary resources) and new laws to tackle novel challenges (eg soil erosion). There were also policy shifts, including recognition of the economic benefits of resource stewardship (eg with water and soils), the notion of community 'amenities' (eg in town planning) and a 'scientific' approach to managing natural resources (eg forests).[16] Yet, in some areas little changed, including the marginalisation of Aboriginal people.

As the theory of path dependency postulates, where past institutions shape and constrain options for future reform,[17] the young nation's environmental laws

[13] J McDonald, 'Mapping the Legal Landscape of Climate Change Adaptation' in T Bonyhady, A Macintosh and J McDonald (eds), *Adaptation to Climate Change: Law and Policy* (Federation Press, 2010) 1.

[14] WR Johnston, 'An Environmental Education for a Local Community: Knowing the Border Ranges' in S Dovers (ed), *Environmental History and Policy: Stilling Settling Australia* (Oxford University Press, 2000) 146, 158.

[15] See eg T Orgill, *The Forgotten Decade: The Legislative Conservation of Game, Fish and Timber in 1860s Victoria* (LLB thesis, ANU, 2014).

[16] AB Costin and TG Marples (eds), *Conservation* (Penguin, 1971) 208, 242.

[17] O Hathaway, 'Path Dependence in the Law: The Course and Pattern of Legal Change in a Common Law System' (2001) 86 *Iowa Law Review* 601.

worked within that colonial edifice and the nation's anthroparchic underpinnings rather than springing from a blank slate open to radical change. There was limited teleological imperative to environmental law's evolution, as reforms were 'seldom normative, but usually procedural and administrative and highly discretionary and, very often, … subject to political control', explains Douglas Whalan.[18] Whilst the mainstream political parties governed with some policy variances (eg Labor's interest in improving urban amenities), they shared a commitment to economic growth and supporting extractive industries. It wasn't until the 1970s that a distinct green agenda entered Australian politics with the United Tasmania Group (forerunner to the Australian Greens).[19] Before then, individual politicians sometimes were environmental advocates, such as Robert Martin Collins, elected as an independent to Queensland's Legislative Council who helped found the state's national park system in the early 1900s. But proponents of environmental protection rarely if ever challenged the political and economic *system* driving environmental degradation,[20] just stimulated reform *within* that system.

The motif of coloniality doesn't furnish a complete overview of this book's history because nature's agency needs credit. Colonisation of landscapes wrought upheavals including plagues of invasive pests, dust storms of eroded soils and depilated landscapes shorn of their vegetation. Non-Indigenous Australians weren't ignorant of nature's agency, but New World settlers' assumptions of fertile lands and watered environments were often ill-matched to the continent's ecologies. The nineteenth-century acclimatisation societies, who imported plants and animals to anglicise the land, compounded this failure to adapt to nature.[21] Occasionally some landholders thought differently, such as farmers in Gippsland and the Atherton Tablelands saving pockets of scenic rainforest, points out Warrick Frost.[22] And in cities, explains Andrea Gaynor, a culture of backyard agriculture developed where households growing vegetables and poultry learned to appreciate the vicissitudes of the environment.[23]

Many environmental laws were designed not to save remnants of an unadulterated nature but to manage nature's unruly reaction to colonisation. Wars waged against so-called 'vermin' reflected a struggle to tame a continent whose natural balance was upset. Nature's backlash made it particularly difficult for

[18] DJ Whalen, 'The Structure and Nature of Australian Environmental Law' (1977) 8 *Federal Law Review* 194, 316.

[19] P Manning, *Inside the Greens* (Schwartz Books, 2019).

[20] D Hutton and L Connors, *A History of the Australian Environmental Movement* (Cambridge University Press, 1991).

[21] A few historians however suggest that the societies' work wasn't entirely detrimental, such as valuing the land's soil and climate: P Osborne, 'The Queensland Acclimatisation Society: Challenging the Stereotype' (2008) 20(8) *Royal Historical Society of Queensland Journal* 337.

[22] W Frost, 'Did they Really Hate Trees? Attitudes of Farmers, Tourists and Naturalists towards Nature in the Rainforests of Eastern Australia' (2022) 8(1) *Environment and History* 3, 9–11.

[23] A Gaynor, *Harvest of the Suburbs: An Environmental History of Growing Food in Australian Cities* (UWA Press, 2006).

environmental law to succeed because of the uncertainties and complexities introduced by disturbed ecological and biological processes shifting in unprecedented ways. Nature's backlash created economic and social problems that contemporary Australia has still to solve. Climate change, the most virulent repercussion conceivable, now exacerbates many of these long-standing permutations, such as the massive bushfires and then floods in eastern Australia during 2019 to 2022. This discrepancy between the powers of the legal system to colonise and protect the environment owing in part to nature's agency permeates this book's history.

In the next section, I introduce the modes of governance, and their relationship to law, in shaping environmental outcomes. 'Environmental law', whose definition scholars often debate,[24] includes not only the legal norms, tools and agencies of the nation-state for use or protection of the natural environment including human settlements, but also has tendrils spread ubiquitously across many other domains of the legal system including in property tenure and constitutional law. The notion of 'governance' beneficially expands our enquiry, by highlighting decision-making power beyond the state, and especially the interactions between government and non-government actors.[25]

This approach to this book's history is particularly apt in an era where the body of official environmental law was relatively small, a void filled by many other actors and processes. Australian environmental laws before the late 1960s didn't owe much to the law profession – judges, legal academics or other law-related actors – unlike the prominent position the profession holds today through dedicated environmental lawyers and specialist tribunals, matched in the academic world by numerous scholars and students in this field. Non-lawyer constituencies including scientists, town planners, trade unions, the media and community groups were occasionally quite influential shapers of environmental governance. Concomitantly, the instruments or tools of environmental decisions went beyond conventional legal institutions such as legislation and court cases to include policy-making processes, public inquiries, economic incentives and much more.

## II. Tendrils of Governance

Several modes of governance were operative in this book's history, distilled in Figure 1.1: scientific expertise, enlightened despotism, polyarchy and markets. Still applicable today with some adjustments, these modes straddle two axes: authoritarianism versus pluralism, and environmental exploitation versus protection. The modes represent *tendencies* associated with their assigned quadrants rather than

[24] E Fisher, B Lange and E Scotford, 'What is Environmental Law?' in *Environmental Law: Text, Cases and Materials* (Oxford University Press, 2013) 5–20.

[25] C Holley, N Gunningham, and C Shearing, *New Environmental Governance* (Earthscan, 2012).

rigid trajectories, and sometimes they co-existed or operated in tension depending on the political, economic, cultural and legal context. Science tended to assist decisions to protect nature but could facilitate practices and technologies to exploit it, and even in its more benign guise science might surreptitiously aid nature's subjugation. Likewise, markets serve economic expansion but could moderate profligacy where they helped convey the economic value of using natural resources frugally. And whilst market mechanisms could counter-weight the power of state bureaucracies and legislatures, market actors themselves can acquire coercive dominance. Moreover, governments themselves participated heavily in markets in ways unfamiliar to contemporary Australians, through Crown corporations, ownership of railways, energy and many other vital parts of the nation's economic infrastructure, in addition to intrusive economic planning, as in many other nations before the rise of neo-liberalism.[26] These modes of governance applied to both the state and federal spheres of the nation, but their salience varied in time and place. For example, during and after World War II the nation saw a rise in 'big government'.

**Figure 1.1** Antinomies of Australian environmental governance

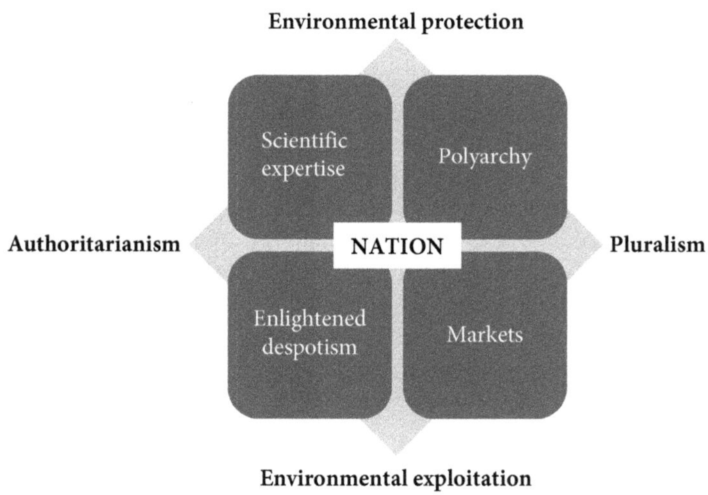


To elaborate on these modes, ***scientific expertise*** refers to how scientific knowledge and its practitioners contribute to environmental decision-making. Thomas Dunlap's seminal history of nature in settler societies contends that the changing role and increased value of the natural sciences in the early twentieth century, especially the shift from amateur naturists to professionalisation in domains such as soil and forestry management, helped settlers in Australia and other societies

[26] L Bernier, M Florio and P Bance (eds), *The Routledge Handbook of State-Owned Enterprises* (Taylor and Francis, 2020).

to seek accommodation with their land and its wildlife in contrast to the prevalent attitudes in the previous century of 'man versus nature' and the concomitant attempts to remake their new environs in the image of their countries of origin.[27] Science could aid environmental regulation by setting standards for 'rational' resource use, wildlife management and control of destructive pests. The natural sciences were advanced through many actors, including natural history museums and field naturalist clubs, including the Australian Academy of Science,[28] plus government-run scientific institutions for advancing agriculture and other resource uses. Whilst they didn't design laws, these actors helped shape societal understandings of environmental threats and impacts to which regulators could respond. Some stakeholders opposed these scientific approaches, such as bushmen and graziers who preferred their own learned experience, or what Chris Soeterboek calls a 'folk ecology', in contrast to the 'theoretical' understandings of academic scientists.[29] Furthermore, Aboriginal environmental knowledge was not widely respected by mainstream scientists in this history, with a few exceptions.[30]

By invoking the assumption that through science humankind could master its environmental adversities, science was also complicit in coloniality. In creating a new Advisory Council in 1915, Prime Minister Billy Hughes declared 'in the destiny of this great country … Science can lend a most powerful aid. Science can make rural industries commercially profitable [and] develop great mineral wealth'.[31] The Commonwealth went on to establish in 1926 the Council for Scientific and Industrial Research, renamed in 1949 the Commonwealth Scientific and Industrial Research Organisation (CSIRO), which Joseph Powell argues 'represented the consummation of the visionary schemes for the future dominion of science'.[32] They and other federal bodies collaborated with the states in promoting a scientific approach to managing the continent's natural resources, though often in ways that helped lessen damage (eg soil conservation and control of invasive pests).

Whilst this turn to science partly reflected the increasing complexity of the nation's modernisation, it was attractive to authorities wishing to depoliticise issues by placing them in the hands of trusted, 'value-neutral' experts.[33] The authoritarian potential of science is accentuated when government agencies

[27] TR Dunlap, *Nature and the English Diaspora: Environment and History in the United States, Canada, Australia, and New Zealand* (Cambridge University Press, 1999).

[28] L Robin, 'Nature Conservation as a National Concern: The Role of the Australian Academy of Science' (1994) 10(1) *Historical Records of Australian Science* 1.

[29] C Soeterboek, '"Folk-Ecology" in the Australian Alps' (2008) 14 *Environment and History* 241.

[30] See eg HH Finlayson, *The Red Centre: Man and Beast in the Heart of Australia* (Angus and Robertson, 1935).

[31] Quoted in G Currie and J Graham, *The Origins of the CSIR: Science and the Commonwealth Government 1901–1926* (Melbourne University Press, 1966) 15.

[32] JM Powell, *Environmental Management in Australia 1788–1914* (Oxford University Press, 1976) 111.

[33] RC Lewontin, *Biology as Ideology* (Harper, 1991).

mobilised science to restrict public dissent; science was enlisted in the 1950s for managing the 'safety' of atomic bomb testing and allay public concerns, for instance. Scientists working for government who refused to toe the official line could find themselves out of favour. The self-taught Edward Swain, a forester in the NSW and Queensland governments between 1918 and 1948, who campaigned against the indiscriminate allocation and permanent clearance of forested lands, became alienated from government land departments favouring land for agriculture. Another who was out of step was Walter Froggatt, an entomologist in the NSW agricultural portfolio, who in the 1930s opposed the introduction of South American cane toads into Queensland sugarcane plantations because of the risk the omnivorous species posed to non-target biota.

Thus, science has played a dyadic role in environmental governance, being an empowering tool to challenge pernicious dogma, as Rachel Carson did in the 1960s in critiquing the dubious science behind agricultural pesticides,[34] yet also a means by which authorities can foster elitist decision-making that excludes lay persons. 'Expert' perceptions of environmental problems are likely to be judged as rational and more consistent with societal interests than the 'subjective' opinions of lay public. The scientific priesthood thus stifles open debate of the values that must accompany decisions.[35]

A second, more authoritarian mode of governance is ***enlightened despotism***, a term coined by Leonard Krieger,[36] though it was Thomas Hobbes in the seventeenth century who first valorised it.[37] In its contemporary formulation serving the collective welfare, enlightened despotism serves to legitimate government interventions to maintain law-and-order, manage national emergencies, safeguard national security and mitigate economic downturns. World history since 1901 has provided numerous pretexts for it: the Great Depression, two World Wars, a Cold War and the COVID-19 pandemic. Some historians argue that Australia's origins as a penal colony embedded a 'strong tradition of government initiative' and centralisation of authority.[38] In the economic sphere particularly, this notion has sometimes been called 'high modernism', defined by leading theorist James Scott as a 'strong … muscle-bound, version of self-confidence about scientific and technological progress, the expansion of production … [and] the mastery of nature' in meeting the collective welfare.[39] High modernism commonly takes the form of authoritarian, large-scale planning and administrative re-orderings.

[34] R Carson, *Silent Spring* (Houghton Mifflin, 1962).

[35] R Keat, *The Politics of Social Theory: Habermas, Freud, and the Critique of Positivism* (Basil Blackwell, 1981) 3.

[36] L Krieger, *An Essay on the Theory of Enlightened Despotism* (University of Chicago Press, 1975).

[37] T Hobbes, *Leviathan* (Penguin Books, 1968, first published 1651).

[38] G Bolton, *Spoils and Spoilers: Australians Make their Environment 1788–1980* (Allen and Unwin, 1981) 17.

[39] JC Scott, *Seeing Like a State: How Certain Schemes to Improve the Human Condition Have Failed* (Yale University Press, 1998) 4.

This book's history is punctuated by authoritarian interventions. The colonial and successor state governments' punitive surveillance of Aboriginal people was one domain, and included sequestering their lands for more 'productive' development.[40] At the national level, 'big government' took off during the 1940s, especially during the nation's post-war reconstruction, explains Stuart Macintyre.[41] It includes the Commonwealth's leadership in the Snowy Mountains Scheme and atomic bomb testing, both purported exercises of its constitutional power over national defence. Each had momentous environmental legacies. Precedents set during World War II included regulations promulgated under the National Security Act 1940 to bolster Commonwealth control over many sectors of domestic industry and natural resources. The Commonwealth also sought (unsuccessfully) in 1944 to amend the Constitution to give itself legislative authority over many matters including soil conservation, a national concern after successive droughts and land degradation. Nonetheless, the High Court's wide interpretation of Commonwealth constitutional powers to meet the needs of nation building already facilitated its growing share of power despite a few setbacks, such as when the Court disallowed the Menzies government's outlawing of the Communist Party.[42]

Enlightened despotism could also have seemingly pro-environmental objectives, as seen lately where state governments have coercively restricted landowners' rights to clear native vegetation. Interference in property rights has a longer history, whereby water, minerals, forests, wildlife and the like were brought under Crown ownership. Illustratively, Victoria's Water Act 1905 declared 'the right to the use and flow and to control of the water' in any river or lake shall 'vest in the Crown', for management by its state-wide State Rivers and Water Supply Commission.[43] In Western Australia, the state government took control of some logging and opened its own sawmills in the early twentieth century to supply materials for construction of its railways.[44] Concomitantly, state governments sometimes shielded themselves from accountability in their control of such resources by taking advantage of the long-standing doctrine of Crown immunity.[45] Conflict over increasingly scarce natural resources may engender more neo-Hobbesian responses in the future, warn environmentalists.[46]

On the pluralist ledger of governance, Australian governments have operated within two modalities. ***Polyarchy*** refers to the institutions that support a

[40] A Armitage, *Comparing the Policy of Aboriginal Assimilation: Australia, Canada, and New Zealand* (UBC Press, 2011).
[41] SF Mcintyre, *Australia's Boldest Experiment: War and Reconstruction in the 1940s* (NewSouth, 2015).
[42] *Australian Communist Party v Commonwealth* [1951] HCA 5.
[43] Section 4(1).
[44] M Calder, *Big Timber Country* (Rigby, 1980) 134.
[45] *Dean v Attorney-General of Queensland* [1971] Qld R 391.
[46] W Ophuls, 'Leviathan or Oblivion' in H Daly (ed), *Toward a Steady State Economy* (WH Freeman, 1973) 215.

democratic polity, including parliamentary elections, political parties, recourse to the courts and freedoms of assembly and speech.[47] Polyarchy can be supplemented in the executive branch of government by mechanisms to engage the community such as public inquiries and stakeholder representation on advisory committees. In theory, polyarchal mechanisms enable more diverse voices to contribute to environmental decisions and to nurture a vibrant civil society including the formation of nature conservation groups, learned societies and a free press. In turn, a democratic polity can aid environmental governance by making authorities more accountable to society. Polyarchal processes were important for articulating growing community interest in Australian nature conservation for public amenity, recreation and aesthetic appreciation.[48]

Opportunities for public participation have been unequal, however. Aboriginal people historically lacked equivalent rights to vote or stand for election: the first federal electoral law, the Commonwealth Franchise Act 1902, gave women the right to vote and stand for election but excluded Aboriginal people (unless already enfranchised as voters in their state), a gap which would not be fully rectified until the Commonwealth Electoral Act 1962. At the state level, enfranchisement of Aboriginal people and women was also incomplete at the time of Federation.[49] The discriminatory franchise for local governments, which favoured property owners, also marginalised the voice of the impecunious.

Furthermore, equal enfranchisement didn't mean equal political influence. Women and Aboriginal people historically were in practice excluded from much political life. Electorates in some states were gerrymandered to give (conservative) rural seats more weight in legislatures.[50] And in a political system where money talks, business interests had (and still have) the ear of lawmakers. Notoriously, for instance, areas of Tasmanian national parks were excised in 1939, 1950 and 1967 for mining, forestry and dams respectively, a pattern known as 'regulatory capture'.[51] The problem is exacerbated in executive agencies wielding broad discretionary powers subject to limited parliamentary or judicial oversight.

In this history, lay people had limited recourse to the courts, as private litigants typically needed to have affected property or pecuniary interests, even in town planning law where people's own communities were at stake.[52] Victoria's Town and Country Planning Act 1961 heralded a shift towards wider community rights to

[47] R Dahl, *Polyarchy: Participation and Opposition* (Yale University Press, 2008).

[48] Powell (n 32) 115.

[49] J Chesterman and B Galligan, *Citizens Without Rights: Aborigines and Australian Citizenship* (Cambridge University Press, 1997); A Oldfield, *Woman Suffrage in Australia: A Gift or a Struggle?* (Cambridge University Press, 1992).

[50] JR Kelly, 'Vote Weightage and Quota Gerrymanders in Queensland, 1931–1971' (1971) 43(2) *Australian Quarterly* 39.

[51] M Levine and J Forrence, 'Regulatory Capture, Public Interest and the Public Agenda: Toward a Synthesis' (1990) 6 *Journal of Law, Economics and Organization* 167.

[52] PA Management Consultants, *Guide to Environmental Law in Australia* (1974) passim.

participation in decision-making, a shift that gathered momentum in other states in the following decades (albeit with some unevenness). Until then, third parties could petition their elected representatives to express grievances. Public inquiries by royal commissions or parliamentary committees allowed some public submissions and deliberation. Nongovernmental constituencies such as scientists or farmers sometimes also had a voice in advisory committees and boards constituted under statutes to aid their administration. The necessity to routinely legitimate environmental governance with public participation did not become well established until after the late 1960s.[53]

As earlier noted, in this era the law profession was largely a bystander to the vanishing continent. A few practising lawyers shone, however. One was Marie Byles (1900–79) who with NSW bushwalking clubs in the 1920s and 1930s lobbied for enlarging the conservation estate, becoming a trustee on the governing board of one she helped create in 1935, the Bouddi Natural Park.[54] Another pioneer lawyer was Rae Else-Mitchell (1914–2006), who was an energetic contributor to the early years of the NSW National Trust (established 1945), helping it secure protection of historic buildings and scenic natural places for public benefit.[55] Yet, in the bigger picture, the law profession (including the judiciary) was not a major stakeholder in environmental law. Tellingly, a compendium of 85 leading, all-time environmental law cases for Australia, published in 2012, lists just three before 1970, and all foreign judgments.[56] Courts occasionally adjudicated tort and property cases touching on environmental issues,[57] and enforced regulations concerning wildlife hunting, vermin control and pollution abatement.[58] Some legal professionals also served on public inquiries appointed to investigate land management issues.[59] This deficit in the law profession's role wasn't unique to environmental law however, in an era before the growth in legal education and access to legal services seen from the 1960s onwards.

The biggest champions for defending nature in this book's history tended to be far removed from legislatures or courtrooms – scientists, journalists, travel writers, bushwalkers and artists were among disparate constituencies questioning remaking the continent, though much less so Aboriginal dispossession. They engaged the mass media (eg, letters to newspaper editors and participation in radio broadcasts), undertook scientific research into environmental problems, and

[53] BJ Richardson and J Razzaque, 'Public Participation in Environmental Decision-making' in BJ Richardson and S Wood (eds), *Environmental Law for Sustainability* (Hart Publishing, 2006) 165.

[54] A McLeod, *The Summit of Her Ambition: The Spirited Life of Marie Byles* (Anne McLeod, 2016) 50–58.

[55] C Logan, 'The National Trust and the Heritage of Sydney Harbour' (2015) 16(1) *Landscape Review* 63, 67.

[56] B Jessup, *Environment Law* (LexisNexis, 2012).

[57] See M Lunney, *A History of Australian Tort Law 1901–1945* (Cambridge University Press, 2017).

[58] See eg *Browne v Button* (1923) Tas LR 52; *Winterton v Wilson* (1929) 29 SR (NSW) 186.

[59] See eg *Royal Commission to Inquire into the Condition of the Crown Tenants of the Western Division of New South Wales* (NSW Legislative Assembly, 1901).

promoted appreciation of the outdoors through bushwalking and field naturalist associations. Individual personalities sometimes were pivotal in specific environmental controversies. Myles Dunphy was one, helping to save NSW's Blue Gum Forest and enlarge its national parks system. Another was zoologist David Fleay, who by managing wildlife sanctuaries and public advocacy helped awaken societal interest in native fauna, especially endangered varieties. The stories of individuals' achievements 'emphasises the importance of appreciating human agency, under even limited space to manoeuvre', in leveraging social change, explains legal historian Susan Carle.[60]

The last key mode of governance is ***markets***. Like polyarchy, markets can counterbalance authoritarian rule. Yet they have a much stronger economic bias than polyarchy. Markets in a capitalist system aid its logic of indefinite growth, thereby creating a fundamental tension with an environmental agenda of restraint and sustainability.[61] Markets need to be understood as a governance institution because they are shaped politically and legally. Governments manipulate markets to promote specific economic policies; for example, Prime Minister Stanley Bruce's mantra 'Men, Money and Markets' (1922) signalled a programme of government-stimulated development to populate the continent's 'empty' spaces and grow prosperous industries trading in the British Empire.[62] Two areas of law most germane to state-leveraged markets are property rights and corporate governance.

Property rights are fundamental to the history of the continent's colonisation.[63] Crown grants of freehold or leasehold were often conditional on landholders' clearing forests and other 'improvements', evident particularly in the soldier settlement schemes.[64] Through its ownership of minerals, governments allocated rights to mining ventures to leverage development and raise revenue. Allocation of water rights have the same effect. Countervailing efforts to protect the environment have tended to operate by limiting private property rights, such as obliging landholders to control pests and protect soils, thereby representing a partial nationalisation of the bundle of property rights.[65]

Property law has also aided dispossession of Australia's First Nations, with environmental ramifications. The notion of *terra nullius*, a land without owners, was the fig-leaf of colonisation;[66] the courts before 1992 didn't recognise

[60] SD Carle, *Defining the Struggle: National Organizing for Racial Justice, 1880–1915* (Oxford University Press, 2013) xiv.

[61] The literature is vast here; see recently A Buller, *The Value of a Whale: On the Illusions of Green Capitalism* (Manchester University Press, 2022).

[62] D Lee, *Stanley Melbourne Bruce: Australian Internationalist* (Bloomsbury, 2016).

[63] See N Graham, *Lawscape: Property, Environment and Law* (Taylor and Francis, 2010).

[64] B Scates and M Oppenheimer, *The Last Battle: Solder Settlement in Australia 1916–1939* (Cambridge University Press, 2016).

[65] MJ Davies, *Property: Meanings, Histories and Theories* (Routledge-Cavendish, 2007).

[66] H Reynolds, *The Law of the Land* (Penguin, 1992).

Aboriginal title.[67] Even the small reserves set aside for disposed Aboriginal people were during the twentieth century attenuated to reallocate land for mines or farms, and in South Australia, to make way for testing atomic weaponry. The creation of national parks was also problematic, for the mythology of an unpeopled wilderness erased its Aboriginal history. It's no coincidence that justice for Aboriginal peoples gained to some extent in recent decades, such as via the federal Native Title Act 1993, has coincided with growing recognition that their customs for 'caring for country' can aid environmental rehabilitation and conservation.[68]

Property also shapes the business corporation, a market institution that both owns property and itself is property for investors. As in other societies, the corporation is a ubiquitous part of Australia's commercial landscape, and as the primary agent of economic development it has been deeply complicit in the vanishing continent. The phenomenal success of the corporation relies heavily on its legal framework including separate legal personality, limited liability for its members and transferable shares, that became established in English law in the mid-nineteenth century. The first Australian companies operated under less flexible frameworks, such as the Royal Charter issued for businesses aiding government policy. While no Australian chartered company was as large as Canada's famous Hudson's Bay Company,[69] a local version was the Van Diemen's Land Company, founded in 1825 with a 250,000-acre grant to develop the colony's agricultural base. The UK's Joint Stock Companies Act 1844 and Limited Liability Act 1855 created many of the building blocks of modern company law, along with the House of Lords' landmark 1897 ruling that upheld the company's separate legal personality.[70] Australian parliaments transplanted the British reforms,[71] including specifically to facilitate natural resources development such as Victoria's Act for the Better Regulation of Mining Companies 1855. Federation gave the Commonwealth some power to legislate in this field, doing so in piecemeal fashion in an attempt to promote a national unified system that was not complete until 2001.[72]

Corporations law is vital for economic growth by encouraging pooled investment in business ventures. Legal historian Phillip Lipton argues that 'mining companies, and ultimately the mining industry itself, benefited greatly from the

[67] *Milirrpum v Nabalco Pty Ltd* (1971) 17 FLR 141. Explicit judicial discussion of the *terra nullius* however didn't occur until *Coe v Commonwealth* [1979] HCA 68, and the doctrine was explicitly rejected by the High Court in *Mabo v Queensland (No 2)* [1992] HCA 23.

[68] JC Altman and S Kerins, *People on Country: Vital Landscapes, Indigenous Futures* (Federation Press, 2012).

[69] VH Sukdeo, *Regulating the Corporation from Within and Without* (PhD dissertation, York University, 2022) 214–18.

[70] *Salomon v Salomon Co Ltd* [1897] AC 22.

[71] See eg Companies Act 1864 (Vic) and Companies Act 1874 (NSW).

[72] Corporations Act 2001.

introduction of a general incorporation system and limited liability legislation'.[73] Australia's largest corporation today, BHP, was founded in 1885 to undertake mining. In the agricultural sector, many Australian farms were, and continue today to be, family affairs but large corporations took control of much of the processing and retail side including Colonial Sugar Refining (founded 1855), Arnott's (1865) and Rosella (1895). The forestry industry also flourished with incorporation, such as Associated Pulp and Paper Mills founded in 1936. Governments themselves formed statutory corporations to operate commercial businesses and manage economic infrastructure, such as Tasmania's dam-building, political citadel, the Hydro-Electric Commission (created in 1929–30).[74]

Harnessing the corporation to further economic goals was not matched by a commitment to include social justice or environmental responsibilities in the corporate mandate. The movement for corporate social responsibility (CSR) is largely a post-1970 phenomenon, although there were sporadic antecedents. Researchers have found evidence of CSR-related disclosures by Australian companies such as BHP since the early twentieth century.[75] So too academics in this era began to reflect on the importance of CSR, such as American Howard Bowen's landmark book in 1953.[76] Yet overall, prior to the late 1960s, corporations took their cues from government regulation (or tried to limit it) rather than seek any societal licence beyond such regulation as is more commonly sought today.

The foregoing modes of governance were means of articulating competing considerations of environmental protection and exploitation but they weren't of even significance or influence. In a young nation bereft of heroic or revolutionary deeds, an outpost of the British Empire forged out of a convict colony that sought to erase the continent's Aboriginal history, the legitimacy of the nation could hardly be sustained by appealing to the manner of its founding. Rather, its legitimacy depended on future outcomes associated with economic, territorial and demographic expansion.[77] Responsible for national housekeeping, the modernising Australian state grew to resemble the *parens patriae*, tasked with encouraging settlement of the continent, building economic infrastructure, lifting living standards and maintaining security. The economy might not always trump environmental considerations, but it usually had the upper hand.

[73] P Lipton, 'A History of Company Law in Colonial Australia: Economic Development and Legal Evolution' (2007) 31(3) *Melbourne University Law Review* 805, 817.

[74] B Davis, 'Adaptation and Deregulation in Government Business Enterprise: The Hydro-Electric Commission of Tasmania 1945–94' (1995) 54(2) *Australian Journal of Public Administration* 252.

[75] J Guthrie and LD Parker, 'Corporate Social Reporting: A Rebuttal of Legitimacy Theory' (1989) 19 *Accounting and Business Research* 342.

[76] HR Bowen, *Social Responsibilities of the Businessman* (New York University Press, 1953).

[77] See also Fraser's analysis of genetic versus telic legitimacy in Australian constitutional law: A Fraser, 'False Hopes: Implied Rights, Popular Sovereignty in the Australian Constitution' (1994) 16 *Sydney Law Review* 213.

# III. 1901 to 1967

This book's history concentrates on 1901 to 1967. Whilst periodisation may provide an incomplete account of any history, and scholars of environmental law will debate its different chapters, 1901 to 1967 is compelling. It begins with Federation, a milestone that created a national government with the Commonwealth of Australia Constitution Act and altered the legal milieu for the subnational states. Some environment-related laws in Australia were adopted by the states' colonial predecessors, as Tim Bonyhady and Joseph Powell have examined,[78] with some continuing after 1901. But in the first two-thirds of the twentieth century the states also embarked on legislative programmes that impacted the natural environment, and some of this governance was influenced by the Commonwealth. An example is the states' environmentally damaging soldier settlement schemes to accommodate veterans of wars to which the Commonwealth had committed the nation. Federalism also necessitated a new governmental territory – the Australian Capital Territory, hosting Canberra – which would become an incubator for new approaches to urban planning. A second territory – the Northern Territory – was separated from South Australia in 1911 and came under federal oversight. The Commonwealth itself began its own direct forays into environmental matters, including brokering an agreement for allocating waters of the Murray-Darling Basin in 1914,[79] and curbing the rapacious international trade in some Australian fauna.[80] And with the transfer to Australia in 1933 of Great Britain's putative Antarctic territories,[81] the Commonwealth acquired the potential to control a vast domain.

Nationhood also influenced the states and territories, and the Commonwealth itself, through a heightened sense of nationalism that culturally began to accommodate the continent's unique wildlife and ecosystems. Australian nationalism had colonial antecedents, aided by self-governance such as the Australian Colonies Government Act passed by the Imperial Parliament in 1850.[82] Nature conservation laws were one domain where this connection between nationalism and the continent's natural heritage was strongly forged, benefiting the charismatic species, such as the lyrebird and koala, and scenic landscapes possessing mountains and waterfalls, that were harnessed as symbols of Australianness.

[78] Bonyhady (n 8); Powell (n 32).

[79] River Murray Waters Agreement 1914; River Murray Waters Act 1915.

[80] Regulated under the Customs Act 1901.

[81] Australian Antarctic Territory Acceptance Act 1933, taking effect on 24 August 1936.

[82] Formally entitled, Act for the Better Government of Her Majesty's Australian Colonies, 1850, coming into effect in 1851.

**Figure 1.2** Lyre-bird stamp, 1932, a species the Commonwealth helped protect by banning international trade in its plumage; Australia Post

Nationhood in 1901 however didn't precipitate an overnight cohesive national identity, let alone one to leverage ambitious federal leadership in environmental affairs, as historian William Coleman cautions in citing Western Australia's secessionist movement.[83] Not until World War II, when Australia faced an existential threat, did the balance of power decisively tilt to the federal sphere, thereby spurring initiatives such as the Snowy Mountains Scheme and the testing of atomic bombs. Even so, not until Whitlam's election in 1972 did national environmental leadership emerge, though serious gaps remain owing to the political wrangling of meddling with the states' economic prerogatives.

The terminus of this study might seem less obvious because of the absence of a discrete milestone equivalent to Federation. The 1960s was a period, now well-documented, of significant social and cultural change in Australia, as in other

[83] WO Coleman, *Their Fiery Cross of Union: A Retelling of the Creation of the Australian Federation, 1889–1914* (Connor Court Publishing, 2021).

Western countries.[84] The year 1967 specifically marked the onset of several environmental campaigns that brought new values and tactics in a decade of heightened political activism, and these campaigns highlighted unprecedentedly the deficiencies of existing environmental laws, thereby helping to inspire extensive reforms including greater national leadership in the following decade. Environmentalists challenged brazen proposals for mining in the Great Barrier Reef and NSW's Colong Caves, plans to farm Victoria's Little Desert and dam Tasmania's Lake Pedder, and urban residential development in Sydney that inspired the 'Green Bans'. Such outbursts of environmental concern shouldn't imply that Australian society previously lacked agitation but it was less intense and less well organised on environmental issues.

Both the Great Barrier Reef and Lake Pedder campaigns led to calls for federal intervention – a shift from viewing environmental entanglements as merely a local or state concern. This growing sense of the national dimension is also exemplified in another significant occurrence of 1967 for Australia in the constitutional amendment to give the Commonwealth concurrent legislative power over Aboriginal affairs; in ensuing decades it would transfer control of the continent's land via the Native Title Act 1993. Environmentalists themselves during this era began to organise themselves nationally. The Australian Conservation Foundation (ACF) was founded in 1965 (though a forerunner was the Wild Life Preservation Society, established in 1909).[85] Seeking political respectability, with its initial president being the High Court Chief Justice, Sir Garfield Barwick, followed by Prince Philip, the ACF was however more conservative than the grassroots campaigners trying to save Lake Pedder or the Colong Caves.[86] Activist groups also flourished at a community level in the major cities in the 1960s, seeking to protect residential life from inappropriate urban development.

Some researchers might prefer to extend this book's history into the 1970s or even early 1980s because of Commonwealth initiatives that solidified cooperative federalism on environmental matters. These include the historic Senate Select Committee reports on air and water pollution in 1969 and 1970 respectively,[87] the House of Representatives Select Committee report on wildlife conservation in 1972,[88] the National Estate report in 1974,[89] and landmark laws of the Whitlam

[84] S Robinson and J Ustinoff (eds), *The 1960s in Australia: People, Power and Politics* (Cambridge Scholars Publishing, 2012).

[85] J Webb, *100 Years of Saving Australia's Wildlife: The History of the Wildlife Preservation Society of Australia 1909–2009* (Wildlife Preservation Society of Australia, 2010).

[86] For a history of the ACF, see B Broadbent, *Inside the Greening: 25 Years of the Australian Conservation Foundation* (Insite Press, 1999).

[87] Australia, Parliament, Senate, *Report from the Senate Select Committee on Air Pollution* (Government Printing Office, 1969); Australia, Parliament, Senate, *Report from the Senate Select Committee on Water Pollution, Water Pollution in Australia* Government Printer, 1970).

[88] Australia, Parliament, House of Representatives, *Wildlife Conservation – Report* (Government Printing Office, 1972).

[89] Committee of Inquiry into the National Estate, *National Estate: Report of the Committee of Inquiry* (Government Printer, 1975).

government including the Environmental Protection (Impact of Proposals) Act 1974 and the National Parks and Wildlife Conservation Act 1975. And there were parallel developments with the judiciary, such as the High Court's decision in 1976 upholding the Commonwealth's power to block export licences for mineral sands taken from Queensland's Fraser Island,[90] and the Court's ruling in 1983 upholding federal prohibition on Tasmania damming the World Heritage-listed Franklin River.[91] Whilst these developments between 1968 and 1983 fortified a new era of environmental federalism in Australia for the coming decades,[92] I exclude them from the core of this book's history because they differ markedly from the Commonwealth's earlier, more parsimonious role. Moreover, this book's purpose isn't to examine an era that researchers already recognise, and have written about, as part of *modern* environmental law. Whilst this book highlights national issues and patterns, it's also far from just regarding Commonwealth developments. Much content considers the environmental law histories of the states and territories.

The book is also not a treatise on all facets of Australia's history of environmental law but investigates selected examples that illuminate the overarching themes of modes of governance, colonisation and nature's agency. The case studies span diverse subjects including town planning, soil conservation, invasive species, pollution control, national parks and wildlife management. Nature conservation garners much attention because it attracted many of the earliest law reforms and has been the focus of contentious environmental disputes. Unlike some nations such as Great Britain where industrial development and town planning were especially formative influences in the evolution of their environmental laws,[93] Australia's development, said to have 'rode on the sheep's back', is where rural and natural resource issues dominated. That said, given that the majority of Australians even a century ago were urban dwellers, governance issues relating to town planning and urban pollution control are certainly not ignored in this book.

I now turn to the story of the vanishing continent, beginning with my maternal family's experiences as property owners colonising one landscape. It's valuable to illustrate in this detailed manner some broad themes that otherwise might seem too abstract for the unfamiliar reader.

## IV. Orchardfield: Fragment of a Vanishing Continent

My mother Margaret Richardson (née Jackes) was raised on a farm in the New England Tableland of northern NSW. Known as 'Orchardfield', the 260-hectare

[90] *Murphyores v Commonwealth of Australia* [1976] HCA 20.

[91] *Commonwealth v Tasmania* [1983] HCA 21; and see World Heritage Properties Conservation Act 1983 (Cth).

[92] R Fowler, 'Environmental Law and its Administration in Australia' (1984) 1(1) *Environmental and Planning Law Journal* 10.

[93] See B Pontin, 'Integrated Pollution Control in Victorian Britain: Rethinking Progress within the History of Environmental Law' (2007) 19(2) *Journal of Environmental Law* 173.

property near Armidale – a town once touted as the nation's capital – furnished one of the largest and most prosperous orchards in the state. My great, great grandfather Franklin Jackes founded Orchardfield in the 1860s, and it stayed in the Jackes lineage until 1950. Although one generation removed, I know of the farm's history from stories shared by my mother and her siblings, and from archival records including many in the National Library's *Trove* database.[94] I also visited Orchardfield twice, although long after its farming days, and its dishevelled, empty paddocks now overseen by the local municipality face encroachment by Armidale airport's business park.

Orchardfield typifies many of the environmental permutations of a vanishing continent. The emptying of landscapes of their trees and wildlife began before Orchardfield, but during its tenure those transformations dramatically intensified. Before the 1860s, Australia didn't suffer from rabbits, foxes or cane toads, and retained most of its forests. When my grandparents relinquished Orchardfield nearly a century later, the continent had incurred vast environmental upheavals. Much had vanished.

**Figure 1.3** Franklin Jackes (1830–84); author's family collection

[94] See trove.nla.gov.au. It contains approximately 650 newspaper entries for Orchardfield until the mid-1950s.

Orchardfield began in 1866 when the land was acquired by Canadian-born Franklin Jackes, a member of the first Armidale City Council in 1863, and thus emulating his father, with the same Christian name, who in 1834 was elected to the inaugural Toronto City Council. Franklin junior travelled extensively in Australia before settling in New England in 1856, drawn by its gold rush. After a stint at Rocky River and Uralla, he moved to Armidale, the hub in this relatively fertile region straddling the western slopes of the Great Dividing Range. Besides operating small businesses in Armidale including a hotel, Franklin Jackes developed an orchard, about eight kilometres south.[95] Originally named 'Skedaddle',[96] the orchard prospered, and in its final years with the Jackes family in the 1940s it was air-freighting produce interstate and even internationally.[97] In the late nineteenth century the region was being transformed into a simulacrum of Mother England, though letters from Franklin suggest he had southern Ontario more in mind as the prototype for Orchardfield, including its Canadian-designed homestead.

The colonisation of the New England Tableland began with the 1818 expedition of NSW Surveyor-General John Oxley, whose journal recalls: 'the finest open country, or rather park, imaginable … where art, so far as it is an auxiliary of beauty, would have been detrimental to the fresher and simpler garb of nature'.[98] This landscape had been managed for eons by its Aboriginal inhabitants, whom Oxley occasionally glimpsed. Squatters began to steal their territory in the early 1830s, aided by a 'large body' of police 'to employ coercive measures' against any resistance.[99] 'By the late 1860s', explains Aboriginal historian Callum Clayton-Dixon, 'the New England tribes found themselves in a set of circumstances very different from those in 1831'.[100]

Environmental change ensued. Like much of the colonised continent, the New England landscape was scarred by cropping and livestock grazing. Orchardfield was among these transformers, as the *Armidale Express* enthused: 'it is men like Mr. Jackes … who have the enterprise to introduce new industries at their own risk, that the district is indebted'.[101] Deforestation was the most telling sign of a vanishing nature, including at Orchardfield as one newspaper reported: 'when Mr Jackes bought the ground it was a dense mass of gum trees. A great deal of labour was spent in clearing, grubbing, fencing, etc'.[102] Much of the Armidale

[95] EM Jackes, *A Genealogy of the Jackes Family in Australia* (Society of Australian Genealogists, undated).

[96] 'Armidale and Grafton Road' (*Armidale Express*, 7 July 1866) 2.

[97] 'Air Transport Possibilities for Fresh Fruit. Tests by Progressive Armidale Orchardist' (*Land*, 11 November 1949) 8.

[98] J Oxley, *Journals of Two Expeditions into the Interior of New South Wales* (John Murray, 1820) 8 September.

[99] 'Ship News' (*Sydney Gazette*, 6 February 1832) 2.

[100] C Clayton-Dixon, *Surviving New England* (Newara Aboriginal Corporation, 2020) 132.

[101] 'Orchardfield' (*Armidale Express*, 10 December 1880) 4.

[102] 'Orchardfield, New South Wales' (*Australasian*, 5 January 1878) 26.

hinterland today remains depilated of its original vegetation, with just scattered, dishevelled groves left for shading sheep, separated by swathes of pasture amidst veins of eroded, distressed land. These were also scenes encountered across much of eastern Australia, as poet Dorothea Mackellar evoked in 1908 in the famous stanza from *My Country:* 'the stark white ring-barked forest All tragic to the moon'.

**Figure 1.4** Spraying a cherry orchard, Orchardfield, 1947; author's family collection, and NSW State Archives and Library

Cropping imprinted particularly deep scars. Orchardfield hosted 12,000 exotic fruit trees, including cherries, pears, plums, quinces and apples. Trespassing insects were repelled with pesticides, typically sprayed with little appreciation of the collateral damage.[103] My grandfather Ronald Jackes' hands and arms were 'oddly speckled', recalled my mother, owing to his carefree spraying without protective gloves (see Figure 1.4). Marauding flying foxes drawn to the fruits were likewise persecuted by Jackes and fellow orchardists; a tabloid in 1942 mentioned that 'the [flying] foxes come out just at dusk and it is then that orchardists are busy with guns'.[104] Shooting parties would massacre roosting bat colonies in surprise raids.

[103] 'War to the Death Against the Pests of the Orchard' (*Sydney Mail*, 27 May 1931) 39.
[104] 'Flying Foxes: Armidale Orchards' (*Inverell Tines*, 7 December 1942) 4.

Orchardists equally abhorred frugivore birds. The *Australian Town and Country Journal* remarked how they fared on Orchardfield and its adjoining property, the 'Croft', managed by another of the Jackes clan:

> One of the worst pests [they have] to contend with is a species of green parrot, which destroys more fruit than any other enemy. ... War is waged ruthlessly upon them with the gun, but still they come in thousands. Mr Jackes tried putting stuffed hawks on poles, but the parrots were shy for two or three days only, and then came along and cheekily roosted alongside the hawks. Shooting ... it seems the only way to keep them down.[105]

Many other native creatures faced farmers' guns, snares or poisons in a society typically oblivious to the welfare of wildlife. The Armidale Pastures Protection Board, part of a network of NSW rural agencies, periodically declared open seasons on kangaroos and other species it considered pestiferous, though interestingly a kangaroo was kept as a pet on Orchardfield that my mother and her brother befriended, as shown in Figure 1.5.[106]

**Figure 1.5** Pet kangaroo and my mother and her brother at Orchardfield, 1941; author's family collection

[105] Rega, 'The Fruitgrower' (*Australian Town and Country Journal*, 5 December 1906) 27.
[106] 'Open Season: Kangaroos and Wallabies' (*Armidale Express*, 14 September 1938) 4.

Most landholders were less sentimental about macropods or other native fauna. Illustratively, the 1909 official kill tallies for wildlife in the New England district, which omitted the likely extensive, unofficial hunting, included 19,667 rat kangaroos (known today as bettongs), 3,754 crows, 41,836 wallabies and 352 dingoes.[107] In the 1930s and 1940s wombats were added to the noxious list owing to their fence-damaging habits.[108] Equally detrimental to native fauna, and flora were the foxes, rabbits and other exotics introduced by settlers – creatures that ironically often proved more costly to farmers than any native species.

It wasn't unrestricted, wanton slaughter however: the story of Australia's vanishing nature reveals countervailing efforts to safeguard some of it. We must jettison any ameliorant narrative that purports to credit the present with environmental wisdom and care lacking in the past, as though our predecessors were mindless vandals of ancient landscapes. Regulations in the early twentieth century sought to protect some wildlife and their environs for aesthetic, recreational, scientific or economic reasons. Wildlife protection improved in the early twentieth century, ending the indifference to wholesale destruction of native fauna, with even the killing of common species sometimes subject to licensing owing to their skins and meat having commercial value. Prosecutions of unlicensed hunters increasingly occurred in the New England Tableland, such as one fined £88 by the Walcha Police Court in 1920 for possession of 346 skins of various marsupials,[109] and a poacher fined £75 by the Uralla Police Court in 1922 for 75 possum skins (both fines worth about A$7,000 in 2023 money).[110] Some wildlife habitat of scenic or recreational value was also saved. In 1935 the New England National Park of 17,000 hectares was gazetted, which the press announced: 'afford[s] one of the finest panoramic views in the world'.[111] Yet then, as now, there were limits to what lawmakers would protect if agricultural or other economic interests might be jeopardised. Thus, insects, birds and marsupials that feasted on the produce of orchards remained fair game,[112] and national parks including the aforementioned remained potentially open to mining.

Farmers' own environmental practices were not beyond scrutiny where they had economic ramifications. The strongest controls tended to apply to Crown lands, such as to limit removal of trees: in 1910 the Burdarrn Court, sitting 75 km west of Armidale, fined a violator £6.3s.4d (about $980 today) for ring-barking 370 trees on a Crown leasehold, contrary to the Forestry Act 1909.[113] Ring-barked and overgrazed landscapes suffered erosion, especially during

[107] 'Pestiferous Armidale' (*Inverell Times*, 27 May 1901) 2.
[108] 'Wombats Noxious' (*Armidale Express*, 15 January 1937) 7.
[109] 'Skinman Fined £88' (*Bathurst Times*, 7 June 1920) 1.
[110] 'Illegal 'Possum Hunting' (*Scone Advocate*, 11 April 1922) 4.
[111] 'New England National Park, Armidale' (*Sydney Morning Herald*, 13 October 1933) 12.
[112] 'War to the Death Against the Pests of the Orchard' (*Sydney Mail*, 27 May 1931) 39.
[113] 'Important Land Case' (*Intercolonial Courier*, 16 December 1910) 7.

droughts, and noxious weeds such as blackberry and prickly pear could render land unfarmable. Orchardfield had its fair share of these problems.[114]

By the 1940s, after much of the New England region had already been deforested, the Armidale Pastures Protection Board debated saving remaining trees as a soil erosion measure.[115] Separate soil conservation regulations were introduced in NSW's Soil Conservation Act 1938. The first prosecution in NSW to address soil erosion involved a landholder who ring-barked trees along protected waterways northwest of Armidale.[116] The miniscule fine, here just £2.10s (about $150 in 2023 money), would hardly deter others. A 1953 report from the NSW government estimated that 60 per cent of New England was 'affected by accelerated soil erosion to an appreciable extent'.[117]

Landowners were also obliged to control rabbits for a similar reason. It was a 'heavy burden', as the NSW Supreme Court conceded in a 1910 case where it confirmed the Pastures Protection Board's authority to oblige an Armidale Shire landholder to suppress rabbits on public roadsides, for if they were 'not kept clean the provisions in regard to the destruction of rabbits on the runs might be useless'.[118] In fact, the legalised war waged against rabbits was rather useless until the lethal myxomatosis was introduced by Australian scientists in the 1950s. The law could also be blind to its contradictions in dealing with rabbits, however. Illustratively, in 1903 up to 300 'native cats', which were not listed under NSW's Native Animals Protection Act 1903, were reportedly killed at Orandumby Station, in the southern Tableland;[119] yet the carnivorous eastern quoll (*Dasyurus viverrinus*), as it's known today, might have helped farmers control rabbits.[120]

As the pre-1788 ecosystems and their wildlife retreated, another landscape emerged as settlers recreated their own version of the Mother Country. The very name 'New England', where my ancestors settled, of course evokes this sentiment. William Cleghorn, another from my family tree who came here, wrote in the 1860s of his vision for a 'country covered with farms and vineyards with many happy homes and neat villages … [on] fertile plans which are now a barren wilderness'.[121] Settlers like Cleghorn and Jackes sought not simply to colonise the land with an imported agrarian economy but to imbue it with aesthetic flourishes to evoke their ancestral homes. In 1880 Orchardfield was chosen for the release of English skylarks into New England.[122] A gifted avian diva and enduring subject

[114] 'PP Board Cleans Out Saumarez Reserve' (*Armidale Express*, 18 July 1952) 4.
[115] 'Armidale Debate on Tree Clearing' (*Daily Examiner* (Grafton), 12 July 1946) 2.
[116] 'First State Prosecution Affecting Erosion' (*Armidale Express*, 19 April 1950) 15.
[117] 'Large Area of New England Erosion Affected' (*Warialda Standard*, 30 September 1953) 4.
[118] *Rae v Simmons* (1910) 10 NSW SR 582, 593.
[119] 'Topics of the Day' (*Armidale Express*, 27 February 1903) 4.
[120] The eastern quolls apparently became extirpated on the mainland by the 1960s, until reintroduced to NSW's Booderee National Park in 2018 from a Tasmanian quoll population.
[121] Letter of William Cleghorn to wife Isabella, 1 July 1868, quoted in G Baines et al, *Colonial Cleghorns. Lineage and Letters* (John Vickery, 2011).
[122] 'Orchardfield' (*Armidale Express*, 10 December 1880) 4.

of affection of English poets, skylarks were released across eastern Australia to remind newcomers of their homeland. Many trees and plants were imported for similar reasons. A gardening feature in the *Glen Innes Examiner* in 1938 praises the 'many stately elms of immense size throughout the New England', and nominates those at Orchardfield as among the 'very fine[st]'.[123]

Franklin Jackes more specifically wished to create something reminiscent of southern Ontario. Acquiring the land soon after NSW's Robertson Land Acts (includes the Crown Lands Alienation Act) were passed in 1861, he planted an elm drive with a circular terminus like that at his parents' house in Toronto. The elms, and pines too, still adorn the property, flanking its 400-metre driveway to the site of the original homestead, partly resembling an Ontarian log house. (Sadly, the homestead was demolished in the early 1980s.) A 1906 edition of *Australian Town and Country Journal* enthuses over Orchardfield's floral ambience:

> 'Orchardfield' is approached by a magnificent drive, about 400 yards in length. It is beautifully graveled and excellently kept ... Lilac and hawthorn, one with its delicate heliotrope flower and the other with a bloom of dazzling whiteness, bathe the surroundings in color; while flower beds in which are pansies, wallflowers, and other rich-looking blooms, gem the walks with Nature's jewels.[124]

Another description exclaimed: 'the perfume of hawthorn was borne everywhere on the breeze carrying with it a feeling of lassitude such as one would associate with the lotus-eater'.[125] In 1934 the *Sydney Morning Herald*, reporting on the marriage of Ronald Jackes to his American bride Elizabeth Kennedy, admired how they would be returning to Orchardfield 'renowned for its lovely old-world garden with its English trees and avenue of elms'.[126]

In these refashioned and repurposed landscapes, the Aboriginal people were swept aside. The Anēwan (also written Anaiwan/Anaywan) are the traditional owners of the New England region who by the 1860s had been evicted. Some who remained dwelled on Armidale's outskirts in a squalid enclave derided by locals as 'the Dump'. One of their members lived at Orchardfield as a maid and nanny during the late 1930s and early 1940s. From the late 1950s authorities sought to improve living conditions at the Dump, then officially called the 'East Armidale Aboriginal Reserve', following the intervention of the Armidale Association for the Assimilation of Aborigines created by staff of the University of New England. While the Association embraced an ethos of cultural assimilation that few find palatable today, it was ahead of its time in some ways.

[123] PE Stramberg, 'The Garden. Outstanding Trees of the North' (*Glen Innes Examiner*, 8 October 1938) 2.
[124] Rega, 'The Fruit Grower' (*Town and Country Journal*, 5 December 1906) 27.
[125] Rega, 'The Fruit Grower' (*Town and Country Journal*, 28 November 1906) 27.
[126] 'Social and Personal' (*Sydney Morning Herald*, 5 July 1934) 13.

## V. The Big Picture

Orchardfield is a fragment of a vanishing continent, a glimpse into entire ecosystems and assemblages of wildlife that disappeared or degraded as landscapes were refashioned for settlers' aesthetic and economic preferences. The vanishing continent's ecological permutations has already been documented extensively, including in Don Watson's *The Bush*,[127] Jock Marshall's, *The Great Extermination*[128] and Barbara York Main's *Twice Trodden Ground*,[129] among much literature. The pillaging has also been contrasted with the millennia of Aboriginal environmental husbandry by Bill Gammage and Bruce Pascoe[130] and Matthew Colloff.[131] In thinking about anthropogenic changes, Eric Rolls' *A Million Wild Acres*[132] matters, for he questions European settler assumptions that simplistically distinguish between a pristine and disturbed nature, for in NSW's Pilliga Forest he finds a creative ecology adapting to invasive pressures. The implications of this caution for understanding 'wilderness', a concept treasured by settler nature conservationists, are examined in chapter nine.

The continent's colonisation began with great profligacy, a free-for-all as sealers, whalers, cedar getters and the likes plundered the most accessible resources, aided by the misguided belief of the continent's inexhaustible riches. The first wave of colonisers were 'casually destructive', suggested historian Geoffrey Bolton,[133] whose impacts were constrained by insufficient financial capital, rudimentary technology and limited labour. During the second half of the nineteenth century, the colonies intensified their grip on the land as gold rushes, broad-acre cropping and logging expanded. The following century unleashed more pressure through population growth, greater economic investment and technological changes from chainsaws to motor vehicles. The Commonwealth's seminal 1975 inquiry into the National Estate reported on the legacy: an estate 'downgraded, disregarded and neglected. All previous priorities accepted at various levels of government … have been directed by a concept [of] uncontrolled development'.[134] The impacts were uneven however, with northern Australia 'remaining relatively unmodified' because of failures in settlement and economic ventures.[135]

Much data is now available to quantify what has vanished. Australia has lost 34 terrestrial mammal species since 1788, with the severest losses accruing

[127] D Watson, *The Bush* (Penguin, 2014).

[128] J Marshall, *The Great Extermination: A Guide to Anglo-Australian Cupidity, Wickedness and Waste* (Heinemann, 1966).

[129] B York Main, *Twice Trodden Ground* (Jacaranda, 1971).

[130] B Gammage and B Pascoe, *Country: Future Fire, Future Farming* (Thames and Hudson, 2021).

[131] M Colloff, *Landscapes of Our Hearts: Reconciling People and Environment* (Thames and Hudson, 2020).

[132] E Rolls, *A Million Wild Acres* (Thomas Nelson, 1981).

[133] Bolton (n 38) 58.

[134] Committee of Inquiry into the National Estate (n 89) 334.

[135] B Griffiths, *Deep Time Dreaming: Uncovering Ancient Australia* (Black Inc, 2018) 148.

during the first two-thirds of the twentieth century, especially between 1930 and 1960 when the cumulative known extinctions jumped from 15 to 25 species.[136] Numerous more invertebrates and plants have likely been lost. As native wildlife declined, the nation's livestock population ballooned, from 82 million (horses, sheep, cattle and pigs) in 1900 to 185 million animals by 1967.[137] Vast areas were also deforested, though this is difficult to quantify owing to definitional and data problems.[138] Most deforestation in NSW occurred between the late nineteenth and mid-twentieth century in the wake of the Crown Lands Alienation Act 1861 and the Crown Lands Occupation Act 1861, which opened areas to settlement with obligations on landholders to 'develop' their tenures. Land clearing in the northern and western areas of the continent intensified between the 1920s and 1970s as the frontiers of settlement shifted, aided by similar legislation such as Western Australia's Homestead Act 1893. One metric of the extent of clearance is the area under agricultural production, such as croplands that grew from 8,814 million acres nationwide in 1901 to 39,553 million acres in 1967.[139] The continent's human population likewise grew from 3.8 million to 11.8 million. Increased urbanisation placed Australian cities under increasing environmental pressure as well: Sydney's population enlarged from 482,000 in 1901 to 2,550,000 in 1967, and its share of NSW's population over this period jumped from about 36 per cent to 61 per cent.[140]

The mythology of a 'big country' suited the young nation's aspirations for a growing economy and population but the uncritical assumption of a bountiful land meant that lawmakers were slow to recognise the need to impose limits. While legal historians have documented attempts to moderate wantonness from the earliest days of White settlement,[141] those with the plough or axe wielded far more influence in the corridors of power than the dissenting voices among natural scientists, artists, bushwalkers and others favouring restraint.

The shift from exploiting to defending nature rested heavily on appeals to the natural world's contribution to the nation's identity and prosperity. Geoffrey Bolton identifies the aesthetic and spiritual values of the bush as helping to inspire nature conservation.[142] Scenic landscapes and charismatic fauna were earlier beneficiaries of this stance. The very sovereign identity of the nation – for instance, the fauna and flora represented in the Commonwealth's coat of arms and bank notes, and the creation of the 'bush capital' in Canberra – could make nature conservation a patriotic cause. This growing affinity with nature in the young nation was also evident

[136] JZ Woinarski et al, 'Ongoing Unraveling of a Continental Fauna: Decline and Extinction of Australian Mammals Since European Settlement' (2015) 112(15) *PNAS* 4531.

[137] Australian Bureau of Statistics (ABS), *Year Book Australia 1968* (ABS, 1968) 913.

[138] CJA Bradshaw, 'Little Left to Lose: Deforestation and Forest Degradation in Australia Since European Colonization' (2012) 5(1) *Journal of Plant Ecology* 109.

[139] ABS (n 137) 862–63.

[140] C Argus, 'Trends in NSW Population Growth' (NSW Parliamentary Research Service, 2019) 3.

[141] Bonyhady (n 8).

[142] Bolton (n 38).

in the assorted native wildlife, especially kangaroos, that became morale-boosting mascots to soldiers in the World Wars (see Figure 1.6). Aesthetics however could also aid the pernicious remaking of the Australian bush, refashioning it to make settlers' surroundings more familiar, such as through the work of acclimatisation societies and land clearers. Moreover, Tim Bonyhady notes 'the difficulty of finding a legal basis for … an aesthetic argument against "improvement", as development was generally known'.[143]

**Figure 1.6** Kangaroo mascot with Australian diggers, World War I: Australian War Memorial

Another strategy to stem the vanishing continent cited the economic costs. Indiscriminate ring-barking began to be questioned as the continent's timber resources weren't found to be inexhaustible. Deforested landscapes that left soils open to erosion could also hurt farmers. And better designed cities with more greenery and less pollution could improve the livelihoods of their denizens and boost urban Australia's productivity. But this logic could also release additional sources of environmental pressure in the name of nation building. Indeed, some degradation was precipitated under the misguided belief that a superior environment could be rendered through human intervention: examples include agricultural settlement for war veterans and the hydropower project that reshaped

[143] T Bonyhady, 'An Australian Public Trust' in Dovers (n 14) 258.

the Snowy Mountains. This enlightened despotism was undertaken by governments supplying the technologies, funds, lands and legal frameworks.

A third pathway to adapting Australian society to its vanishing continent came from scientific knowledge, but again it was a mixed blessing for science could be availed to help remake, not save, the natural world. Scientific knowhow was instrumental in controlling the menace of prickly pear and rabbits that once ravaged much of the continent, and although the control was motivated to assist agriculture, it indirectly benefited natural ecosystems. Likewise, advances in pedology aided agricultural production with spin-off benefits for native flora and fauna by reducing land degradation. Soil science was mobilised by authorities through legislation such as NSW's Soil Conservation Act 1938. Science was also helpful in building appreciation of unique native fauna and flora, which translated into the creation of national parks and regulations protecting some wildlife. And science assumed a prominence in the consolidation of Australia's presence in its Antarctic Territory, with the establishment of several research stations. Yet harnessing scientific knowhow was part of the mix of behemoth nation-building projects such as dams and atomic weapons.

The adaptive capacity of Australia's early environmental laws was also shaped by the availability of foreign legal precedents. The nation's legal system primarily reflected the impost of British colonialism, which introduced the common law and a constitutional monarchy whilst sweeping aside Aboriginal legal traditions. After Federation, Australian lawmakers became more attentive to governance trends in other jurisdictions, especially the United States. The design of the national capital began with an international competition won by Chicagoan architects Walter and Marion Griffin, whose innovative blueprint for Canberra brought the principles of the global 'city beautiful' and 'garden city' town planning into the city's future. Soil conservation legislation adopted by the states in the 1930s was also directly influenced by US legal responses to its 'Dust Bowl' crisis. Yet some relevant foreign innovations that could have helped failed to take root in Australia, notably the US public trust doctrine, a lapse that Bonyhady blames on Australian courts' failure to appreciate the concept's former emerging place in the country's colonial legal history.[144]

The foregoing shifts, to defend rather than exploit Australian nature, didn't however gain the upper hand. A disparity continued between the efficacy of legal governance for environmental subjugation versus conservation. Laws defending nature in the first two-thirds of the twentieth century were often rudimentary and unwieldy, emphasising procedures rather than obligatory standards or outcomes, and insufficient institutional support to facilitate implementation. With regulators often retaining broad discretionary powers, environmental law tended to remain heavily susceptible to political control and the economic forces of colonisation

[144] ibid 258.

rather than being able to offer an independent governance space with effective accountability.

## VI. The Book's Synopsis and Sources

The chapters that follow cover many subjects, discussed thematically rather than chronologically in four parts, as a chronological history wouldn't illuminate the book's motifs so clearly and the legal changes didn't unfold evenly across Australia during this period.

For the rest of Part I, chapter two begins with the legal implications of a new sovereign nation and its federalist constitutional structure for environmental law, and then considers the implications of nationhood for how Australian nature was valued culturally, economically and politically. This place of nature in the Australian polity in 1901 is contrasted in chapter three with events from 1967 when a wave of environmental disputes inspired by community activists forged alternate values of the natural world and tactics to defend it that exposed the cumulative limitations of Australia's environmental laws. The date also marks an important constitutional amendment when the Commonwealth gained nationwide power to legislate on Aboriginal affairs.

Part II examines how Australian nature was adversely transformed through legal frameworks governing agricultural settlement, nation building and economic expansion. Case studies cover taming the bush and land clearing through imported property tenure regimes and the concomitant disavowal of Aboriginal land rights (chapter four), the disastrous consequences of invasive species introduced by settlers and the legalised war against native 'vermin' perceived to threaten agriculture (chapter five), government-led industrial, hydropower projects (chapter six) and atomic weapons testing in the Outback (chapter seven). Each case study illustrates different combinations of governance modalities albeit sharing to various degrees a colonising orientation.

Part III examines how colonisation was challenged out of a desire to defend Australian nature for reasons that included national pride in the continent's natural heritage, aesthetic and recreational benefits, plus the economic value of scientific husbandry of natural resources. With legal institutions and instruments, these case studies examine conservation of wildlife (chapter eight), the national parks (chapter nine), town planning including the development of Canberra (chapter ten), pollution control and regulation of resource use including forestry and mining (chapter eleven), and finally the environmental governance issues that arose as Australia extended its territorial ambitions to the South Ocean and Antarctica (chapter twelve).

Part IV returns to the recent history of Orchardfield, as a portal into the wider environmental upheavals in Australia of our generation to show that it would be a mistake to assume that environmental law and governance, as measured by biodiversity, the climate and other indicia, has improved in Australia. One solution is to prioritise ecosystem restoration, now in the spotlight since the United Nations declared its Decade on Ecosystem Restoration for 2021–30, and considerable opportunities exist for governments and nongovernmental institutions to collaborate here. Some projects are already demonstrating best practice, such as Western Australia's Gondwana Link. In a sense, therefore, the vanishing of Australia's nature is not just a story of a history gone but a future to be shaped.

My final introductory remarks concern the sources researched for this book. Of course, I'm not the first to acknowledge this formative legal history, as for instance perspicaciously done by the Honourable Justice Brian Preston, Chief Judge of the NSW Land and Environment Court,[145] but the literature authored by specialist scholars of environmental law is meagre. Beyond the core field, I consulted constitutional law, property rights, Aboriginal law and other areas of law that shaped environmental practices. The primary sources were cases and legislation from the AustLII databases, archival records of regulatory agencies, and reports of public inquiries and parliamentary proceedings, which helped reveal the motivations behind and debates surrounding legal developments. The legal history of other countries, especially in North America and Western Europe, were also considered to help understand how foreign precedents shaped Australia's history.

While this book was written primarily for readers interested in law, I take a multidisciplinary approach because an analysis of legal doctrine and affiliated governance alone wouldn't make sufficient sense of the subject. Because legal history at its most fundamental concerns the relationship between law and social change – understanding how and why the law changes, and whether it leads or follows society – it was important that my research be informed by a variety of sources outside legal scholarship. I consulted considerable literature from the environmental humanities; Tom Griffiths, Libby Robin, Andrea Gaynor, Heather Goodall, Stephen Dovers, William Lines and others have written extensively about subjects relevant to this book.[146] Scholars of environmental policy and governance, such as Ken Walker and David Mercer, have examined some more recent phases of this history.[147] Non-academic work that informs this book includes travel writings, poetry, films and popular media. The artistic, literary and scientific representations of landscapes and country, and their influence on environmental

[145] BJ Preston, 'Environmental Law 1927–2007: Retrospect and Prospect' (2007) 81 *Australian Law Journal* 616.

[146] See Australian and Aotearoa New Zealand Environmental History Network, www.environmentalhistory-au-nz.org/members.

[147] DC Mercer, *A Question of Balance: Natural Resources Conflict Issues in Australia* (Federation Press, 1995); KJ Walker, *The Political Economy of Environmental Policy: An Australian Introduction* (UNSW Press, 1994).

laws and policies, are germane to the research in revealing evolving public attitudes on environmental issues that shaped law and governance. I considered Aboriginal Australians' role and voice in this history as far as relevant and known from the sources. The available literature however is overwhelmingly from White Australians, and reflects a preoccupation with how a settler culture was coming to terms with the limitations of the environment.

# 2

# 1901: Nature for Nation

## I. Governing a Federation

Australia became an independent nation on 1 January 1901, a legal milestone but far from a complete break from the past. It didn't translate into a mature, self-determining nation for some decades. The Constitution was adopted, explains Bruce Kercher, 'at a time of ambivalence about Australia's place in the world, whether it was an independent country or a child of England'.[1] Whilst its framers sought greater independence from Britain, the Constitution, which itself formed part of an Act of the Imperial Parliament, maintained connections to the 'Mother Country'. White Australians still saw themselves stalwarts of the British Empire, sang 'God Save the Queen', and the Union Jack was retained in the Australian flag. English law continued to pervade Australia: the legislature, executive and judiciary branches of the Commonwealth and states were subject to the control of Westminster, British Ministers and the Privy Council, and Queen Victoria was Australia's head-of-state.[2] In 1935, Australia's then Attorney-General and future Prime Minister wrote, 'Australia sees no future outside the British Empire'.[3] World War II challenged that connection as Britain's setbacks meant it could no longer assure national security, a void that Australia would look to the United States to fill. In 1942 Australian lawmakers took the opportunity to remove one important British legacy, with the implementation of the Statute of Westminster that ended the Imperial Parliament's capacity to override Commonwealth law.

Whilst birth of the Australian nation didn't entirely remove the penumbra of Britain's oversight, nationhood was aesthetically and culturally curated to identify with the continent's unique landscapes and wildlife. Governments, along with other constituencies including in the arts, scientific community and media, contributed to this affiliation of nationhood with nature, although national identity was also shaped by other factors including economic expansion that worked against that affiliation. This chapter examines Australian nature in nationhood,

[1] B Kercher, *An Unruly Child: A History of Law in Australia* (Allen and Unwin, 1995) 157.
[2] ibid 158.
[3] RG Menzies, 'Australia's Place in the Empire' (1935) 14(4) *International Affairs* 480, 485.

beginning with the impact of federalism; although the Constitution hardly acknowledges environmental issues, it would eventually have important consequences for environmental law. We then look at how nature's treasures acquired cultural and political salience that would, as later chapters explore, shape the law's colonisation or conservation of the continent.

Australia is a single nation but its sovereign authority to regulate environmental issues is shared among different tiers of government. Borrowing federalism and separation of powers from the United States and the Westminster systems of responsible government from Britain, Australia was founded as a federal, representative democracy with governance shared between the national sphere, the Commonwealth, and the subnational sphere of six states that were successors to the colonial administrations.[4] Unlike the American model, however, and that of some other liberal democracies, the Constitution of Australia lacks a bill of rights, instead enumerating a few, ad hoc individual rights (eg right to vote, trial by jury, and protection against taking on property on unjust terms). Though there was growing Australian patriotism and some resentment of the country's colonial status in the late nineteenth century, as historians John Hirst and Helen Irving argue,[5] federalism was influenced by pragmatic considerations including the desire for a trading and customs union to facilitate commerce across the continent.[6] This preoccupation is reflected in that many enumerated legislative powers of the Commonwealth relate to markets and business, such as interstate trade and commerce (section 51(i)), corporations (section 51(xx)), currency and coinage (section 51(xii)), copyright, patents and trademarks (section 51(xviii)), banking (section 51(xiii), and postal and telegraphic services (section 51(v)). Equally important, the Constitution prescribes that trade within the Commonwealth shall be free (section 92). The section 51 heads of power are held with the states but section 109 provides that Commonwealth law prevails if there's an inconsistency between it and a state law.

Australia's Constitution left the state governments in charge of managing most natural resources. They also had exclusive authority over Aboriginal people until the Constitution was amended in 1967 to give the Commonwealth concurrent power, a lacuna that Jennifer Eastick suggests owed partly to the perception by the Constitution's drafters that Aboriginal Australians were a 'dying [race] whose future need not require protection beyond that which the States would provide'.[7]

[4] For useful introductions, see: J Steelios, *Zines and Stellios's The High Court and the Constitution* (Federation Press, 2022); N Aroney et al, *The Constitution of the Commonwealth of Australia* (Cambridge University Press, 2015).

[5] J Hirst, *The Sentimental Nation: The Making of the Australian Commonwealth* (Oxford University Press, 2000); H Irving, *To Constitute a Nation: A Cultural History of Australia's Constitution* (Cambridge University Press, 1997).

[6] J La Nauze, *The Making of the Australian Constitution* (Melbourne University Press, 1972).

[7] JE Eastick, 'The Australian Aborigine: Full Commonwealth Responsibility Under the Constitution' (1980) 12 *Melbourne University Law Review* 516, 518.

**Figure 2.1** Opening of First Parliament of the Commonwealth of Australia, 9 May 1901, oil on canvas, Tom Roberts, 1901–03; National Library of Australia

Later, the 1929 Royal Commission on the Constitution received suggestions by some politicians that the Constitution should give the Commonwealth power over 'aborigines, fauna and flora, fisheries and forestry'.[8] Ultimately, the Commonwealth's only explicit power on environmental matters is 'fisheries in Australian waters beyond territorial limits' (section 51(x)). Early Commonwealth laws in this domain include the Beaches, Fishing Grounds and Sea Routes Protection Act 1932, regulating ship discharges, and the Fisheries Act 1952. Some of its other laws were potentially counterproductive, however; bizarre by today's standards, the Navigation Act 1912 allowed a shipmaster without liability to 'throw overboard any dangerous goods shipped without his knowledge'.[9]

Water management was a contentious issue in the constitution's drafting because of intergovernmental rivalries over the Murray-Darling basin.[10] Whilst section 51 omits water management, section 98 clarifies that the Commonwealth's trade and commerce power (section 51(i)) extends to water navigation and state railways. This clause was included to appease South Australia's interest in maintaining river trade. To allay concerns of NSW and Victoria that

[8] 'Constitution Alteration (Power of Amendment) Bill, Second Reading, House of Representatives, Parliamentary Debates, 26 March 1930, 525.

[9] Section 250.

[10] SD Clark and IA Renard, 'Constitutional, Legal and Administrative Problems' in HJ Firth and G Sawer (eds), *The Murray Waters* (Angus and Robertson, 1974) 263, 268–70.

any Commonwealth laws might constrain their interests in drawing water for irrigated agriculture, the Constitution has the proviso in section 100 that the Commonwealth not interfere with the rights of states and their residents to make 'reasonable use of the waters of rivers for conservation or irrigation'.[11]

Despite its paucity of environmental provisions, the constitutional landscape has dramatically shifted over the past century, 'with the Commonwealth holding political powers that would have amazed the founding fathers', explains Kercher.[12] Nonetheless, the Commonwealth has often pursued cooperation on environmental matters to avoid the political repercussions of encroaching on what the states' regard as their turf.

One source of federal action is the external affairs power (section 51 (xxix)), permitting legislation to implement international treaties and other global affairs of concern to Australia. Whilst the High Court's decision in the *Franklin Dam* case (1983) was a watershed for the Commonwealth's invocation of an international environmental treaty to override a state's economic project,[13] this potential was planted far earlier. In the *Burgess* case of 1936, the Court interpreted the external affairs power broadly. In the most expansionist interpretation, Justices Evatt and McTiernan held that subject to some express and implied limitations such as section 92 (freedom of trade), the Commonwealth could implement any treaty whatever its subject.[14] Between 1901 and 1967 however there were few international environmental treaties; for instance, the Commonwealth ratified the International Whaling Convention 1946, International Plant Protection Convention 1951 and the Convention for the Prevention of Pollution by Sea by Oil 1954.[15] Thus, the full potential of the external affairs power for environmental governance wouldn't become apparent until the 1980s.

The *Franklin Dam* case also affirmed the Commonwealth can avail the corporation power (section 51(xx)) to address the environmental activities of business corporations. The decision was possible because of the High Court's 1971 ruling in the *Strickland* case,[16] which overturned its 1909 decision in *Huddart, Parker*[17] that the corporation power was constrained by the (since discredited) doctrine of the reserved states' powers. The Commonwealth however has generally eschewed embedding environmental standards directly in corporate governance; today, the meagre exceptions include provisions in its lodestar Corporations Act 2001 for a company director's report to disclose the entity's performance regarding any

[11] P Kildea and G Williams, 'The Constitution and the Management of Water in Australia's Rivers' (2010) 32(4) *Sydney Law Review* 595.

[12] Kercher (n 1) 162.

[13] *Commonwealth v Tasmania* [1983] HCA 21.

[14] *R v Burgess; Ex parte Henry* [1936] HCA 52.

[15] Cited in E Brown Weiss, 'The Evolution of International Environmental Law' (2011) 54 *Japanese Yearbook of International Law* 1, 3.

[16] *Strickland v Rocla Concrete Pipes* [1971] HCA 40.

[17] *Huddart, Parker & Co Pty Ltd v Moorehead* [1909] HCA 36.

significant environmental regulation that affects it, and for investment corporations to disclose to the public the extent to which they take environmental matters into account in their investment products.[18]

In conceptualising the ambit of Commonwealth powers, the High Court's ruling in the *Engineers* case of 1920 is particularly germane, holding that its constitutional powers are *plenary*, unqualified by any implied reservation of powers to the states.[19] This interpretation was reaffirmed in the *Murphyores* case of 1976, which involved an unsuccessful Queensland challenge to a Commonwealth ban on the export of mineral sands in order to protect Fraser Island's beaches.[20] Also, the fact that Commonwealth legislation could be characterised as related to several subject matters did not invalidate the legislation so long as at least one matter could be pegged to a constitutional head of legislative power (here, trade and commerce power).

Another legal avenue for Commonwealth aggrandisement is the executive's nationhood power sourced in section 61, enabling actions pursuant to Australia's character and status as a nation, beyond the scope of the legislative heads of power. High Court jurisprudence suggests the nationhood power furnishes the federal executive with 'a capacity' to 'engage in enterprises and activities peculiarly adapted to the government of a nation and which cannot otherwise be carried on for the benefit of the nation'.[21] The implied nationhood power has helped support Commonwealth initiatives including environment-related ones such as establishment of the CSIRO (Commonwealth Scientific and Industrial Research Organisation). The Commonwealth's express and implied incidental powers also are recognised by constitutional law experts as 'expand[ng] the totality of Commonwealth power'.[22] Furthermore, via the incidental power in section 51(xxxix)), the Commonwealth can enact legislation in aid of the exercise of the section 61 executive power. The High Court in the *Airlines of NSW* case of 1965 upheld federal regulations over safety of domestic air navigation – a matter without express power but considered as reasonably incidental to the power to govern interstate and overseas trade.[23]

Increased Commonwealth authority has flowed heavily from the fiscal imbalance, leveraged by its concurrent power over taxation (section 51(ii)) and to grant financial assistance to any state on such terms it wishes (section 96). The fiscal imbalance shifted during World War II as the Commonwealth hiked income taxes to fund the war effort, with the states correspondingly retreating. Through the financial grants power, experts suggest that the Commonwealth can 'treat the

[18] Sections 299(1)(f) and 1013D(1).

[19] *Amalgamated Society of Engineers v Adelaide Steamship Co Ltd* [1920] HCA 54.

[20] *Murphyores v Commonwealth* [1976] HCA 20.

[21] *Victoria v Commonwealth* (1975) 134 CLR 338, 397.

[22] GA Rumble, 'Section 51(xxxix) of the Constitution and the Federal Distribution of Power' (1982) 13 *Federal Law Review* 182, 186.

[23] *Airlines of New South Wales v New South Wales* (1965) 113 CLR 54.

states largely as conduits of Commonwealth spending on matters lying outside the limits of its legislative power'.[24] Section 96 grants have been used for environment-related purposes, such as drought assistance and soil conservation, but also for leveraging environmentally impactful development. In subtle ways too, however, the Commonwealth's financial levers have sometimes been counter-productive for environmental policy, such as until 1983 giving farmers' tax breaks for land 'improvements' such as tree clearing.[25]

The Commonwealth's most unencumbered power, furnished by section 122 of the Constitution, concerns Australia's territories outside the states. These presently comprise six external territories (several islands and the Australian Antarctic Territory), three internal territories (the Australian Capital Territory, Northern Territory and Jervis Bay Territory) and one territory with a bespoke status (Norfolk Island). The massive Australian Antarctic Territory covers 5.896 million $km^2$ or 42 per cent of the continent, although many nations dispute Australia's sovereignty and its governance is mediated by the Antarctic Treaty 1959.[26] In its territories the Commonwealth has enacted bespoke environmental legislation or applied its general environmental laws such as currently the Environment Protection and Biodiversity Conservation Act 1999. Formerly, the Australian Antarctic Territory Act 1954 provided that the laws of the Australian Capital Territory would apply to its Antarctica domain.[27]

Another avenue for nation building has been cooperative federalism. Curiously, the Constitution is largely bereft of formal intergovernmental machinery. Whilst it provided in section 101 for an Inter-Sate Commission to facilitate cooperation on trade and commerce, just two years after its establishment in 1912 the High Court ruled that the Commission's adjudicative functions were constitutionally impermissible, thus emasculating its potential, and the Commission died in 1920.[28] Despite that setback, cooperative federalism was articulated institutionally through other statutory and executive mechanisms. An Interstate Royal Commission on Murray Waters was convened in 1902 to inquire into the 'conservation and distribution of the waters of the Murray and its tributaries for the purpose of irrigation, navigation and water supply'.[29] In 1914 the Prime Minister and three state premiers concluded the River Murray Waters Agreement, whereby NSW and Victoria agreed to limit their constitutional powers to manage the River Murray and to provide South Australia with a share of its flow. Cooperative

[24] B Gogarty, 'Making Sense of s 96: Tied Grants, Contextualism and the Limits of Federal Fiscal Power' (2019) 42(2) *Melbourne University Law Review* 455, 458.

[25] MG Kirby and MJ Blyth, 'Economic Aspects of Land Degradation in Australia' (1987) 31(2) *Australian Journal of Agricultural Economics* 154, 163.

[26] 402 UNTS 71.

[27] Section 6(1).

[28] A Bell, 'Inter-State Commission' in T Blackshield, M Coper and G Williams (eds), *The Oxford Companion to the High Court of Australia* (Oxford University Press, 2001) 353.

[29] Murray-Darling Basin Authority, 'History of Water Management in the Basin' (2022) 2.

federalism in this sphere continued by other means over the century using other constitutional powers, leading for instance to the creation in 1962 of the Australian Water Resources Council.

Agriculture, including soils conservation and pest control, was another domain of early cooperative federalism.[30] The Council for Scientific and Industrial Research – the CSIRO's precursor – was established in 1926 to undertake and coordinate research into issues of national importance,[31] and in 1927 its chief executive joined the relevant heads of state and Commonwealth departments in a Standing Committee on Agriculture to define priorities and methods for cooperation in agricultural research. In 1935 the Standing Committee expanded its remit inter alia to pests and diseases, and to support the then recently established Australian Agricultural Council to facilitate intergovernmental consultation on agricultural matters. The latter Council was convened in response to growing national concerns about land degradation impacting farming. Creation of institutions and expressions of concern, however, don't necessarily translate into effective cooperative federalism, which has suffered some major failures, notably, explains Daniel Connell, in the decades of mismanagement of the Murray-Darling basin.[32]

The Commonwealth also partook in development projects and other activities that brought adverse environmental consequences. One domain is the Commonwealth's control of immigration policy – a powerful lever to influence Australia's population growth and size. After the national insecurity provoked by World War II, the Commonwealth expanded immigration, absorbing by 1965 two million persons, many from war-torn Europe, under the slogan 'populate or perish' coined by Arthur Calwell, Australia's first Minister for Immigration (appointed in 1945).[33] The influx brought cultural and economic benefits but also intensified environmental pressures, most evident in sprawling cities, urban congestion and increased land clearing for food production. Many migrants also came to work on nation-building projects. The Snowy Mountains hydropower scheme was launched in 1949 and was justified as an exercise of the Commonwealth's authority over national defence (section 51(vi)).[34] Senator Frederick Katz explained in the parliamentary debates on the enabling legislation, the Snowy Mountains Hydro-Electric Power Bill, that:

> This Government is making use of the defence power of the Commonwealth to initiate the Snowy Mountains project, not because it is fearful of an immediate attack upon

[30] J Williams, *Soils Governance in Australia: Challenges of Cooperative Federalism* (UTS ePress, 2015).

[31] CB Schedvin, *Shaping Science and Industry: A History of Australia's Council for Scientific and Industrial Research, 1926–49* (Allen and Unwin, 1987).

[32] D Connell, *Water Politics in the Murray-Darling Basis* (Federation Press, 2007).

[33] Department of Immigration, 'All States Pledge Support for Immigration Policy' *Tomorrow's Australians: Bulletin of the Department of Immigration* 15 (5 June 1949) 2.

[34] BP MacFarlan and AR Taylor, 'Legal Opinion 1856: Validity of Snowy Mountains Hydro-Electric Power Bill (1949)', legalopinions.ags.gov.au/legalopinion/opinion-1856.

> the nation, but in order to prepare Australia for any future eventuality of that nature. Should we ever be involved in war again, we must have plenty of electric power.[35]

That assertion was never tested in court, and subsequent views suggest the Snowy scheme had a 'tenuous link to the defence power'.[36] Also never judicially challenged was the Commonwealth's collaboration with Britain to test atomic bombs in the Outback. However, it was a more obvious exercise of the Commonwealth's defence, and external affairs powers, but a chapter in the nation's history that illustrates how Commonwealth constitutional mandates have also been instruments of environmentally destructive, 'enlightened' despotism. Yet, the mandates were not unlimited, as when the High Court denied the Commonwealth's attempt to rely on its defence power to outlaw the Communist Party.[37]

Public expectations that the Commonwealth should assume national environmental leadership wouldn't start to become widely expressed until the late 1960s or even later. An early example was petitions from community groups that the government restrict international export of Australian fauna and their skins or feathers. From the late 1960s, environmentalists began to appeal more systematically for Commonwealth intervention in matters hitherto regarded as states' responsibilities, as considered in the following chapter, such as to save Lake Pedder from a Tasmanian hydropower project.

Another channel for expanded federal involvement in environmental matters is the Commonwealth parliament's convening of public inquiries, and even if they raise issues outside federal competence such inquiries at least can stimulate public debate and encourage action by other actors (governmental or nongovernmental). In 1963 a parliamentary select committee inquired into Aboriginal grievances in Arnhem land.[38] In the late 1960s and early 1970s several groundbreaking inquiries were held by parliamentary select committees on air pollution, water pollution and wildlife conservation.[39] They all found serious deficiencies in the states' environmental laws and advocated Commonwealth involvement to coordinate comprehensive protections. Another landmark was in 1973 when the Whitlam government initiated an inquiry into the flooding of Tasmania's Lake Pedder after Moss Cass, Australia's first ever Minister for Environment and Conservation, declared 'we have no rights in the matter at all'.[40] Commentators of

[35] Senate, Official Hansard, 18th Parliament, 2nd Session, 30 June 1949, 1782.

[36] Parliamentary Library, 'Bills Digest No. 70 1997–98 Snowy Hydro Corporatisation Bill 1997', Commonwealth of Australia, 1997.

[37] *Australian Communist Party v Commonwealth* [1951] HCA 5.

[38] House of Representatives, Select Committee, *Grievances of Yirrkala Aborigines, Arnhem Land Reserve* (Government Printing Office, 1963).

[39] Senate, *Report from the Senate Select Committee on Air Pollution* (Government Printing Office, 1969); Senate, *Report from the Senate Select Committee on Water Pollution, Water Pollution in Australia* (Government Printer, 1970); House of Representatives, *Wildlife Conservation – Report* (Government Printing Office, 1972).

[40] Quoted in PA Management Consultants, *Guide to Environmental Law in Australia* (1974) 522.

this era however cautioned against the Commonwealth convening public inquiries (eg a Royal Commission) that would exercise compulsive powers, such as to demand information, save where it acts pursuant to direct constitutional authority.[41]

## II. The States

Whilst the Constitution, explains Geoffrey Sawer, put 'overwhelming financial resources' under Commonwealth control, the states retained primary control over natural resources.[42] They also retained authority over Aboriginal people. The states thus had considerable leverage over the nation's economic development, especially through property tenure (including eviction of Aboriginal landholders), allocation of resource licences (eg mining and forestry) and, in areas of major human settlement, via town planning and creation of municipal authorities.

The states' legal regimes were poorly adapted to address the accreting environmental problems of the young nation. The common law inherited from Britain was unfit as a framework for their regulation.[43] Justice Windeyer of the High Court in 1962 cautioned, 'The conditions of settlement, of climate and geography in which this body of customary law developed are very different from those prevailing in many parts of Australia. And this is to be borne in mind when particular decisions of English courts are brought forward as analogies'.[44] One difficulty with the common law is that where environmental damage ostensibly is confined within a single property, such as soil erosion or deforestation, there may be no other party with a legally-recognised interest to challenge the problem. Moreover, the long latency of some environmental problems not only obscures liability but inhibits long-term preventive solutions.

Statutory responses to fill these lacunae often didn't radically improve the situation, owing to environmental legislation typically being procedural and administrative in character, with extensive discretionary powers subject to political rather than legislative or judicial control, and governing agencies operating in silos that inhibited coordination of cross-cutting environmental considerations.[45] Occasional departures from the latter inflexibility included NSW's Conservation Authority established in 1949 to coordinate soil, water and forestry management across the state and to direct other agencies to undertake specific initiatives.[46] Their normative frameworks were also weak, as the emerging concept of 'wise use' was yet to be developed into a robust legal standard.

[41] G Sawer, 'Conservation and the Law' in AB Costin and HJ Firth (eds), *Conservation* (Penguin, 1971) 262, 269.

[42] ibid 262.

[43] J Bradsen, 'Soil Conservation: History, Law, and Learning' in S Dovers (ed), *Environmental History and Policy: Still Settling Australia* (Oxford University Press, 2001) 273, 287–90.

[44] *Gartner v Kidman* (1962) 108 CLR 12, 23.

[45] PA Management Consultants (n 40) passim.

[46] Conservation Authority of New South Wales Act 1949.

Another realm where the states sought to improve and coordinate action was in town and land use planning where, explains AS Fogg, 'they found it convenient to borrow' foreign planning precedents.[47] Whilst many Australian towns were established during the colonial period, their governing frameworks evolved in the late nineteenth and early twentieth century under international precedents and trends, notably the public sanitation reforms in industrialising Britain, then the 'city beautiful' vision of US planners and the 'garden city' ideals associated with Ebenezer Howard.[48] Equally importantly, town planning was harnessed to facilitate commerce and material progress, as evident for example in the Royal Commission for the Improvement of the City of Sydney and its Suburbs convened in 1908 'to fully inquire into the whole subject of the remodelling of Sydney'.[49]

Comprehensive urban planning, however, was delayed by the Great Depression and World War II, but rebounded in the post-war construction boom, such as with NSW's Local Government (Town and Country Planning) Amendment Act 1945, which enabled municipalities to prepare comprehensive local plans aided by zoning. Some cities also adopted wider, regional plans, such as Sydney's County of Cumberland Plan 1949 and Melbourne's Metropolitan Board of Works Plan 1953 that aimed to improve urban amenities, create well-serviced neighbourhoods and convenient transport networks.[50] Not only were cities being planned to grow horizontally, their vertical expansion was also being overhauled; a 1957 amendment to NSW's Height of Building Act 1912 removed the 150-foot heigh limit, thereby enabling a surge in high-rise construction in Sydney.

The renaissance in town planning had limitations, however. It didn't extend to Aboriginal communities who, dispossessed from their traditional territories, were shunted into reserves, missions and fringe camps in often squalid conditions.[51] Even for the non-Aboriginal beneficiaries of the new planning ideologies and laws, their drawbacks became palpable by the early 1970s as community backlash grew against freeways and other mega-developments of modernist planning that put business before people. The story of urban planning continues in chapter ten, focusing on Canberra's history.

The potential for enlightened despotism manifested in another guise during this era in special 'indenture' legislation that created bespoke governance

[47] AS Fogg, *Australian Town Planning Law* (University of Queensland Press, 1974) 10.

[48] On Australian urban planning history, see R Freestone, *Designing Australia's Cities: Culture, Commerce and the City Beautiful Movement, 1900–1930* (Routledge, 2007); B Gleeson and N Low, *Australian Urban Planning: New Challenges, New Agendas* (Allen and Unwin, 2000); S Hamnett and R Freestone (eds), *The Australian Metropolis: A Planning History* (Allen and Unwin, 2000).

[49] P Ashton and R Freestone, 'Town Planning' (2008) 1(2) *Sydney Journal* 11, 14.

[50] See I Alexander, 'The Post-war City' in S. Hamnett and R. Freestone (eds), *The Australian Metropolis: A Planning History* (Allen and Unwin, 2000) 98.

[51] S Jackson, L Porter and LC Johnson, *Planning in Indigenous Australia: From Imperial Foundations to Postcolonial Futures* (Routledge, 2018).

agreements for major resources and industrial projects, typically exempting them from ordinary land use or other environmental controls including liability for common law torts. Such exceptionalism of course undermined the integrity of environmental law. Two examples, from South Australia, were the Pulp and Paper Mill Agreement Act 1958 and the Pulp and Paper Mills (Hundreds of Mayurra and Hindmarsh) Act 1964.[52] The latter Act provided that the beneficiary company, Apcel:

> shall not be liable in any way for discharging effluent from the mill into a drain … or for discharging smoke, dust or gas into the atmosphere or creating noise or odours … if such discharge, flow or creation or such consequences is or are reasonably necessary for the efficient operation of the works of the Company and not due to negligence on the part of the Company, its servants or agents.[53]

Apcel's waste was discharged into Lake Bonney, the state's largest freshwater lake; it was described in 1971 as a 'porridge of death'.[54] A Victorian example of bespoke deals is the Westernport (Oil Refinery) Act 1963, which bequeathed the beneficiary company control of extensive public foreshore rezoned and allowed it 'to dispose of all effluent waters … without fee charge'.[55] In Tasmania special legislation was enacted to facilitate forestry concessions, such as the Huon Valley Pulp and Paper Industry Act 1959. Indenture legislation however had the potential downside of arousing public attention, and criticism, as happened with NSW's Clutha Development Pty Ltd Agreement Act 1970 to fast-track approval of a new coal loading facility near Wollongong. The company abandoned its environmentally controversial plan in the wake of massive community opposition.[56]

Plausibly, the very structure of much environmental regulation including pollution licensing can be construed as a state-sanctioned concession to private business, for it has typically served to authorise pollution within technologically and economically viable criteria. One indicium is the ubiquitous regulatory standard of 'best practicable means' or equivalent terms.[57] NSW's Clean Air Act 1961, modelled on the UK's Alkali Act 1863, required use of 'all practicable means' for preventing air pollution. Victoria's Clean Air Act 1958, likewise qualified compliance if the source premises used 'any practicable means there may be for minimizing the emission of air impurities'.[58] An analysis of Queensland's water pollution regulations of this era concluded that 'controls were imposed that were

[52] A Chalklen, 'Indentures and Pollution Control at Lake Bonney' (1990) 7(3) *Environmental and Planning Law Journal* 234.
[53] Section 6.
[54] D Whitelock, *A Dirty Story: Pollution in Australia* (Sun Books, 1971) 80.
[55] Schedule 4(n)(ii).
[56] J Hagan, 'Clutha: The Politics of Pollution' in R Dempsey (ed), *The Politics of Finding Out* (Cheshire Publishing, 1974) 29.
[57] J.L Sullivan, 'Australian Air Pollution Legislation' (1965) 15(9) *Journal of the Air Pollution Association* 429, 431.
[58] Section 8.

cheap to implement or useful to the pollution agency, but which were ineffective in stopping pollution outright'.[59] Environmental licensing historically thus rarely vetoed economically beneficial projects, at best mitigating the worst consequences in an era of unscientific faith in a 'dilute and disperse' solution which relied on tall smokestacks or long effluent pipes to shift pollution out of sight.

Governments could give themselves similar concessions where they undertook major developments on the assumption that they were furthering the 'public interest'. In legal terms, this could be achieved by reliance on the traditional doctrine of Crown immunity, by which the Crown was presumed not to be bound by legislation in the absence of express language or necessary implication.[60] Crown immunity thus helped exempt some state-sponsored projects from environmental rules or other legal constraints. The doctrine was altered by the High Court in the *Bropho* case of 1990 – involving the application of Western Australia's Aboriginal Heritage Act 1972 to Crown lands – where it ruled that this presumption applies in a more limited manner, by considering whether parliament intended for the statute to bind the Crown, as ascertained from the statute's terms and purposes.[61] The High Court's shift, rationalised by government organs' growing involvement in social and economic affairs, is all the more interesting given that just the year before the UK House of Lords reaffirmed the traditional presumption of Crown immunity.[62]

Another legal strategy by which the states sought to pursue their economic and political agendas unshackled from environmental controls was bespoke legislation to facilitate prestige projects. One particularly brazen example, considered in the following chapter, is when Tasmania's Hydro-Electric Commission's dammed the sublime Lake Pedder in the island's southwest wilderness pursuant to special enabling legislation: the Hydro-Electric Commission (Power Development) Act 1967. When opposing environmental groups pointed out that the Commission had probably contravened Tasmania's National Parks and Wildlife Act 1970, the state premier in 1972 rushed through parliament the Hydro–Electric Commission (Doubts Removal) Act to retroactively legalise the flooding.

In sum, federalism distributed powers to exploit the continent's natural resources but without imprinting on the nation corresponding duties for overarching environmental stewardship, a lacuna little different to any nation of that era but now a jarring gap given vast constitutional reform on the environment, as David Boyd's work documents.[63] The Constitution formalised Australia's political

[59] J Wegner, 'Sludge on Tap: Queensland's First Water Pollution Legislation, 1944–1985' (2009) 15 *Environment and History* 199, 199.

[60] See eg the Privy Council's decision in *Province of Bombay v Municipal Corporation of Bombay* [1947] AC 48.

[61] *Bropho v Western Australia* [1990] HCA 24.

[62] *Lord Advocate v Dumbarton District Council* [1989] 3 WLR 1346.

[63] DR Boyd, *The Environmental Rights Revolution: A Global Study of Constitutions, Human Rights, and the Environment* (UBC Press, 2011).

independence but left its ecologies open to intensification of an existing coloniality begun in 1788. By protecting interstate trade and commerce, and equipping the Commonwealth with new powers for nation building, the Constitution enabled that path. And equally detrimental for Aboriginal people, the Constitution just ignored them, leaving their lands and cultures to be subjugated by the states. Yet despite these shortcomings in the nation's founding legal architecture, from the inception of nationhood, Australia's landscapes and wildlife were increasingly sequestered as sources of national pride, a story taken up in section IV of this chapter.

## III. The Penumbra of English Law

The formality of an independent nation in 1901 didn't unleash in Australia a wave of legal innovations. Instead, it was a period of 'creeping legal independence' according to one historian.[64] Law-makers, practitioners and the legal academy continued to operate within the penumbra of 'Mother England's' legal traditions, or what former High Court Justice Michael Kirby once called 'a branch office of the English law and its judges',[65] and this shadow inhibited autochthonous legal solutions adapted to Australian needs and conditions across many domains including the natural environment. The Constitution of 1901, an Imperial statute, didn't remove the Privy Council in London as the highest court of appeal, Australian judges continued for some years to treat English House of Lords decisions as influential, if not binding, precedents, and homegrown legislation had yet to be enacted in many fields to modify, supplement or replace the English common law. For instance, in 1974 the Privy Council decided an important case from NSW concerning the relationship between mining law and environmental law.[66] And Australian courts in the 1970s were still closely following English precedents on municipal authorities' wide discretionary powers in planning matters,[67] and companies' liability for pollution damage.[68] In an era where Australian legal professionals were trained by academics who hesitated to question legal traditions, promote law reform or engage with the wider public beyond the classroom, the law was often behind societal pressures for addressing the nation's environmental challenges along with related issues such as the grievances of Aboriginal Australians.

[64] Kercher (n 1) 176.

[65] M Kirby, 'Beyond Noble Drudgery: Pioneering Australian Legal Scholars, by Susan Bartie: Foreword' (2019) 8; www.michaelkirby.com.au/2019-speeches.

[66] *Associated Minerals Consolidated v Wyong Shire Council* [1975] AC 538.

[67] TL Bryant, 'Conditional Town Planning Permits' (1979) 12 *Melbourne University Law Review* 139, 142.

[68] DE Fisher, *Environmental Law in Australia* (University of Queensland Press, 1980) 69–72.

The Australian judiciary was steeped in the traditions of English positivism. Influential High Court Justice and later Chief Justice Sir Owen Dixon espoused what he called a 'strict and complete legalism'[69] that eschewed judicial activism.[70] He also once famously said, in 1942: 'no good can come of divergence between the common law in one jurisdiction of the British Commonwealth and as administered in another. We think that it can be best avoided by continuing to recognise the high persuasive authority of the decisions given in the Strand and at Westminster'.[71] By 1963 Dixon conceded his court shouldn't necessarily follow House of Lords rulings,[72] and the Privy Council in 1967 likewise affirmed that Australian case law should guide its judiciary.[73]

Likewise, with few exceptions, law academics reliant on English textbooks habitually expounded legal rules rather than critiqued them.[74] University-based law schools were established in the Australian colonies or states between 1855 and 1927, whose staff were mostly legal practitioners, teaching part-time. The standard textbook on Australian history was Windeyer's treatise, published in 1938,[75] which Horst Lucke observes actually focused on UK legal history, with just 12 out of its 280 pages devoted to the 'introduction of English law into Australia'.[76] There were negligible Australian scholarly literature on the law relating to the environment, which was addressed obliquely via property tenure, town planning, public health and tort law.[77]

Legal historians thus see 1901 as part of the journey rather than culmination of Australia's unshackling from Great Britain, a process initiated when the colonies gained some self-governance from the 1850s. The 1901 Constitution certainly marked a decisive milestone but the break from the UK's legal order was incomplete. There were two further key steps although their relative significance is debated.[78] One was the imperial parliament's Statute of Westminster Act 1931, which the Commonwealth adopted in 1942, thereby gaining full, independent

[69] O Dixon, *Jesting Pilate and Other Papers and Addresses* (LBC, 1965) 247.

[70] O Dixon, 'Concerning Judicial Method' in SHZ Woinarski (ed), *Jesting Pilate* (Law Book, 1965) 155.

[71] ibid 104.

[72] *Parker v Queen* (1963) HCA 14.

[73] *Australian Consolidated Press v Uren* (1967) All ER 523.

[74] See S Bartie, *Free Hands and Minds: Pioneering Australian Legal Scholars* (Hart Publishing, 2019).

[75] WJV Windeyer, *Lectures on Legal History* (Halstead Press, 1938); revised in 1949.

[76] H Lucke, 'Legal History in Australia: The Development of Legal/Historical Scholarship' (2010) 34 *Australian Bar Review* 109, 113.

[77] See eg E Campbell, 'Regulation of Australian Coastal Fisheries' (1960) 1 *University of Tasmania Law Review* 405; TP Fry, 'Land Tenures in Australian Law' (1946–47) 3 *Res Judicatae* 158; DP O'Connell, 'Problems of Australian Coastal Jurisdiction' (1958) 34 *British Yearbook of International Law* 199; CC Reade, 'Town Planning Legislation in South Australia: A Retrospect' (1921) 9(3) *Town Planning Review* 157; FW Ledgar, 'Town Planning in Victoria with Particular Reference to the Aim and Scope of the Melbourne Metropolitan Planning Scheme' (1959–60) 2 *Melbourne University Law Review* 283; AR Southwood, 'Public Health Legislation: Its Evolution in South Australia' (April 1938) *Medical Journal of Australia* 726.

[78] A Twomey, 'Independence Day' (2011) 36(1) *Alternative Law Journal* 2.

legislative powers. Until then, some UK legislation still applied, such as the Whaling Industry (Regulation) Act 1934. The Statute provided that a law of the Dominions of the British Empire isn't 'void or inoperative on the ground that it is repugnant to the law of England', that Dominions can make laws of extraterritorial application, and UK laws only extend to a Dominion if the Dominion consents.[79] Whilst the Statute thus negated the Colonial Laws Validity Act 1865 – whereby Imperial legislation had retained paramountcy, as demonstrated by the High Court's decision in 1925 finding invalid provisions of the Commonwealth's Navigation Act 1912 for being contrary to British Merchant Shipping Acts[80] – the Statute didn't cover the states' parliaments, and furthermore the Crown on the advice of British ministers could disallow laws passed in the states, and appeals to the Privy Council could still occur in limited circumstances.[81]

The latter fetters were removed in 1986 by the second major milestone, the Australia Acts, passed separately by the Australian and British parliaments.[82] The legislation repealed all capacities for the British Parliament to make laws for the Commonwealth and the states, ended the Crown's powers to disallow a state law, ended appeals from any Australian court to the Privy Council, ended the UK's role in the appointment of the state governors, and transferred the power to alter UK statutes that form Australia's Constitution to the Commonwealth and the state parliaments.[83] However, because the British monarchy still has a notional place in the Australian nation, commentators suggest 'the severance of ties with Britain is incomplete' until Australia becomes a republic.[84]

The question of the legal status of prior Aboriginal occupation of the continent for millennia also remains not conclusively resolved. It was entirely ignored in Australia's Constitution. It was accepted common law doctrine of the time that colonised territory was either conquered or settled. If the former, the laws of the conquered peoples remained in place until altered by British law. If the latter, the coloniser's laws applied immediately upon annexation of the territory, and such territory could either be one entirely without people (as in Antarctica) or, in the nomenclature of English jurist William Blackstone, the land was 'desart (sic) and uncultivated'.[85] By this dogma, the 'settled' continent of Australia was considered *terra nullius*. There were few scholarly works on Australian Aboriginal legal issues during the first half of the twentieth century; early publications, albeit not

[79] Sections 2–4.
[80] *Union Steamship Co of New Zealand Ltd v Commonwealth* (1925) 36 CLR 130.
[81] M Gleeson, 'The Privy Council – the Australian Experience' (Anglo-Australasian Lawyers Society, London, 18 June 2008).
[82] Australia Act 1986 (Cth) and Australia Act 1986 (UK).
[83] D Gare, 'Dating Australia's Independence: National Sovereignty and the 1986 Australia Acts' (1999) 29(113) *Australian Historical Studies* 251.
[84] Kercher (n 1) 188.
[85] W Blackstone, *Commentaries on the Laws of England: A Facsimile of the First Edition of 1765–1769* (University of Chicago Press, 1979) vol I, 104.

from lawyers, were authored in 1932 by John Sexton, a Baptist clergyman active in Aboriginal affairs in South Australia,[86] and then another in 1941 by Edmund Foxcroft, a federal civil servant.[87] The successful challenge to *terra nullius* that culminated in the High Court's 1992 ruling in the *Mabo* case[88] arose from a land rights conference at James Cook University in 1981 where the eventual plaintiff, Eddie Mabo, met lawyer Greg McIntyre who recommended a test case to confirm Mabo's customary land rights on Murray Island. Whilst Australian common law belatedly recognises 'native title' as surviving British colonisation, it raises the unresolved demand to recognise unceded Aboriginal sovereignty of the continent.[89]

## IV. Curating Nationalism

Whilst Australia's federation in 1901 didn't sever the nation's umbilical cord to British law, it helped cultivate the nations' cultural identity, as evoked in representations of its land and people in poetry, paintings, the media and other cultural outputs, and these representations included greater appreciation of the continent's landscapes (though Aboriginal culture was yet to receive the same respect). Political historian Benedict Anderson argues that such cultural expressions matter in creating an 'imagined community' for a national consciousness.[90] Australian governments themselves sought to connect the continent to nation. Authorities' expropriation of legitimating symbols supportive of the dominant political and economic ideologies, argues Tiffany Jenkins, is a valuable form of soft intervention that complements the harder governance of law.[91]

Affiliating nationhood with the natural world didn't, however, necessarily equate to greater legal protection of it, as this book's later chapters will show. Many decades later, during a Queensland parliamentary debate to amend the Badge, Arms and Floral Emblem of Queensland Act, one politician ironically suggested it would be apt to choose as the state's emblem a 'kangaroo, hotly pursued by a shooter, dashing over a strip of beach that had been destroyed by sand-miners, and looking out towards a Barrier Reef liberally straddled with oil rigs'.[92] Affiliating

[86] JH Sexton, *Legislation Governing the Australian Aborigines* (Aborigines Friends' Association, 1932).

[87] EJB Foxcroft, *Australian Native Policy: Its History, Especially in Victoria* (Melbourne University Press, 1941).

[88] *Mabo v Queensland (No 2)* [1992] HCA 23.

[89] H Reynolds, 'After Mabo, What About Aboriginal Sovereignty?' (1996) *Australian Humanities Review*, australianhumanitiesreview.org/1996/04/01/after-mabowhat-about-aboriginal-sovereignty.

[90] B Anderson, *Imagined Communities: Reflections on the Origin and Spread of Nationalism* (Verso, 1983).

[91] T Jenkins (ed), *Political Culture, Soft Interventions and Nation Building* (Routledge, 2015).

[92] Queensland Parliamentary Debates, 1971, quoted in J Wanna and T Arklay, *The Ayes Have It: The History of the Queensland Parliament 1957–1989* (ANU Press, 2010) 430.

national identity with the continent's natural heritage in other words didn't necessarily entail questioning the nation-building colonisation of it. The orthodoxy of the times was that Australia 'rode on the sheep's back', where economic prosperity grew from agriculture and other extractive industries. Furthermore, in creating its own insignia, the curatorial practices were highly selective however, not just in the limited variety of animals and plants showcased as emblems of sovereign identity but that Australia's Aboriginal heritage was ignored whilst monuments to colonial figures who committed atrocities against them continued to grace city parks and thoroughfares.

**Figure 2.2** Commonwealth coat of arms; Melbourne Museum; photograph by author

The nation's official inauguration wasn't accompanied by any immediate relinquishing of symbols of the Mother Country, as British coins and currency remained in circulation, as did colonial-era postage stamps, along with ubiquitous references to the empire in public life. The Commonwealth's coat of arms, the premier insignia of sovereign authority, was a priority to develop. It denotes the Crown's ownership of property, to authenticate documents, certify national legislation and other official purposes. The first armorial bearings were authorised in 1908, then amended in 1912. The revised design integrated symbols of the six states on a shield braced by a kangaroo and an emu. (It's ironic that in 1932 the Commonwealth agreed to supply machine guns and soldiers to help Western Australia destroy crop-damaging emus,[93] and kangaroos likewise were often outlawed vermin.[94]) The coat of arms also featured a golden wattle under the seven-pointed Commonwealth Star (symbolising the country's federation). The wattle's inclusion was a request from then Prime Minister Andrew Fisher, who believed that as the plant occurs throughout Australia it would best embody its unification.[95] References to Australian nature also grace the coat of arms of some states, territories and municipalities, though without implying their enhanced legal protection; Tasmania's features the thylacine, the state's most iconic beast yet probably extinct owing to state-sanctioned persecution until the early twentieth century.

Official animal and plant emblems are another way the nation has been connected with nature. The states have animal emblems, such as the koala for Queensland and the platypus for NSW, but the Commonwealth lacks one so far. The golden wattle was selected as Australia's official floral emblem in 1988 after a history of national veneration. In 1899 the Victorian naturalist Archibald James Campbell founded the Victorian Wattle Club, and soon he was advocating for a national celebration of the resplendent plant. He got his wish when on 8 January 1913 Wattle Day was declared. Today it's widely recognised in medals of honour, stamps and tourist paraphernalia. The golden wattle wasn't a foregone choice, however, as some admirers find more striking and unique the waratah, which in 1962 became NSW's floral emblem.

Waratahs, wattles and other plants, as well as animals, have also adorned Australian stamps. Australian philately began in 1913 when the Commonwealth, having a constitutional power in this domain,[96] issued the country's first official stamp, bearing a kangaroo superimposed on a map of Australia. The stamp was intended to derive from a design competition convened in 1911 but Charles Frazer, the then Postmaster-General, disliked the winning entry featuring King George V. He therefore commissioned artist Blamire Young to design a new stamp showing a map of the continent (featured on this book's cover). Frazer defended his intervention, asserting 'a postage stamp is one of the best advertising mediums the country can have'.[97] The absence of the King's head was controversial, so this design was reinstated in 1913 and the two stamps co-existed in circulation.

[93] 'Destruction of Emus', House of Representatives, Parliamentary Debates 22 November 1932, 2634.

[94] K Boom et al, 'Pest and Resource: A Legal History of Australia's Kangaroos' (2012) 1(1) *Animal Studies Journal* 17.

[95] WJ Sowden, 'Outline History of the Wattle Blossom Celebration in Australia. History of the Wattle Day Movement' (Australian Wattle Day League, 1913) 11.

[96] Section 51(v).

[97] M Maloney, '"One of the Best Advertising Mediums the Country Can Have:" Postage Stamps and National Identity in Canada, New Zealand and Australia' (2014) 77–78 *Material Culture Review* 21.

**Figure 2.3** Wattle Day celebrations, South Australia, 1914; State Library of South Australia

Many other Commonwealth stamps since then have showcased native plants and animals. In 1914 a kookaburra stamp was released, the black swan was depicted in a 1929 stamp commemorating the centenary of Western Australia, and the lyrebird and emu graced stamps in 1932 and 1942 respectively. Likewise, native animals were and remain a popular choice for stamps, including the koala (1940), bilby (1959) and the thylacine (1962). But equally, stamp designs have linked national identity to attributes of coloniality, including merino sheep, British Royalty and heroic wars. One curious discrepancy is the 1934 stamp commemorating Victoria's centenary that depicts an Aboriginal man gazing at Melbourne's skyline – perhaps offensively signifying a relic of a 'doomed' race admiring the ascendancy of his coloniser.

Surprisingly, Australian flags rarely reflect the continent's natural heritage. South Australia's flag, adopted in 1904, has a so-called 'piping strike', modelled on the Australian magpie. A black swan graces Western Australia's flag, designed in 1953, a majestic bird symbolically affiliated with the state from the earliest days of White settlement – originally called the Swan River Colony. The other states' flags, all tied to the British blue ensign, and pre-federation in origin, omit local environmental symbols (the Tasmanian and NSW state flags show a lion).

Environmental motifs adorn some Australian bank notes and coins, although they equally celebrate economic commodities like gold and wool. The Australian Notes Act 1910 authorised the Commonwealth to issue its own currency.[98] The first £1 banknote depicted gold mining in Bendigo, the £10 banknote featured wheat and the £50 banknote a flock of sheep. Timber-cutting in Tasmania was the subject of the £20 banknote. Australian landscape and scenery were also depicted; the rare £100 banknote depicts waterfalls at Leura, NSW, and on the Yarra River, Victoria. Of coinage, from 1938 the Australian one penny displayed the head of the monarch (George VI) on one side and a kangaroo on the other. The 1954 florin depicted Queen Elizabeth II and, on its reverse, a kangaroo and lion. It wasn't until the decimal system, introduced in 1966, that Australian fauna took precedence in the nation's coinage.

Another way national identity and natural heritage were married was army mascots.[99] Stationed abroad, some soldiers in the World Wars wished to take unique emblems of their homeland to provide entertainment and strengthen morale, though some animals didn't survive the ship voyages. Kangaroos and wallabies were popular but other native fauna to serve as solders' companions included sulphur crested cockatoos, a cassowary and a wombat. One of the most unusual mascots was a Tasmanian devil with the 12th battalion Australian Imperial Force stationed in Egypt in 1914–15. Yet, dogs, cats, donkeys and other non-natives were just as common army companions, along with exotic fauna collected from theatres of war.

Despite their status as army mascots and national emblems in stamps, banknotes and other official realms, native fauna continued to be legally persecuted, sometimes due to the creed that hunting was a 'noble' pastime that honoured the quarry.[100] Aficionados of natural history could likewise avidly hunt. Their interest in acquiring specimens meant they often killed to collect, and guns were standard equipment on field expeditions. Indeed, some naturalist groups hunted for pleasure in its own right, on par with bushwalking.[101] Animal trophies were also collected to showcase the nation's culture and resources. The Australian pavilion at the 1924 British Empire Expedition in London featured a cabinet of marsupial furs, as depicted in Figure 2.4. The fisheries stand in the pavilion featured native turtle and dugong products, and another stand displayed samples of prestige Australian hardwood timbers such as red mahogany and spotted gum.[102] Exploitation of native fauna and flora thus seemingly aligned well with the image Australian authorities wished to curate internationally.

[98] Reserve Bank of Australia, 'A New Currency: 1910–1920', museum.rba.gov.au/displays/a-new-currency.

[99] N Allsopp, *Anzac Mascots* (Big Sky Publishing, 2023).

[100] EJ Brady, *Australia Unlimited* (George Robertson and Company, 1918) 132–34.

[101] Cited in D Quarmby, *The Politics of Parks. A History of Tasmania's National Parks 1885–2005* (PhD thesis, Murdoch University, 2006) 73.

[102] *Official Catalogue: Australian Pavilion, British Empire Exhibition, April – October 1924 Wembley, Middlesex, England* (Australian Exhibition Commission, 1924).

**Figure 2.4** Australian animal furs at the British Empire Exhibition 1924; State Library of Queensland

The iconography of Australian nationalism was also strongly tied to imagery of other forms of environmental exploitation. Nation-building projects, especially after World War II, harnessed forests, waterways, minerals and other natural riches to enlarge the economy in ways that scarred the continent. One way that authorities sought to legitimate this agenda was through government film units commissioned to produce documentaries celebrating Australia's economic ascendancy.[103] During the 1920s and 1930s a Cinema and Photographic Branch of the Commonwealth government created films for international audiences to encourage migration and economic investment in the antipodes. The Australian National Film Board (operative 1945–55) and its successor, the Commonwealth Film Unit (operative until 1973) continued this mission whilst engaging Australians about the nation's challenges and triumphs.

[103] B Smaill, 'From Extraction to Wilderness: Australian Film History, Environmental History, and The Last Wild River' (2023) *Journal of Media and Cinema Studies*, forthcoming.

The documentary film's potential in the mid-twentieth century was, explains Trish FitzSimons and others, recognised by its sponsors as 'a powerful medium' for 'promoting a national viewpoint'.[104] Film historians Albert Moran and Tom O'Regan argue government film units helped to construct a discourse of 'a unified nation' that would 'get away from the clichés of "kangaroos, koala bears and fields of waving wheat"'.[105] Films of this era covering more varied themes of the nation's modernisation and economic development included *The Timber Getters* (1949), *Millions for the Finding* (1954), *Power from the Snow* (1955), *North-west Horizon* (1958) and *Oil: Our Hidden Wealth* (1962). Some state governments also established film units with a similar agenda; Western Australia's produced *Farms in the Making* (1959) to celebrate clearing the bush. Tasmania's film unit created numerous works honouring the state's forestry and hydropower development, such as *Logging for Newsprint* (1956) and, like their federal counterparts, such films downplayed or ignored the environmental costs. A few government films acclaimed the nation's natural heritage such as *The Splendour and the Peaks* (1962) that showcased the scenic wonders of Tasmania's national parks.

Governments however didn't have a monopoly in this space, but their influence could extend by financing others' work. The independent documentary film maker Frank Hurley, who journeyed to Antarctica with explorer Douglas Mawson and Australia's protectorate in Papua New Guinea, was influential in curating imagery of heroic expeditions that aided the nation's international ambitions.[106] Hurley also did domestic work, such as *A Nation is Built* (1938), funded by the NSW government to celebrate its sesquicentenary.[107] Films were also created by some groups to challenge narratives of national cohesion and prosperity, such as the film unit established by the Waterside Workers in the 1950s to propagate a trade union perspective on workplace safety, housing shortages and other concerns.[108]

The moving image as an instrument of colonisation of the continent was preceded by the still image. Jarrod Hore's history of landscape photographers and settler colonialism in the late nineteenth and early twentieth centuries in the Pacific Rim, including Australia, argues that photographers such as Tasmania's John Watt Beattie mirrored the extractive economies by capturing images of impressive mountains, lakes and other natural scenery framed as beautiful, unpeopled environs for settlers' enjoyment.[109] Photographers, like film producers,

[104] T FitzSimons, P Laughren and D Williamson, *Australian Documentary* (Cambridge University Press, 2011) 49.

[105] A Moran and T O'Regan, 'Two Discourses of Australian Film' (1983) 15(16) *Australian Journal of Screen Theory* 166.

[106] A McGregor, *Frank Hurley: A Photographer's Life* (NLA Publishing, 2019).

[107] FitzSimons, Laughren and Williamson (n 104) 16.

[108] L Miller, *Fighting Films: A History of the Waterside Workers' Federation Film Unit* (Pluto Press, 2003).

[109] J Hore, *Visions of Nature: How Landscape Photography Shaped Settler Colonialism* (University of California Press, 2022).

helped construct an image of nature framed as empty wilderness, without ancestral Aboriginal history, available for settlers' gratification. Indeed, Beattie himself collaborated with Tasmania's tourism industry and government to promote the island's appeal as a drawcard for adventure seekers. Landscape photographers, argues Hore convincingly, continued the colonisation project of establishing dominion over those parts of the continent not taken up by pastoralists, miners or other resource extractors, a type of dominion that would likewise become a commodified experience.

## V. Celebrating Nature

Connecting national identity with the continent's wildlife, landscapes and resources was not only curated by officialdom but by a new generation of Australian nature writers, artists and researchers, some of whom are what Martin Mulligan and Stuart Hill call 'ecological pioneers'.[110] Through their novels, travel writings, paintings and other creative outputs they accentuated the aesthetic and scientific qualities of Australian nature, nourishing popular interest as well as awareness of threats including bushfires and droughts. They thereby, explains Joseph Powell, 'assisted the adaptation and orientation of the emerging nation' in connecting to the continent's nature and closing the gap between mere national symbolism and active nature protection.[111] Governments were not bystanders here however, due to creating or supporting art galleries and natural history museums (see further chapter eight).

Unlike the landscape photographers who sought to endear themselves to Australians with images of dramatic scenery, some nature writers such as Alec Chisholm (1890–1977) preferred the more prosaic variety that readers might encounter in their vicinity, like the wildflowers and birds observed in household gardens.[112] From his first book, *Mateship with Birds*, one of 20 written, and his frequent lectures to school children, Chisholm sought to foster this kinship with local nature.[113] Eschewing the language of 'wilderness', Chisholm could admire environments that had a gentle human presence, where people coexisted benignly with nature, and could place it into the heart of an emerging Australian nationalism.

Like Chisholm who wished to engage young Australians, botanical illustrator May Gibbs (1877–1969) also valorised nature in her children's books. Unlike

[110] M Mulligan and S Hill, *Ecological Pioneers: A Social History of Australian Ecological Thought and Action* (Cambridge University Press, 2001).

[111] JM Powell, *Environmental Management in Australia 1788–1914* (Oxford University Press, 1976) 53.

[112] See R McGregor, *Idling in Green Places: A Life of Alec Chisholm* (Australian Scholarly Publishing, 2019).

[113] AH Chisholm, *Mateship with Birds* (Whitcombe and Tombs, 1922).

some of her peers who idolised European scenery, Gibbs' characters are set in the Australian bush. In *Gumnut Babies* (1916) and *The Tales of Snugglepot and Cuddlepie* (1918), she created cherubic, anthropomorphised figures, the homonculi 'gumnut' babies', resembling eucalyptus (gum tree) nuts. Gibbs not only celebrated the bush but occasionally also conveyed her concerns about its abuse. In her time koalas and possums were coveted for their furs; offended, she pleads in one book, 'Humans: please be kind to all bush creatures'.[114] Noel McLachlan identifies the creation of snugglepot and cuddlepie as an 'outstanding nationalist event',[115] helping a new generation of young Australians identify with and take pride in the bush. Bill Gammage found that World War I soldiers 'wrote wistfully of scented gums and golden wattle, and carefully preserved in their wallets and notebooks a leaf or a sprig to remind them of their distant homeland'.[116]

Another author of nature-oriented, children's books, plus adult literature, was Elyne Mitchell (1913–2002), best known for her prodigious *Silver Brumby* series. Mitchell explored environmental ethics and the symbiosis between human and ecological health. Whilst historians often cite American pioneers, such as Aldo Leopold's *A Sand County Almanac*, published in 1949,[117] Mitchell also stirred this awakening: 'Does not the strength of a nation need roots in the soil? And this land could reject a people who are without understanding and who rob the soil of all good, cut down its forests, let silt fill its streams'.[118] Mitchell's insights came from firsthand experience, mustering livestock, in between horse riding and skiing, on Towong Hill Station in the foothills of the Snowy Mountains. She lauded the majestic setting: 'an everlasting outlet for one's thoughts, a freedom from the hampering clasp of custom and civilization'.[119] Beyond her spiritual and aesthetic veneration of nature, Mitchell wrote about the downfall of civilizations, from the Persians to Egyptians, that disrespected their ecological foundations. Her prophetic aim was to cajole Australians to respect the soil and water on which their livelihoods also depended.[120]

Some travel writers were similarly apprehensive. One prescient voice was William Hatfield, who reflected on ruinous land degradation sighted during his journeys across the continent. In South Australia he observed, 'Fallow land was feet deep under sand; even the fence post tops were out of sight. It was not even sheep country – just a barren waste of sand'.[121] In western Queensland he distilled the destructive forces as play: 'Pastoral land in Australia has been

[114] M Gibbs, *The Complete Adventures of Snugglepot and Cuddlepie* (Angus and Robertson, 1947) foreword.

[115] N McLachlan, *Waiting for the Revolution: A History of Australian Nationalism* (Penguin Books, 1989) 210.

[116] B Gammage, 'Voices from the Frontline' *Age* (Melbourne, 24 April 2010) 7.

[117] A Leopold, *A Sand County Almanac: And Sketches Here and There* (Oxford University Press, 1949).

[118] E Mitchell, *Speak to the Earth* (Angus and Robertson, 1945) 213.

[119] ibid 60–61.

[120] E Mitchell, *Soil and Civilization* (Angus and Robertson, 1946) 53.

[121] W Hatfield, *Australia Through the Windscreen* (Angus and Robertson, 1939) 248.

exploited in much the same manner as an alluvial goldfield'.[122] At odds with the ebullient nationalism of some of his generation such as Edwin Brady, Hatfield recommended 'the whole of the interior be abandoned'[123] and the unemployed of the Great Depression be put to 'work on reclamation on a tremendous scale'.[124]

Bush poetry also helped endear Australians to its landscapes. Henry Lawson (1867–1922) is known as a poet of the bush, though his oeuvre didn't extend to being an explicit voice for conserving the bush. Dorothea Mackellar (1885–1968) is another closely affiliated with the bush, and her 'My Country' poem, (1908), with its 'wide brown land' and 'thirsty paddocks', is according to the NSW State Library the 'universal statement of our nation's connection to the land'.[125] For Judith Wright (1915–2000), poetry wasn't merely an expression of biophilia but part of her political activism. Wright's collection *Birds*,[126] inspired by her residency in the rainforest-clad Tamborine Mountain in the Gold Coast hinterland in the 1950s, captures the beauty and loss of birds she encountered. In her poem *Extinct Birds*, Wright bemoans how they 'All now vanished with the fallen forest'.[127] In 1968 Wright published an essay in *Quadrant*, where she hoped that nature conservationists would nurture awareness of a 'new kind of creative relationship with Nature'.[128]

Unsurprisingly thus, wildlife protection in the early twentieth century was heavily influenced by sentimental considerations. Birds were the first to benefit, especially beautiful avian divas, and some also happened to be nonthreatening to politically influential agriculturalists. Similarly, the creation of national parks was easiest for scenic landscapes, though their status was always contingent on the absence of any competing economic agenda, as examined in chapter nine.

A further impetus to connecting nature with nationhood, explains Thomas Dunlap, and nurturing a more environmentally conscious society, was expanding scientific knowledge and popularisation of the natural sciences.[129] From the beginning of colonisation, some settlers were curious about Australia's unique flora and fauna, and a few collected on behalf of naturalists in Europe. Later, museums and natural history societies were organised to sponsor research and collect specimens. The popularity of natural history was also evident in increasing newspaper coverage of sightings of rare wildlife and other environment-related stories. Some scientists also clamoured for tougher legal protection; Herbert Finlayson's study of the Outback documented in *The Red Centre* called for 'sanctuaries where

[122] ibid 42–43.
[123] ibid 126.
[124] ibid 279.
[125] 'Dorothea Mackellar My Country', www.sl.nsw.gov.au/stories/dorothea-mackellars-my-country.
[126] J Wright, *Birds* (Angus and Robertson, 1962).
[127] ibid 182.
[128] J Wright, 'Conservation as a Concept' (1968) 12(1) *Quadrant* 29.
[129] TR Dunlap, *Nature and the English Diaspora: Environment and History in the United States, Canada, Australia, and New Zealand* (Cambridge University Press, 1999).

conditions are such that stock and all the disturbing factors of settlement cannot operate'.[130]

During the nineteenth century, natural history societies and field naturalist associations were established across Australia with missions to study, and increasingly to protect, native flora and fauna. They included the Royal Society of Tasmania (established 1843), Field Naturalists Club of Victoria (1880), Field Naturalists section of the Royal Society of South Australia (1883), Royal Society of Queensland (1883), Natural History Association of NSW (1887) and the Western Australian Natural History Society (1891). They were eminent bodies, drawing on the professional and learned classes; for instance the patrons of Western Australia's society in 1906 included the state Governor and the society's president was the Bishop of Perth.[131] Likewise, numerous community and professional groups for the study and protection of nature and wildlife flourished, and whilst they eschewed the strident political activism of contemporary environmentalists, they at least nurtured public awareness and debate, and occasionally sought to influence law makers.

One still active today is the Gould League of Bird Lovers, formed in 1909 and named in honour of John and Elizabeth Gould.[132] It was established to prevent the wanton collecting of native bird eggs and to educate the public to protect Australian birds. Also established in 1909, the Wild Life Preservation Society of Australia – now known as the Australian Wildlife Society – campaigned against the gluttonous trade in animal products for fashion, especially bird feathers and animal furs. According to one historian, the Society 'was largely responsible for the passage of the Birds and Animals Protection Act 1918' in NSW.[133] Similarly, members of the South Australian branch of the UK-based Society for the Protection of Birds helped draft the then colony's Birds Protection Act 1900.[134] Some groups focused on flora conservation and management, from the Tasmanian Wattle League active in planting the flowering tree in civic parks, to the Australian Forest League, established in 1912 by foresters and scientists. National parks associations were also established in most states during the first half of the twentieth century, becoming lobbyists for protected areas.

These bodies' public outreach included field excursions, public lectures, conferences and publication of literature. Still in circulation today, the *Victorian Naturalist* was launched by the Field Naturalists Club of Victoria in 1884. Another trailblazer was the Royal Australasian Ornithologists Union's *Emu*, published since 1901 to 'provide a recognized means of intercommunication

[130] HH Finlayson, *The Red Centre: Man and Beast in the Heart of Australia* (Angus and Robertson, 1936) 17.

[131] R Chapman, *Fighting for the Forests. A History of the Western Australian Forest Protest Movement 1895–2001* (PhD, Murdoch University, 2008) 56–75.

[132] Gould League, www.gould.org.au/about-us.

[133] BJ Stubbs, 'From "Useless Brutes" to National Treasures: A Century of Evolving Attitudes Towards Native Fauna in New South Wales, 1860s to 1960s' (2001) 7(1) *Environment and History* 23, 50.

[134] BC Newland, 'From Game Laws to Fauna Protection Acts in South Australia: The Evolution of an Attitude' (1961) 23 *South Australian Ornithologist* 52, 56.

between all interested in ornithology … and afford all an opportunity of recording facts and valuable observations, and of giving publicity to those and their own deductions'.[135] The most well-known of its genre in the mid-twentieth century was *Walkabout*, produced from 1934 to 1978 by the Australian Geographical Society (from 1946) with the Australian National Travel Association. It offered lavishly illustrated stories on natural history and travel, such as lively tales about close encounters with crocodiles and diving in coral reefs. Historians Mitchell Rolls and Anna Johnston, who studied the monthly-issued magazine's impact, observe: 'Marked throughout by a belief that the "real" Australia was to be found outside of the cities, *Walkabout* nevertheless did not succumb to bucolic pastiche or nostalgia for the so-called pioneering values of yesteryear', and it conveyed 'a palpable sense of concern for Australia's unique flora and fauna that transcended crude instrumentalist interests of, say, the touristic potential of the koala'.[136]

Nature science writing also figured increasingly in the mainstream media, then dominated by newspapers and radio. Nature writers such as Donald Macdonald and Charles Barrett active in the early twentieth century were vital contributors. As historian Tom Griffiths has explained, they helped in 'finding, or creating, local symbols of sentiment' whereby settlers could, in contrast to the alienation their predecessors felt towards the continent's landscapes and wildlife, begin to identify with their surroundings.[137] Nature essayists active in the mainstream newspapers not only helped readers appreciate native flora and fauna, some also reminded them of the ugly side of colonial history including wanton environmental degradation and even oppression of Aboriginal people. Media-savvy naturalists thus helped shape public attitudes, and thereby lay the groundwork for eventual reforms to environmental laws and practices. In discussing measures to save the lyrebird, for instance, a 1936 newspaper mentioned 'the favourable public sentiment created by nature writers, and the more stringent protection by the law in recent times'.[138]

Donald Macdonald (1859–1932) was one to promote this more complex view of Australia's natural history. A self-taught naturalist and gifted journalist, he authored a weekly column in Melbourne's *Argus* called 'Nature Notes and Queries' and several books.[139] The eclectic scope of his successful weekly column led Macdonald to divide it into separate 'Nature Notes' and 'Notes for Boys', with the latter, he explained, to make 'no reference to school work, excepting where it relates to nature study'.[140] Macdonald offered more than sentimental thoughts, commenting on some unsavoury aspects of Australian history, such as: 'The

[135] 'The Emu' (1901) 1(1) *The Emu: Official Organ of the Australasian Ornithologists' Union* 5.
[136] M Rolls and A Johnston, *Travelling Home, Walkabout Magazine and Mid-Twentieth Century Australia* (Anthem Press, 2016) 3.
[137] T Griffiths, *Hunters and Collectors: The Antiquarian Imagination in Australia* (Cambridge University Press, 1996) 122.
[138] ELR, 'Nature Study, Birds in the Zoo. The Wonderful Lyrebird' (*Queensland Times*, 4 June 1936) 4.
[139] For instance, D Macdonald, *At the End of the Moonpath* (Whitecombe and Tombs, 1922).
[140] 'Death of Mr Donald Macdonald' (*The Australasian*, 26 November 1932) 9.

reason we know so little about these aborigines is that instead of studying we shot them'.[141] His obituary explains that such was his popularity as measured by readers' correspondence, that 'Macdonald's share of letters received through the post almost exceeded that of a Prime Minister'.[142]

Another nature essayist promoting a 'sensuous engagement with nature' that inspired readers to marvel at their environs, explains Griffiths,[143] was Charles Leslie Barrett (1879–1959), a portly man and habitual pipe smoker, who as a Melbourne *Herald* journalist spent over three decades from 1906 sharing anecdotes. His varied subjects included the habits of termites, earthworms, ants and monotremes, and publicising governments' failures to protect wildlife. He remonstrated against pilfering of protected wild flowers, observing that the law 'had not proved sufficiently effective' to stamp out the 'greedy collector'.[144] Sharing with readers a wildlife safari he had in the 'Top End' in 1939, Barrett pleaded for 'full protection and strict enforcement of the Game Laws' and for authorities to end the 'cruel, ugly trade' in taking parrots, finches and other colourful birds for the pet trade.[145] In 1932 Barrett called for legal controls over native fauna and flora to be transferred to the Commonwealth owing to the 'toll taken by fur trappers, by the plume trade and by dealers in live birds'. His stated reasons included that such wildlife 'belong not to any State, but to Australia', and that there 'birds protected in one State but not in another, which need to be under the Commonwealth's wing [in order to] close these loopholes in the game laws'.[146]

Of trained scientists, one standout is Edith Coleman (1874–1951), a prize-winning orchidologist described by biographer Danielle Clode as the 'foremost female naturalist and nature writer of her generation'.[147] An ardent gardener, Coleman amassed extensive botanical knowledge and in 1922, at the relatively late career age of 48, delivered her first research paper on Australian orchids, to the Field Naturalists Club of Victoria. Writing for diverse outlets from the popular press to scientific periodicals, Coleman pioneered understandings of orchid pollination by insects. She was almost equally fascinated by the animal kingdom, entertaining readers with observations on courtships of huntsman spiders, the feeding habits of tawny frogmouths and the perambulations of echidnas (she once even kept one as a pet). Like her peers, Coleman occasionally acknowledged the need for environmental laws, such as new regulations 'to prevent depredation [of orchids] by the thoughtless and selfish'.[148]

[141] D Macdonald, 'From a Western Hill-Top' (*Argus*, 10 January 1885) 14.

[142] 'Mr Donald Macdonald. Death at Black Rock. Nature Lover and Journalist' (*Argus* (Melbourne), 24 November 1932) 6.

[143] Griffiths (n 137) 127.

[144] C Barrett, 'Vandals at Work. Robbing Bush of Wild Flowers' (*Herald* (Melbourne), 2 February 1934) 19.

[145] C Barrett, 'Hunting Crocodiles with a Camera' (*Courier-Mail* (Brisbane), 7 January 1939) 7.

[146] C Barrett, 'Control of Fauna. Federal Powers Needed' (*Herald* (Melbourne), 17 November 1932) 14.

[147] D Clode, *The Wasp and the Orchid. The Remarkable Life of Australian Naturalist Edith Coleman* (Pan Macmillan, 2019) synopsis.

[148] E Coleman, 'Springtime Among the Orchids. The Benefits of Protection' (*Age* (Melbourne), 14 November 1931) 8.

Australia's best-known naturalist in this era was arguably Philip Crosbie Morrison (1900–58).[149] A zoologist who like Coleman won the Australian Natural History Medallion, Morrison turned to journalism where he enthralled audiences. He's most well-known for his Sunday radio programme *Along the Track*, running from 1938 to 1954 in Melbourne; at his height of popularity, Crosbie reputedly had an astonishing 70 per cent of radios tuned in to him. He was also editor of *Wild Life*, a seminal monthly magazine on Australia's natural history and conservation. For those who witnessed his public lectures, Crosbie was a memorable sight, with his thick moustache and fat-rimmed, black glasses. His followers flooded him with fan mail, some even sending flora and fauna specimens for identification that sometimes caused consternation in the postal service.

Morrison was concerned not only with studying nature's curiosities but conserving them.[150] He remonstrated 'against the indiscriminate export of protected birds' apparently condoned by Commonwealth authorities.[151] In his later years Morrison promoted national parks in Victoria, and in 1952 was appointed the foundation President of the Victorian National Parks Association, and in 1957 the inaugural Director of Victoria's National Parks Authority. A year before his untimely death from a cerebral haemorrhage, Morrison spoke of national parks as the 'only true portrayal of the national character'.[152] Though raising public awareness of Australia's natural wonders, Morrison, like his peers, didn't live to see sufficient changes in practice; as Morrison's biographer wrote, in 1992, 'had Morrison's broad advice been acted on … Australia could have more effectively handled or even avoided some of the ecological disasters we are now seeing'.

In 1901 Australia was inaugurated as a nation whose founding Constitution lacked explicit guidance on how its federal system would govern environmental issues, and its legal order was left incompletely separated from its colonial roots. Yet during this period Australia's national identity was increasingly connected to the continent's geography. The natural environment was a beneficiary of this process but it also was to suffer as economic expansion and national security assumed pre-eminence in meeting the needs of the national household. Australia First Nations, its Aboriginal people, were also to suffer in making way for the settler nation. Before we delve into the ensuing history of how a continent increasingly vanished, we must fast-forward to 1967 to examine several environmental controversies that would help raise the importance of conserving the continent and reforming its laws in a more decisive manner than achieved earlier that century.

[149] G Pizzey, *Crosbie Morrison. Voice of Nature* (Victoria Press, 1992).
[150] See eg C Morrison, 'Tiger Cat Makes a Comeback' (*Argus* (Melbourne), 16 June 1956) 33.
[151] C Morrison (*Argus* (Melbourne), 15 December 1965) quoted in Pizzey (n 149) 206.
[152] Conclusion to the first Annual Report of the National Parks Authority (1957) 11, cited in L Robin, *How a Continent Created a Nation* (NewSouth Books, 2007) 31–32.

# 3

# 1967: Nature for Nature

## I. Protesting for Better Environmental Laws

This book's history of 'before environmental law' takes us to 1967. That year several major environmental disputes erupted across the nation, with a more belligerent character than found in previous environmental controversies, and they eventually spawned wide-ranging law reforms. Governments were at the epicentre of these disputes not only because they directly sponsored or facilitated the opposed developments but because they presided over and manipulated the legal regimes that approved them with minimal public consultation or environmental assessment. The focus on 1967 as a turning point however isn't intended to imply that it was a complete break from the past or that the seeds of change hadn't been planted many decades earlier.

Cosy relationships between government and business elites wedded to a philosophy of industrialisation and unbridled economic growth came under unprecedented scrutiny and critique from a politically animated civil society seeking better environmental laws. The willingness to challenge this corruption of governance was, explains historian Liz Young, tied to a 'growing political culture of dissent [that] emerged within Australia during the 1960s',[1] and was facilitated by a populace better educated and sensitised to the gravity of environmental decline within Australia and the planet. Pioneering international books that helped stoke this awareness of a nature under siege were Rachel Carson's *Silent Spring* (1962)[2] and Paul Ehrlich's *The Population Bomb* (1968).[3] They utilised knowledge from the natural sciences developed over at least the past century to highlight the interrelated and fragile properties of ecosystems under anthropogenic pressure. Film and television also assisted. David Attenborough began producing natural history work for mass audiences from the 1950s. Australia's first television documentary series of this genre, *Nature Walkabout*, was launched in the mid-1960s by Channel 9 and starred Vincent Serventy, an ornithologist active in conservation groups, and who authored in 1966 the prescient book *Continent in Danger*.[4] Engagement with

[1] L Young, 'The Rise of Environmentalism in Australia' (1996) 18 *Flinders Journal of History and Politics* 67, 77.

[2] R Carson, *Silent Spring* (Houghton Mifflin, 1962).

[3] P Ehrlich, *The Population Bomb* (Sierra Club and Ballantine Books, 1968).

[4] V Serventy, *Continent in Danger* (Andre Deutsch, 1966).

a wider public also ensued with complementary changes to the organisation of environmental groups, with a proliferation of new regional and local organisations in the 1960s as well as establishment in 1965 of the Australian Conservation Foundation, the country's first national such body in this era. This institutionalisation of environmental advocacy, research and public engagement paralleled global advances such as the founding of the World Wildlife Fund in 1961 and Friends of the Earth in 1969.

Environment-related protest wasn't unprecedented before 1967 however, as evidenced by the public disquiet from the 1950s regarding Australia's atomic bomb testing in the Outback. But unlike the anti-nuclear protests that focused on risks to human health, the controversies from 1967 that this chapter discusses were steps towards realising *nature for nature*. In 1967 the Tasmanian government initiated plans to flood Lake Pedder in the state's southwest wilderness for a hydropower project, in defiance of the lake's national park status. In NSW, the state government granted mining leases in a conservation reserve at Mount Colong, threatening the area's geologically precious limestone caves. In Queensland, Premier Joh Bjelke-Petersen was eyeing the Great Barrier Reef for mining and oil exploration, whilst in Victoria, authorities were consolidating plans to open the Little Desert mallee scrub to wheat and livestock farms. The opposing environmentalists sought to conserve nature far from cities, but there was another controversy erupting in the heart of the nation's biggest metropolis in the battle to save the foreshore bushland remnant known as 'Kelly's Bush' that sparked Sydney's famous 'Green Bans'.

This chapter's stories are Australian but similar turning points vented in many countries. New Zealand environmentalists waged an ultimately successful campaign between 1969 and 1972 to save Lake Manapouri from inundation by a dam to supply a power station.[5] In the US in 1965 an environmental group sued to protect New York's scenic Storm King Mountain from a power project, creating a major judicial precedent for public interest litigation to stop environmental harm.[6] A grassroots, anti-nuclear movement took off in West Germany and France in the early 1970s opposed to nuclear power plants.[7] In India, peasants in the Himalayan region of Uttarakhand in 1973 launched the Chipko movement to save their forests from logging.[8] The Hindi word 'chipko' means 'to hug', and reflects the protesters' tactic of embracing trees to hinder the loggers. I could give numerous more examples.

[5] N Peat, *Manapouri Saved! New Zealand First Great Conservation Success Story* (Longacre Press, 1995).

[6] *Scenic Hudson Preservation Conference v Federal Power Commission* (1965) 354 F.2d 608.

[7] AS Tompkins, *Better Active Than Radioactive! Anti-nuclear Protest in 1970s in France and West Germany* (Oxford University Press, 2016).

[8] R Guha, *The Unquiet Woods: Ecological Change and Peasant Resistance in the Himalaya* (University of California Press, 2000).

Unbridled economic growth was now being questioned by a new generation of environmentalists, introducing values and tactics rarely seen in earlier struggles. They idealised the natural world as inherently valuable for its ecological and biological qualities apart from collateral benefits to people. In her account of the Little Desert campaign, historian Libby Robin argues that conservationists were defending a nature for itself, a nature they did not experience or know directly, unlike an earlier generation who defended nature for their personal aesthetic and recreational pleasure.[9] Likewise, poet Judith Wright, involved in the Great Barrier Reef cause, wrote in 1968 of her hope for a 'new kind of creative relationship with Nature' born out of respect for its inherent values that required a new approach to environmental activism.[10] However, there were a few conservationists well before then espousing similar views, such as NSW lawyer Marie Byles who helped secure Bouddi Natural Park in 1935 and, according to her biography, 'believed passionately that nature had intrinsic value and was not merely for the use of humans'.[11]

This idealisation of an unadulterated nature has since been overtaken by a more complex picture that recognises the history of Aboriginal environmental stewardship.[12] As Western Australian archaeologist Sylvia Hallam eloquently said in 1975, in opening her pioneering book about Aboriginal use of fire in the continent's southwest: 'The land the English settled was not as God made it. It was as the Aborigines made it'.[13] Commentators such as Val Plumwood and Timothy Neale have problematised the 'wilderness' agenda of non-Indigenous conservationists for perpetuating the colonial mentality of an unpeopled continent in its original state, without any human history prior to Western culture.[14] Aboriginal people weren't generally part of the conservation campaigns of the late 1960s, and this absence is a seminal difference from contemporary Australian environmental politics where First Nations are sometimes at the forefront, such as in anti-mining disputes. Nonetheless, Aboriginal activism was taking off in this era in relation to land rights, as the final section of the chapter discusses, which would eventually have direct consequences for environmental governance. Conceptually, this Aboriginal self-determination would also help to break down the culture – nature divide that has accompanied White colonisation.

Equally memorable during the late 1960s, environmentalists campaigned with greater political tenacity: no longer content just to sign petitions or write

[9] L Robin, *Defending the Little Desert: The Rise of Ecological Consciousness in Australia* (Melbourne University Press, 1998) 14.

[10] J Wright, 'Conservation as a Concept' (1968) 12(1) *Quadrant* 29.

[11] A McLeod, *The Summit of Her Ambition: The Spirited Life of Marie Byles* (Anne McLeod, 2016) 99.

[12] See eg B Gammage and B Pascoe, *Country: Future Fire, Future Farming* (Thames Hudson, 2021).

[13] S Hallam, *Fire and Hearth: A Study of Aboriginal Usage and European Usurpation in South-western Australia* (Australian Institute of Aboriginal Studies, 1975) vii.

[14] V Plumwood, 'Wilderness Scepticism and Wilderness Dualism' in J Baird Callicott and MP Nelson (eds), *The Great New Wilderness Debate* (University of Georgia Press, 1998) 655; T Neale, *Wild Articulations: Environmentalism and Indigeneity in Northern Australia* (University of Hawaii Press, 2017).

polite letters to newspaper editors, they now flagrantly protested, invading electoral politics, defying corporations and resorting to the courts where possible. In this sense their tactics brought into question the adequacy of the polyarchal institutions that created law and allowed for such problematic projects and developments. This politicisation of environmental issues also brought into sharp relief the question of who benefited from development that degraded natural or cultural heritage.

Although none of these rows involved the Commonwealth directly as a regulator, in a way they soon would, 1967 was also a national turning point for another reason that directly impacted the Commonwealth. On 27 May, Australian voters approved overwhelmingly to amend the Constitution to allow the Commonwealth to make laws in regard to Aboriginal people. This popular mandate would enable future national leadership in Aboriginal affairs that would eventually have ramifications in the environmental sphere as well, following the 1992 *Mabo* decision of the High Court[15] and the returning of stolen lands through the Native Title Act 1993. Legal justice for Aboriginal Australians would allow them to reassert their 'caring for country', applying knowledge and custom to heal some of the environmental trauma of colonialism. Historian Heather Goodall argues Indigenous knowledge is best understood 'as a process rather than as an archive' in which despite the White invasion such knowledge has continued to evolve and remain relevant, even for urban Aboriginal communities.[16]

Unveiling these turning points and their legacies yields a richer perspective of the preceding decades of the last century. Understanding the strategies, opportunities and constraints to defending a vanishing continent during that earlier period becomes clearer when we can compare them to those associated with the controversies that erupted from 1967 onwards. But it wasn't a fundamental rupture with *everything* from the past. Environmental degradation remains, and in some ways has worsened, notably due to further land clearing and invasive species, as well as intensifying climate change, as documented grimly in Australia's 2021 State of the Environment report.[17] Conversely, like today, in the earlier years of the last century there were scientists warning about environmental risks, along with nature conservation groups advocating increased protection. Nascent attitudes about valuing the natural world less instrumentally were also emerging in nature writing, such as by Elyne Mitchell in the 1940s.[18]

Several systemic problems with the governing laws fed these disputes. One was few opportunities for the general public to have a say in decision-making.

[15] *Mabo v Queensland* (No 2) [1992] HCA 23.

[16] H Goodall, 'Riding the Tide: Indigenous Knowledge, History and Water in a Changing Australia' (2008) 14(3) *Environment and History* 355, 356.

[17] See soe.dcceew.gov.au.

[18] E Mitchell, *Speak to the Earth* (Angus and Robertson, 1945); *Soil and Civilization* (Angus and Robertson, 1946).

Regulation governing approval of dams, mines, urban developments or other projects habitually trivialised public input, with few statutory obligations on regulators to take into account community opinion.[19] Minor exceptions included public input into mining warden's courts and public inquiries. Polyarchal institutions allowed the public to elect parliamentary representatives but otherwise the assumption was that their laws would be administered in the 'public interest', or with advice from scientific 'experts', without the need for any further social licence.

Equally pernicious, the law ratified development proposals with minimal or no assessment of their environmental sequelae. Whilst project approvals sometimes included environmental conditions, they were commonly not based on scientifically established standards. Land use planning, a potential safety net to spatially contain environmental impacts, was also flawed because governments could rewrite plans and allowable zoned uses with few procedural obstacles. Without a clear, overarching normative agenda, such as sustainable development or nature conservation, environmental laws of this era were deeply susceptible to manipulation and becoming mere window-dressing.

These lacunae were compounded by the paucity of legal checks and balances via judicial oversight of executive decision-making, or freedom of information rights, resulting in agencies being able to build their own empires, as occurred with Tasmania's notorious Hydro-Electric Commission, or to become victims of 'regulatory capture' by the interests they were meant to regulate.[20] Business elites informally enjoyed considerable influence in the corridors of power, yet their corporate law framework shielded them from social accountability beyond their investors.

## II. The City: Kelly's Bush

The 1960s saw rapid urbanisation, from highways to high rises, obliterating much cultural and ecological heritage. Melbourne's 1969 Transportation Plan was one contentious modernist blueprint for urban 'renewal' that met with fierce community resistance.[21] Whilst many Australian towns and cities can furnish examples, Sydney offers a seminal history lesson. There, the Builders Labourers Federation allied with community groups to save urban heritage from predatory developers. The story that began in 1967 highlights serious deficiencies in the land use planning law of that era where community opinion was marginalised whilst decision-making processes privileged municipal administrators and property

[19] T Bonyhady, *Places Worth Keeping* (Allen and Unwin, 1993) 21.
[20] E Dal Bó, 'Regulatory Capture: A Review' (2006) 22(2) *Oxford Review of Economic Policy* 203.
[21] G Rundell, 'Melbourne Anti-freeway Protests' (2008) 3(4) *Urban Policy and Research* 11.

entrepreneurs. Despite ostensible progress in Australian town planning law over the twentieth century, it still prioritised development over green spaces, such as the well-intended 1948 Cumberland Plan (discussed in chapter ten) that failed to prevail in the face of demographic and development pressures.

Kelly's Bush occupies about five hectares on the foreshore of Woolwich Peninsula, the only sizeable enclave of bush left along this area of Sydney's Parramatta River. Besides its rich plant diversity that includes shrubland and coastal health, Kelly's Bush contains traces of its original Wallumedegal people such as engravings and middens. The bush was next to a smelting works established in 1890s, and when it closed in 1967, real estate developer AV Jennings acquired the site with plans to erect nearly 150 housing units including some up to eight-stories. The Hunters Hill Council rejected the conspicuous proposal in the hope of acquiring the site to enlarge the adjacent parkland it already owned. After this plan was rejected by NSW's State Planning Authority because it clashed with its own vision of medium-density housing for the area, Jennings submitted a modified application for 56 townhouses that in 1969 was accepted by the Council (without public consultation). The plan was controversial, as the year before the Hunters Hill Trust was established to preserve the suburb's historic heritage, and the Trust led efforts to have the Jennings project scaled back to just 25 housing units.

**Figure 3.1** Sign at Kelly's Bush introducing bushwalkers to its history, 2022; photograph by author

This didn't settle the growing community furore, and on 27 September 1970 some local women formed the 'Battlers for Kelly's Bush'. It recognised the need for a new style of activism when the NSW Minister of Local Government rezoned the area from reserved open space to residential use. In addition to writing numerous letters soliciting support, they engaged with the media by novel means, such as holding 'boil the billy' days in the bushland in which journalists were satiated with baked foods, and running essay competitions for school children about saving the bush. But above all, the Battlers took the unusual step of asking a trade union for help.

The Builders' Labourers Federation (BLF) agreed to impose a ban on any bush clearance or development on the contested site if the Battlers could demonstrate they had community backing. They did: over 600 people attended a public meeting in August 1971 called to formally request a ban. It was an unlikely alliance given that the trade union's leaders such as Jack Mundey were outspoken communists. The BLF prevailed over AV Jennings by threatening to impose stop-work orders on another of its development sites if the company developed Kelly's Bush with non-union, scab labour. The dispute continued during the 1970s, as although Jennings eventually sold the land to Hunter's Hill Council, its councillors voted to retain the site as a residential zone. The impasse ended when the new State Premier, Neville Wran, decided to protect Kelly's Bush indefinitely from any development – a move perhaps also influenced by the discovery of radioactive waste from the former smelter, which made any housing nearby very problematic. On 4 September 1983 the site was purchased by the NSW government for retention as a public reserve, with control assigned to the Hunters Hill Council a decade later.[22] Since 1999 Kelly's Bush has also been listed on the NSW State Heritage Register.

Kelly's Bush was one of 54 Green Bans imposed by the BLF in and around Sydney, uniting trade union members and urban residents in saving historic buildings, bushland and other sites.[23] The actions inspired Green Bans elsewhere in Australia too, from Perth to Adelaide.[24] Saving Kelly's Bush stood for the proposition that there are other, non-materialistic values that mattered to Australians that warranted protection. The larger legacy of the Green Bans was in law reform, eventually prompting the NSW government to overhaul its environmental legislation to enable far greater community input and environmental assessments and protection, with the introduction of the Heritage Act 1977, Environmental Planning and Assessment Act 1979 and Land and Environment Court Act 1979.[25] Federally, the Whitlam government in 1975 sponsored the Australian Heritage Commission

[22] See M Shaw, *The History of the Battle to Save Kelly's Bush and the Green Ban Movement in the Early 1970s* (Buckleys, 1996).

[23] M Burgmann and V Burgmann, *Green Bans, Red Union: The Saving of a City* (UNSW Press, 1998).

[24] WJ Lines, *Taming the Great South Land* (Allen and Unwin, 1991) 230.

[25] J Cole, 'Environmental Law and Politics' (1981) 4(1) *UNSW Law Journal* 55. Although, not all of the Green Ban agenda was legislated: A Thorpe, 'Public Participation in Environmental Law: Lessons from the Green Bans' (2013) 30 *Environmental and Planning Law Journal* 93.

Act to improve the identification and protection of built and natural items of national significance. Another legacy of the Green Bans was that they inspired political parties in Australia and abroad to adopt the name 'Green'. Petra Kelly, a German political activist visiting Australia in the 1970s took the name 'Green' (Grün) when in 1980 she helped found the German Greens (Die Grünen). Green parties in Australia opted the same nomenclature in the 1980s and 1990s. Whilst the Kelly's Bush campaign is less obviously an example of fighting for nature for nature, it certainly represents a rebuke of the ideology that privileged economic expansion.

## III. Hydropower: Lake Pedder

The flooding of the iconic Lake Pedder in southwest Tasmania for an industrial energy scheme was deeply grievous for environmentalists. The dam was built by the Tasmanian Hydro-Electric Commission (HEC, now called Hydro Tasmania), a then behemoth presence in Tasmanian political and economic affairs, and whose influence we will encounter later in this book. The HEC's damming of the Serpentine and Huon rivers drowned Lake Pedder, originally some 12 $km^2$ in extent, under a huge but shallow impoundment stretching over 250 $km^2$. Situated in a rugged wilderness, the lake's flooding was astonishing given that in 1955 it was the centrepiece of the newly created Lake Pedder National Park. The park's creation on the recommendation of the state's Scenery Preservation Board is all the more intriguing given that Allan Knight, the HEC head who later championed the dam that flooded Pedder, was a member of the Board.[26]

The dam was the single largest case of loss of wilderness in Tasmania's history, a tragedy that spurred a new generation of environmental activism in Tasmania, and elsewhere in Australia, which a decade later was strong enough to halt another calamitous proposal – to flood Tasmania's Franklin River for more hydropower. The Pedder dispute was also historically notable for environmentalists' appeal for Commonwealth intervention, following the election of the Whitlam government in 1972.[27] Although it didn't succeed in stopping the dam, his administration soon initiated unprecedented legislative reform to increase the Commonwealth's role in protecting Australia's natural heritage. His government also commissioned a public inquiry into the loss of Lake Pedder, where future options, including restoration of its former condition, were investigated.[28]

[26] BW Davis, 'Waterpower and Wilderness' in R Dempsey (ed), *The Politics of Finding Out* (Cheshire Publishing, 1974) 42, 43.

[27] ibid.

[28] Lake Pedder Committee of Enquiry, *Final Report, April 1974, the Flooding of Lake Pedder* (AGPS, 1974).

In the mid-1960s the HEC unveiled plans to dam Pedder as a key plank in its ambitious hydro-industrialisation of the island's economy. The ubiquitous power of the HEC as a surrogate arm of the Tasmanian government was evident in the then close alliance between Premier Eric Reece and the HEC's Allan Knight, who jointly advocated the damming of Lake Pedder. (The Premier's enthusiasm for this project and other hydro-energy schemes earned him the nickname 'Electric Eric'.) Extraordinarily by the legal standards of today, no environmental impact assessment of the HEC's proposal was conducted, and the Commonwealth's subsequent inquiry concluded that Tasmanian authorities sought 'to limit public knowledge and foreclose public discussion of the proposal to flood Lake Pedder'.[29]

Environmentalists became concerned when, in May 1967, the government tabled plans in parliament for approval of expenditure on a major hydropower dam that would flood Lake Pedder. The South West Committee, formed in 1962 by bushwalking and community bodies, initially led calls to save Pedder, and later a dedicated Lake Pedder Action Committee was created to step up opposition. Unable to unseat the dogmatic support among Tasmania's elites for the dam, environmentalists organised the world's first green values political party – the United Tasmania Group, launched on 23 March 1972. Although it didn't win a seat in the state's election that year, it became the forerunner to the Tasmanian Greens, who went on to become a political force. The Pedder disaster also led to the establishment of the South West Tasmanian Action Committee, the precursor to the Wilderness Society that has become a major environmental activist organisation in Australia.

Lake Pedder was widely acclaimed for its outstanding ecological and geological values. A relic glacial lake without peer in Australia, it was heralded by scientists as 'one of a kind, with no replicate in the southern hemisphere and probably on a global scale'.[30] It was a sanctuary for a distinctive biota including the endemic *galaxias pedderensis* fish and crustaceans.[31] The lake was also more than just a singular landform – it was nestled within a wider geomorphological and biological community in the surrounding mountains, button grass plains and flanking sand dunes. The United Nations Educational, Scientific and Cultural Organization (UNESCO) recognised Pedder's exemplary qualities when it deplored the impending dam 'as the greatest ecological tragedy' since the White colonisation of Tasmania.[32]

[29] ibid 11.

[30] K Kiernan, 'The Geomorphology and Geoconservation Significance of Lake Pedder' in C Sharples (ed), *Lake Pedder: Values and Restoration* (University of Tasmania, 2001) 14, 45.

[31] T McDonald, 'Visions of Stream Restoration: The Need for Long-term, Big Picture Projects: Interview with Sam Lake' (2007) 8(1) *Ecological Management and Restoration* 5, 6.

[32] Quoted in K Kiernan, 'I Saw My Temple Ransacked' in B Brown, I Lowe and C Milne (eds), *The Rest of the World is Watching* (Pan Macmillan, 1990) 20, 26.

**Figure 3.2** Lake Pedder and environs, c. 1971; photograph by Stefan Karpiniec; CC BY 2.0 licence

Lake Pedder was particularly renowned for the intoxicating beauty of its dazzling pink, quartzite beach and rolling sand dunes, a splendour that inspired writers, artists and bushwalkers to pay homage to the wilderness before it disappeared.[33] One was nature photographer and HEC-employee Olegas Truchanas (1923–72), who tried to save Lake Pedder by impressing Tasmanians with his photography of its sublime grandeur. Shortly before his tragic death in January 1972 on a canoeing expedition near Lake Pedder, Truchanas asked: 'is there any reason why, given enlightened leadership, the idea of beauty could not become an accepted goal of national policy?'.[34] The intervention of artists like Truchanas to leverage nature's aesthetic values for conservation outcomes was not an Australian first, as antecedents earlier in the century occurred through poetry, children's illustrated books, and landscape painting. But with Lake Pedder, the connections between art and nature conservation were more explicit.

The fate of Lake Pedder matters to this book as it took place when the role of the Commonwealth in enabling or preventing environmental destructive

[33] T Bonyhady, 'Lake Pedder 1871' (1993) 55 *Island* (1993) 16.

[34] O Truchanas, 'Shining Beacon' speech, at the exhibition 'Lake Pedder 1971', Saddlers Court Gallery, Richmond, 19 November 1971. See further T Bonyhady, 'No Dams: The Art of Olegas Truchanas and Peter Dombrovskis' in R Butler (ed), *The Europeans: Émigré Artists in Australia 1930–1960* (National Gallery of Australia, 1990) 236.

developments was beginning to arouse public debate. In 1967 the Commonwealth agreed to provide special financial assistance for Tasmania's hydropower project, so it already had a material role in the scheme. With Whitlam's election, having professed greater federal environmental leadership, conservationists saw an opportunity. Brenda Hean, a campaigner against Pedder's flooding, on 8 September 1972 flew to Canberra in a vintage Tiger Moth to gain support by skywriting 'Save Lake Pedder' above the nation's parliament; tragically, her plane mysteriously disappeared en route.[35] Whitlam wouldn't intervene but initiated an inquiry into Lake Pedder, which recommended a moratorium on the flooding and consideration of an alternate, less environmentally destructive option, such as a canal to channel waters around the lake. Interestingly, the inquiry believed the HEC's statutory regime, the Hydro-Electric Commission Act 1944, allowed and likely obliged it to consider the environmental impacts of any dam it proposed.[36] Whitlam's proposal was rebuffed by the recalcitrant Tasmanian Premier, despite ostensibly being of the same (Labor) political stripes. The lake was completely flooded by 1973, retrospectively legalised with the sweeping Hydro–Electric Commission (Doubts Removal) Act 1972, and the area is now submerged under 16 metres of water, forming one of Australia's largest freshwater reservoirs.

The furore over the damming of Lake Pedder hasn't disappeared, with increasing calls for the site's restoration. The Restore Lake Pedder group, to which I am affiliated, continues to lobby for this goal and has furnished evidence that restoration is technically feasible and economically affordable.[37] If successful, the restoration would be one of the most ambitious projects of its kind, and a fitting national achievement for the United Nations Decade on Ecosystem Restoration 2021–2030.[38]

## IV. Mining: Colong Caves

New South Wales had disputes over nature conservation during the twentieth century, such as those regarding commercial activities in the Royal National Park in the 1920s and the threat to clear the Blue Gum Forest in the Blue Mountains in the 1930s. But a proposal for limestone mining at Mount Colong and Mount Armour in the southern Blue Mountains in the mid-1960s triggered a far bigger backlash, described by the leading environmental organisation in the region

[35] S Millwood, *Whatever Happened to Brenda Hean?* (Allen and Unwin, 2008).

[36] Specifically s 16(2)(a), which obliged the HEC to consider 'the necessity or desirability of the new power development'.

[37] Restore Lake Pedder, www.lakepedder.org.

[38] See www.decadeonrestoration.org.

today, the Colong Foundation for Wilderness, as 'the first politically focused high profile wilderness campaign in NSW'.[39] One newspaper of the time summed up its significance: 'NSW has never seen a conservation protest like the Save Colong campaign'.[40]

The dispute centred on the threat to the Colong Caves, in the then Kanangra-Boyd reserve, set aside for conservation in 1891 but without precluding mining. A limestone cave system, the Colong Caves are one of the largest in NSW, dating from the Silurian period 430 million years ago, with impressive stalagmites and speleothem formations. A geologist writing in the Australian Museum's house magazine in 1928 concluded that he hoped 'that at some not far distant day, a generous government will make this rugged area … a sanctuary for wildlife. Its scenic wonders warrant its reservation, and its furry and feathered occupants claim it as their heritage'.[41]

Proposals for mining the caves had been lodged in 1939 and 1956 but hadn't been progressed. In 1967 a lease was granted by the Minister for Lands, adding to three smaller leases in the area issued over the previous decade, which were now held by the Australian subsidiary of the Associated Portland Cement Manufacturers Australia (APCMA). In May 1968, Milo Dunphy, son of the famous conservationist Myles Dunphy, formed the Colong Committee to coordinate opposition to any mining. Conservationists were incensed not just at the risk of serious pollution but that the government had excised a portion of an area reserved for conservation for mining. The Colong Committee deployed a variety of strategies to publicise its concerns, energising a broad coalition of supporters as diverse as Catholic priests to medical doctors.

Its most innovative and novel protest strategy targeted the offending company. The Colong Committee began purchasing shares in APCMA, which it transferred to numerous individual protesters so as to allow them to attend the company's annual general meeting (AGM) in April 1969 in Sydney to publicise their opposition. They were unsuccessful in moving the company's managers other than a promise to review the need for its proposed mine at Colong. Conservation-minded shareholders attended the company's 1970 AGM to again voice their concerns. Attempting to avoid a repeat at the 1971 AGM, the company's heads switched the venue to Melbourne in the hope that most of the anti-mining shareholders, based in Sydney, wouldn't show up. The tactic wasn't successful: the Colong Committee recruited allies in Victoria's caving community who were asked to enlist others as shareholders' proxies to attend the AGM. More media publicity was secured when

[39] Colong Foundation for Wilderness, 'Mountains – 1861 to 2014', www.colongwilderness.org.au/about-wilderness/dunphy-kowmung-centenary-walk/history.

[40] M Dunphy, 'On Colong, the Premier and Political Vandalism' (*Tharunka*, 17 June 1969) 20.

[41] CJ Barnes, 'The Colong Caves' (1928) 3(6) *Australian Museum Magazine* 211, 216.

one protester abseiled down the seven-storey building in the Melbourne downtown where APCMA had its offices, followed by some 200 protester shareholders, outnumbering other attendees two to one, gate-crashing the AGM on 28 April, monopolising several hours of the meeting to attack the company's management and submit a vote of no-confidence against its chairman, Sir Grant Ferrier.[42] The recalcitrant company's managers conceded nothing more than to 'review' the need for the mine.

The Colong Committee also recognised the need to target the government itself. It had already secured the support of the NSW Labor Party to revoke the leases if it won power, and three members of the Committee chose to stand as Labor Party candidates in the 1971 state election. The NSW government, then in the hands of the Liberal and National parties, tried unsuccessfully to defuse the protest by enacting new national parks legislation in 1967, followed by the gazettal of a major national park in 1968. The NSW Liberal Party itself had some supporters for the conservationists' cause, passing resolutions for protection of the caves at the party's state council meetings in 1968 and 1969.[43] Some party members also visited the caves in 1970, apparently coming away suitably impressed.

The campaign was ultimately successful, with the mining leases relinquished by APCMA in 1972 without the necessity of government intervention, although it helped by giving the company permission to expand its limestone quarry at Marulan in the Southern Tablelands of NSW. In their assessment, environmental historians Drew Hutton and Libby Connors saw the Colong as 'a landmark campaign of the Australian environment movement. It marked a clear break between old and new protest forms … and was the first time Australian environmentalists had used shareholder rights to confront a corporation'.[44]

## V. Agriculture: Little Desert

Conservationists also prevailed in another major dispute of this era, concerning Victoria's 'Little Desert', about 375 km northwest of Melbourne. It's not what one would ordinarily regard as a true desert of treeless, rolling sand dunes but the region is named after its sandy soils and that it's 'little' relative to the neighbouring Big Desert. The Little Desert has a rich biota, harbouring at least 670 native plant species, 220 bird species and 60 types of mammals and reptiles.[45]

[42] 'Colong Protesters Vocal at APCM Meeting' (*Sydney Morning Herald*, 26 April 1971) 2; 'Colong Protesters Assail APCM' (*Sydney Morning Herald*, 30 April 1971) 26.

[43] D Hutton and L Connors, *History of the Australian Environment Movement* (Cambridge University Press, 1999) 116–17.

[44] ibid 118.

[45] 'Little Desert National Park: Visitor Guide', vicsouth.info/little-desert-np.pdf.

**Figure 3.3** Clearing mallee, Murrayville district, 1925; National Library of Australia

Though lacking the scenic grandeur of Lake Pedder, and perhaps even outright dull in its flat, repetitive terrain, the Little Desert attracted an ardent campaign from conservationists on par with the other causes in the late 1960s. The story goes back to 1955 when 218 hectares were reserved as the Kiata Lowan Sanctuary for protecting the mound-building malleefowl (*Leipoa Ocellata*), a species then and still in decline owing to predatory foxes and land clearing. In 1967 the Victorian government announced plans to develop the Little Desert for agriculture. The public uproar which caught the scheme's backers off guard led in 1968 to the protected area being increased to 1,162 hectares and the declaration of the Little Desert National Park. The park expanded the following year to 35,300 hectares, and in 1988 another 96,700 hectares were added to make Little Desert one of Victoria's largest protected areas.

The Little Desert had been occupied and managed sustainably by the Wotjobaluk people for thousands of years until the mid-1800s when settlers started colonising the mallee lands.[46] Richard Broome has documented Aboriginal land

[46] R Broome et al, *Mallee Country* (Monash University Publishing, 2019).

use of the mallee in this colonial period, helping to challenge the 'narrative of settler triumphalism' in the mallee (and other regions colonised).[47] Initially the 'scrub country' was overlooked for serious farming but by the 1870s the mallee was being cleared by dauntless pioneers, whose pressures on the landscape intensified after the first and second World War soldier settlement schemes.[48] Another emerged from the 1950s when remaining mallee country, owned by the Crown, was eyed for agriculture. In 1951 the Australian Mutual Provident Society (known today as the AMP) sought tenure from the government over 100,000 hectares of the Little Desert for conversion and subdivision into agricultural enterprise.[49] In 1950, CSIRO scientists advised it would be 'unwise to encourage or to permit the removal of vegetation' given the mineral-deficient sandy soil, modest rainfall and prevalence of rabbits.[50] Declining agricultural commodity prices in the 1960s undermined the project's feasibility, but by June 1967 Victoria's Minister of Lands, William McDonald, a local pastoralist, renewed interest in the plan and in early 1968 he announced the Little Desert Settlement Scheme to establish 48 wheat and sheep farms covering 80,000 hectares with new road connections. Opposition stirred from many quarters, including agricultural experts, economists and conservationists.

The Save our Bushlands Action Committee, representing eight conservation groups, spearheaded the campaign, holding public meetings in Melbourne, bombarding newspapers with letters, and petitioning the Victorian Premier. One touching letter published by the media in 1969 from two teenagers declared 'The Little Desert is an area unique in Australia as an undisturbed natural habitat for our wildlife. Now the Government wants to destroy this … It is appalling to realise that decisions such as these can be made by one man who will not listen to the naturalists' warning'.[51]

Support from farmers weakened after Alan Lloyd, a specialist in agricultural economics at Melbourne University, argued the land parcels to be allocated under the scheme were not financially viable.[52] The campaign was soon winning concessions when, in mid-1969, the Minister of Lands agreed to reduce the size of the scheme to 12 farms while expanding the national park to 35,300 hectares. Aboriginal people also called for the land to be returned to them, with the 'right to live and hunt in the Little Desert'.[53] The scheme was wholly abandoned in December 1969 after the government lost a byelection in the seat of Dandenong partly due to the controversy and the prospect of its budget legislation being blocked by hostile

[47] R Broome, 'Changing Aboriginal Landscapes of Pastoral Victoria, 1830–1850' (2011) 31(2) *Studies in the History of Gardens and Designed Landscapes* 88, 88.
[48] 'Develop Little Desert' (*Horsham Times*, 30 June 1953) 2.
[49] 'To Reclaim "Little Desert"' (*Age* (Melbourne), 11 September 1951) 4.
[50] 'Little Desert Settlement is Inadvisable' (*Weekly Times* (Melbourne), 8 February 1950) 23.
[51] L McFarlane and G McFarlane, 'The Little Desert' (*Canberra Times*, 6 August 1969) 2.
[52] '"Gag" on Little Desert Report' (*Canberra Times*, 24 December 1969) 3.
[53] 'Little Desert Rights' (*Canberra Times*, 5 February 1970) 1.

parliamentarians in the Upper House unless work on the scheme ceased. Since then, the Little Desert National Park has flourished with additional territory, and an Indigenous Land Use Agreement negotiated in 2005 has enabled the traditional owners to be formally recognised in its stewardship.

The campaign's success shook the Victorian political landscape, a catalyst for wider reforms for nature conservation and environmental protection that gained traction in the policy agenda of the mainstream parties. According to the Victorian National Parks Association, 'the Little Desert National Park controversy is often considered to mark the beginning of widespread environmental awareness and activism in Victoria …, ultimately leading to changes in political processes and a rise in environmental consciousness, which still has impact today'.[54] Likewise, historian Libby Robin argues the Little Desert was nationally significant, asserting a non-instrumental ethos of nature conservation.[55] The ensuing legal reforms included the establishment in 1971 of Australia's first specialist Environment Protection Authority with the passing of the Environment Protection Act 1970. The national parks system was also eventually expanded with new legislation in 1975. Environmental groups in 1969 formed the Conservation Council of Victoria (later known as Environment Victoria) to improve coordination and campaigning for nature conservation.

## VI. Mining: Great Barrier Reef

Another environmental controversy that took off in 1967 was in Queensland, where the 'Save the Reef Campaign' was born to challenge the state government's interest in opening the Great Barrier Reef to mining.[56] Its current World Heritage listing and marine park status can be traced to pioneering efforts from the 1960s to block mining, and later oil exploitation. The establishment in 1962 of the Wildlife Preservation Society of Queensland by concerned citizens, including poet Judith Wright, its inaugural president, was vital in building coordinated agitation for greater environmental protection that mobilised later that decade.

The reef campaign began in 1967 when North Queensland artist and conservationist John Busst saw a notice in his local tabloid of an application from a cane grower to harvest 2,000 tonnes annually of coral from the supposedly dead Ellison Reef, near Innisfail, for making agricultural fertiliser. Busst and 14 others lodged objections to the mining application, to be heard in the Innisfail Mining Warden's Court, and tendered evidence that the reef was alive and worth saving.

[54] Victorian National Parks Association, 'Celebrating 50 Amazing Years of the Little Desert National Park', media release 10 December 2018, vnpa.org.au/celebrating-50-amazing-years-of-the-little-desert-national-park.

[55] Robin (n 9) 4.

[56] R Lloyd, *Saving the Reef* (University of Queensland Press, 2002) ch 5.

The application was opposed not only because of the prospect of damage to the reef but, for the long term, it 'would establish a dangerous legal precedent which could allow complete commercial exploitation of the Reef'.[57] Collaborating with environmental organisations including the Wildlife Preservation Society, Busst wrote to government ministers and coaxed the press to cover the controversy.[58]

The campaign scored an early success when, to the surprise of many and annoyance of some, the presiding Mining Warden, JW Ashfield, recommended against the mining application after hearing evidence that the Ellison Reef had living coral.[59] The Queensland Minister for Mines declined to overrule the Warden's decision yet had his department survey the Great Barrier Reef for other development options. Buoyed by advice from Harry Ladd, a US geologist, that protection of the reef did not bar some exploitation, the Bjelke-Petersen government was quick to unveil plans to open much of the reef for oil drilling, with a public tendering process initiated. Off-shore exploratory drilling began in 1967.[60] Yet the prospect of commercial exploitation of the Great Barrier Reef had ignited public debate about the merits of exploiting its resources, bringing such development under greater scrutiny and doubt. In addition to the environmental risks, there was public disquiet over the discovery that the Queensland Premier himself held shares in one of the oil companies wishing to exploit the reef.

The Commonwealth's Petroleum (Submerged Lands) Act 1967 had foreshadowed the possibility of oil drilling in Australian coastal waters with its preamble stating: the 'exploration for and the exploitation of the petroleum resources of submerged lands adjacent to the Australian coast would be encouraged by the adoption of legislative measures applying uniformly'. Yet, the Commonwealth's Continental Shelf (Living Natural Resources) Act passed the following year suggested the federal government might be able to protect the reef. Environmentalists' campaign was aided by several overseas catastrophic oil spills, including the Torrey Canyon incident in British waters in 1967, and the Santa Barbara spill in Californian waters in early 1969. By September 1969 a Save the Barrier Reef Committee was formed to coordinate lobbying, attracting a diverse membership including many with no background in environmental organisations. Using well-known campaigning measures today, the Committee distributed car bumper stickers and conducted opinion polls to raise public awareness of its concerns. The Australian Engineers Union backed the campaign, threatening to withhold work on one of the drilling ships owned by Ampol. This growing opposition prompted the Queensland and Commonwealth governments to convene

[57] DW Connell, 'The Great Barrier Reef Conservation Issues – A Case History' (1971) 3(4) *Biological Conservation* 249, 250.

[58] R Lloyd, M Newlands, and T Petray, 'Coral Battleground? Re-examining the "Save the Reef" Campaign in 1960s Australia' (2017) 3(1) *Environmental Sociology* 54.

[59] 'Protection for Reef' (*Canberra Times*, 9 September 1967) 1.

[60] Lines (n 24) 206.

a royal commission into oil drilling in the reef, which by taking four years to complete its inquiry, helped to alleviate political pressure on both governments.[61]

The Commonwealth was taciturn about intervening. Although he expressed unease about offshore oil drilling, Prime Minister John Gorton cited constraints to the Commonwealth's constitutional powers to act.[62] Gough Whitlam, however, promised to intervene if elected, pointing to the High Court's decision in a 1969 case in which some of its justices observed that state jurisdiction effectively ended at the low-tide mark, and that all waters (save the states' internal waters) were within the Commonwealth's sphere of control.[63] In 1975 the High Court confirmed this view more decisively in further litigation over control of coastal waters,[64] a decision made in the wake of the Commonwealth's Seas and Submerged Lands Act 1973, which vested in the Commonwealth all of the territorial sea (now encompassing up to 12 nautical miles from the coastline). This legislation paved the way for the Commonwealth's Great Barrier Reef Marine Park Act 1975.

Today the reef, listed under the World Heritage Convention,[65] remains under much environmental stress from new sources – coral bleaching from climate change and pollution runoff from coastal farming. These are stories of a different era and context that don't concern us here. The Save the Reef campaign demonstrated to conservationists that success depended on at least two conditions: presenting robust evidence of their case and generating widespread publicity of the issues.[66] The role of the Commonwealth would also eventually prove decisive, as a potential counterweight to the more development-driven state governments prone to 'regulatory capture'.

## VII. Recognising Aboriginal People

An account of 1967 wouldn't be complete without acknowledging another milestone. The struggle to save a vanishing continent cannot ignore its momentous environmental changes have been intertwined with the violent dispossession of its Aboriginal peoples. The fiction of *terra nullius* – land belonging to no one – was the legal contrivance by which White settlers could render Australia's first peoples

[61] Australian Government and Government of the State of Queensland, *Report: Royal Commission into Exploratory and Production Drilling for Petroleum in the Area of the Great Barrier Reef* (Government Printer, 1974).

[62] M Newlands, T Petray and R Lloyd, '*"Save the Barrier Reef" from 1967 to 2013: A Forty-six-year-old Campaign that Changed the Great Barrier Reef* (Great Barrier Reef Marine Park Authority, 22 January 2014).

[63] *Bonser v La Macchia* (1969) 122 CLR 177.

[64] *New South Wales v Commonwealth* (1975) 135 CLR 337.

[65] Convention Concerning the Protection of the World Cultural and Natural Heritage, (1972) 1037 UNTS 151.

[66] Connell (n 57) 250.

invisible in their own country. Their dispossession had environmental ramifications, as Indigenous environmental stewardship skills and wisdom honed over tens of thousands of years were lost or ignored.

The persecution of Aboriginal people, began from the earliest years of colonisation. Reserves designed to quarantine the dispossessed – grossly insufficient in their original state – were further reduced incrementally, such as the halving of Aboriginal reserve land in NSW from 26,000 acres to 13,000 acres between 1913 and 1927 to make way for settlers' farms and towns.[67] A popular assumption in the early 1900s was that the Aboriginal population would literally die out or that its 'primitive' culture would disappear through the 'civilising' influences of the church and state. The segregation of Aboriginal communities into small reserves and the placement of their children into White families were consequences of this prejudice, influenced by the fad of Social Darwinism. By the 1920s, when it became apparent that the Aboriginal population was growing not dying, authorities began to intensify their policy of removing Aboriginal children, especially 'half castes', to be put in state or religious 'care'.

Whilst Aboriginal resistance to colonisation occurred from its earliest days, as documented extensively by historians such as Henry Reynolds,[68] the early twentieth century marked a new phase with the development of a pan-Australian consciousness and organisational scale.[69] Whilst there were White-run advocacy groups, such as the Association for the Protection of Native Races, founded in 1911, the Australian Aboriginal Progressive Association (AAPA) formed in 1924 was the country's first politically focused, national Aboriginal group.[70] Its demands were similar to those championed by Aboriginal leaders a generation later: land rights, racial equality and cultural identity. Other pioneering groups soon followed. The Australian Aborigines' League was established in 1933 to advocate for a separate Aboriginal state governed by Indigenous law within the Australian federation and for guaranteed Aboriginal representation in the Commonwealth Parliament. With the AAPA, the League staged a Day of Mourning on Australia Day, 26 January 1938, to oppose celebrations of the sesquicentennial anniversary of colonisation. An Aborigines Progressive Association was formed in 1937 in NSW, aiming to secure full citizen rights for Aboriginal people and to repeal all racially discriminatory legislation. It sent a ten-point manifesto of its demands to Prime Minister Joseph Lyons.

[67] National Museum Australia, 'Formation of the AAPA', www.nma.gov.au/defining-moments/resources/formation-of-the-aapa.

[68] H Reynolds, *The Other Side of the Frontier: Aboriginal Resistance to the European Invasion of Australia* (James Cook University, 1981).

[69] See generally B Attwood and A Markus, *The Struggle for Aboriginal Rights – A Documentary History* (Allen and Unwin, 1999).

[70] J Maynard, *Fight for Liberty and Freedom – The Origins of Australian Aboriginal Activism* (Aboriginal Studies Press, 2007).

**Figure 3.4** Australian Aboriginal Progressive Association logo, 1924

Some Aboriginal resistance was impromptu. When no Aboriginal people were invited to the opening of Canberra's parliament house in May 1927, two elderly Wiradjuri men from southern NSW, Jimmy Clements and John Noble, known as 'King Billy' and 'Marvellous' respectively, walked 150 kilometres to gate-crash the ceremony. When the police tried to evict them the assembled crowd defended King Billy and Marvellous, resulting in the event marshals acquiescing, and even allowing them to meet the attending Duke and Duchess of York.[71] Sympathetically, the press reported on 'an ancient Aborigine, who calls himself King Billy and who claims sovereign rights to the Federal Capital Territory'. Despite these and other efforts, many in Australia still then assumed that its Aboriginal population was a 'dying race'. The *Adelaide Mail* observed: 'today a few scattered remnants of a dying race are left … When another hundred years have passed, the only record of the black man is likely to be in museums and in distorted place names'.[72]

Paralleling or preceding the environmental protests that erupted in the late 1960s, Aboriginal peoples also became more defiant. A seminal precedent

[71] 'Parliament at Canberra. Imposing Ceremonies' (*Australasian*, 14 May 1927) 1220.
[72] 'The Passing of the Aborigine Since the Settlement of the State' (*Mail* (Adelaide), 21 March 1936) 5.

was in 1946 when 800 Aboriginal pastoral workers in the Pilbara region of Western Australia went on strike for three years over unfair labour conditions.[73] The more well-known example is the Wave Hill walk off. On 23 August 1966, scores of Gurindji stockmen and other workers at the Wave Hill cattle station in the Northern Territory walked off the job after negotiations with their employers broke down. The Gurindji people's homelands were confiscated in 1883 by colonial authorities who reassigned some 3,000 km$^2$ of land to pastoralists. Their thousands of cattle impacted an environment managed sustainably for thousands of years by the Gurindji. The dispute wasn't just about oppressive labour conditions but about reclaiming land rights, as demonstrated in April 1967 when the strikers moved their base camp 20 km to Daguragu, closer to their community's ancestral home. The Gurindji's petition for Commonwealth assistance went unheard until the 1970s when Whitlam was elected, who paved the way for landmark Aboriginal land rights legislation for the Northern Territory.[74]

Until 1967 the Commonwealth lacked the constitutional power to legislate with regard to Aboriginal peoples, except in the Northern Territory and the Australian Capital Territory. That changed on 27 May that year, when over 90 per cent of voters supported a referendum to amend the Constitution to allow the Commonwealth to act. It's the highest 'yes' vote ever in Australia's constitutional referendums, and a major milestone towards the taking of national leadership in Aboriginal affairs. The success of the referendum owed much to the groundwork laid by the Federal Council for Aboriginal Advancement, established in 1958.

Now mythologised as a landmark in the maturing of the nation, the 1967 referendum did not immediately lead to any major innovations in Commonwealth policy towards Aboriginal people, let alone any improvement in their conditions, which over half a century later still lag behind those of non-Aboriginal Australians. The constitutional change 'did not require any federal government to use that power', 'let alone take over responsibility for [Aboriginal affairs] from the state governments', explains Bain Attwood, a leading historian on the 1967 referendum.[75] Yet the national plebiscite would eventually leverage some momentous changes. It emboldened the Commonwealth to introduce the Aboriginal Land Rights (Northern Territory) Act in 1976, and later the Native Title Act in 1993 to give effect to the High Court's *Mabo* ruling.[76] These and other law reforms have

[73] M Hess, 'Black and Red: The Pilbara Pastoral Workers' Strike, 1946' (1994) 18(1–2) *Aboriginal History* 65; see also D Rose, *Hidden Histories: Black Stories from Victoria River Downs, Humbert River and Wave Hill Stations* (Aboriginal Studies Press, 1991).

[74] B Attwood, 'The Articulation of "Land Rights" in Australia: The Case of Wave Hill' (2000) 44(1) *Social Analysis: International Journal of Anthropology* 3; Aboriginal Land Rights (Northern Territory) Act 1976 (Cth).

[75] B Attwood and A Markus, *The 1967 Referendum: Race, Power and the Australian Constitution* (Aboriginal Studies Press, 2007) vi–vii.

[76] *Mabo v Queensland* (No 2) [1992] HCA 23.

been instrumental in returning approximately half the continent to its traditional owners, albeit not always with exclusive possession. Many Aboriginal activists still rightly seek further reform as the Constitution does not recognise the special status of Aboriginal people as Australia's First Nations whose sovereignty was never ceded. A treaty with Aboriginal people is one option to address this lacuna.

Although the 1967 referendum did not in itself have any direct bearing on environmental policy, it legitimated a shift for the Commonwealth to take leadership in an important domain of national affairs that would eventually have consequences for environmental governance. The Commonwealth was now expected to assume a more assertive role in negotiating with and intervening for Aboriginal people across Australia. This legitimation of Commonwealth leadership would within a short time spill into other domains, including environmental policy. The Whitlam government of 1972 to 1975 introduced a new generation of environmental laws that marked the first serious national insertion into this policy domain, including the Environment Protection (Impact of Proposals) Act 1974, Australian Heritage Commission Act 1975, and National Parks and Wildlife Conservation Act 1975 – enacted through reliance on assorted constitutional heads of power given the absence of an explicit constitutional power on environmental matters. These statutes could address some Aboriginal issues, such as the provisions in the National Parks and Wildlife Conservation Act for the administering Commonwealth agency to cooperate with Aboriginal landowners in conserving wildlife.[77]

The Commonwealth's power gained from the 1967 referendum would eventually also have great significance for environmental policy through measures to promote opportunities for Aboriginal people in environmental management ('caring for country') on returned lands. Today, over 1,000 Indigenous Land Use Agreements, negotiated under the auspices of the Native Title Act, are helping Aboriginal people engage with their traditional territories. Many Aboriginal lands are also included in the Indigenous Protected Areas network – some 85 million hectares nationwide were managed in 2022 for biodiversity conservation, through voluntary agreements with the Commonwealth.[78] Some national parks, such as at Kakadu and Uluru, are also jointly managed by Crown and Aboriginal representatives.[79]

Above all, the empowerment of Aboriginal people in environmental stewardship has left a legacy of growing popular awareness that nature shouldn't be regarded as a realm separate from humankind but rather as an integral part of

[77] Section 18.

[78] Commonwealth Department of Agriculture, Water and the Environment, 'Indigenous Protected Areas', www.environment.gov.au/land/indigenous-protected-areas.

[79] T Bauman and D Smyth, *Indigenous Partnerships in Protected Area Management in Australia: Three Case Studies* (AIATSIS, 2007).

human life. Writers such as Matthew Colloff and Bill Gammage are awakening mainstream Australia to Aboriginal people's role in socialising the continent's landscapes for eons.[80] Australian ecosystems and their biota have co-evolved with them, and the increasing restoration of the continent's lands and waters to their traditional inhabitants is helping to re-establish that symbiosis. The turning points of 1967 thus paved the way not just to appreciate nature for nature but to recognise humankind's place within not apart from the natural world.

[80] M Colloff, *Landscapes of Our Hearts* (Thames and Hudson, 2020); B Gammage, *The Biggest Estate on Earth: How Aborigines Made Australia* (Allen and Unwin, 2012).

# PART II

# Transforming a Continent

# 4

# Taming the Bush

## I. Remaking the Land

The 'bush' in Australian *lingua franca* often denotes the countryside at large, though some observers might distinguish between the forested, coastal fringes and the 'Outback'. Most Australians don't live in the bush in either sense and some rarely encounter it, for the nation is highly urbanised. Today, 88 per cent of Australians reside in towns and cities,[1] mostly sprawling metropolises such as Sydney and Melbourne. In 1901 about 65 per cent of Australia's population inhabited such places – still many, relatively.[2] Yet such skewed demography belies the bush's economic, historical and cultural salience, and it has been of great interest to lawmakers in building the nation culturally and economically.

Australian society has long idolised rural life. The bush infuses national folklore, where men and women develop mateship, industriousness and other virtues lauded as indelible to the national psyche. The city, contrastingly, was often damned as a seedbed for slums, squalor and sin.[3] The bush also had miscreant connotations, notably bushrangers, though some viewed outlaws as folk heroes rebelling against despotic rule.[4] Today, the bush has acquired other connotations in White culture, sometimes pilloried for reactionary or outdated thinking unlike the creative and cosmopolitan vibe of the big smoke. These narratives don't speak for those of Aboriginal Australians, where the bush – or 'country', as it's known – has traditionally embodied their cultural psyche but now includes towns where many live.[5]

[1] According to the Australian Bureau of Statistics, 'urban' means a town of at least 1000 residents.

[2] Department of Infrastructure and Regional Development, *The Evolution of Australian Towns*, Report 136 (Commonwealth of Australia, 2014) 2.

[3] L Sandercock, *Property, Politics and Urban Planning: A History of Australian City Planning 1890–1990* (Transaction Publishers, 1990).

[4] G Seal, *The Outlaw Legend. A Cultural Tradition in Britain, America and Australia* (Cambridge University Press, 1996).

[5] J Altman and S Kerins (eds), *People on Country: Vital Landscapes Indigenous Futures* (Federation Press, 2012); L Behrendt, 'The Urban Aboriginal Landscape' (*PostSuburban Sydney: The City in Transformation* conference, Sydney, 2005).

The reverence of rural life, however, didn't initially attach to so-called 'wilderness', and indeed until the mid-twentieth century wilderness was often termed by nature conservationists themselves as 'primitive' places. The terminology also has a transnational history; the US Forest Service in 1929 introduced 'primitive area' as one of its land-type designations, 'to maintain primitive conditions of transportation, subsistence, habitation, and environment to the fullest degree compatible with their highest public use'.[6] The Australian bush in its rugged, 'primitive' form was commonly viewed in the early twentieth century as needing to be cleared and civilised in a society that equated the national interest with agriculture.

Also remaking the land was the once prevalent view that the continent abounded in natural resources, a 'big country' that White settlers were best equipped to exploit. Scottish immigrant and writer, James Collier, in his 1911 book *The Pastoral Age in Australasia*[7] proclaimed the 'greater inherent capability on the part of the whites; the only real wrong on the part of the blacks is their all-round inferiority and their inability to toll the ground or even make use of its natural pastures. Their disappearance was a natural necessity'. (Ironically, observes Tom Griffiths, 'the grasslands and woodlands that Europeans found attractive had been sculptured by Aborigines who regularly fired the landscape to keep it open for hunting'.[8]) Another to glorify settler triumphalism was Edwin Brady, an influential journalist, who challenged the 'desert myth' in advocating colonisation of the Outback.[9]

A contrasting, sobering view came from Thomas Griffith Taylor, a University of Sydney geographer who argued that there are insurmountable environmental and climatic constraints to expanding Australia's population and economy.[10] He wasn't the first to claim so, as 'Goyder's Line', proposed in 1865 by Surveyor-General of South Australia, GW Goyder, suggested a line beyond which perennial cultivation of wheat wouldn't be possible owing to unfavourable rainfall.[11] To challenge the optimists who had circulated maps of Australia superimposed with outlines of European countries, showing that much of Western Europe could fit into the Outback to imply Australia's untapped riches, Taylor produced maps of Australia overlaid with Saharan and sub-Saharan Africa – a better choice in terms of soil and climate.[12] In arguing for economic activity to concentrate on Australia's richer coastal fringes, Taylor's stark views seemed unpatriotic to his evangelical rivals,

[6] Forest Service, Experimental Forests and Ranges, Natural Areas and Primitive Areas, Regulation L-20. After 1939 the Forest Service switched to the terminology of wilderness area or wild areas.

[7] J Collier, *The Pastoral Age in Australasia* (Whitcombe and Tombs, 1911) 37.

[8] T Griffiths, *Hunters and Collectors: The Antiquarian Imagination in Australia* (Cambridge University Press, 1996) 14–15.

[9] EJ Brady, *Australia Unlimited* (George Robertson and Company, 1918) 14.

[10] T Griffith Taylor, 'Australia as a Field of Settlement' (1927) 5(4) *Foreign Affairs* 679. On his feud with Brady, see JM Powell, *Griffith Taylor and 'Australia Unlimited'* (University of Queensland Press, 1993).

[11] DW Meinig, 'Goyder's Line of Rainfall' (1961) 35(4) *Agricultural History* 207.

[12] M O'Connor, 'Boundless Plains to Share: Why No Population Policy?' in K Crowley and KJ Walker (eds), *Environmental Policy Failure* (Tilde Publishing, 2012) 146, 147.

and he incurred public opprobrium including in the Commonwealth Parliament for being 'so pessimistic about the future of Australia'.[13]

**Figure 4.1** Edwin James Brady, c. 1909, a leading advocate of settling Australia's interior; National Library of Australia

These lively debates influenced the political establishment. Brady's views resonated with Western Australia's Premier in the early 1920s, James Mitchell, who was passionate about land clearing to fulfill his belief in this state's vast agricultural potential.[14] Federally, Prime Minister Stanley Bruce orchestrated reforms

[13] 'Development and Migration Bill', Second Reading, House of Representatives, Hansard, 1 July 1926, 3745 (per John Perkins).

[14] WJ Lines, *Taming the Great South Land* (Allen and Unwin, 1991) 168.

during the 1920s to bolster primary industries' economic contribution to the nation's ascendancy, such as closer agricultural settlement (considered later in this chapter).[15] Yet whilst Brady's vision was 'the political orthodoxy' of his time,[16] he became, suggests one historian, 'something of a whipping boy for the failures of the closer settlement schemes introduced during World War I and the environmental damage that came with the expansion of farming into marginal land'.[17] His vision was never applied to the Outback, where it would have proved disastrous.

The fate of the vanishing bush was intertwined with the dispossession of its Aboriginal inhabitants, whose ejection also removed or impaired their environmental stewardship. Few nature lovers of this era acknowledged this nexus, but one who did was mammalogist Herbert Finlayson. In 1936 he praised the environmental knowledge of the Luritja people of the Outback: 'in obtaining his quarry he has at his command every relevant detail of its life-history and habits, and to what he has personally seen and remembered, is added that great store of knowledge which is the communal gain of long generations of observation'.[18] The impact of White settlers was also not lost on Finlayson: 'surely in no other country in the world, have the aboriginal people assisted so materially in facilitating the process of European occupation – and so frequently to their own undoing'.[19]

Settlers' remaking of the bush reflected not just their wilful ignorance of the limitations of Australia's climate, water and soil but the influence of government policy. Paul McGuire, a public servant and diplomat, remarked in his *Australian Journey* that the 'slaughter of trees in Australia is … equivalent to a slow process of national suicide'[20] and 'I decline to have any respect whatsoever for Australian politicians while this madness runs riot'.[21] The attitude of the time was that the axe was an instrument of civilisation.[22] This chapter tells the story of the subjugation of the bush through two types of government interventions – property tenure and closer/soldier settlement schemes. It concludes with their environmental ramifications. The extensive ring-barking and burning of forests unleashed a cascade of changes, including hard-hooved grazing livestock, exotic pests and weeds, and then agri-chemicals to control these exotics, and eventually nature's backlash that hurt agriculture itself. In 1943 Samuel Wadham, a Melbourne University professor of agriculture and member of the Commonwealth's Rural Reconstruction

[15] W Frost, 'Australia Unlimited: Environmental Debate in the Age of Catastrophe 1910–1939', working paper (Faculty of Business and Economics, Monash University, 2004).

[16] S Mirams, 'The Attractions of Australia: EJ Brady and the Making of *Australia Unlimited*' (2012) 43(2) *Australian Historical Studies* 270, 279.

[17] ibid 271.

[18] HH Finlayson, *The Red Centre: Man and Beast in the Heart of Australia* (Angus and Robertson, 1936) 78.

[19] ibid 92.

[20] P McGuire, *Australian Journey* (William Heinemann, 1942) 169.

[21] ibid 46.

[22] R Chapman, *Fighting for the Forests. A History of the Western Australian Forest Protest Movement 1895–2001* (PhD, Murdoch University, 2008).

Commission, mourned: 'the country side of Australia has been an area of disillusionment and not an area of steady progress'.[23] Yet despite the failure of many land settlement schemes that trespassed environmental limits, historian Graeme Davison explains that 'Australians were still reluctant to surrender their vision of a more populous and prosperous countryside'.[24] Where such limits were acknowledged, 'many people believed that science and technology' such as irrigating the Outback by rerouting rivers inland could overcome obstacles to an agrarian nirvana.

## II. Property Tenure

The subjugation of the Australian bush was facilitated by property tenure imported from England. Australian property tenure originated in the common law, with statutory adjustments including land titles statutes and the distinctly Australian regime of pastoral leases.[25] Property tenure influences environmental practices as it determines to whom natural resources are allocated and proprietors' rights and duties. Conceptually, property also seminally helps constitute raw spaces into lived 'places' – the values or uses people ascribe to a specific locality, such as their heritage, history or economic utility.[26] Conversely, 'empty' spaces, without effective ownership, may encourage abuse and degradation, as postulated by Garrett Hardin's 'tragedy of the commons' thesis.[27]

The Crown became the ultimate or 'radical' owner of all land and water in Australia when the continent was annexed by Britain. Therefore, no one including Aboriginal people could acquire any property rights except from the Crown. Federation in 1901 left largely undisturbed the colonies'/states' proprietorship of land and other natural resources although the Commonwealth acquired some land (eg Australian Capital Territory) as well as eventually coastal waters and their seabed. The Commonwealth also acquired the capacity to legislate in some domains that could interfere with property by promoting particular uses (eg Snowy Mountains Scheme) or restricting uses (eg controlling export of harvested natural resources). The state governments themselves, however, have not been the primary exploiter of land or other natural resources, preferring to collect economic rents such as from pastoral leases and mining ventures.

[23] SM Wadham, *Reconstruction and the Primary Industries* (Melbourne University Press, 1944) 4.

[24] G Davison, 'Country Life: The Rise and Decline of an Australian Ideal' in G Davison and M Brodie (eds), *Struggle Country: The Rural Ideal in Twentieth Century Australia* (Monash University Press, 2005) 32, 44.

[25] TP Fry, 'Land Tenures in Australian Law' (1947) *Res Judicatae* 159, 161–62; see also AR Buck, *The Making of Australian Property Law* (Federation Press, 2006).

[26] E Relph, *Place and Placelessness* (SAGE, 1976); YF Tuan, *Space and Place* (University of Minnesota Press, 1977).

[27] G Hardin, 'The Tragedy of the Commons' (1968) 162(3859) *Science* 1243.

The biggest change to this arrangement came with the native title revolution of recent decades, but it had yet to make its mark by 1967.

Whilst there's no comprehensive database of Australian land tenure, studies of its impact on environmental management have found that in 2021 an estimated 28.7 per cent of the landmass was held privately as freehold, 38.2 per cent managed privately as leasehold of Crown land, and the balance of 33.1 per cent held mostly by the Crown for purposes such as national parks, forestry and defence.[28] An accurate picture of land tenure is complicated by overlapping tenures, of which the biggest element now is Aboriginal property held exclusively or non-exclusively (eg co-existing with pastoral leases) and the Crown's ownership of minerals regardless of the surface tenure.

Property law doesn't operate in a vacuum but interacts with other legal provisions. As Paul Martin and Miriam Verbeck explain, 'property rights are defined by whatever legal instruments create and govern that right'.[29] Whilst leaseholders of Crown land were historically subject to more restrictions on land use, the relative liberties enjoyed by freeholders also declined during the twentieth century as governments reacquired and regulated part of the bundle of property rights to obtain resource rents (eg minerals) or manage conflicting uses (eg town planning and water consumption). For instance, a NSW court in 1909 declared that the plaintiff's common law riparian rights had been curtailed by the state's Water Rights Act 1896, placing water rights under the Crown's control for enabling waterways' 'more equal distribution and beneficial use' and their 'protection from pollution'.[30] A 1955 ruling of the High Court on NSW's water legislation concurred: 'to exercise full dominion over the waters of rivers and lakes … it was necessary to give to the Crown, or to some statutory authority, overriding rights to which private rights must, if need arise, give way'.[31] Another domain where the Crown expropriated or limited private property rights was wildlife, by restricting landholders' common law rights to hunt game.[32]

It would be misleading, however, to imply that this reassertion of state authority over land and water was inherently environmentally beneficial. English property tenure had other environmental consequences. It superimposed a new spatial and temporal division on the landscape, with tenures fixed in time and parcels fixed in place. Pastoral leases, occupying the majority of rural land in Western Australia and Queensland, incentivised resource use within the available term of the lease or making 'improvements' in the hope of it maturing into

[28] SG Kearney et al, 'Saving Species Beyond the Protected Area Fence' (2002) 4(3) *Conservation Science and Practice* e617.

[29] P Martin and Mi Verbeek. 'Property Rights and Property Responsibility' in C Mobbs and K Moore (eds), *Property: Rights and Responsibilities. Current Australian Thinking* (Land and Water Australia, 2002) 1, 2.

[30] *Hanson v Grassy Gully Gold Mining* (1900) 21 NSWLR 271, 275–76.

[31] *Thorpes v Grant Pastoral Co* (1955) 92 CLR 317, 331.

[32] *Yanner v Eaton* [1999] HCA 53, paras 24, 46.

a freehold estate, and even freehold had a temporal constraint in that failure to utilise unimproved, 'waste land' over a given time frame (eg 20 years) could lead it to being lost to a squatter under the doctrine of adverse possession.[33] Landscapes of interconnected and dynamic ecological properties became compartmentalised into discrete units of property. For example, the separation of proprietary rights over land and water allowed for the diversion or use of river waters to the deprivation of surrounding landscapes, such as when floodplains and other wetlands were drained. One legacy today is particularly evident in the distressed Murray-Darling rivers system.[34] Moving wild animals also don't respect the boundaries of property ownership set by the law. The tenure system also encouraged sedentism among settlers, limiting their capacity to adapt to variations in climate and environmental conditions such as the availability of water in droughts. Aboriginal people, by contrast, traditionally moved and adapted to nature's permutations, thus maximising their survival and minimising over-exploitation of any locality.[35] Land use planning in recent decades has attempted to counter some of the foregoing problems, by enabling authorities to 'reconnect' spaces fragmented by property tenure, such as to manage watersheds holistically.

Scholars of environmental law have in recent years debated ideas for a more radical overhaul of property law out of concern that it still remains problematically subservient to economic and other utilitarian interests.[36] A few recent legal innovations to improve environmental outcomes have already been enacted. One is conservation covenants placed on private land of high natural values, as I did for a patch of forest I formerly owned in Tasmania: conservation covenants are offered in all Australian states through special statutory regimes that aim to overcome the limitations of non-statutory, restrictive covenants in Equity.[37] The most radical new legal innovation is to replace human ownership of nature with nature owning itself by affirming its legal personality and intrinsic value, as already implemented in New Zealand and Ecuador.[38] These legal reforms however take us outside the scope of this book's history.

The role of property tenure in Australia's environmental changes cannot be divorced from its devastating consequences for the continent's First Nations. When Governor and commander of the First Fleet, Arthur Phillip, formally inaugurated the new colony on 7 February 1788 at Sydney Cove, he asserted imperial authority over not just the resident Gadigal people but other Aboriginal people

[33] *Harnett v Green* (1883) 4 NSWLR 292.
[34] R Beasley, *Dead in the Water* (Allen and Unwin, 2021).
[35] I Keen, *Aboriginal Economy and Society: At the Threshold of Colonisation* (Oxford University Press, 2003).
[36] See eg D Grinlinton and P Taylor, *Property Rights and Sustainability* (Brill, 2011); N Graham, *Lawscape: Property, Environment, Law* (Routledge, 2011).
[37] See eg, Tasmania's Nature Conservation Act 2002, ss 33–38.
[38] M Tănăsescu, 'Rights of Nature, Legal Personality, and Indigenous Philosophies' (2020) 9(3) *Transnational Environmental Law* 429.

including some 3,000 km away in Arnhem Land. Not only was Aboriginal sovereignty ignored, their traditional territories were deemed to be 'Crown land' on the legal fiction that the continent was *terra nullius*. In 1889 the Privy Council ruled that the creation of the NSW colony concerned 'a tract of territory practically unoccupied, without settled inhabitants or settled law, at the time when it was peacefully annexed to the British dominions'.[39]

The British annexation was initially accompanied by limited physical occupation, and it was not until the mid-nineteenth century that extensive tracts were taken up by pastoralists and other settlers.[40] As explorers opened more territory to occupation, sales of stolen Aboriginal land supported further colonisation; under the Australian Colonies: Waste Lands Act 1842 proceeds of land sales financed increased British immigration. When the Mother Country granted the colonies self-government from the 1850s, their parliaments acquired the power to dispose of 'waste' lands and waters, a capacity retained after Federation.[41] Titles to freehold or leasehold estates were issued by colonial (and later state) legislatures to reward settlers and incentivise development of their lands, although some pastoral leases included provisions reserving areas for access, camps and subsistence use by Aboriginal residents.[42] State governments also claimed ownership of minerals,[43] which in turn were reallocated through leases and licences to enterprising developers but not to Aboriginal peoples.

It would be a mistake to equate Aboriginal dispossession as belonging only to Australia's colonial period. Heather Goodall has researched a 'second dispossession' during the early- and mid-twentieth century. In NSW, ongoing revocation of Aboriginal reserves in whole or part occurred, along with the removal of children and relentless state surveillance via the Aborigines Protection Board.[44] In the 1920s many reserves were lost as governments reassigned property to war veterans under solider resettlement schemes, with 74 per cent by acreage of reserve land revoked between 1915 and 1926 in the NSW North Coast.[45] Some Aboriginal reserves were also moved to other land not desired by settlers, as documented in the Northern Territory.[46]

The Australian judiciary was asked in the seminal *Gove* case whether Aboriginal land title existed. The case originated in 1963 when the Yolngu people

[39] *Cooper v Stuart* (1889) 14 App Cas 286, 291.

[40] J Clarke, 'Australia: The White House with Lovely Dot Paintings whose Inhabitants have "Moved On" from History?' in BJ Richardson, S Imai and K McNeil (eds), *Indigenous Peoples and the Law: Comparative and Critical Perspectives* (Hart Publishing, 2009) 81, 92–93.

[41] Sections 106–07, Australia Constitution Act 1900.

[42] J Fulcher, 'The Wik Judgement, Pastoral Leases and Colonial Office Policy and Intention in NSW in the 1840s' (1998) 4(1) *Australian Journal of Legal History* 33.

[43] See eg Western Australia's Land Act 1933, s 15(1).

[44] H Goodall, *Invasion to Embassy: Land in Aboriginal Politics in New South Wales, 1770–1972* (Sydney University Press, 2008).

[45] H Goodall, *A History of Aboriginal Communities in New South Wales, 1909–1939* (PhD thesis, University of Sydney, 1982) 216–17.

[46] GL Crough, *Aboriginal Land and Development in the Northern Territory* (ANU North Australia Research Unit, 1992) 24.

of eastern Arnhem Land petitioned the Commonwealth House of Representatives after federal authorities sold without consultation part of their reserved land to Nabalco, a bauxite miner. After granted it a mining lease in 1968, the Yolngu led by Milirrpum Marika asked the Supreme Court of Northern Territory to uphold the ownership of their lands on the basis of Aboriginal (native) title – which means the right to the lands and waters they had traditionally possessed in accordance with their laws and customs.[47] They were unsuccessful.[48] Justice Richard Blackburn concluded that Australia's common law did not allow his court to recognise the Yolŋgu's lands rights. While acknowledging the Yolgnu people's enduring connections to country, the claimants' connections weren't of a character that the prevailing property legislation could recognise. Moreover, since Blackburn believed Australia was a colony founded by settlement rather than conquest, sovereignty and ultimate title to the land vested in the Crown on the continent's 'discovery'. Although Blackburn didn't explicitly refer to *terra nullius*, his judgment effectively rendered this claimants' land as such.[49] This ruling in 1971 thus put Australian law at odds with Canada, where its Supreme Court shortly afterwards, in 1973, ruled Canadian law must recognise the traditional property rights of the country's First Nations.[50]

The judicial extinguishment of 60,000 years of Aboriginal rights to country also shunted aside valuable Aboriginal ecological wisdom and husbandry skills.[51] They were radically unlike those introduced by Britain, being based on hunting and gathering, supplemented by bartering and reciprocity. Whilst they had delineated homelands, Aboriginal lifestyles were nomadic and communities were small outside of well-resourced areas such as fertile coastal strips, riparian areas and the Torres Strait islands. Given resource scarcities and harsh climates, Aboriginal people honed sophisticated environmental stewardship.[52] These attributes were acknowledged by Justice Blackburn himself in *Milirrpum* where he described the Yolngu traditions as 'a subtle and elaborate system highly adapted to the country in which the people led their lives, which provided a stable order of society'.[53]

Native (Aboriginal) title – as recognised since the Native Title Act 1993 giving effect to the High Court's annulment of *terra nullius* in the *Mabo* case[54] – differs

[47] K McNeil, *Common Law Aboriginal Title* (Clarendon University Press, 1989).
[48] *Milirrpum v Nabalco* (1971) 17 FLR 141.
[49] D Lavery, 'Not "Purely of Law" – the Doctrine of Backward Peoples in *Milirrpum*' (2017) 23 *James Cook University Law Review* 53.
[50] *Calder et al v British Columbia* [1973] SCR 313.
[51] Such knowledge and practice are being reclaimed through initiatives such as Indigenous Protected Areas and Indigenous Land Use Agreements: H Ross et al, 'Co-management and Indigenous Protected Areas in Australia: Achievements and Ways Forward' (2009) 16(4) *Australasian Journal of Environmental Management* 242.
[52] B Gammage, *The Biggest Estate on Earth: How Aborigines Made Australia* (Allen and Unwin, 2012).
[53] *Milirrpum* (n 48) 267.
[54] *Mabo v Queensland (No 2)* (1992) 175 CLR 1.

markedly from Anglo-Australian property tenure that conceives property as a fungible, economic asset.[55] Derived from Crown grants, freeholders enjoy the greatest rights, including to sell, lease, mortgage, build or trade on land.[56] While native title isn't a common law tenure, it's recognised by it.[57] Like freehold, native title custodians can use and enjoy their land but constrained by the owning group's traditional laws and customs, such as to where to hunt, gather or fish.[58] Native title is also not alienable,[59] and the courts have construed it as typically not encompassing commercial uses.[60] Egregiously, native title cannot revive Aboriginal ownership once extinguished, such as by the granting of contrary freehold estates,[61] although financial compensation for loss may be possible for dispossession since 1975 owing to the federal Racial Discrimination Act 1975. Native title may continue to be lost in the future, as the Australian Constitution does not protect it from extinguishment or compulsory acquisition – unlike Canadian constitutional law since 1982.[62] As of 2023, about 50 per cent of the Australian mainland had been formally recognised as under either exclusive or non-exclusive native title, or other forms of Aboriginal land rights granted under legislation in the states or the Northern Territory.[63]

## III. Bush Settlement Schemes

In the second half of the nineteenth century the colonial property regime faced pressures to better support economic expansion. As historian Stephen Roberts stated in explaining the bottleneck, 'there was a demand for land and a need to put the people on the land, but the land itself was alienated and lying idle'.[64] Pastoralists with large holdings, such as in the Riverina and Hunter Valley districts of NSW, were perceived by authorities to be hindering efficient farming attainable through more compact land holdings. The taming of the bush was thus regarded as incomplete. Consequently, colonial governments began unveiling 'closer settlement' schemes that involved re-acquiring territory, voluntarily or compulsorily, for subdivision and redistribution.[65] Enabling legislation was driven not just by facilitating the economic and demographic flourishing of the countryside but also belief in the

[55] E Wensing, *Comparing Native Title and Anglo-Australian Land Law*, Discussion paper (Australian Institute 1999).
[56] S Hepburn, *Australian Property Law Cases, Materials and Analysis* (LexisNexis, 2021) 253–54.
[57] *Mabo* (n 54) 59, 61.
[58] Native Title Act 1993, s 223.
[59] *Mabo* (n 54) 60.
[60] But see *Akiba v Commonwealth* (2013) 250 CLR 209.
[61] *Yorta Yorta Aboriginal Community v Victoria* [2002] HCA 58.
[62] Constitution Act 1982, s 35(1).
[63] National Indigenous Australian Agency, 'Land and Housing' (2022) www.niaa.gov.au/indigenous-affairs/land-and-housing.
[64] SH Roberts, *History of Australian Land Settlement (1788–1920)* (Macmillan, 1968; original 1924) 357–58.
[65] T Connors, 'Closer Settlement Schemes' (1970) 42(1) *Australian Quarterly* (1970) 72.

moral virtues of small-scale, family-run farms.[66] In this world Aboriginal people who had hitherto sometimes co-existed with pastoralists were, explains Heather Goodall, increasingly displaced as new settlement patterns cemented exclusive rather than shared spaces.[67]

Closer settlement laws also had environmentally disastrous consequences. John Holmes' argues that long-term pastoral leases in NSW and Queensland fostered 'severe land degradation' due to 'undersized holdings', 'insufficient usable grazing areas and high rents' that encouraged overstocking by economically stressed pastoralists.[68] Environmental degradation was compounded by conditional purchase schemes in which acquisition of freehold estates was conditional on 'improving' the land, which typically meant to clear bush, erect fences and build a homestead.[69] NSW's Crown Lands Alienation Act 1861 provided for the purchase of Crown lands of between 40 and 320 acres, subject to the purchaser making specified improvements and taking up residence for three years.[70] NSW's Closer Settlement Act 1904 provided that if the assigned land was unimproved in its original state, 'the purchaser shall make substantial and permanent improvements thereon to the value of ten per centum of the capital value thereof, within two years'.[71] In the 1908 case of *Ex parte Phillips* heard by the NSW Supreme Court, involving an unsuccessful prosecution of the holder of an 'improvement lease' of Crown land for ring-barking too many trees, Justice Pring noted sympathetically 'there are large areas of land covered with thick scrub, waterless, full of noxious animals, etc, and in order to deal with them it is necessary to offer great advantages to would-be leases'.[72] A slight shift in environmental emphasis appeared with NSW's Crown Lands Amendment Act 1916 that introduced the option to require the 'preservation or planting of timber'.[73] Similar trajectories occurred in other jurisdictions. Western Australia's Land Act 1898 made vacant Crown Land available for conditional purchase leases that included obligations to clear, fence and crop a minimum proportion of the lease over a number of years.[74] Its Group Settlement Scheme, launched in 1921, subsidised migrants from Great Britain with the offer that upon clearing parcels of karri and jarrah forests they would own the land to farm.

A collateral policy lever for closer settlement was to tax the unimproved capital value of land, in its natural state. The initiative began in South Australia in 1884,

[66] Department of Infrastructure and Regional Development, *The Evolution of Australian Towns*, Report 136 (Commonwealth of Australia, 2014) 37.

[67] Goodall (n 44) 85.

[68] J Holmes, 'Pastoral Lease Tenures as Policy Instruments, 1847–1997' in S Dovers (ed), *Environmental History and Policy: Still Settling Australia* (Oxford University Press, 2001) 212, 227.

[69] As detailed for instance in B Bunbury, *Invisible Country. Southwest Australia: Understanding a Landscape* (UWA Publishing, 2015).

[70] Section 18.

[71] Section 29(c).

[72] (1908) 8 SR (NSW) 52, 56.

[73] Section 18.

[74] Section 78.

aiming to incentivise economic use or to subdivide and sell-off big, underutilised estates.[75] Under the federal Land Tax Act 1910, the Commonwealth also taxed (until 1952) the unimproved value of all land in the country not specifically exempted. Land taxes gave subject landholders an incentive to clear native vegetation in order to reap, higher, untaxed property values and, in some cases, to claim the deduction of the costs of such improvements against their income tax. As the High Court acknowledged in the important *McGeoch* case of 1929, involving a disputed tax assessment, 'the greater portion of the land occupied for pastoral purposes in Australia would have been of little value unless it had been cleared of many of the trees growing on it', and 'clearing the timber from the land has uniformly been regarded as an improvement'.[76] However, as *McGeoch* further decided, an 'improvement' could also be made by eradicating noxious weeds, in this case prickly pear, so land taxes could also aid the environment albeit usually where weeds were eradicated to boost agricultural productivity.

In the 1920s closer settlement morphed into soldier settlement schemes, a policy Australia adopted like other British dominions for returning soldiers. Typically, war veterans were offered on concessional terms small parcels of leasehold or freehold land, mostly undeveloped bush. The schemes rewarded veterans for their sacrifice, along with the aim to create a morally superior 'property owing yeomanry'.[77]

From World War I onwards, each of the Australian states, with Commonwealth aid, introduced such schemes, resulting in 23,300 farms over 9 million hectares nationwide. Beneficiaries were also assisted with purchase of farm machinery through soft loans. Enabling legislation, such as NSW's Returned Soldiers Settlement Act 1916 and Victoria's Discharged Soldiers Settlement Act 1917, offered freehold title to veterans for dairying and other agricultural enterprises. Queensland's scheme offered perpetual leasehold, which the Secretary for Public Lands hoped would enable settlers to productively use the 'immense tracts of forests that are being neglected'.[78]

These settlement schemes began with much fanfare and optimism. Western Australia's guidebook boasted: 'ex-soldier settlers will be provided with the best land and will be afforded every facility to develop same under the most favourable conditions. The Department merely requires consistent industry on the part of the settler'.[79] Accompanying marketing materials typically showed lush landscapes and comfortable homesteads, such as in the Victorian example depicted in Figure 4.2.

[75] H Heaton, 'The Taxation of Unimproved Value of Land in Australia' (1925) 39(3) *Quarterly Journal of Economics* 410.

[76] *McGeoch v Federal Commissioner of Land Tax* (1929) 43 CLR 277, 286, 288.

[77] R Waterhouse, 'The Yeoman Ideal and Australian Experience, 1860–1960' in K Darian-Smith et al (eds), *Exploring the British World: Identity, Cultural Production, Institutions* (RMIT Publishing, 2004) 453.

[78] 'Land Act Amendment Bill', Second Reading, Queensland Legislative Assembly, Hansard, 1 December, 1915, 2537.

[79] Department of Lands and Surveys, *Soldier Settlement Guide* (Government Printer, 1920) 4.

**Figure 4.2** Victorian Government poster promoting soldier settlement, 1920s; Public Record Office Victoria

Such optimism was often dashed.[80] The parcels of allocated lands, sometimes just 10 acres to each beneficiary, were frequently economically unviable for

[80] B Scates and M Oppenheimer, *The Last Battle: Soldier Settlement in Australia 1916–1939* (Cambridge University Press, 2016).

farming, and many first-time farmers lacked the skills to live off the land or carried debilitating war injuries, as documented in Victoria's Royal Commission.[81] Weak agricultural prices after World War I and the high cost of farm equipment compounded settlers' struggles. Thus many eventually walked off the land, looking for better prospects. In the worst affected state, Tasmania, 61 per cent of the first 1,976 soldier settlers left within the first decade. Australia-wide, 29 per cent of veterans had quit by 1929, and more would do so in the coming years when the Great Depression proved to be the last straw.

Despite such setbacks, soldier settlements were repeated after World War II, though with some tweaks including bigger land parcels, more generous assistance for houses and fences, and requirements that land recipients be certified as physically able, and to remain in residence for at least five years. However, the environmental consequences of settlement schemes remained a low priority. Consider Victoria's Heytesbury Settlement Scheme, established in the 1950s and 1960s to create a dairy industry in the Otway Ranges. It cleared 43,000 hectares of forest; the 2,500 hectares left untouched, explained the Minister for Lands, was 'to ensure adequate firewood supplies for the future'.[82] The project was fortunately the last in Victoria in terms of large land settlement schemes.

State-run agricultural banks were complicit in abuse of the bush, as indebted farmers sought to boost yields unsustainably so they could repay loans. According to one Western Australian account of a bankrupt farmer's plight: 'the Agricultural Bank officials had compelled him to keep trying to grow wheat on soil that had officially been analysed as unsuitable'.[83] His 90-acre property had been completely cleared, such that by 1925 'he finally had to give up … and his place, like the other nine, now stands deserted, with the homesteads and all going to ruin'.[84]

A few veterans became endeared to the bush, creating another obstacle to the wishes of settlement scheme planners. One was Leslie Gordon Chandler (1888–1980), a World War I soldier who settled in the mallee lands of northwest Victoria, and preferred photographing nature rather than farming his allotted 18 acres. Chandler's biophilia began in his youth, often exploring the Dandenong Ranges, near Melbourne, and at age 18 he began giving talks to school children. Chandler went to great lengths to photograph birds, even erecting tall ladders to observe wedge-tailed eagle nests. Chandler participated in nature groups such as the Field Naturalists' Club of Victoria, the Bird Observers Club and the Australasian Ornithologists Union, and wrote frequently in natural history periodicals such as *The Emu* and *Walkabout*, publishing over 100 articles. He also helped form the Sunraysia Naturalists' Club, through which he lobbied for the Hattah-Kulkyne to

[81] Victoria, Royal Commission on Soldier Settlement, *Report* (Government Printer, 1925) 16–17.
[82] 'Start to be Made Soon on Heytesbury Settlement Plan' (*Camperdown Chronicle*, 15 September 1952) 2.
[83] 'A Farmer's Story of Failure to Grow Wheat on Unsuitable Land' (*Daily News* (Perth), 10 June 1925) 1.
[84] ibid.

become a national park, which was achieved in 1960. This is the same area that in the late 1960s would be the battleground for the Little Desert conservation battle, as discussed in chapter three.

## IV. Land Clearing

The bush began to be rolled back from the earliest days of colonisation to meet demands for firewood, building material and, most importantly, land for crops or livestock. The clearing was hastened by technological innovations, such as wire fences and railways, with the greatest assault occurring from the late nineteenth to mid-twentieth centuries. In NSW, some 9.6 million hectares had been cleared by 1892 (a period of 104 years since 1788), yet between 1893 and 1921 (just 29 years) a staggering 25.7 million hectares were cleared or substantially degraded.[85] One national *State of the Environment* report found that as much land clearing across the continent had occurred between 1895 to 1945 as in the 150 years since the nation's founding.[86] Many existing forests are also not old growth but new growth, a generally inferior ecosystem for biodiversity.[87] Another indicium of change has been the corresponding expansion of farmland: from 1890 to 1930 it quadrupled, leaping from 2.2 million hectares to nearly 8.9 million hectares.[88] Much of the continent was vanishing.

Ring-barking and fire were the principal tools of land-clearing zealots, who often made little use of the wood.[89] A cheap and effective method of razing a landscape, ring-barking excises a narrow ring of bark around the tree trunk that prevents the flow of essential nutrients.[90] Because ring-barking enabled rapid and extensive clearing, and wasted valuable timber, some began to demand its regulation.[91] Public figures such as Charles Moore, the Director of the Sydney Botanic Gardens, warned that rapacious deforestation could alter regional climates by reducing precipitation, an impact of economic detriment to farmers themselves.[92]

[85] P Reed, 'An Historical Perspective on Conserving What? The Basis for Nature Conservation Reserves in New South Wales 1967–1989' (1990) 26(2) *Australian Zoologist* 85, 85.

[86] State of the Environment Advisory Council, *State of the Environment 1996* (CSIRO Publishing, 1996) 4–6.

[87] D Mercer, *A Question of Balance: Natural Resources Conflict Issues in Australia* (Federation Press, 2000) 135–36.

[88] G Bolton, *Spoils and Spoilers: Australians Make Their Environment 1788–1980* (Allen and Unwin, 1981) 135.

[89] See T Griffith, *Secrets of the Forest: Discovering History in Melbourne's Ash Range* (Allen and Unwin, 1992) 16–19.

[90] The practice was not unique to Australia; in the United States it was also widely done, where it was known as 'girdling'.

[91] BJ Stubbs, 'Land Improvement or Institutionalised Destruction?' (1998) 4 *Environment and History* 145, 154–58.

[92] 'Ring-barking' (*Australian Town and Country Journal*, 2 December 1876) 15; 'Trees and Climate. Ringbarking and Rainfall' (*Cobargo Chronicle*, 22 May 1914) 4.

Later, soil erosion was recognised as another collateral cost. Regulators gradually began to take notice. In NSW, modest controls over ring-barking were introduced in 1875 under the Lands Acts Amendment Act, which required holders of pastoral Crown leases to obtain permission from the Minister (of course, the question of the efficacy of such a requirement is another matter, and such requirements were difficult to supervise in remote areas).

**Figure 4.3** Youth taught how to ring-bark a tree, Riverview, Queensland, 1927; National Archives of Australia

Regulatory restrictions on ring-barking could work at cross-purposes to tax regimes that incentivised ring-barking, as mentioned earlier in discussing the effect of taxes on the 'unimproved' value of land. In 1881 the NSW Supreme Court confirmed that ring-barking amounted to a land 'improvement',[93] a concept enshrined by NSW lawmakers in the Ringbarking on Crown Lands Regulation Act 1881 and subsequent legislation for many decades but in a narrow formula in which financial compensation was payable for the actual tree clearance work

[93] *Ex parte George Thomas*, (1881) 2 NSWLR 39.

rather than, as the court held was necessary, for the underlying, improved capital value of the land. The effect of classifying 'improved', ring-barked land more generously gave lessees of such Crown property the right to recover from future selectors of such land more financial compensation for their efforts. The court's stance was welcomed by some NSW parliamentarians, such as James Douglas, a former pastoralist, who explained: 'it is only by means of ringbarking that a large area of the public estate can be rendered fit for settlement'.[94]

Lawmakers could moderate clearing by reserving Crown land for forestry. It was perceived as a relatively lesser environmental threat in this era compared to the opprobrium it attracts today. Forestry became more economically significant after World War II when housing construction spiked demand for timber. The political influence of the forestry industry thereby increased, though governments often chose the politically easy route of opening native forests to harvesting rather than creating plantations on marginal or degraded farmland. The story of forestry is discussed further in chapter eleven.

The onslaught against the bush generated some public debate and disquiet. Visitor Elspeth Huxley in the mid-1960s wrote of landscapes being a 'boundless morgue of dead trees'.[95] Observing the defacement firsthand in the late nineteenth century, geologist and clergyman William Clarke lamented how 'many a sylvan scene of beauty' faced 'desecrat[ion]'.[96] In the 1930s, William Hatfield wrote of 'mute skeletons of the Australian pioneer's deadliest enemy, the living tree. … They were ringbarked, and left to die'.[97] In a similar era, visiting British zoologist Francis Ratcliffe observed, 'Australians revel in felling trees. It is the pulse of the pioneer still beating in their systems I suppose. … The big trees have always been foes in the eyes of the Australian settler; and he has treated them with scant mercy'.[98]

Yet the mass media often praised (uncritically) land clearing for lifting nature's productivity. In 1923 the *Nambour Chronicle*, covering Queensland's Sunshine Coast, rejoiced in the refashioned landscape: 'rich pasture lands, with dairy herds grazing in the deep grass; fruitful banana plantations … well-built comfortable-looking houses – all these meet the gaze wherever one turns, stamping the district with the hall-mark of prosperity'.[99] The newspaper went on to contrast this idyllic scene with that '30 years ago [when] the district was clothed in virgin scrub, heavy scrub festooned with vines and creepers'.[100] Such sentiments helped

[94] J Douglas, NSW, Hansard, *Parliamentary Debates*, 3 August 1881, 463.

[95] E Huxley, *Their Shining Eldorado. A Journey Through Australia* (Chatto and Windus, 1967) 64.

[96] Quoted in JM Powell, *Environmental Management in Australia, 1788–1914* (Oxford University Press, 1976) 91.

[97] W Hatfield, *Australian Through the Windscreen* (Angus and Robertson, 1939) 300.

[98] F Ratcliffe, *Flying Fox and Drifting Sand: The Adventures of a Biologist in Australia* (Chatto and Windus, 1938) 64.

[99] 'The Dulong District. Scrub to Prosperous Farms', (*Nambour Chronicle and North Coast Advertiser*, 14 December 1923) 5.

[100] ibid.

support the political status quo of leaving landowners free to clear without legal sanction.

After World War II the front-line of land clearing shifted to Western Australia's Wheatbelt and Queensland's Brigalow Belt, both showing reliance upon support from the state to mobilise resources, including making available heavy machinery, and to furnish conducive legal frameworks. The Brigalow is named after the dominant vegetation, the brigalow tree (*Acacia harpophylla*), whose canopy attains 50 feet. The infestation of the Brigalow Belt with the prickly pear before the 1930s stalled clearing, but once the weed was conquered the onslaught took off. One observer describes how the brigalow was banished with 'heavy duty tractors advancing in pairs through the bush like trawlers, dragging steel cables and heavy chains' and then 'hormone weedkiller sprayed from the air, which checks the regeneration of the suckers'.[101] Cattle now graze these areas. Efforts to conserve even small pockets met with political resistance and legal obstruction. A proposal to reserve 62,000 acres failed after one of the many government departments required to consent refused because it believed the area might contain valuable minerals.[102] Today only about 2 per cent of the original Brigalow Belt is ostensibly safe in conservation reserves.

Similar environmental ruin unfolded in Western Australia's Wheatbelt, a wedge in the state's southwest.[103] Government-subsidised settlement for an agrarian vision of populating the land and boosting economic opportunities resulted in vast clearing, and decimation of the culture of the Noongar people.[104] Government aided the colonisation through conditional purchase schemes and construction of railway services to facilitate movement of goods and settlers,[105] and the state's Agricultural Bank provided large-scale rural credit. Science was enlisted by authorities to facilitate the empire of wheat, such as establishment of government demonstration farms to experiment in maximising crop yields.[106] Farmland acreage grew from 6.48 million hectares in 1949 to 13.77 million hectares in 1969, and continued to grow at a lesser pace until the mid-1980s.[107] A few settlers disagreed with the region's transformation, however. Defending the aesthetic and ecological virtues of untrammelled landscapes, war veteran James Pollard wrote of 'the beauty of powdered silver mallee', and 'the songs of tomtit and honeyeater, and the chatter of wagtail, the carol of magpie and the raven's lament … [a] friendly

[101] Huxley (n 95) 343.

[102] ibid 345.

[103] T Hughes-d'Aeth, *Like Nothing on this Earth: A Literary History of the Wheatbelt* (UWA Publishing 2017).

[104] A Haebich, '"Clearing the Wheat Belt": Erasing the Indigenous Presence in the Southwest of Western Australia' in D Moses (ed), *Genocide and Settler Society* (Berghahn Books, 2004) 267.

[105] S Glynn, 'The Transport Factor in Development Policy: Pioneer Agricultural Railways in the Western Australian Wheat Belt, 1900–1930' (1969) 15(2) *Australian Journal of Politics and History* 61.

[106] Lines (n 14) 148.

[107] A Gaynor, 'How to Eat a Wilderness' (*Inside Story*, 6 February 2015) insidestory.org.au/how-to-eat-a-wilderness.

world, the mallee, full of charm'.[108] Pollard went on to warn, 'Clear this country and the soil will likely begin to drift and blow away'.[109] His advice went unheeded. Today the region can only support, explains Andrea Gaynor, 'industrial farming' sustained on fossil fuels and agrochemical inputs'.[110] The Wheatbelt is visible from space: satellite maps show a swathe of tan-coloured farmland flanked by green forest to the west and brown scrubland to the east. Only 7 per cent of its original vegetation remains.

## V. Nature Bites Back

Land clearing not only unbalanced nature, it unsettled settlers themselves. Settlers' idolisation of rural life clashed with the reality of a 'sunburnt' country – drought-prone, as well as fire-prone. The continent has just one major river system, in the Murray-Darling basin. Australia's soils are also generally poor, with little comparable to the rich alluvial plains of Europe or the eastern United States. Combine fragile soils, droughts and land clearing, and one has a recipe for a desiccated and degraded landscape. Eroded hillsides and creeks, with soil shorn away, were the most telling signs of troubled landscapes. Another was salinisation; the removal of native vegetation, which can hold water, resulted in groundwater rising, and with it, damaging salts surfacing.[111] Nature's backlash was observed not only by those working the land but distant city dwellers. A succession of severe droughts in southeast Australia in the early to middle twentieth century stirred huge dust storms, with newspapers reporting on the choking and blinding sand that caused havoc to residents of Melbourne and Adelaide.[112]

Despite experiencing many droughts since 1788, it took settlers and lawmakers until well into the twentieth century to truly appreciate that insufficient rain is a recurring and often frequent, natural event.[113] Rainfall records from the 1850s reveal the continent suffered extensive droughts from 1895 to 1903 (the mega 'Federation Drought'), and then again from 1942 to 1944, intermittently between 1957 and 1968, and several more in each decade from the 1980s. Historical reconstruction of the effects of the Federation Drought by the CSIRO suggests it precipitated numerous ecosystem collapses and severely affected 60 genera of birds, mammals, reptiles and plants over 2.8 million km$^2$, or about

[108] J Pollard, 'In the Mallee Country' (*Western Mail* (Perth), 26 February 1948) 60.

[109] ibid.

[110] ibid.

[111] 'The Salt Menace. Value of Growing Timber' (letter to the editor) (*Western Australian*, 18 October 1935) 17.

[112] 'City's Worst Dust-storm' (*Advertiser* (Adelaide), 30 December 1944) 1; 'Worst Dust Storm in Memory' (*Argus* (Melbourne), 8 January 1942) 3.

[113] M McKernan, *Drought: The Red Marauder* (Allen and Unwin, 2005).

over one-third of the continent.[114] And 2019, the year of unprecedented bushfires saw more records for parchedness broken across the continent. Indeed, some part of Australia at any time is in drought.[115] The delay in understanding and respecting the limitations of the world's driest, inhabited continent may have owed, suggests drought-historian Michael McKernan, to the former optimism that new areas would be available to settle to replace those that became degraded.[116]

This struthious, short-sighted attitude, in turn delayed introduction of laws to instil better land stewardship. The authorities were reluctant to concede that large swathes of the continent shouldn't be farmed, and that some areas already colonised should be allowed to revert to their original condition. Both federal and state governments encouraged agriculture in marginal areas since the early twentieth century through costly 'drought proofing' irrigation schemes such as in the NSW Riverina, by concessional loans in hard times such as under Victoria's Cultivation Advances Act 1927 and NSW's Farmers' Relief Act 1933, and doling out 'disaster' relief like fodder and water subsidies.[117] The assumption of policy makers was that droughts were deviations from the norm, akin to random acts of God. Astonishingly, it wasn't until the 1992 National Drought Policy that 'the emphasis [shifted] away from drought being classified as a natural disaster and towards that of a normal component of the operating environment'.[118]

Climatic variations underline Australia's vulnerability to degradation. Recurring drought is associated with the El Niño-Southern Oscillation, denoting variations in sea surface temperatures and weather patterns across the Pacific Ocean that engender shifts in the climate of eastern Australia.[119] Floods and cooler conditions come with the La Niña phase of the Southern Oscillation. Major La Niña events in Australia last century occurred in 1917–18, 1955–56 and 1975–76. The continent is unevenly affected by the Southern Oscillation. As with vulnerability to droughts, the devastation wrought by floods is exacerbated by reckless planning decisions by authorities that allowed development in vulnerable riparian areas and floodplains.[120] Major damaging floods for the young nation occurred

[114] CSIRO, 'Megadrought Caused Mega Biodiversity Loss' (16 July 2019), www.csiro.au/en/news/news-releases/2019/megadrought-caused-mega-biodiversity-loss.

[115] 'Drought' is not an absolute concept but defined with reference to context – the environment and the uses one wishes to avail of it: insufficient rainfall for an expected bountiful crop in one locality may be viewed as a 'drought' but not otherwise if the same country were left for nature conservation. Hence, the discrepancy between water needs and water availability makes for a drought.

[116] McKernan (n 113).

[117] K Downing, R Jones and B Singley, 'Handout or Hand-Up: Ongoing Tensions in the Long History of Government Response to Drought in Australia' (2016) 62(2) *Australian Journal of Politics and History* 186.

[118] Department of Agriculture, Fisheries and Forestry, *Drought in Australia* (Australian Government, 2012) 6.

[119] FHS Chiew et al, 'El Nino/Southern Oscillation and Australian Rainfall, Streamflow and Drought: Links and Potential for Forecasting' (1998) 204(1–4) *Journal of Hydrology* 138.

[120] See M Cook, *A River with a City Problem* (QBD Books, 2019), examining the history of floods in the Brisbane River catchment including their political context.

in Queensland at Clermont and Peak Downs (1916), Mackay (1918) and Cairns and Townsville (1927), as well as in northern Tasmania (1929), Melbourne (1934) and the NSW Hunter Valley (1955).[121] As with drought aid, government financial assistance to flood victims encourages settlement in risky, low-lying areas.

**Figure 4.4** Receding river with dead livestock, Woolamit, Queensland, 1900; State Library of Queensland

The insouciance, naivety or plain arrogance of colonising settlers contrasts with the caution and adaptability of Aboriginal people. Glenn Albrecht and fellow drought researchers at Murdoch University argue: 'Aboriginal peoples responded to the changing climate by altering their settlement patterns, local economies and by developing new technologies. … they also planned ahead and provide evidence of adaptive management in the face of major change'.[122] Examples of such practices include, in western Victoria, fish weirs erected to hold water in the summer and manage flows during high rainfall, with one such structure covering six hectares. Bruce Pascoe's *Dark Emu* documents many other examples.[123]

[121] D Carbone and J Hanson, 'Top 10 Worst Floods in Australia' (*Australian Geographic*, 8 March 2012), www.australiangeographic.com.au/topics/history-culture/2012/03/floods-10-of-the-deadliest-in-australian-history.

[122] G Albrecht et al, *Historical Case Studies of Extreme Events: Resilience and Water Security in Two Outback Cities* (National Climate Change Adaptation Research Facility, 2010) 10.

[123] B Pascoe, *Dark Emu: Aboriginal Australia and the Birth of Agriculture* (Magabala Books, 2018).

The extent of land degradation by the mid-twentieth century nonetheless wasn't lost on non-Aboriginal Australians, and it generated considerably public anxiety among scientists, popular writers and the press. Judith Wright in her poem *Dust* (1945),[124] and Elyne Mitchell in her book *Soil and Civilization* (1946)[125] challenged the credence of a peaceful and prosperous rural Australia. Mitchell explicitly linked unchecked soil erosion to the prospect of civilisational collapse.[126] Resorting to spiritual ideas and romantic language to engage readers, she argued that soil erosion fuelled 'a man-made alteration in the rhythm of the universe'.[127] That such writers, who aren't scientific experts, could identify with reasonable sophistication the dimensions and causes of rural land degradation indicates the considerable public awareness of the problem. The press contributed to this narrative, especially during World War II's disruptions to food security. The *Newcastle Herald* wrote of 'Soil Erosion Enemy of the Nation',[128] and another paper warned of 'The Enemy Within'.[129] One called 'the menace … even more deadly than the Jap invader'.[130]

The causes of land degradation were thus increasingly recognised by some as not a result of natural variability but decisions of settlers and, potentially, government policies. In 1944 the *Sydney Morning Herald* explained: 'Mankind is inherently destructive of Nature's bounty', and that soil erosion owes to farmers' 'excessive over-stocking and easy-going land management'.[131] The success of US authorities' handling of the Dust Bowl crisis of the 1930s was cited in the Australian media as evidence of what its own governments might achieve.[132] The development of soil conservation laws in response to such concerns is examined in chapter eleven.

Other forms of land degradation accompanied agriculture. One to mention, as it relates to my mother's Orchardfield, is chemical pollution. The environmental and health risks of herbicides and pesticides were not widely publicised or known until Rachel Carson's polemic *Silent Spring*, published in 1962.[133] Before World War II, agri-chemicals were an unquestioned valuable 'weapon' in the proverbial struggle of 'man versus insects'.[134] Orchards were the most heavily sprayed areas. In apple groves of southern Tasmania, observed Elspeth Huxley in the 1960s, 'growers have to spray their orchards about sixteen times a season … these valleys

[124] J Wright, *A Human Pattern: Selected Poems* (Angus and Robertson, 1990) 239–40.
[125] E Mitchell, *Soil and Civilization* (Angus and Robertson, 1946).
[126] ibid.
[127] ibid 26.
[128] 'Soil Erosion Enemy of the Nation' (*Newcastle Herald*, 16 October 1941) 2.
[129] '"The Enemy Within". Soil Erosion a Major Problem' (*National Advocate* (Bathurst), 22 July 1943) 1.
[130] J MacDonald Holmes, 'Disease of Soil Erosion Can be Cured and Prevented' (*Sydney Morning Herald*, 3 January 1945) 2.
[131] Martingale, 'Soil Erosion. Cost of Wartime Food Drive' (*Western Mail* (Perth), 20 January 1944) 33.
[132] HS Pearson, 'The Dust Bowl Grows Green' (*Daily Mercury* (Mackay), 26 October 1942) 4; 'America Tackles Soil Erosion' (*Adelaide Chronicle*, 16 June 1938) 9.
[133] R Carson, *Silent Spring* (Houghton Mifflin, 1962).
[134] 'Man Versus Insects' (*Toowoomba Chronicle and Darling Downs Gazette*, 12 December 1933) 12.

must be well saturated with chemicals that have persistent residues. What of the effects on soil bacteria and animals on birds, bees and butterflies?'[135] Carson's findings were acknowledged in the Australian press in the early 1960s, reporting on collateral animal deaths from insect sprays and implications for human health.[136] A decade earlier, the media were reporting sanguinely on the findings of US scientists – later discredited by Carson – that the public 'need not fear harmful effects from DDT and other scientifically tested pesticides used by farmers'.[137] Just a minority of journalists voiced caution, citing the lack of Australian regulation (in the 1950s) for the safe handling of pesticides.[138]

[135] Huxley (n 95) 168.

[136] 'Cats Killed by Insect Sprays' (*Sydney Morning Herald*, 29 July 1962) 15; 'Pesticides a Threat to Human Life?' (*Canberra Times*, 11 May 1963) 18.

[137] 'Pesticides Safe for Food Crops US Scientists Say' (*Singleton Argus*, 9 May 1952) 6.

[138] JV Mertin, 'Health Hazards of the New Pesticides' (*Adelaide Chronicle*, 21 August 1952) 13.

# 5

# Prickly Pears to Toxic Toads

## I. Invasive Species

Australia has a long and dismal history of introducing, inadvertently or deliberately, animals and plants that have gone on to cause mayhem. Cats, cane toads, foxes, pigs, rabbits, camels, assorted species of fish such as carp, and countless invertebrates and plants, are among the exotica now at home in Australia.[1] Many were introduced to improve agriculture, and some for sport or ornamental embellishments. Acclimatisation societies established before Federation, and enjoying the imprimatur of the law, spearheaded the invasion. Their members, explain scholars such as Guy Hall, Alistair Paton and Pete Minard who have analysed this history closely, believed that Australian nature was somehow deficient but could be improved through importation of superior plants and animals, along with other methods of colonisation such as tree clearing.[2] The corollary of the importation of 'superior' species was campaigns to destroy native species considered harmful to agriculture. Such pests or weeds in the eyes of farmers were readily classified by lawmakers as 'vermin' or 'noxious', and thereby punitively controlled; but apart from a few success stories, they have continued to defy control. Introduced in the nineteenth century, rabbits have probably been the worst invader for farmers and nature alike. Two other destructive interlopers, especially in Queensland, are the prickly pear and cane toad.

The introduction and management of these pests is revealing for the role, and sometimes misguided use of, scientific expertise. It was mobilised by authorities to help control weeds and pests, as it was with finding solutions to soil erosion, and whilst science helped tame some of Australia's most damaging exotics, its misuse by authorities also sometimes had disastrous results. Even the environmental success stories harboured a darker side. Popular narratives of scientific ingenuity enabling biological control of destructive pests such as prickly pear are problematic, suggests historian Jodi Frawley, as they can 'support a fantasy about human

[1] See T Low, *Feral Future: The Untold Story of Australia's Exotic Invaders* (Penguin Books, 2001).

[2] P Minard, *All Things Harmless, Useful and Ornamental* (University of North Carolina Press, 2019); G Hull, *The Ferals that Ate Australia* (HarperCollins, 2021); A Paton, *Of Marsupials and Men* (Schwartz Books, 2022).

control over Australian environments' and hold people 'at arm's length from the accountability for degraded ecosystems'.[3]

Strictly speaking, weeds and pests are just species that people don't want, usually because they harm agriculture such as by feeding on or damaging crops. Yet many plant and animal introductions to Australia, from livestock to improved pastures, that have precipitated enormous environmental change, are considered benign by those who benefited economically. The tens of millions of beef cattle and merino sheep, suggests Geoffrey Bolton, engendered the most 'profound transformation of the Australian environment' of any exotic invader.[4] That some introductions, whether or not classified as weeds or pests, are inimical to native wildlife has been of far less importance to most Australians, at least until recent decades. Indeed, for much of the twentieth century native wildlife were commonly considered pests themselves, and subject to persecution, as discussed later in this chapter. The most egregious weeds or pests have typically been declared by lawmakers to be 'noxious' or 'vermin', with consequential restrictions on their sale, movement or release, and collateral obligations on landholders to destroy them.

To understand the roots of this bias, we must look at the acclimatisation societies established in the nineteenth century to bring plants and animals, especially English varieties, to a continent they considered bereft of attractive or useful species.[5] The societies were imbued with nostalgia for 'mother' England and the desire to assist antipodean settlers in civilising their new land. Historian Pete Minard argues their proponents believed misguidedly they would also make their new homelands more economically productive.[6] The colonial administrations aided acclimatisation most directly by protecting some species introduced for game hunting: the preamble of NSW's Animal Protection Act 1879 declared its purpose 'to encourage the importation and breeding of game not indigenous to the Colony'. Deer were one success story, with a variety of species (red deer, fallow and sambar) readily establishing in the wild. Acclimatisation societies also sponsored birds, of which three – the Indian myna, English starling and house sparrow – have become pestiferous. Fish were also introduced, notably varieties of trout and carp to provide food and sports hunting, and many now dominate Australian waterways.

Numerous plants were imported, some deliberately, others as stowaways. Approximately 2,750 exotic plant species are now naturalised in Australia, amounting to about 12 new naturalisations per year since 1788.[7] Not all however are regarded as a problem: the needs of agriculture have been the principal yardstick

[3] J Frawley, 'A Lucky Break: Contingency in the Storied Worlds of Prickly Pear' (2014) 28(6) *Continuum: Journal of Media and Cultural Studies* 760, 762 and 770.

[4] G Bolton, *Spoils and Spoilers: Australians Make Their Environment*, 2nd edn (Allen and Unwin, 1992) 81.

[5] Minard (n 2).

[6] ibid.

[7] Invasive Species Council, 'Stopping Weed Invasions: A "White List" Approach' (2014).

for differentiating between plants deemed 'weeds' or 'useful'. One widely recognised villain is *Lantana camara La*, a shrub native to the American tropics that was introduced to Australia in the mid-nineteenth century for decorating gardens. By the early twentieth century lantana was flourishing in unwelcome places, having colonised five million hectares of the east coast.[8] Today, botanists deride the weed as a national 'catastrophe'.[9]

My maternal ancestors, who in the 1860s established 'Orchardfield' on the outskirts of Armidale, were complicit in this history (see Fig. 5.1). They planted stately English elms (*Ulmus procera*) to flank the driveway to the homestead, creating a majestic entrance reminiscent of what one might find in a posh English or Canadian estate. The homestead gardens were adorned with many imports including ivy, walnut and mulberry trees, and abundant shasta daisies. The depth of cultural attachment to imported flora that has grown over time is also evident in another site near Orchardfield, where the local community recently complained about the clearing of an exotic pine plantation as tantamount to being shorn of some of their 'heritage'.[10]

The legacy of acclimatisation societies and their collaborators is now viewed rather differently by many. The most biting epithet came from farmer and historian Eric Rolls who exclaimed: 'there was never a body of eminent men so foolishly, so vigorously, and so disastrously wrong'.[11] Rabbits, foxes and carp are among the most catastrophic for native biota. The foolishness of the acclimatisers would have been even more calamitous were it not for a 'shortage of money and the failure of some animals to adapt' to Australian conditions.[12] One could take a more charitable view of acclimatisation as simply reflective of an era where colonisers had insufficient knowledge of the risks their practices posed. Yet, there were dissenting voices at the time, even in official circles. For instance, Tasmania's Game Protection Act 1879 banned the introduction of foxes,[13] a move supported by the island's Colonial Secretary who observed that 'all of the nuisance of the mother country were (sic) being imported into the colony'.[14] Equally pernicious were some naïve beliefs about how to control invasive pests. Edwin Brady pompously pronounced: 'For rabbits, prickly pear and other foreign introductions, which become pests in Australia, here is one explanation – and a remedy. … [They] spread because

[8] SA Bhagwat et al, 'A Battle Lost? Report on Two Centuries of Invasion and Management of *Lantana camara L.* in Australia, India and South Africa' (2012) *PLOS ONE* journals.plos.org/plosone/article?id=10.1371/journal.pone.0032407.

[9] 'Lantana Removal Expert Warns Spread of the Poisonous Weed is a "Catastrophe" for Australia' (ABC News, 10 June 2019), www.abc.net.au/news/rural/2019-06-10/poisonous-lantana-weed-a-catastrophe-removal-expert-warns/11190098.

[10] K Wright, 'Pining for the Present: Ecological Remembrance and Healing in the Armidale State Forest' (2012) 9(1) *Environmental Philosophy* 109.

[11] E Rolls, *They All Ran Wild: The Animals and Plants that Plague Australia* (Angus and Robertson, 1969) 270.

[12] ibid.

[13] Section 25.

[14] 'Parliament of Tasmania' (*Mercury* (Hobart), 30 October 1878) 3.

wide, waste lands afford them unique opportunities to increase and multiply. Closer settlement forms the one effective check to these evils'.[15] To the contrary, closer settlements that cleared the countryside were more likely to have aided such species than healthy, intact ecosystems with more resilient to exogenous threats.

**Figure 5.1** Caring for Orchardfield's English-style gardens, 1935; author's family collection

[15] E Brady, *Australia Unlimited* (George Robertson and Company, 1918) 272.

This chapter examines efforts to remake the continent's wildlife through introduction of foreign species and destruction of native ones. It discusses three examples of national significance during the first half of the twentieth century – the cane toad, prickly pear and rabbit – the latter two attracting significant attention from authorities because they harmed agriculture. The chapter then looks at the vermin wars waged against native fauna for similar reasons. It shows several modes of governance at work, but primarily the role of science in pest control, for good and bad, and how property tenure proved to be an ineffective mechanism. Many of the environmental impacts of invasive species could have been avoided had proper scientific due diligence been conducted, and the war waged against native fauna could also have been avoided had wildlife management been put on a scientific basis to understand species' habits and ecological roles.

## II. Prickly Pear

Prickly pear is a genus of the cactus family, a couple of species of which colonised millions of hectares of eastern Australia in the early twentieth century. These prickly leaved plants were introduced to many countries, including Australia, as garden ornamentals, and some varieties became feral, eventually smothering the countryside in dense thickets. The plant's history in Australia matters both for the magnitude of its suffocating, rapid spread and conversely the speed and efficiency with which it was eventually tamed.[16]

Prickly pear arrived in Australia with the First Fleet after some were collected en route at Rio de Janeiro in the hope of establishing a local cochineal dye industry. More varieties of prickly pear were later imported for use as a hedge plant or for stock feed. Two types – *Opuntia inermis and Opuntia stricta* – ultimately became established in the wild, prospering in the drier plains west of the Great Dividing Range. At the peak of their dominion the weeds covered about 25 million hectares (about the size of Great Britain), with 80 per cent of the infestation in Queensland and the remainder in NSW.[17] Half of these infested areas became useless for agriculture. The successful colonisation was not just due to the plants' ease of propagation but also their hardy qualities, withstanding extremes of drought, flood or fire, and even their ability to regenerate despite direct mutilation or poisoning.

Authorities' efforts to control prickly pear were generally ineffectual, and indeed historians suggest their 'policies unwittingly promoted the spread of the pest rather than arrested it'.[18] The earliest interventions involved clearing prickly

[16] For a fuller discussion of the prickly pear story, see T Domico, *The Great Cactus War: True Story of the Greatest Plant Invasion in Human History* (Turtleback Books, 2018).

[17] A Dodd, *Biological Campaign Against Prickly Pear* (Commonwealth Prickly Pear Board, 1940) 2.

[18] D Freeman, 'Prickly Pear Menace in Eastern Australia 1880–1940' (1992) 82(4) *Geographical Review* 413, 415.

pear in small areas by manual digging, slashing or burning. These hardly made a difference. Chemical control through arsenic pentoxide was more effective but as the poison is highly toxic and financially expensive it couldn't provide a landscape-wide solution.

Legislative responses grew from the late nineteenth century, using property tenure to interpose pest management. Increasing statutory obligations on landholders to eradicate prickly pear stemmed in part from an important interpretation of the common law by the High Court in 1908 that there was no duty on a landholder to control prickly pear that was invading and damaging a neighbour's property; in the words of Justice Higgins, 'the prickly pear is not [his] agent or instrument'.[19] Thus, lawmakers began to oblige landholders to undertake eradication, and disobliging tenants of Crown lands risked forfeiture of their lease. Queensland's Local Authorities Act 1902 also conscripted local governments to help control prickly pear, by now declared a 'noxious' weed, but few municipalities had the resources to assist. By 1925 Queensland authorities adopted a compromise that did not require wholesale weed removal, by requiring landholders to create a one-mile, cleared buffer zone, thereby separating habitable (weed free) and unhabitable areas.

In NSW, the Prickly Pear Destruction Act 1886 likewise was the start of periodic official efforts to deal with the menace through a mix of coercion and suasion. In 1924 the state government overhauled its legislation to gain greater control over eradication efforts. The Prickly-pear Act established the Prickly-pear Destruction Board with wide-ranging powers. Like other land management legislation, it delegated to landholders the primary responsibilities, in this case 'to keep and maintain entirely free from prickly-pear any land of which he is the owner or occupier … and if he fails to do so without reasonable excuse such owner or occupier shall be liable to a penalty'.[20] The Act also empowered the Board's agents to eradicate the weed from properties where landowners had failed, and to charge such costs to the landowner, in addition to any statutory fines if enforcement notices had been ignored.[21]

These regulations made little difference. New South Wales authorities should have paid attention to the 1923 report of a Royal Commission appointed by the Queensland government to investigate the situation; it decried that 'unless existing methods of holding the pear in check are radically changed, there is little hope but that the spread will continue'.[22] The poor coordination of regulations across different tenures contributed to the malaise. The obligations on private landholders left unoccupied Crown lands untreated, and thus they frequently became reservoirs

[19] *Sparke v Osborne* (1908) 7 CLR 51, 75.
[20] Section 9.
[21] Section 10.
[22] BD Steele, *Report of the Royal Commission Appointed to Inquire into Certain Matters Relating to the Prickly Pear Problem* (Government Printer, 1923) 4.

for reinfestations of neighbouring property. Leaseholders of Crown land sometimes abandoned their tenancy when the weed infestations became too extensive and costly to control. Government forfeiture of neglected, weed-infested lands was also no solution as authorities lacked the resources to do anything, and control on road verges was generally ignored. Infested lands, in turn, became unmarketable to new tenants or buyers. The 1923 Royal Commission summed up the problem: 'The evidence discloses, in the minds of many tenants of these lands, a reluctance to deal energetically with the prickly-pear because of a conviction that their efforts might not be duly appreciated or rewarded by the State'.[23]

**Figure 5.2** Four men standing on a road between prickly pears, NSW, 1930s; National Library of Australia

Almost as deficient as these 'sticks' were the 'carrots' to incentivise weed control. Financial rewards to landholders for clearing the weeds were miserly and no subsidies were available for defensive measures to prevent encroachment. In debating possible controls, the Queensland parliament heard advice that 'one of the reasons

[23] ibid 8.

why freeholders have not cleared their land of pear is that it would not be worth anything when they cleared it; and where they cleared it the shire council immediately raised the rates and it was uneconomical for them to hold the land'.[24] The 1923 Royal Commission recommended that 'the basis of local authority valuation of such lands be adjusted so that regard be had to the existence of pear on or near the holding and to the lessee's efforts towards keeping his land clean; in other words, the tenant of clean country should not be taxed more heavily than the tenant of neglected country'.[25] Helpfully, the High Court in a 1929 case involving a disputed land tax assessment held that the costs of eradicating prickly pear were an 'improvement' that entitled the subject landowner to claim to offset his tax liability.[26]

Another financial carrot were the bounties paid by authorities for extermination of native fauna blamed for spreading the prickly pear seed. Queensland declared an open season on emus, accused of seed spreading. The Queensland Prickly Pear Land Commission offered bounties of 2 shillings and 6 pence per dead bird or 1 shilling for an emu egg. Bounties were also paid for destruction of other presumed offenders: crows (6 pence a head) and scrub magpies (4 pence each). Yet, domestic livestock that contributed to the weeds' dispersal were ignored.

With the failures of earlier interventions, the federal and state governments searched for biological control of prickly pear. This history, argues Jodi Frawley, should jettison treating the devised entomological solution as a matter of the unadulterated virtue of science because the portrayal of 'invasive species as villains … displac[es] responsibility for the environmental degradation associated with settler society, … [and] reiterates the ability of science to solve such problems'.[27] The narrative that the prickly pear was conquered by scientists' 'lucky' find, in the form of the cacti-eating *Cactoblastis* moth imported from South America, obscured the complex assemblage of events including assisted reproduction that enabled the *Cactoblastis* to thrive in Australia, yet the 'blind faith' that took hold in a 'single species saviour' was to prove disastrous when it came to the cane toad, as considered later in this chapter.

The turn towards biological control was uncharted waters, for in the early twentieth century such experiments anywhere in the world were in their infancy. In 1912 Queensland established the Prickly pear Travelling Commission, tasked to visit countries to look for insects that could be recruited to spearhead the weed's eradication in Australia.[28] The onset of World War I stalled research as

[24] Queensland, Legislative Assembly, Hansard, 30 October 1923, per J Peterson, 2028.
[25] Quoted in ibid.
[26] *McGeoch v Federal Commissioner of Land Tax* (1929) 43 CLR 277, 286.
[27] Frawley (n 3) 769.
[28] AP Dodd, 'The Biological Control of Prickly Pear in Australia' in A Keast, RL Crocker and CS Christian (eds), *Biogeography and Ecology in Australia* (Springer, 1959) 565.

resources were shifted to the war effort, and it wasn't resumed earnestly until 1920 when the newly established Commonwealth Prickly Pear Board (CPPB) – with participation of the Queensland and NSW governments – provided funding to test biological agents. Other government-supported institutions around this time also began to strengthen their interest in biological control, including the Council for Scientific and Industrial Research established in 1926 with a programme to investigate solutions to livestock predators such as blowflies and ticks and various noxious weeds. The Queensland government's Bureau of Sugar Experiment Stations, established in 1900, also stepped-up investigations into biological control.

The march of the prickly pear was stopped by the *Cactoblastis*, a South American moth that Australian scientists discovered could effectively control the weed, showing an exclusive preference for prickly pear, and being able to breed quickly. The Sherwood quarantine research station of the CPPB was the epicentre of efforts to trial biological agents and breed the *Cactoblastis*. It was then released in a government-sponsored campaign from 1925 to the early 1930s, with millions of moth eggs distributed freely to landholders. The results were astonishing such that by the end of 1931 the prickly pear menace in eastern Australia had been dramatically turned around. Millions of hectares of rotting vegetation were left where impenetrable thickets of the weeds had stood only months before, and these were soon taken up with crops or livestock pasture. By 1933 the CPPB declared victory. The prickly pear didn't completely disappear however, persisting in small numbers, though it was no longer a serious pest to farmers or the environment.

Unfortunately, the success in conquering the prickly pear would encourage authorities to pursue another experiment in biological pest control that would become one of Australia's worst environmental disasters.

## III. Cane Toads

Few stories epitomise the reckless indifference to Australia's natural endowment than that of cane toads, an ugly amphibian imported to control pests but ultimately becoming a much larger pest itself. Native to South and Central America, the cane toad (*Bufo marinus*) was deliberately released in the 1930s to protect Queensland's sugarcane crops from hungry beetles. While Australia has a variety of frog species, before 1935 it was toad-free. The consignment of 102 cane toads to north Queensland that year has today swelled to some 200 million, occupying at least one-eighth of the continent, and still spreading. It's hard to imagine a worst dystopia for nature: the toads failed to control the beetles, they spread beyond the cane fields to become voracious predators of non-target, native insects and other small creatures and, worst of all, many larger native species from goannas to quolls that attempt to eat the toads die from ingesting their poisonous secretions. Invasive species are now widely recognised as one of the gravest threats to Australia's biodiversity, with the cane toad among the worst villains. So how did this disaster come about?

**Figure 5.3** My brother inspecting a cane toad, Northern Territory, 2005; author's family collection

Sugarcane (a cluster of species from the genus *Saccharum*) came to Australia with the First Fleet. It failed to thrive until the 1860s when its cultivation in north Queensland began. Apart from variable climatic conditions, the biggest threat to the sugarcane industry was the larvae of native beetles that fed on the plant's roots. The politically influential cane farmers lobbied for solutions, leading in 1900 to the establishment of the Bureau of Sugar Experiment Stations (BSES), whose entomologists researched methods to control cane beetles, as they became known. The stations operated under the auspices of Queensland's Sugar Experiment Stations Act 1900, with regulators empowered to control sugar-cane plantations to manage disease and insect pests. Australian scientists' success at taming the prickly pear with a biological agent rather than chemical warfare encouraged BSES staff to consider a similar strategy for managing sugarcane pests. Unfortunately, the strict biosecurity controls associated with trialling the *Cactoblastis* weren't replicated with the release of the cane toad as the folklore had already taken hold that the prickly pear was subjugated by a lucky find, a single biological saviour, leading to a naïve faith the cane beetles menacing Queensland sugar cane farmers could be subdued once scientists found a similar magic bullet.[29]

Although voracious eaters of anything they can swallow, the cane toads' reputation as an efficient pest controller was based on flawed studies of limited scope and wildly optimistic hopes. A seminal moment was the Fourth Congress of the International Society for Sugar Cane Technologists, convened in Puerto Rico in 1932, which was attended by Australian Arthur Bell under the aegis of the Queensland government and the sugarcane industry. Perhaps mindful of the need to justify his trip, which might have been perceived as a junket by a public sensitised to economic austerity during the Great Depression, Bell was impressed by a presentation at the conference by entomologist Raquel Dexter on the toads' apparent efficacy in devouring sugarcane pests. Returning home, Bell assigned the BSES's researcher Reginald Mungomery to pursue further enquiries into the toad's pest-control potential. The subsequent research was rudimentary.

Apparently satisfied of their potential, Mungomery travelled to Hawaii in June 1935 to collect and ship some toads to Australia. On their arrival in Sydney on 17 June the rapturous press hailed 'Toad Army Lands: American Foes of Cane Beetles'.[30] The toads flourished in their special breeding enclosure at the Meringa experimental farm in far north Queensland: within the first week the toads were laying eggs, and within a few further weeks thousands swarmed in their pen. By August, 2,400 toads were released into the fields around Gordonvale, with further releases near Cairns and Innisfail, and other coastal areas soon afterwards.

Extraordinarily, no studies into the potential environmental impacts of the toads were undertaken by the BSES or any other body in Australia. The BSES also failed to research whether the toads would in fact control the native grey-backed cane beetle (*Dermolepida albohirtum*) and French's beetle (*Lepidiota frenchi*), relying instead on spurious reports from overseas. The beetles that the toads were meant to control were Australian species, unlike the insect pests in Puerto Rico and Hawaii. The exceptionally short interval between the toads' arrival and release in Australia wouldn't have provided enough time to study their impacts. Yet at the time of introduction, entomologists understood that the toads could control the beetles only when they were on or near the ground, and that in the case of the grey-backed cane beetle, they descended briefly only at oviposition and emergence, or otherwise accidently during mating. It was as though the release of the toads into the wild was itself the means of experimentation into their efficacy as a pest controller. Indeed, in December 1939, four years after the toads were first released, the BSES reported 'some ideas of how effective the giant toad would be in the control of the cane grub should be obtained next year'.[31] Good grief!

[29] Frawley (n 3) 769–70.
[30] 'Toad Army Lands: American Foes of Cane Beetles' (*Courier-Mail* (Brisbane), 21 June 1935) 16.
[31] 'Giant Toads to Attack Cane Beetles in 1940' (*Courier-Mail* (Brisbane), 5 December 1939) 23.

This insouciance is puzzling given that Mungomery had as recently as 1934 called for caution. In his paper in the *Cane Growers' Quarterly Bulletin*, Mungomery warned:

> Biological control does not consist in rushing off to a foreign country, bringing back a number of parasites, and letting them loose upon the unsuspecting pest; to ensure the success of biological forms of control a whole complex of factors must be independently favourable. Such a project is not to be embarked upon light-heartedly, but only after the most mature consideration, since a false step may have disastrous economic consequences through the upsetting of the whole biological balance.[32]

One scientist actively dissented. Walter Froggatt, a retired entomologist who had worked for the NSW government, warned that 'this great toad, immune from enemies, omnivorous in its habits, and breeding all year round, may become as great a pest as the rabbit or cactus'.[33] Froggatt persuaded the Commonwealth Department of Health in November 1935 to ban further introductions or release. But the ban didn't last long, and in any event was probably futile given that thousands of toads were already freed and breeding. The ban was quickly challenged by the Queensland Minister for Agriculture and State Premier, who lobbied the Prime Minister, Joseph Lyons. And the national scientific authority, the Council for Scientific and Industrial Research (CSIR), known as the CSIRO today, sided with the cane growers. The CSIR harboured an interest in importing toads as well, specifically the common European toad (*Bufo bufo*), to control other pest insects in the cooler parts of the continent.[34] Any ban on cane toads might have jeopardised the CSIR's plans.

The media was also against Froggatt's stance. Brisbane's *Telegraph* gleefully proclaimed 'The giant toad is a most remarkable creature in a dozen different ways. Nature seems to have made him precisely for the sugar industry and for no other'.[35] It went on to identify the toad's 'many virtues', including 'an insatiable appetite for the right kind of insects', that 'he multiplies enormously', 'does no damage whatever to humans or animals unless grossly attacked' and 'he costs nothing to maintain, and he is a permanent bodyguard to our crops'.[36] The press also collaborated in presenting the government's position; the *Courier-Mail* published an essay entitled 'Giant Toad Not A Menace' that sought to reassure readers:

> From careful inquiries made before the introduction of giant toads into Northern canefields there was nothing to suggest that they would ever become a potential danger to human life, said the Minister for Agriculture and Stock (Mr. Bulcock) yesterday.[37]

[32] Quoted in Richard Shine, *Cane Toad Wars* (University of California Press, 2018) 19.

[33] WW Froggatt, 'The Introduction of the Great Mexican Toad Bufo Marinus into Australia' (1936) 9 *Australian Naturalist* 163.

[34] CSIR, *Tenth Annual Report* (Commonwealth Government, 1936) 27.

[35] 'Enter the Giant Toad. Exit Our Sugar Grub Pests. Amazing Canefield Immigrant' (*Telegraph* (Brisbane), 10 September 1935) 7.

[36] ibid.

[37] '"Giant Toads Not a Menace", Minister Emphatic' (*Courier-Mail* (Brisbane), 20 January 1938) 16.

Froggatt was also going against a long history of national insouciance regarding exotic imports, let alone the many who supported active introductions such as the acclimatisation societies. Unsurprisingly, the upshot of all this pressure was the Prime Minister rescinded the ban, and the toad releases resumed in September 1936 in north Queensland.

Although Froggatt was an isolated voice against the ecological folly unfolding, his name is honoured today. The 'Froggatt Awards' are bestowed each year by the Invasive Species Council, a nongovernmental organisation, to persons making exemplary efforts to protect Australia's fauna and flora from harmful exotics.

It didn't take long for others to realise that the toads were becoming more a vice than virtue, and ironically a vice for the agricultural sector itself. From the early 1940s reports of the toads destroying beehives in Queensland were circulating.[38] In the late 1940s pastoralists began complaining of the 'alarming spread of the giant sugar cane toads into grazing areas, resulting in the pollution of water supplies for stock'.[39] Ironically, in 1951 pastoralists voiced concern that the cane toad might be eating the *Cactoblastis* – the grub introduced to control prickly pear.[40]

Around this time the toad, which had been known as the Giant American Toad or just Giant Toad, became known as just the 'cane toad'. An Australian expert on them, Richard Shine, explains that the name change was 'driven by interstate politics'.[41] As the ugly toads spread and became increasingly seen as a nuisance, they began to be identified by the NSW public as the 'Queensland cane toads', and then for brevity, just 'cane toads'. As the toads neared the NSW border in the late 1940s, the *Sydney Morning Herald* advised readers: 'everything about it – its very name – is vile. Its huge belly is always distended. The angry glitter in its eye is revolting. It had legs that do not raise it from the mire. … Its habitation is filthy. Its habits disgusting. Its colour dingy. Its breath foul'.[42]

The toads' impact on native fauna took longer to discern. It is poisonous throughout its life cycle – eggs, tadpoles and adults – but mature adults are the most lethal, emitting toxin from glands over their upper body. While some wily birds and other clever native predators have learned to avoid the poisonous parts when feasting on the toads' entrails, many have not, and they die quickly. Yet in 1936, belated toad enthusiast Reginald Mungomery sanguinely claimed that the cane toad wouldn't adversely affect Australian fauna.[43] Isolated warnings or

[38] 'Cane Toads Becoming a Pest' (*Maryborough Chronicle*, 23 November 1943) 3; 'Cane Toads Destroy Bees' (*Northern Miner* (Charters Towers), 12 August 1946) 3.

[39] 'Toad Menace to Stock Water' (*Townsville Daily Bulletin*, 15 April 1947) 3.

[40] 'Is Cane Toad Wiping Out Cactoblastis?' (*Queensland Country Life*, 29 March 1951) 5.

[41] Shine (n 32) 14.

[42] I Brown, 'Giant Toad Comes Marching South' (*Sydney Morning Herald*, 2 August 1947) 9.

[43] RW Mungomery, 'A Survey of the Feeding Habits of the Giant Toad {*Bufo marinus* L.) and Notes on its Progress Since Introduction to Queensland', *Proceedings of the Queensland Society of Sugar Cane Technologists* (Annual conference, 1936) 63.

queries to the contrary were expressed during the 1940s and 1950s.[44] The toads eat a variety of small native fauna, such as frogs, and poison other, larger wildlife that attempt to eat them (eg snakes and goannas), as well as compete with other species for food and shelter. Though as some of the toads' victims such as crocodiles and snakes were also unpopular, some welcomed the toads' success.

By the 1950s any jubilation about the toad was rare. Even Queensland authorities were more reticent. Tellingly, a 1950 book commemorating 'fifty years of scientific progress' by the BSES , which describes its work as 'eminently justified', hardly mentions the cane toad.[45] Its commemorative report however does venerate the BSES's control of three species of 'pest' native rodents blamed for spreading diseases harmful to sugarcane.[46] A few vocal supporters lingered, such as the Queensland Minister for Agriculture and Forestry, Otto Madsen, who in 1961 defended the toad in parliament: 'This animal has been shown to feed avidly on a number of pests that attack sugar cane and other crops … it is not considered to be a pest of any primary industry except perhaps beekeepers'.[47] Yet other states had already decided otherwise, at least recognising its impacts on agriculture; on 21 April 1950 Western Australia became the first state to declare the toad to be vermin, under its Vermin Act 1918.[48] If it's any consolation to the failures of Australian officialdom in allowing the cane toads, the species has become, with human aid, an immigrant to some 138 countries and islands outside their original habitat in South America and Central America.[49]

## IV. Rabbits

Rabbits today are not quite the ubiquitous scourge they once were in Australia but their environmental legacy remains one of the country's worst blunders. Introduced to provide a cheap source of food and fur, rabbits survived the voyage on the First Fleet, and evidently persisted in modest numbers in the first 80 years of colonisation without being a nuisance except in a few localities.[50] The game changer came in the late 1850s when a hardier breed was released into the wild by

[44] AL Ormsby, 'Notes on the Giant Toad *(Bufomarinus)*' (1955–56) *Journal and Proceedings of the Royal Society of NSW* 54; GC Hewitt, 'The Giant American Toad' (1956) 22(1) *Walkabout* 45.

[45] Bureau of Sugar Experiment Stations, *Fifty Years of Scientific Progress* (Department of Agriculture and Stock, 1950) 7, 43–45.

[46] ibid 47.

[47] Queensland, Legislative Assembly, Hansard, 24 November 1961, 1853.

[48] MJ Tyler, 'Cane Toad Control Research: The First Decade' in K Molloy and W Henderson (eds), *Proceedings of the Invasive Animals CRC/ CSIRO/Qld NRM&W Cane Toad Workshop* (Invasive Species Cooperative Research Centre, 2006) 3, 3.

[49] N Turvey, *Cane Toads: A Tale of Sugar, Politics and Flawed Science* (Sydney University Press, 2013) xii.

[50] They were reportedly a nuisance in Tasmania's Midlands in the 1820s: 'Van Diemen's Land News' (*Australian* (Sydney), 1 June 1827) 2.

sports hunters in Victoria. The pivotal moment, suggest historians, was in 1859 when Thomas Austin, an enterprising farmer near Geelong, imported 24 of the wild British sub-species of the European rabbit (*Oryctolagus cuniculus cuniculus*). They adapted easily.

By the early 1860s the 'extraordinary fecundity' of these rabbits – able to reproduce up to four litters annually, from a young age – was being observed by gleeful landholders anticipating a bumper side-industry selling rabbit meat and skins.[51] Their hopes were aided by an ebullient media reporting of the 'pleasant facts' that the 'English wild rabbit is now spreading'.[52] By the late 1860s the mood was cooling, as accreting evidence suggested the rabbits could be a costly nuisance, devouring and digging up grazing lands. Mass culling began. The *Geelong Advertiser* in 1869 reported that 2 million were killed the previous year.[53] In 1883, the Victorian Minister of Lands reported that 5 million acres of mallee country had been abandoned in the last decade 'owing to the ravages of rabbits and wild dogs'.[54] By the 1920s, just 60 years after it had established in the wild, some 10 billion rabbits were estimated to roam across the southern two-thirds of the continent. Not all Australians were unhappy about the plague, however; in the Outback, Herbert Finlayson observed, 'as a factor in the general economy of the blacks, the importance of the rabbit as an accessory food-supply can hardly be overestimated. … [and they] eat more of rabbits probably than of any other mammals'.[55]

Owing to the press and popular writers, the impact of rabbits became widely known. William Hatfield described the following scene he saw in South Australia in the 1930s: 'not a living being stirred in Port Augusta when we drove through, nothing but the rabbits. Rabbits all over the main streets through the town. Rabbits in drove, toddling and scampering'.[56] Whilst farmers and politicians readily blamed rabbits for soil erosion,[57] some scientists deciphered a more complex aetiology. Zoologist Francis Ratcliffe suggested rabbits were secondary to the pernicious influence of sheep.[58] He recommended destocking, 'based on an accurate knowledge of the behaviour and natural regeneration of the main fodder plants'.[59] Ratcliffe also counselled about the compounding effects of

[51] 'A Most Useful New Industry' (*Leader* (Melbourne), 18 October 1962) 8.
[52] 'Saturday, September 23, 1865' (*Argus* (Melbourne), 23 September 1865) 4.
[53] 'The Rabbits of the Western District' (*Geelong Advertiser*, 9 April 1869) 3.
[54] 'The Mallee Country' (*Kyneton Observer, 22* May 1883) 2.
[55] HH Finlayson, *The Red Centre: Man and Beast in the Heart of Australia* (Angus and Robertson, 1936) 80.
[56] W Hatfield, *Australia Through the Windscreen* (Angus and Robertson, 1939) 246.
[57] NSW parliamentarian Joseph Cahill blamed rabbits as the prime cause of soil erosion: 'Rabbits Cause Soil Erosion' (*Weekly Times*, 16 November 1949) 14.
[58] F Ratcliffe, *Flying Fox and Drifting Sand: The Adventures of a Biologist in Australia* (Chatto and Windus, 1938) 323–24.
[59] ibid 325.

droughts: 'The Australian must expect a smashing drought once every decade, and lesser droughts more often. … good seasons are the exception, drought the rule'.[60]

The war against rabbits through poisoning, shooting, trapping and other methods hardly dented their behemoth numbers. Governments tried to help. In 1902 plans were unveiled to erect a massive, 1800 km long fence in Western Australia to contain the rabbits' march westwards, but when construction began rabbits were already found across the proposed fence line.[61] Additional fences were layered in the southwest of the state to protect its agricultural heartland, albeit also of limited efficacy. Long fences were also erected in various parts of NSW, Victoria and Queensland, also largely ineffectual, and many required ongoing maintenance owing to damage by wombats and emus.[62]

As with prickly pear, legislators turned to property tenure to leverage control of rabbits. In 1869 Joseph Connor, a member of the Victorian Legislative Assembly, suggested landowners be obliged to destroy rabbits found on their properties.[63] Adopting this idea, Tasmania in 1871 enacted the bespoke Rabbit Destruction Act, authorising the designation of districts for rabbit control and providing financial rewards for successful efforts. Uncooperative landholders could be overridden by authorities empowered to 'use all such means and take all such measures as may be necessary for taking or destroying any rabbits'.[64] Other colonies adopted similar legislation, such as South Australia's Rabbit Destruction Act 1875. Consequently, vigilant rabbit inspectors became a familiar sight in rural neighbourhoods, checking on control measures and monitoring rabbit populations.

Negligent landholders could be fined, though the token fines sometimes dished out suggest that magistrates were sympathetic to farmers' difficulties in controlling the plague. A landowner in Dungog, NSW, whose property was discovered in 1948 by authorities to be in an 'infested state', was fined two pounds, equivalent to $145 in 2023 (plus the equivalent sum in court costs).[65] Diligent landholders' efforts could easily be undermined by lack of rabbit control along railway easements, road verges and other Crown lands without active pest control. Property holders thus had to maintain constant vigilance against rabbit reinvasion. Unsurprisingly, the press acknowledged 'the present law and machinery to fight the rabbit pest are inadequate. Otherwise these rodents would not be swarming over many of our richest districts in unprecedented numbers'.[66]

[60] ibid 329.
[61] E Stodart and I Parer, *Colonisation of Australia by the Rabbit* (CSIRO, 1988) 13.
[62] Rolls (n 11) 163.
[63] 'The Rabbits of the Western District' (*Geelong Advertiser*, 9 April 1869) 3.
[64] Section 5.
[65] 'Fined for Not Destroying Rabbits' (*Gloucester Advocate*, 25 May 1948) 3.
[66] 'Campaign Needed Against Rabbits' (*Sydney Morning Herald*, 13 October 1949) 2.

Not only were methods of rabbit destruction ineffective in overall population control, they wrought much collateral damage. Poisons and traps were the most indiscriminate killers. Strychnine was commonly mixed with oats or wheat; it killed many rabbits, but also many kangaroos, wallabies, possums, birds and other herbivorous wildlife, as well as raptors that ate the poisoned rabbits. Pressure grew during the twentieth century to restrict such practices.[67] One newspaper voiced 'strong protest … against the abominable practice of laying trails of poisoned seed bait for rabbits, which is resulting in the wholesale slaughter of wild bird life in our district'.[68] Some critics rightly blamed lawmakers, because of landholders' obligations to control rabbits by any means they chose as most cost effective.[69]

Some landholders exacerbated the situation by exterminating native fauna that preyed on rabbits, such as quolls (known as the native cat or tiger cat) and raptors.[70] A few recognised that quolls should be protected at a time when their numbers were declining precipitously in the early twentieth century due to introduced predators and disease.[71] Alternatively, some farmers released domestic cats to control rabbits, with one reporting: 'the next morning … we found not one-tenth of the rabbits seen on the open hillside the previous day'.[72] Some local authorities also declared cats a protected species, for it 'is very useful now in destroying young rabbits playing around the burrows'.[73] Saner persons recognised the 'disastrous consequences' of releasing cats into the wild because of their penchant for indiscriminate hunting.[74] The catastrophic impact on feral cats on native wildlife is now well known. The collateral damage of using exotic predators would have been much greater had a proposal to introduce weasels and stoats been implemented. After New Zealand's disastrous experience with these mustelids, which was cited by the Ornithologists' Union of Australia in vigorously opposing their introduction, the plan was dropped.[75]

A breakthrough in rabbit control came in the early 1950s. Rivalling the success in controlling prickly pear, at least initially, biological control of rabbits came with the release of the myxoma virus, which causes myxomatosis. It was released in Australia in 1950 with phenomenal initial success, killing 99.8 per cent of infected rabbits. Australia's introduction of a biological control of rabbits was more carefully conceived than previous efforts with many years of trials. The Commonwealth Institute of Science and Industry (CISI) – a forerunner to the CSIR and

[67] 'Intended for Rabbits. But Birds Take Poison' (*Examiner* (Launceston), 11 February 1937) 6; 'Poison and Birds' (*Evening News* (Rockhampton), 20 October 1925) 4.

[68] 'Protest Against Slaughter of Bird Life by Poisoned Rabbit Bait' (*Wellington Times* (NSW), 3 June 1948) 1.

[69] 'Poisoning of Rabbits' (*Age* (Melbourne), 13 February 1925) 7.

[70] Rolls (n 11) 151, 299.

[71] 'The Vanishing Native Cat' (*Northern Star* (Lismore), 10 October 1901) 4.

[72] 'Cats as Rabbit Destroyers' (*Albury Banner and Wodonga Express*, 9 March 1888) 11.

[73] 'Protection of Cats' (*Albury and Wodonga Express*, 18 November 1904) 29.

[74] 'Cats, Rabbits, Etc' (*Bairnsdale Advertiser and Tambo and Omeo Chronicle*, 7 November 1905) 4.

[75] 'War on Rabbits' (*Herald* (Melbourne), 24 April 1909) 3.

CSIRO – was aware as early as 1920 when it was established that myxoma might be an effective agent in this regard after advice from a Brazilian expert. Government scientists researched its potential over the following three decades, with limited success. State authorities such as the NSW Department of Agriculture were also involved, with many setbacks owing in part to inappropriate release conditions. Major trials involving the CSIRO began on a few properties in Victoria in 1950, using mosquitoes to transmit the virus. The myxoma then finally took off, and by 1953 most of the continent was virtually free of rabbits. Some however developed resistance to myxomatosis, necessitating release of other viruses, notably the calicivirus in 1996. Today wild rabbit populations in Australia are about 20 per cent of their former peak.

## V. Vermin Wars

Settlers' desire to improve Australian nature with foreign additions had a corollary that native wildlife considered as noxious or a hindrance to colonisation were persecuted. From the second half of the nineteenth century a variety of indigenous fauna were systematically persecuted officially or informally, such as emus, macropods, raptors, flying foxes and marsupial carnivores. The war against them was often ineffective because of the ecological disturbances wrought by settlers' own changes to the land, such as the enlarged populations of macropods that thrived on the additional grazing lands and water points. Settlers' persecution of dingoes and marsupial carnivores was also counterproductive by removing a valuable natural mechanism to control populations of native herbivores.

Vermin destruction legislation continued to apply even as parliaments introduced more inclusive fauna protection laws (examined in chapter eight). Vermin governance typically had two tiers. Unwanted species were listed as 'unprotected' in fauna conservation laws, so they could be killed with virtual impunity, subject (if at all) to animal welfare standards to curb the worst barbarity. Concomitantly, dedicated vermin-control statutes offered bounties for eradication or obliged landholders to control pests at their own expense. Such legislation often encompassed both exotic and native species although the control mechanisms usually differed depending on the type of species or impact. The methods of control ranged from direct killing, such as poisoning and shooting, to indirect means including erection of exclusion fences.[76] Legislation could even oblige landholders to remove wildlife habitat; Victoria's Vermin and Noxious Weeds Act 1949 specifically singled out mallee country to be cleared if the shrubs were found to provide 'cover for vermin'.[77]

[76] TL Knight, 'Barrier Fencing for Vermin Control in Australia' (1969) 59(3) *Geographical Review* 330.
[77] Section 10(a).

Both herbivores and carnivores were outlawed where they were perceived to compete with farmers' livelihoods, whether by grazing pastures, pilfering crops or preying on poultry or lambs. Improvements to wildlife conservation in the early twentieth century could clash with many landholders' interests. Large kangaroos bore the brunt of farmers' wrath. So too, were orchard-raiding flying foxes ruthlessly targeted. Among maligned birds, the emu was often pursued, as well as eagles and hawks. Marsupial carnivores such as the Tasmanian tiger and devil, as well the larger quoll species, were demonised for many years. Of marine life, 'man-eating' sharks were, and still are, persecuted. Unsurprisingly, snakes were widely despised, even by avowed conservationists; snake-killing campaigns such as that depicted in Figure 5.4 were not uncommon. The only situations where vermin might enjoy respite were in Crown conservation reserves, though even here exceptions were sometimes allowed, such as to kill venomous snakes.

**Figure 5.4** Snake hunt on the Murray River, early 1900s; National Library of Australia

Because of its close association with agriculture, vermin control was commonly incorporated into rural land governance. The long-title of NSW's Pastures and Stock Protection Act 1880 stated its goal as to 'protect pastures and livestock from the depredations of certain noxious animals'.[78] Even more to the point, the

[78] 1880, 44 Vic. No. 11, s 1.

Act's preamble elaborated: 'whereas the depredations of Rabbits, Native Dogs and Marsupials in many Districts of this Colony have inflicted serious damage and loss on stockowners and it is necessary … to encourage the destruction of such animal'.[79] By the 1890s, all the colonies had vermin-control legislation evoking similar sentiments, along with separate laws for weed control. They served to coordinate pest destruction, with officious inspectorates supervising landholders' compliance, occasionally with financial inducements. Some species were listed as vermin on a state-wide basis whilst others put on the vermin inventory on a district or seasonal basis depending on when or where they were regarded as most troublesome.[80]

**Figure 5.5** Vermin inspectors, Hopetoun, Victoria, 1917; State Library Victoria

The emu and thylacine are contrasting examples of the failure or success of vermin control. In Western Australia's bizarre 'Emu War', as it was dubbed, a plan was devised in 1932 to drive the emus towards fences and shoot them en masse with

[79] ibid.
[80] See eg NSW's Pastures Protection Act 1934, s 79.

the aid of the Royal Australian Artillery. The operation began on 1 November when its crack machine gunners assumed positions in the emu-infested fields around Campion, 320 kms northeast of Perth. It was a comical fiasco. Defying expectations, the emus adroitly dispersed into smaller flocks and dodged the volleys. The media prematurely gloated of the campaign's success, declaring '300 Killed in First Duel'.[81] The mood soon soured, and Major GPW Meredith, who oversaw the operation, eventually conceded: 'They can face machine-guns with the invulnerability of tanks. They are like Zulus who even dum-dum bullets could not stop'.[82] Persecution of emus, however, persisted for several more decades. A Western Australian newspaper in 1953 derided the bird as a 'national pest of immense proportions', and an 'enemy' that 'has invaded some of the finest fields'.[83] In that year, the state government devised plans for a 220-km long, 'emu-proof fence' to protect its prized wheat-belt. In the east of Australia, emus suffered as well, especially after they were accused of spreading the seeds of prickly pear.[84] Today, the emu is protected and numbers about 700,000 nationwide.

Contrastingly, Tasmania's thylacine was exterminated. The *Thylacinus cynocephalus* was demonised by the colonial press as a 'mischievous and rapacious carnivorous brute'[85] and 'cowardly in proportion to its size'.[86] After sheep farming came to Van Diemen's Land in the 1820s, the 'tiger' was scapegoated as a bloodthirsty sheep killer, and thereafter mercilessly persecuted with the inducement of bounties.[87] They were collected on 2,184 animals, and in 1909 the government bounty scheme closed as the species evidently had become so scarce as to no longer pose a threat. But the so-called 'tiger' was still open to unrestricted destruction until 10 July 1936 when it became officially protected, just 59 days before the last known specimen, in Hobart's zoo, died on 7 September 1936. This date is now commemorated annually as Australia's Threatened Species Day, with the thylacine furnishing the single most potent symbol of a continent's a vanished nature. Today, the thylacine exhibition at the Tasmanian Museum and Art Gallery in Hobart is the institution's premier attraction, displaying taxidermy specimens, film clips and other memorabilia. The prospect of one day harnessing biotechnology advances to reinstate the thylacine has added to the public's fascination with the animal and hope to ameliorate the 'extinction guilt' of a country with the world's worst record of mammal extinctions.[88] It is a curious irony that a species once subject

[81] 'Emu War Again. 300 Killed in First Duel' (*Canberra Times*, 12 November 1932) 1.

[82] 'Fence Plan Recalls When Machine-Gunner Got Bird from WA Emus' (*Sunday Times* (Perth), 5 July 1953) 16.

[83] ibid.

[84] 'Getting Rid of Emus' (*Warwick Examiner and Times (Qld)*, 23 August 1911) 2.

[85] 'The Kangaroo Bill' (letter to editor) (*Mercury* (Hobart), 21 October 1873) 2.

[86] 'The Royal Society of Tasmania' (*The Courier*, 16 June 1858) 2.

[87] R Paddle, *The Last Tasmanian Tiger: The History and Extinction of the Thylacine* (Cambridge University Press, 2000).

[88] PB Banks and DF Hochuli, 'Extinction, De-extinction and Conservation: A Dangerous Mix of Ideas' (2017) 38(3) *Australian Zoologist* 390.

to such official persecution graces Tasmania's coat of arms, which were officially proclaimed in 1919 when the thylacine was still legally unprotected.

The war against vermin levied considerable collateral damage from liberal use of strychnine-laced baits, traps, snares and other indiscriminate means, as acknowledged by the media.[89] It was a high price to pay given that vermin control was often woefully ineffective in eradicating its targets, let alone appreciably reducing their numbers. Neither massive fences nor military-style campaigns dented their populations.

One instrument of impressive kills of canines was sodium fluoroacetate (1080). Controlling wild dogs and dingoes through aerial baiting of 1080 enabled large areas, especially remote country, to be cost effectively controlled, albeit with collateral damage to some native fauna. An interesting part of the 1080 story is that many native species in southwest Western Australia have a natural tolerance to the poison because 1080 occurs naturally in relatively high amounts in some of the region's flora. That adaptive advantage has been exploited by Western Australian conservation authorities since the mid-1990s to conduct aerial baiting over 3.5 million hectares in a programme known as 'Western Shield' to protect wildlife against foxes and feral cats.[90] So, methods of pest control designed to serve agricultural interests have in some instances been repurposed to assist native wildlife, a story that this book returns to in its closing chapter on restoring Australia's ecosystems and wildlife.

## VI. Science, Law and Nature's Backlash

Wars waged against vermin were a potent expression of the quest to colonise the Australian continent and subjugate anything perceived to be hostile to settlers' livelihoods. Animals were likely to be classified by lawmakers as vermin if they fell within one of three categories: a competitor with livestock for food or water, such as kangaroos; secondly, a predator on livestock, such as the thylacine; or thirdly, a source of some adverse effect on agriculture such as flying foxes (which eat fruit). The techniques of vermin control were diverse, and broadly involved three approaches: direct killing, exclusion fencing and habitat clearing. Whilst vermin control aimed to influence the behaviour of landholders with sticks or carrots, in many cases they possessed strong economic self-interest to destroy animals, plus the side-benefit of providing 'cheap meat, fur and feathers', explains animal law historian Steven White.[91]

[89] M Wilson, 'Destroying Native Fauna' (*Sydney Mail*, 20 July 1927) 18.

[90] NJ Marlow et al, 'Lethal 1080 Baiting Continues to Reduce European Red Fox (*Vulpes vulpes*) Abundance After More than 25 Years of Continuous Use in South-west Western Australia' (2015) 16(2) *Ecological Management and Restoration* 131.

[91] S White, 'British Colonialism, Australian Nationalism and the Law: Hierarchies of Wild Animal Protection' (2013) 39(2) *Monash University Law Review* 456, 462.

Vermin control had modest success. Several vast barrier fences were developed in Western Australia from the early twentieth century to keep emus, dingoes as well as introduced rabbits away from prime agricultural lands – with dubious efficacy but costly construction and upkeep.[92] Even deployment of army gunners, in the campaign against emus, was ineffectual. Control efforts might temporarily alleviate pressures at a local level but were often ineffective on a broader landscape scale. Vermin control's biggest success was to kill off the thylacine, although even here other factors also likely mattered including epidemic disease.[93] The large macropods, wombats, raptors and much other vermin to be exterminated survived, and some species thrive today. One major problem was that vermin control lacked sound scientific underpinnings. Regulations relied on anecdotal evidence rather than systematic environmental surveys, and thus could be highly inaccurate in their assumptions and ineffective in their results. Sometimes the designation of vermin status was directly counter-productive for farmers because it encouraged the killing of species such as carnivores that could control introduced pests (rabbits) or control native herbivores (kangaroos) that damaged farmers' interests. None of the foregoing is to imply however that Australian wildlife easily weathered the continent's colonisation; its record of mammal species extinction is the worst of any country, and owes particularly to the impacts of uncontrolled invasive species introduced by settlers.

Authorities had some success dealing with invasive species. The prickly pear, rabbits and cane toads are contrasting tales of how government policy dealt with nature's backlash. The first generation of controls that relied on a property-law solution, where landholders were conscripted to control pests, failed because of the lack of supervision of unmanaged, vacant Crown lands, poor incentives for private landholders to act, and difficulties coordinating action on a landscape scale. The turn to science as a solution focused on biological control, which for prickly pear and rabbits involved the need for government leadership because of the considerable resources that had to be mobilised for scientific research, which governments were prepared to invest because of the economic impacts to agriculture at stake. Here, harnessing science to solve environmental problems deftly helped to distance responsibility of Australian settlers from the original source of the problem, rooted in the nineteenth-century ethos of acclimatisation societies and remaking the continent.

The cane toad, whose impact was more concentrated on native fauna, did not elicit the same response. Their introduction in the 1930s at the service of sugarcane farmers was done with indifference to any collateral damage and with the flimsiest of prior scientific research. Yet at the time there was already enough evidence in Australia of how plant or animal imports could wreak environmental damage,

[92] A Vlachos, 'Fortress Farming in Western Australia?' (2020) 13(2) *Global Environment* 368.

[93] R Paddle, 'The Thylacine's Last Straw: Epidemic Disease in a Recent Mammalian Extinction' (2012) 36(1) *Australian Zoologist* 75.

such that regulators should have done due diligence before releasing the toads, who also failed spectacularly to control the sugarcane-eating beetles. The success in biological control of the prickly pear unfortunately directly contributed to misplaced faith that cane toads were another lucky find that scientific ingenuity could harness to achieve the same results against native insect foes.

Finally, this chapter's case studies on nature's backlash bring into relief the lop-sided efficacy of government regulation. Vermin-control obligations on landholders coupled with an army of inspectors and a labyrinth of regulations tied to property, were extraordinarily cumbersome and unwieldy. Legislative interventions could do too little to stop insidious environmental threats when the means of control weren't practical or cost effective. The impacts of invasive species show how nature's own agency, its backlash when ecosystems are disturbed, can be crippling. Australian authorities needed to turn to scientific expertise rather than legal regulation to achieve some progress, but it too has never fully resolved all the problems. Cane toads remain a growing scourge over the top third of the continent, and even rabbits persist as they build up immunity to viruses, periodically threatening to return in plague proportions.

# 6

# Engineered Landscapes

## I. Environmental Engineering Mania

The latest scientific advances and engineering were embraced with gusto by the nation's exuberant planners' visions of exercising control over nature's pathological elements to promote Australia's prosperity and security. Unfortunately, their exuberant, 'think big' mentality – that modern knowledge and technology could tame nature – often proceeded with insouciance regarding the possible environmental ramifications of their plans, even though science of another kind, relating to the natural world, was increasingly recognised by many as vital for the nation's agriculture, including for tackling soil erosion and controlling invasive species.

Plans for major infrastructure today routinely require an environmental impact assessment before deciding whether it should proceed. Until the 1970s, such projects typically passed with minimal or no such assessment, although occasionally some prescient planners took notice. One of Australia's most momentous projects that engineers and politicians conjured was to harness the country's waterways. Despite being the world's second driest continent, after Antarctica, Australia's meagre water resources weren't seen as a deterrent to technocrats' grandiose visions of hydropower and irrigated agriculture.

This chapter tells the story of how science and enlightened despotism coalesced as governments sought to re-engineer some of Australia's waterways via the Snowy Mountains Scheme (SMS) and Tasmania's hydro-industrialisation. The SMS remains a source of great national pride; historian Brad Collis valorises it as 'an incredible feat for a young country' that put Australia 'at the forefront of world construction technology'.[1] Tasmania's hydro-industrialisation, undertaken over a longer timescale, has been just as salient economically and environmentally. Both examples unveil the role of government as not merely a regulator but an agent of economic activity, with hydropower companies established to build dams and sell electricity – a legal status that was to prove pivotal in the 1983 *Franklin Dam* case when the High Court ruled that Tasmania's Hydro-Electric Commission was a 'trading corporation' for the purpose of section 51(xx) of the Constitution, thereby

[1] B Collis, *Snowy: The Making of Modern Australia* (Coretext Books, 2015) preamble; see also J Butcher, *Australia Under Construction* (ANU E-Press, 2008).

enabling the Commonwealth to make laws to prohibit the Commission from damming the World Heritage-listed river.[2]

Early last century was a fertile era for national dreaming about reengineering nature, inspired by a desire to develop Australia beyond its more fertile coastal belt. With large-scale irrigation in mind, a variety of schemes were touted to overcome the vicissitudes of the continent's harsh climate and to populate the 'empty' Red Centre. The environmental engineering mania was stoked not just by local zealots but also reflected broader, international faith in technocratic approaches to benignly transform nature, which American political scientist James C Scott calls the movement for 'authoritarian high modernism'.[3] Visions of harnessing rivers were sometimes tied to closer settlement schemes sponsored by governments seeking to populate the interior, as discussed in chapter four. Hopes for populating the interior were also increasingly embraced as a matter of national security, especially when Japanese aggression in the 1940s fermented a sense of national vulnerability in the sparsely settled north.

Enthusiasts ranged from professional engineers to grand-standing politicians, buoyed by an often naïve but sympathetic media. At the dawn of Federation, one tabloid exclaimed: 'there are thousands of acres of land in the interior of the "island continent" only awaiting water to produce abundantly, for the soil is prolific, but moisture is lacking'.[4] Popular authors, without civil engineering expertise, also stirred the public's imagination. Bush poet Henry Lawson dreamed of 'reservoirs and grand canals where the sad dry lands had been, and a glorious network of aqueducts mid fields that were always green'.[5] Lawson, who died in 1922, lived to see his dream fulfilled in the completion in 1912 of the Murrumbidgee Irrigation Area in NSW, which today, with subsequent expansions, comprises 3,200 km of irrigation canals and weirs. Another enthusiast was novelist Ion Idriess.[6] His 1941 nonfiction *The Great Boomerang* envisioned diverting Queensland's coastal rivers westwards into the Lake Eyre Basin, irrigating a vast swathe of inland scrub where a 'forlorn silence hung over this land'.[7] Focusing on Western Australia, journalist Henrietta Drake-Brockman lamented the 'wasteful' emptying of the Ord River into the sea, and advocated its damming to allow irrigated agriculture: 'If we are to expand, to develop as a whole, to lose our present restricted condition of being a fringe-country … we must all develop a water-conscience … Water means growth, growth means wealth, wealth means power'.[8]

Such audacious thinking was shared by some professional engineers. The most grandiose pipe-dreams came from John JC Bradfield (1867–1943), who

[2] *Commonwealth v Tasmania* [1983] HCA 21.

[3] JC Scott, *Seeing Like a State: How Certain Scheme to Improve the Human Condition Have Failed* (Yale University Press, 2020) 97.

[4] 'The Question of Irrigation' (*Examiner* (Launceston), 5 November 1900) 4.

[5] H Lawson, 'In the Storm that is to Come' (1904).

[6] IL Idriess, *Onward Australia, Developing a Continent* (Angus and Robertson, 1945).

[7] IL Idriess, *The Great Boomerang* (Angus and Robertson, 1941) 6.

[8] H Drake-Brockman, 'Water Means Wealth' (1944) 10 *Walkabout* 4, 6.

made a name for himself as the chief engineer of the Sydney Harbour Bridge. His hydrological fantasy, known as the Bradfield scheme, envisioned irrigating and drought-proofing the parched lands of western Queensland. Unveiling his plans in 1938, Bradfield called for a network of dams, pipes and pumps to divert water from Queensland's coastal rivers southwest to Lake Eyre. Projected to irrigate some 7,800 $km^2$, the Bradfield scheme promised to sustain a rich food bowl, reduce soil erosion and generate hydro-electricity. Just as optimistically, Bradfield believed it would create a cooler and wetter climate inland. His plans never materialised, as more level-headed officials and scientists prevailed. Inquiries in 1943 by the Rural Reconstruction Commission, and in 1945 by the Commonwealth Meteorological Bureau, concluded that Bradfield's vision was fanciful and prohibitively expensive.[9]

**Figure 6.1** Engineer John JC Bradfield, 1934; National Library of Australia

[9] Rural Reconstruction Commission, *Irrigation, Water Conservation and Land Drainage* (Government Printer, 1943); Commonwealth Meteorological Bureau, *Bradfield Scheme for 'Watering the Inland': Meteorological Aspects* (Government Printer, 1945).

Whilst these nation-building pipe-dreams never got off the ground, some did, and their proponents looked to officialdom to implement them. Whilst much of the history of the vanishing continent told in this book has involved governments facilitating the work of others, from farmers to foresters, governments sometimes took the lead, as with industrial hydropower projects due to the need to mobilise huge funds, coordinate advanced technologies, oversee extensive lands and waters subject to multiple property tenures, and manage significant project risks. Such complex demands required the creation of not merely a regulatory state but also an *administrative* state. Whilst big government has ostensibly fallen out of fashion, except during international crises such as during the COVID-19 pandemic, it once enjoyed far greater legitimacy. Max Weber proclaimed bureaucracy as the supremely rational form of social organisation, arguing that the functionally specialised and hierarchically ordered structures of bureaucracy made it the most rational and efficient institution for achieving the complex goals of society.[10] As the state's legitimacy became tied to its success in managing the national household, as measured primarily through economic growth, the administrative state grew to manage ever-more complex government responsibilities.

More agencies, more staff, and more controls over the economy are hallmarks of big government. The two World Wars were one source of its growth: the Commonwealth public service began in 1903 with 11,374 staff, increasing to 23,424 by mid-1918,[11] and between 1939 and 1947 it jumped from 47,043 to 100,881.[12] By 1970 the federal public service numbered 333,881.[13] Much larger numbers worked in state and local governments. Another indicium of big government is public expenditure, which as a share of Australian GDP grew from 1.17 per cent in 1901 to 28.81 per cent in 1967, the latter eclipsing the 26.16 per cent peak during the costly World War II.[14] Government agencies undertaking economic development projects recruited huge workforces beyond the above tallies of civil servants; the SMS employed about 100,000 workers from 1949 to its completion in 1974,[15] and Tasmania's Hydro-Electric Commission at its peak employed 5,200 during major dam construction and over 30,000 cumulatively in its history.[16]

[10] M Weber, 'Bureaucracy' in HH Garth and CW Mills (eds), *From Max Weber: Essays in Sociology* (Vintage Books, 1948) 223–34.

[11] Commonwealth, House of Representatives, Hansard, 7 September 1920, 4218.

[12] Australian Public Service Commission, *A History in Three Acts* (Commonwealth of Australia, 2004) 47–48.

[13] A Latif, *The Impact of Staff Ceilings on the Australian Public Services*, (Master thesis, ANU, 1983) 10.

[14] E Ortiz-Ospina and M Roser, 'Government Spending (Our World in Data)', ourworldindata.org/government-spending.

[15] National Archives of Australia, www.naa.gov.au/home/snowy-mountains-hydro-electric-scheme/snowy-mountains-hydro-electric-authority-employment-records.

[16] Hydro Tasmania, 'Our History', www.hydro.com.au/about-us/our-history.

These daring, nation-building imaginings have resurfaced over the years, occasionally attracting political support. Ruth Morgan has revealed a little-known history of how from the mid-1960s Australian scientists proposed hauling Antarctic icebergs to southern Australia to help overcome hydrological limits to agriculture.[17] In 2019, during severe drought conditions, a motley of federal parliamentarians led by Barnaby Joyce called for resurrection of Bradfield's scheme. The suggestion was dismissed by the Commonwealth's Water Resources Minister for the same reasons it was jettisoned during the 1940s – as unaffordable and based on junk science.[18] In 2020, the NSW government announced the so-called 'Snowy 2.0', a second-generation Snowy scheme, lauded on its website as 'a nation-building renewable energy project that will provide on-demand energy and large-scale storage for many generations to come'.[19] Snowy 2.0 envisions increasing the current generating capacity by 2,000 megawatts, or by nearly 50 per cent. Sceptical independent experts believe cost over-runs, pollution and degraded aquatic ecosystems are more likely outcomes.[20] The media in March 2022 denounced the project as a 'white elephant'.[21]

Historians surmise that the periodic revival of such pipe-dreams reflect troubled times of economic malaise, international conflict or severe drought where unconventional thinking gains traction.[22] Robert Wooding cites severe drought as the leading factor: 'the level of faith in the possible panacea of a vast irrigation scheme of the type proposed by Jack Bradfield – waxes and wanes in a labile fashion that parallels the tendency for inland Australia to shift in and out of periods of major drought'.[23] We shouldn't, however, dismiss Bradfield's proposal or others' as entirely rash or naïve, for when proposed in the 1930s and 1940s, they were, argue historians Tom Griffiths and Tim Sherratt, 'a sign of national environmental maturity' that engaged with 'the recurrent reality of drought'.[24]

[17] RA Morgan, 'Dry Continent Dreaming: Australian Visions of Using Antarctic Icebergs for Water Supplies' (2018) 4(1) *International Review of Environmental History* 145.

[18] N Hasham. 'Water Resources Minister Rebukes MPs Pushing "Discredited" 1930s Technology' (*The Age*, 1 August 2019) 34.

[19] Snowy Hydro, 'Snowy 2.0, About', www.snowyhydro.com.au/snowy-20/about.

[20] B Mountain and M Lintermans, 'NSW has Approved Snowy 2.0. Here are Six Reasons Why That's a Bad Move' (*The Conversation*, 21 May 2020) theconversation.com/nsw-has-approved-snowy-2-0-here-are-six-reasons-why-thats-a-bad-move-139112.

[21] T Woodley, 'Five Years On, Snowy 2.0 Emerges as a $10 Billion White Elephant' (*Sydney Morning Herald*, 15 March 2022).

[22] A Gillanders, 'Mirage of the Inland Sea: The Bradfield Scheme' (2009) 95(1) *Journal of the Royal Australian Historical Society* 38; JM Powell, *Plains of Promise Rivers of Destiny: Water Management and the Development of Queensland 1824–1990* (Boolarong Publications, 1991).

[23] R Wooding, 'Populate, Parch and Panic: Two Centuries of Dreaming about Nation-building in Inland Australia' in J Butcher (ed), *Australia Under Construction: Nation-building Past, Present and Future* (ANU Press, 2008) 59, 68.

[24] T Griffiths and T Sherratt, 'What if the Northern Rivers had been Turned Inland?' in S Macintyre and S Scalmer (eds), *What If? Australian History as it Might have been* (Melbourne University Press, 2006) 234, 238.

## II. Planning the Snowy Mountains Scheme

Originating on the slopes of Mt Kosciuszko (also sometimes spelt Kosciusko), in the Snowy Mountains straddling the NSW and Victorian borders, the Snowy River is one of Australia's iconic waterways. Celebrated in Andrew Barton 'Banjo' Paterson's ballad *The Man from Snowy River*, in the 1950s it became the site of the nation's largest engineering project. Its environmental legacies remain contentious, with George Seddon's *Searching for the Snowy: An Environmental History*[25] characterising the project an economic and ecological blunder. The colonisation of the Snowy Mountains began much earlier, however, with the violent dispossession of its Aboriginal inhabitants from the 1840s. From then, the region incurred increasing livestock grazing pressure, accompanied. by weeds and soil erosion. The declaration of the Kosciusko State Park in 1944 was shaped by the NSW Soil Conservation Service and nature conservation groups keen to limit pastoral uses and protect the Snowy catchment.[26] Later, the new Snowy Hydro Authority would support annulment of grazing leases in the high country to protect its dams from siltation from eroded, loose soil, though the grazing continued to some extent until enactment of stricter controls under NSW's National Parks and Wildlife Act 1967.

The Snowy Mountains Scheme (SMS) is the quintessential nation-building venture. A development to support hydropower and agriculture built between 1949 and 1974, the colossus comprises 16 main dams, nine power stations, 145 kms of tunnels, 80 kms of aqueducts, and 1,600 kms of roads, divided into two project areas: – the Snowy-Tumut Development and the Snowy-Murray Development.[27] This labyrinth of infrastructure enabled water from the Snowy, Murrumbidgee and other, smaller rivers to be diverted westward for the production of hydropower and then released into the Murrumbidgee and Murray waterways for irrigation of farms in the Riverina. Agriculture has since flourished there, becoming one of Australia's premier food bowls. First generating power in 1955, today the SMS has a total capacity of 4,100 megawatts, providing about 17 per cent of the electricity capacity of the continent's densely populated south-east.[28]

Launching the behemoth project was the last major initiative of Prime Minister Ben Chifley before he lost office in the December 1949 general election.

[25] G Seddon, *Searching for the Snowy: An Environmental History* (Allen and Unwin, 1994).

[26] M Pearson, 'Thatching the Roof of Australia: Landscape Manipulation and History' (2005) 18(2) *Historic Environment* 29.

[27] S Domicelj, 'The Australian Snowy Mountains Scheme: National Growth and Regional Development' (1980) 5(5–6) *Habitat International* 601.

[28] Data in the paragraph from Snowy Hydro's Discovery Centre, Cooma, December 2020.

**Figure 6.2** Governor-General William McKell pushes the button to denote the first blast of dynamite, Snowy Mountains Scheme, 1949; National Archives of Australia

Though led by government, the SMS came about with support from a variety of vested interest groups, such as the Murrumbidgee Valley Water Users' Association and the Snowy River Hydro-Electric Development League.[29] Its inception was subject to political jostling over whether it would belong to the NSW or Commonwealth governments. As the Australian Constitution allocated responsibility to the states for energy production and irrigation, the Chifley government rationalised its leadership in the scheme as an exercise of its prerogatives over national defence by boosting the country's economic security – a Commonwealth constitutional responsibility.[30] When tabling the enabling legislation, Chifley's Minister for Works and Housing, Nelson Lemmon, declared it was for a 'great national project' that would not only generate considerable electricity but would be 'bringing water to the thirsty inland of Australia'.[31] At the opening ceremony, Chifley heralded the SMS as 'one of the greatest milestones on

[29] D Boadle, 'Regional Water Wars: River Leagues and the Origins of the Snowy Scheme' (1994) 80(3–4) *Journal of the Royal Australian Historical Society* 195.

[30] Australia Constitution Act, s 51(vi).

[31] House of Representatives, Hansard, 23 June 1949, 1440.

the march of Australia to full national development' and 'which are going to make this country truly great'.[32] It was a prophetic call, for in 1967 the American Society of Civil Engineers acclaimed the SMS as one of the world's greatest civil engineering wonders, joining the Eiffel Tower and the Suez Canal in its illustrious list of 'historic landmarks'. And in 2016 the SMS was inscribed by Australia's National Heritage List.

Initiation of the project was the culmination of some 50 years of proposals and debate, rooted in the dogma that nature holds little value until harnessed for 'productive' ends. In 1885 the NSW Royal Commission on the Conservation of Water identified the mountainous country as potential sources of water to enrich the Murray and Murrumbidgee rivers through storage systems.[33] The NSW Surveyor General advised the Royal Commission that 'any permanent system of irrigation in the colony would have to be drawn from snow waters'.[34] In 1913 at an Interstate Conference of Engineers a proposal was tabled for redirecting the Snowy River westwards for irrigation purposes.[35] No concrete plans for such a costly proposition progressed however until the middle of the twentieth century owing to wartime austerity and the Great Depression.

Framing the project as a matter of national defence to justify its involvement, and confident the project could pay for itself through sales of water and hydropower after borrowing $100 million from the World Bank, the Commonwealth legislated in 1949 to establish the Snowy Mountains Hydro-electric Authority to construct and operate the scheme.[36] In 1958 complementary legislation was passed by NSW and Victoria to implement agreements between the participating governments about further details of the operation of the scheme.

## III. Environmental Issues in the Snowy Mountains Scheme

Extraordinary by the legal standards of today, the Snowy development proceeded without first comprehensively assessing its potential environmental impacts. Had the project been proposed today – indeed at any point after 1974[37] – the Commonwealth would have been obliged to undertake a formal environmental impact study and consider its findings in deciding whether to allow the project or

[32] S McHugh, *The Snowy: People Behind the Power* (Angus and Robertson, 1995) 18.

[33] Royal Commission on the Conservation of Water, *First Report* (New South Wales Government 1885).

[34] Quoted from display at Snowy Hydro Discovery Centre, Cooma, December 2020.

[35] M Bergmann, 'The Snowy Mountains Hydro-electric Scheme: How did it Manage Without an EIA?', Discussion paper No. 60 (Australian National University, Graduate Program in Public Policy, 1999).

[36] Snowy Mountains Hydro-electric Power Act 1949 (Cth).

[37] The Commonwealth's Environment Protection (Impact of Proposals) Act was enacted in 1974, introducing an environmental assessment procedure for major projects.

any conditions to it if approved. Flow rates in mountain rivers and streams, and geological conditions, were studied prior to construction so as to understand how best to locate and design the dams. Yet, such geological and hydrological surveys served narrowly to advance the economic yield of the project rather than assess its environmental costs and risks. Water conservation was acknowledged by authorities of the time, but was seemingly tainted by a similar economic agenda. Research by Michael Bergmann found that concerns about water conservation discussed by planning bodies during the late 1940s were shaped by 'ulterior motives' in that the governments of 'Victoria and South Australia in particular, did not want the bulk of water captured by the Scheme to benefit solely New South Wales, and so were pointing out that NSW would probably waste it anyway'.[38]

A few insiders and observers raised apprehensions about possible environmental sequelae, albeit with little success. The Commonwealth and State Snowy River Committee, appointed in 1947 to investigate proposals to utilise the waters of the Snowy Mountains, downplayed suggestions of some risks:

> Although no appreciable irrigation of the rich river flats near Orbost is carried out from the Snowy River, the view was expressed by residents that a considerable reduction in the river flow might cause the following results:
>
> (a) lowering of the water table under the Flats with consequent loss of fertility in the summer;
> (b) deposition of silt in the bed of the river through the Flats;
> (c) the extension further upstream of salt water from the sea, affecting the watering of stock, and the use of wells for water supply; and always;
> (d) the closing of the mouth of the river by a sand-bar at times of low flow, resulting in flooding of low areas before the bar can be broken down by the increased head or by freshets.
>
> After inspection of the area and consideration of the problems, it was decided that there was little justification for the fears mentioned, and moreover, that if any deleterious effects appeared they could be overcome by the construction of relatively minor works.[39]

Subsequent history has deflated such exuberance. The project diverted river flows through tunnels and flooded terrain under 16 major dams. At 116 metres high, Adaminaby Dam (later renamed Eucumbene Dam), was then the biggest impoundment erected in Australia, and now is the country's third largest (capable of holding 4.798 gigalitres or nine times the volume of Sydney Harbour). The accompanying road construction dissected the high country with 1,600 kms of tracks.

It's surprising that the Commonwealth's Snowy Mountains Hydro-electric Power Act 1949 lacked explicit environmental considerations given that the

[38] Bergmann (n 35).

[39] Commonwealth of Australia, *Diversion and Utilisation of the Waters of the Snowy River. Final Report* (Commonwealth and States Snowy River Committee, 1950) 35.

project affected lands and waters in the Kosciusko State Park, established in 1944 over 528,000 hectares, and upgraded to a national park in 1967. One conservation planner described it as the most roaded national park in the world.[40] The Snowy Authority was obliged 'to cause as little detriment and inconvenience and do as little damage as possible'[41] – a nebulous requirement without environmental standards to guide the Authority, which it interpreted as intended to avoid damage to the proprietary interests of affected landholders. Furthermore, the Act's provision for undertaking soil surveys was for 'ascertaining the suitability of the land for the purposes of the Authority' rather than environmental conservation.[42]

Despite these lacunae in the governing legislation, a few environmental issues occasionally received attention by project staff. With input from the NSW Soil Conservation Service and the Water Conservation and Irrigation Commission, plus engineers from the US Bureau of Land Reclamation, water runoff and river-bank erosion were identified as issues to manage so as to minimise siltation or water loss.[43] In these ways, argues researcher Siobhán McHugh, the Snowy Mountains Authority 'implemented erosion control measures that far outstripped contemporary practice. They even inserted clauses into all major projects to ensure that the contractors carried out reclamation programs where necessary'.[44] Not all would agree with her sanguine view, however; University of Sydney botanist Marie (Betty) Phillips was employed by the Authority during the 1950s, but left after conflicts with her superiors over aspects of their development plans. In 1961, other scientists protested against a proposal to excavate a mountain side above Geehi Dam for an aqueduct bench – a proposal eventually ditched in favour of a less environmentally intrusive option.[45] Yet overall, insists McHugh, 'Compared with other public bodies in Australia at the time, the Authority was reasonably sensitive to the environmental damage it might cause'.[46]

Legislation passed in 1958 to implement a supplemental agreement between NSW, Victoria and the Commonwealth, which served to extend or clarify the Authority's powers, and to allocate electricity and irrigation water among the parties, included some explicit environmental provisions and acknowledged the status of the Kosciusko State Park. Whilst intended to protect the water catchment rather than the park as such, the provisions could provide collateral

[40] NC Gare, *Park Master Plan – Position of Summit Road within Kosciusko Primitive Area* (Kosciusko National Park Files, 1966), cited in M McDonald, *The Influence of the National Park Concept on Kosciusko National Park* (Master thesis, Australian National University, 1981) 67.

[41] Section 33(1).

[42] Section 19.

[43] S McHugh, *The Snowy: A History* (NewSouth Publishing, 2019) 104.

[44] ibid 333.

[45] D Slattery, 'Science and Land Use: The Kosciusko Primitive Area Dispute of 1958–65' (2010) 16 *Environment and History* 409, 415.

[46] McHugh (n 43) 334.

benefits to the high country's ecology and biota. Notably, the legislation provided that the Authority shall:

> keep the Kosciusko State Park Trust fully informed of such work to be carried out within the boundaries of the Kosciusko State Park as may affect the Park, and in carrying out of any such work exercise all proper care to pre serve natural assets, including trees, scrub, grasses and beauty spots in the Park.[47]

Other provisions obliged the Authority to take precautions to prevent soil erosion, water pollution or tree damage.[48] However, as by 1958 much of the construction work had already been completed or initiated, and the Authority retained wide statutory discretion to determine its best course of action, these additional clauses were somewhat belated and insufficient.

The supplemental agreement would, however, be relevant to a dispute over the Authority's use of the high-alpine country holding the headwaters of the Snowy River. Known by many as the 'High Tops', this unique area was identified by a group of concerned scientists as warranting protection as a 'primitive area'.[49] The NSW Kosciusko State Park Act authorised the State Park Trust to declare a primitive area of up to 10 per cent of the park. The scientists, who from 1961 enlisted the Australian Academy of Science in their campaign,[50] argued that nature conservation did not mean 'wasteful', non-use of land, but rather its retention for safeguarding and advancing aesthetic, ecological and recreational values. The scientists' position eventually prevailed against the wishes of the development-oriented Authority, with inclusion of High Tops in the national park created in 1967. A leading figure in the campaign was alpine ecologist Alec Costin, who adroitly married conservation science with the cultural and aesthetic values of the landscape in his pitch. Costin highlighted the fragility of alpine country, often steeply sloped, which couldn't be easily restored if disturbed: 'we need such undisturbed areas more than the developments which are possible in them. If we cannot save a few of the best, it does not say much for our scientific, cultural and spiritual standards'.[51] His sentiments differed from the Authority's engineers who saw environmental issues as technical or utilitarian challenges to manage. The successful campaign to save the Snowy headwaters as a conservation area was a seminal precursor to the other major, and better known, environmental activism that erupted in 1967, such as over Lake Pedder and Little Desert.[52] The campaign also implicitly underscored the lack of formal opportunities for

[47] Snowy Mountains Hydro-electric Agreements Act 1958 (NSW), s 13(j).

[48] ibid.

[49] Slattery (n 45) 409.

[50] Australian Academy of Science, 'The Future of the Kosciusko Summit Area: A Report on the Proposed Primitive Area Within the Kosciusko State Park' (1961) 23 *Australian Journal of Science* 391.

[51] Costin and another, 30 April 1962, quoted in Slattery (n 45) 419.

[52] See further G Worboys et al, 'Protected Area Management in the Australian Alps. A Case Study: Kosciusko National Park' in LS Hamilton, DP Bauer and HF Takeuchi (eds), *Parks, Peaks and People* (East-West Center, 1991) 50.

public participation in SMS decision making, and the necessity to exert pressure through other channels.

Protecting the alpine summit for a future national park would be a mixed blessing however as the park encouraged tourist visitation, and thus another type of impact to the Snowy Mountains. The many roads and related infrastructure constructed to support the hydro-scheme brought with it greatly increased tourism and recreation in the region. In 1967, travel writer Elspeth Huxley remarked: 'the Kosciusko State Park … is both a sanctuary for wildlife and a pleasure-ground. The two interests conflict. … Roads and lodges destroy that tranquillity which it is a prime object of a Park to preserve'.[53] Huxley further grumbled that 'a little less than 100 square miles out of 2,000 – no more than five per cent – has been declared a "Primitive Area" which is to be left just as it is, for nature to take its course'.[54]

It would take several decades – belatedly – for the environmental impacts of the SMS to be formally investigated, in response to increasing scrutiny from activists and scientists.[55] One effort was the Snowy River Environmental Flow Scoping Study, prepared in 1994 by NSW and Victorian authorities and the Snowy Mountains Hydro-electric Authority. It examined different water-flow scenarios to assess the likely outcomes, concluding that environmental improvements would accrue only once the flow of the Snowy was restored to at least 12.5 per cent of its original condition. In 1996 the Snowy Genoa Catchment Management Committee also studied water flows, receiving advice from experts that a demonstrable improvement in the ecology of the Snowy required reinstating 28 per cent of the river's original flow.[56] The 1997–98 Snowy Water Inquiry, commissioned in response to the proposed corporatisation of the Authority, also examined some of the project's environmental sequelae and future restoration options.[57] These included declines in habitat for aquatic fauna, poorer water quality and colonisation of riparian areas by weeds.[58] The counter argument to addressing such concerns was that retaining more water for ecological purposes would impair electricity generation and hurt downstream irrigation users.

Some adverse environmental changes have also ensued far from the dams. Widespread salinity in the Riverina district has arisen due a combination of deforestation and mismanagement of irrigation waters fed by the SMS. Increased irrigation drainage along the Murray River has increased salinity in the surface soil, which has also percolated into the river,[59] though once water leaves the SMS,

[53] E Huxley, *Their Shining Eldorado. A Journey Through Australia* (Chatto and Windus, 1967) 57.

[54] ibid.

[55] T Fisher, '30 Years Between Drinks: The Snowy River' (1998) 26(5) *Habitat Australia* 9.

[56] Snowy Genoa Catchment Management Committee (SGCMC), *Expert Panel Environmental Flow Assessment of the Snowy River Below Jindabyne Dam* (SGCMC, 1996).

[57] Snowy Water Inquiry, *Snowy Water Inquiry Final Report. Submitted to the Governments of New South Wales and Victoria* (October 1998).

[58] LJ Martin, 'Total Environment Centre, Australia Conservation Foundation and Snowy River Alliance' (1999) 37(3) *Australian Geographical Studies* 337, 338.

[59] Domicelj (n 27) 607.

the distribution and use of it along the Murray and Murrumbidgee rivers is a matter outside the Authority's remit, for regulation by the Victorian or NSW state governments.

The parsimonious interest of regulators in the project's environmental footprint contrasted with the heightened care for workers' safety, although the project still incurred 121 fatalities and many more injuries. Over 25 years from 1949 to 1974, 100,000 workers toiled on the scheme, with 7,300 workers in 1959 alone at the project's peak of construction. The majority were recruited abroad owing to local labour and skills shortages, coming from war-torn Europe to seek not only job opportunities but a new life in Australia. They were housed in seven towns and over 100 camps established during the life of the project. According to a contemporary information display at Snowy Hydro's Discovery Centre, in the town of Cooma, 'industrial safety was a vital concern for the Authority during construction. Safety practices on the Scheme were well ahead of comparable projects around the world at that time'. For instance, a decade before it became mandatory across the nation, workers had to wear a seat belt when travelling the rough, mountainous terrain.

Apart from the electricity generated, many welcomed the modified Snowy Mountains for its new boating, fishing and swimming opportunities. Lake Jindabyne was one mecca for such recreation. The original lakeside town, dating from the 1840s, was flooded in 1964 and re-established less than one kilometre away on higher ground. The same fate befell Adaminaby, whose 100 houses and other buildings were relocated in the late 1950s to make way for Lake Eucumbene. During drought, relics of the original township eerily re-emerge from the retreating waters of the reservoir. The aesthetic, recreational and economic projects of the SMS were heavily promoted by the Authority itself, which meticulously documented its activities through photography.[60]

The scheme today is promoted by Snowy Hydro – the renamed managing authority – as also being a major contributor to Australia's climate-friendly future. At Snowy Hydro's Discovery Centre, one display lauds the scheme as 'largest supplier of clean, renewable energy' in Australia, and another boasts that it 'saves millions of tonnes of carbon dioxide being released into the atmosphere each year'. Snowy Hydro also boasts on its website that its scheme provides 'one third of renewable energy to the National Electricity Market',[61] and is 'the single largest supplier of greenhouse gas emission free energy in the national grid'.[62] Yet ironically climate change itself may diminish the long-term precipitation in the region to support electricity generation. To combat this threat, since 2004 NSW authorities have conducted cloud seeding, under the Snowy Mountains Cloud Seeding

[60] E Esau, 'Photography and the Snowy Mountains Hydro-electric Scheme' (1998) 22 *History of Photography* 72.

[61] Snowy Hydro, www.snowyhydro.com.au.

[62] Snowy Hydro, *Environment Report for 2014–2015* (Snowy Hydro, 2015) 9.

Trial Act, which under suitable conditions can increase precipitation by an average of 14 per cent without adverse environmental impacts.[63]

## IV. Powering the Tasmanian Economy

Hydropower has been even more economically important – and environmentally controversial – in Tasmania. The island's potential to be the 'battery of the nation', as some politicians boast today, was recognised at least a century ago. Nationalistic commentator Edwin Brady remarked in 1918 that: 'hydraulic generation of electrical force can be greatly extended in Tasmania – the land or lakes and rivers. … With her cool climate and cheap power, the Island State may aspire to become a great manufacturing base for the Commonwealth.'[64] Hydropower in Tasmania began in 1889 with the electrification of the town of Waratah and its Mount Bischoff tin mine, powered by a local hydropower facility.[65] But this milestone was small compared to the hydropower schemes which were to begin some two decades later.

With abundant water and mountainous terrain, Tasmania was viewed by its economic managers as offering ideal conditions to develop hydropower as a way to attract heavy industry and meet households' needs. Roger Lupton's history of the subject observes that 'no other state in Australia matched Tasmania's reliance on hydro power'.[66] The reliance has been so great that the island's governments over many decades, especially after World War II, made hydropower the defining symbol of Tasmania.

The first major step towards this vision was the Great Lake Power Scheme, in the Central Highlands. Its potential was publicised in 1905 when University of Tasmania physicist Alexander McAulay outlined in a letter to the *Mercury* newspaper his vision for an ambitious power scheme, where 'Nature practically makes us a present' that can be readily exploited without any major financial or engineering obstacles.[67] The Great Lake Power Scheme impounded the Shannon and Ouse rivers to service the Waddamana power station, opened in 1916. Perhaps not with too much exaggeration, chief engineer and manager of the project, John Butters, pronounced that starting up the turbines on 6 May 'was probably the most important event in the history of Tasmania'.[68] Yet the private venture ran into logistical

[63] M Simon et al, 'Enhancing the Weather: Governance of Weather Modification Activities in Australia' (2020) 37 *Environmental and Planning Law Journal* 698, 709.

[64] EJ Brady, *Australia Unlimited* (George Robertson and Company, 1918) 746.

[65] K Preston, 'Mount Bischoff Tin Mines: Pioneers of Water Power in the Tasmanian Mining Industry' (2010) 8 *Journal of Australasian Mining History* 150.

[66] R Lupton, *Lifeblood: Tasmania's Hydro Power* (Focus Publishing, 1999) 8.

[67] A McAulay, 'The Water Supply of Tasmania' (*Mercury* (Hobart), 29 June 1905) 7.

[68] Quoted from a display at the Waddamana Museum; see further www.hydro.com.au/things-to-do/waddamana-heritage-site.

and financial difficulties associated with the onset of World War I, leading to the project being taken over by the state government in 1914, marking the beginning of its controversial involvement in the business of building and operating hydro-power projects. Besides expansion of the Waddamana facility from 1919 to 1923, a second power station was added during World War II. Since its decommissioning in 1994, the site has been a heritage-listed museum open to the public, with restored machinery and displays about the 'good old' pioneering days of Tasmania's march into hydro-industrialisation.

**Figure 6.3** Tasmanian Hydro-Electric Commission, advertisement, 1932; University of Tasmania

**Figure 6.4** Turbines of Waddamana power station, 2021; photograph by author

Today Tasmania's Central Highlands cradles a labyrinth of dams and power stations, providing the backbone to the state's electricity generation system, now overseen by Hydro Tasmania which was established in 1998 when the Hydro-Electric Commission (HEC) was disaggregated into three government-owned enterprises. The Hydro-Electric Purchase Act 1914 established a Hydro-Electric Department, which in 1929 became the Commission under updated legislation, with control of Tasmania's waterways and a monopoly over the generation and sale of electricity throughout the island. Its enabling legislation gave the Commission a sweeping mandate, whose dangers for accountable governance would eventually become all-too apparent:

> construct any works, and may operate, manage, control, and generally carry on and conduct any business whatsoever, relating to or connected with the generation, transmission, distribution, and sale of electrical energy, and carry out any purpose in relation thereto which the Commission may deem desirable in the interests of the State.[69]

[69] Section 15(2)(a).

Waddamana was a catalyst for transforming Tasmania's economy and politics. Although the power scheme was designed principally to power the energy-hungry, zinc refinery in Hobart, the provision of electricity for households was increasingly emphasised by authorities keen to portray hydropower as benefitting all Tasmanians. A 1929 newspaper advertisement sponsored by the HEC touted: 'electricity in the home promotes health and comfort, abolishes drudgery and makes time available for recreation'.[70] Tasmanians' growing appetite for electricity buttressed the Commission's plans to develop a state-wide power grid and build more dams.

The HEC quickly became a political behemoth, and an exemplar of enlightened despotism. Historians generally agree that it 'became more powerful perhaps than any government instrumentality that Australia had known in times of peace'.[71] Indicative of its political omnipresence, the 'Minister Administering the Hydro-Electric Commission Act' was usually Tasmania's state premier. With its monopoly over the state's energy system, and central role in powering Tasmania's economic future, the HEC managers enjoyed unprecedented access to and influence over politicians. Although the HEC's 1944 legislation stipulated that 'no new power development shall be undertaken or constructed by the Commission unless and until it has been authorised by Parliament',[72] the two major political parties in Tasmania were ideologically aligned with the expansionist mission of the HEC.

Officialdom's lack of attention to the environmental ramifications of hydropower reflected a wider insouciance in society about the costs accompanying industrialisation. Its environmental effects in the early twentieth century were not unknown but there was naïve belief that natural processes such as wind and water currents could safely remove pollutants. Consider, for instance, the advice of Hobart City Council's chief health officer in 1915 to the then proposed zinc refinery: 'The refuse could be deposited in the river, and would be carried away by the flow of the stream. A further recommendation is that the site is situated to the eastward of the city, and the prevailing winds would carry away the obnoxious fumes from the city'.[73] Reliance on rivers or winds to disperse pollution was accepted best practice in this era. Hydropower schemes introduced impacts that couldn't be so easily dispersed or neutralised however, notably the destruction or alteration of river systems and the flooding of wildlife habitat. By the 1950s, the HEC was starting to acknowledge some of its environmental legacies; for example, its hydro-dam construction towns were being designed to minimise despoiling the landscape and construction sites were repaired by restoring soil and planting trees.[74] But such localised interventions overlooked the broader ecological changes wrought by big dams.

[70] Hydro-electric Department, advertisement (*Mercury* (Hobart), 2 November 1929) 13.
[71] Lupton (n 66) 8.
[72] Hydro-Electric Commission Act 1944, s 16(1)).
[73] *Daily Post* 26 July 1915, quoted in Lupton (n 66) 60.
[74] H Felton, *Ticklebelly Tales and Other Stories from the People of the Hydro* (Hydro Tasmania, 2013) 124, 211.

The 1944 Act gave the HEC the power to control, with consent of the government, the use of waters in lakes, rivers and other waterbodies,[75] and vested the Commission with power to 'raise or lower the level of any lake, river, or stream, and … impound, divert, take, and use the waters thereof … which the Commission deems necessary for the purposes of this Act'.[76] The closest this legislation came to conceding that the Commission's dam and grid-building activities might injure others was the obligation that the 'Commission shall cause as little detriment and inconvenience and do as little damage as possible, and compensation shall be paid by the Commission for damage caused to any property in the course of the execution of such works'.[77] Furthermore, in regard to environmental protection, the legislation stated:

> the Commission shall take steps, so far as possible, to preserve and protect the natural beauty of lakes, falls, rivers, and streams, and shall consult with, and take into consideration the views of, the Scenery Preservation Board in respect of any proposed works which may appear to be likely to affect the natural beauty thereof.[78]

The Scenery Preservation Board however was not politically influential, and as discussed in chapter nine, it failed to stop the excision in 1950 of a premium slice of Mount Field National Park for a forestry concession. The 1944 legislation also preserved the existing right of individuals to 'the supply of water for stock of domestic purposes' and the right to water under mining tenements,[79] but without obliging the HEC to respect environmental flows for healthy ecosystems and biodiversity.

Unlike the Snowy Mountains Authority, the HEC was not directly tasked with facilitating irrigation schemes. That role came under the auspices of the Rivers and Water Supply Commission, established under the Water Act 1957, with the same mentality as the HEC – that Tasmania's rivers were there to be harnessed for economic progress. The Commission's official role was to establish waterworks for domestic, industrial and agricultural purposes, and the legislation (unsurprisingly) omitted environmental considerations.[80] The HEC assisted here by managing river flows, enabling additional water to be drawn by farmers during their growing seasons.

The 1950s was the most pivotal decade for the expansion of Tasmania's hydropower, with five new power stations opened to meet demand for electricity that was then doubling every five years.[81] In 1951, the HEC generated electricity of 1020 million kWh, which rose to 2566 million kWh by 1961, by which time

[75] Section 65.
[76] Section 69(1)).
[77] Section 50(1).
[78] Section 69(2).
[79] Section 68.
[80] See L Griggs, 'The New Regime for Water Management in Tasmania' (2000) 19(2) *University of Tasmania Law Review* 159, 161–63.
[81] Lupton (n 66) 185 and 196.

one-fifth (21 per cent) of all electricity consumed in Australia in manufacturing industries was produced and used in Tasmania with just 1/13 (7.7 per cent) of the nation's population.[82]

Tasmania's hydropower industrialisation reached its apotheosis of environmental controversy in the 1970s and early 1980s with the ignominious damming of Lake Pedder in 1972 and the nearly achieved damming of the Franklin and Gordon rivers in the early 1980s. The former HEC head, Allan Knight, who reigned from 1946 to 1977, had little sympathy for any environmental objections, indeed remarking some years after his retirement that hydropower was an environmental blessing: 'it is unfortunate, in my opinion, that Tasmania has been denied the opportunity to develop the power resources of the Lower Gordon as originally planned. Perhaps when the non-polluting value of water power is more fully appreciated, wiser counsel will prevail'.[83]

[82] RMH Garvie, *A Million Horses: Tasmania's Power in the Mountains* (Hydro-Electric Commission, 1962) 89, 109.

[83] Quoted in Lupton (n 66) 7.

# 7

# Testing Times Over the Outback

## I. The Outback

For many, explains Roslynn Haynes, Australia is synonymous with the Outback.[1] It's an unfathomably vast expanse of 5.5 million $km^2$ that occupies 70 per cent of the continent yet is home to less than one-twentieth of the nation's population. Laden with mythology, folklore and heritage for both Aboriginal and non-Aboriginal Australians, the Outback is an iconic geographical realm characterised by its remoteness, aridity and harsh climate. The very name however has colonial connotations, explains Ann McGrath, for space is measured by distance from White settlement and civilisation.[2] The region has an ancient pedigree, occupied by Aboriginal peoples for some 60,000 years.[3] Its relatively intact ecosystems also make Australia's heartland one of the largest wild areas left on Earth, suggest scientists,[4] and an ancient geological history which delivered the continent so much aridity, explains Steve Martin in *Australian Deserts*.[5] The Outback however is not a singular, monolithic expanse: from monsoonal, tropical savannas to arid barrens it has a diverse biota adapted to its ephemeral and changeable conditions, and variations in land use from enclaves of intensive mining and tourism to spacious, undisturbed national parks, add to the Outback's defiance of simple categorisation.

The region came into unprecedented national consciousness with John Heyer's widely circulated documentary film, *The Back of Beyond* (1954), following a postman's journey over 500 km that helped corroborate 'settler anxieties about the Outback as a place of isolation, brutal indifference, danger and timelessness' but also furnished a realm for individuals' endurance and courage.[6]

[1] RD Haynes, *Seeking the Centre: The Australian Desert in Literature, Art and Film* (Cambridge University Press, 1998).

[2] A McGrath, 'Travels to the Distant Past: The Mythology of the Outback' (1991) 10) *Australian Cultural History* 113.

[3] G Hamm et al, 'Cultural Innovation and Megafauna Interaction in the Early Settlement of Arid Australia' (2016) 539 *Nature* 280.

[4] JEM Watson, 'Protect the Last of the Wild' (2018) 563 *Nature* 27.

[5] S Morton, *Australian Deserts: Ecology and Landscapes* (CSIRO Publishing, 2022).

[6] P De Souza, 'The Back of Beyond', Australian Screen, aso.gov.au/titles/documentaries/back-of-beyond/notes.

The Outback has a long history of New World settlers.[7] Europeans' presence began in the mid-nineteenth century, with the first explorers searching for the mythical 'inland sea'.[8] They were followed by pastoralists, who evicted Aboriginal people and brought additional violence to the land as their hard-hooved cattle trampled the sparse vegetation and fragile soils, accompanied by an entourage of exotics including rabbits, camels and buffelgrass. The twentieth century brought further upheaval with industrial-scale mining.

Settlers' also found aesthetic and spiritual appreciation of Australia's arid interior and, as with the changing receptivity of Whites to the continent's environment, artists and scientists were valuable intermediaries. In contrast to explorer Walter Gregory's description in the *Dead Heart of Australia* of 'the merciless severity of its forces',[9] or the desolate, barrenness of the arid interior depicted in Russell Drysdale's paintings, mammologist Hedley Finlayson (1885–1991) celebrated the Outback's splendid biota and topography, wishing to dispel 'the idea of its flatness, of its treelessness and its monotony'.[10] Another inspired was painter Hans Heysen (1877–1968). Born in Germany, Heysen emigrated as a child and settled in Adelaide, where he took to drawing the gum trees of the Adelaide Hills. On visiting the Flinders Ranges in the 1920s, a harsh landscape lacking large eucalypts, Heysen turned his attention to the ancient, weathered mountains, desiccated terrain and stunted vegetation. Inspired by Modernism, Heysen reduced his renderings of this primeval landscape to simple but powerful tones and forms. Thereby, he helped engage Australians with the aesthetics of the Outback, which had until then hardly attracted the interest of nature conservationists. Painting landscapes in a European style, Aboriginal artist Albert Namatjira (1902–59) also brought to a national audience an appreciation of the Outback's aesthetics, and was a founding member of the Hermannsburg School of art in the Northern Territory. Namatjira and Heysen however, didn't concretely depict the environmental changes and degradation that moved others.

One who was observant of these changes was Hedley Finlayson, who observed first-hand the Outback's degradation. A skilful photographer, Finlayson gave many Australians their first visual impressions of Uluru (or Ayers Rock, as then known), spinifex plains, sand dunes and stunning goannas. But it was in his writings that Finlayson left his greatest impression. He opened *The Red Centre*, his magnum opus published in 1935, with this remark: 'The old Australia is passing. The environment which moulded the remarkable fauna in the world is best on all sides by influences which are reducing it to a medley of semi-artificial environments'.[11]

[7] A Mayne, *Beyond the Black Stump: Histories of Outback Australia* (Wakefield Press, 2008).

[8] D Parker, *Outback. The Discovery of Australia's Interior* (Sutton Publishing, 2007).

[9] W Gregory, *The Dead Heart of Australia: A Journey Around Lake Eyre in the Summer of 1901–1902* (J Murray, 1906) 163.

[10] HH Finlayson, *The Red Centre: Man and Beast in the Heart of Australia* (Angus and Robertson, 1935) 21.

[11] ibid 16.

**Figure 7.1** Hans Heysen working in his garden, 1954; State Library of South Australia

With prescience, Finlayson elaborated: 'if the devastation which is worked to the flora and fauna could be assessed in terms of the value which future generations will put upon them, it might be found that our wool-clips, and beef and timber trades have been dearly bought'.[12] Today, we would recognise such language as associated with the ethos of intergenerational equity, the ostensible touchstone of much environmental policy. Finlayson also recognised his fears and concerns might seem preposterous to the hoi polloi:

> The man in the street has heard and read so much of a vast, empty centre [with] the conception of an untrodden wilderness enduring ... But it must always be remembered that even in those tracts where no stock have been depastured, those enterprising pests, the rabbits, foxes, and feral cats, have ... worked untold change and damage.[13]

[12] ibid.
[13] ibid 17.

One highlight of Finlayson's pioneering fieldwork in the early 1930s was when he found the desert rat-kangaroo, also known as the oolacunta (*Caloprymnus campestris*), a small, elusive marsupial that hadn't been recorded by Europeans since 1843,[14] and since 1935 has never had a confirmed sighting after Finlayson collected his specimens. 'It seemed to scarcely touch the ground', wrote he, and 'almost floated ahead in an eerie, effortless way that made the thundering horse behind seem, by comparison, like a coal hulk wallowing in a heavy sea'.[15]

**Figure 7.2** Desert rat-kangaroos; lithograph by Henry Richter and John Gould, 1845; Australian Museum

The desert rat-kangaroo likely perished due to predators (foxes) and competitors (rabbits), compounded by diminished suitable habitat after dispossession of Aboriginal people. Other Outback wildlife to suffer the same fate were the pig-footed bandicoot (*Chaeropus ecaudatus*), which vanished by the 1950s, the lesser stick-nest rat (*Leporillus apicalis*), last confirmed in 1933, and the lesser bilby (*Macrotis leucura*), unseen since 1931. Their disappearance occurred before governments had a chance to enact conservation laws, though even had they

[14] Although more recent research has confirmed that some specimens collected by HJ Hillier between 1902–05 on the shores of Lake Killalpaninna, South Australia, were the same species: K Vernes, S Ingleby and M Eldridge, 'An Overlooked, Early Record of the Desert Rat-kangaroo (*Caloprymnus campestris*) from Lake Killalpaninna, South Australia' (2019) 42(2) *Australian Mammalogy* 223.

[15] Quoted in T Flannery, *The Explorers: Text Classics* (Text Publishing, 1998) 353.

tried, it's doubtful they would have succeeded given the multiple, insidious threats unleashed by colonisation.

In fact, during the mid-twentieth century the Commonwealth conscripted the Outback for the most environmentally traumatic episode in the country's history: to test atomic bombs, in the name of 'nation building'. It was governance by enlightened despotism and scientific 'progress' at its strongest. The legacy, distills Elizabeth Tynan, Australia's leading researcher into this ignominious chapter of the nation's chronicle, was to turn 'a pristine Australian wilderness into one of the most contaminated places on earth'.[16] Whilst one can quibble with Tynan's reference to 'pristine … wilderness', which Marcia Langton and others point out obfuscates the history of Aboriginal land management of the continent,[17] there can be no argument that the impacted deserts were violated in an unprecedented manner.

## II. Bombs Away

On 27 September 1957, Melbourne's *Argus* published a congratulatory story headlined 'Bombs Away' that epitomised much of the nation's glee at the testing of atomic weaponry on Australian soil.[18] The programme originated in Great Britain's desire to build its own nuclear arsenal after the war, to stay abreast of changing world geopolitics and halt its international decline. After being ostracised from America's atomic weapons programme in 1950, Britain sought a place – outside its own territory, of course – to test its experimental nuclear bombs. It had already been testing long-range, guided missiles at Woomera, South Australia, since 1946, which put Australia on the short-list.

Without any prior environmental assessment, the Commonwealth gave Britain the green light. Over the next 11 years, beginning on 3 October 1952 with the detonation near the Monte Bello Islands off the Western Australian coast, some 700 weapon tests occurred, all under the curiously and innocuously named Defence (Special Undertakings) Act 1952 (it would be misleading however to imply from this legislation that the testing programme incurred serious parliamentary oversight or other public scrutiny). Prime Minister Robert Menzies assured his compatriots in a brief speech on 18 February 1952, that the tests 'will be conducted in conditions which will ensure that there will be no danger whatever from radioactivity to the health of the people or animals in the Commonwealth'.[19] The Commonwealth's stance relied on its constitutional power

[16] E Tynan, *Atomic Thunder: The Maralinga Story* (NewSouth Books, 2016) 1.

[17] M Langton, 'The Conceit of Wilderness Ideology' (*ABC Radio National*, 9 December 2012) www.abc.net.au/radionational/programs/boyerlectures/the-conceit-of-wilderness-ideology/4409022.

[18] I Arnold, 'Bombs Away' (*Argus*, 27 September 1957) 1.

[19] Quoted in P Brown, 'Maralinga: Theatre from a Place of War' in G McAuley (ed), *Unstable Ground. Performance and the Politics of Place* (Peter Lang, 2006) 205, 205.

over national defence, a stance already set by the precedent when it took control of a large area in Woomera, South Australia, for rocket testing. Interestingly, a 1959 parliamentary inquiry recommended the constitution be amended to provide the Commonwealth with an explicit power to govern nuclear energy to facilitate its national leadership.[20]

The inaugural bomb test at the Monte Bello islands, code-named 'Operation Hurricane', released the energy equivalent of 25,000 tonnes of TNT (trinitrotoluene), exhaling a mushroom cloud four kilometres above the ocean and gouging a 300-metre-wide crater in the sea floor. The Australian press were enthralled: 'a magnificent display of a stupendous release of energy' and 'awe-inspiring', summed up the sycophantic media.[21] The front-page of the *Western Australian* elaborated on the visual spectacle:

> The immediate flash resembled the top quarter of a setting sun. A dense and magnificently turbulent cloud almost immediately shot to a height of 2,000 ft. At first deep pink, it quickly changed to mauve in the centre, with pink towards the outside and brilliantly white turbulent edges. Within two minutes the cloud, which still was like a giant cauliflower, was 10,000ft high. A small pure-white milling ball rested on top.[22]

The first detonation on the mainland occurred on 15 October 1953 at Emu Field in the Great Victoria Desert in South Australia, but in 1956 the tests were moved to another, less remote site in South Australia at Maralinga.

**Figure 7.3** Operation Hurricane, first nuclear bomb test in Australia, at Monte Bello Islands, 3 October 1952; Australian War Memorial

[20] Australia, Parliament, Joint Committee on Constitutional Review, *Report* (Commonwealth Government Printer, 1959) 74.

[21] 'Observer's Account of Atomic Explosion' (*Advertiser* (Adelaide), 9 October 1952) 2.

[22] 'Britain Tests Her First Atomic Bomb off W.A. Coast' (*West Australian*, 4 October 1952) 1.

Pending completion of the testing facilities at Maralinga, tests resumed at Monte Bello. It hosted the 'Operation Mosaic' G2 blast on 19 June 1956, the largest nuclear device ever denotated in Australia, and the most controversial. Its cloud rose 14,000 metres, higher than the forecast 11,000 metres, and owing to the winds much of it spread east across the continent. Reports of 'radioactive rain' caused some public consternation, yet Acting Prime Minister, Arthur Fadden, quickly hosed down fears, blithely declaring the 'operation was carried out without risk to life or property on the mainland or elsewhere' and that the small depositions recorded were 'completely harmless'.[23] The Royal Commission into British Nuclear Test in Australia, appointed by the Commonwealth in 1984 to examine the tests' legacy, was critical of this insouciance or disingenuity, calling a report from the Atomic Weapons Tests Safety Committee (AWTSC): 'misleading and did not properly inform the Government of the difficulties experienced [including] the higher than expected levels of fallout on the mainland'.[24]

Maralinga is now etched in Australian history as the place most synonymous with the bomb tests. Occupying 3,200 $km^2$, it refers to an area north of the Nullarbor Plain, some 850 kms northwest of Adelaide, that is arid but certainly not a wasteland. Over 100 bird species have been recorded in Maralinga,[25] and it has a long Aboriginal history, with its relics described by a leading Maralinga researcher as an 'Aboriginal Stone Henge'.[26]

The 1956 agreement between Great Britain and Australia gave the former 10 years of rent-free operations at Maralinga, extendable by mutual agreement. Each individual major test would require a further, separate approval by the parties, and tests on Sundays were banned for religious sensibility. The agreement explicitly forbade testing the behemoth H-bomb (hydrogen or thermonuclear weapon), which would have been too politically controversial. (The British instead tested H-bombs in 1957 at Malden Island and Christmas Island, now part of Kiribati). The 1956 agreement also provided that Britain would share tests data with Australia – something which often didn't happen. The site was managed by the Maralinga Board of Management, a joint British-Australian staffed entity, whilst safety matters were overseen by the AWTSC appointed by the Commonwealth government. Maralinga also hosted a sizeable settlement, with numerous houses and community infrastructure including a swimming pool and theatre, to accommodate some 35,000 military personnel cumulatively based there.[27]

In addition to testing mushroom-cloud bombs at Maralinga, the UK also conducted so-called 'minor trials', the most controversial being the 'Vixen' A and B experiments that detonated TNT to smash simulated nuclear warheads holding

[23] 'That A-Rain is Harmless, He Says' (*Argus* (Melbourne), 26 June 1956) 5.

[24] JR McClelland, J Fitch and WJA Jonas, *The Report of the Royal Commission into British Nuclear Tests in Australia – Conclusions and Recommendations* (AGPS, 1985) 19.

[25] Tynan (n 16) 12.

[26] ibid 92.

[27] ibid 97.

plutonium. The tests and trials ended in 1963 when Britain and Australia signed the Treaty Banning Nuclear Weapon Tests in the Atmosphere.[28] The mushroom-cloud blasts produced the most radioactive fallout, literally falling from the sky, with the dissemination depending on the height of the cloud and the prevailing winds. The Vixen tests also produced a lethal legacy, although it was more geographically confined and concentrated. An estimated 22.2 kilograms of plutonium-239, with a radioactive half-life of 24,100 years, were released from the Vixen B tests. Inhaling just a milligram of it, potentially in the fine dust of the test site, is enough to cause lung cancer.

To understand Australia's acquiescence to such folly, one has to look to the Cold War politics and Australia's relations with Great Britain. In 1950 its Prime Minister Clement Attlee asked Robert Menzies for his government's agreement. Menzies obsequiously obliged without referral of the request to his Cabinet, let alone putting it to parliament for approval. (Later, the Minister for Supply, Howard Beale, unknowingly twice misled parliament in 1951 when advising there were no plans for British tests in Australia).[29] Prime Minister Menzies was a notorious Anglophile, though also sufficiently nationalistic that he sought advantages for Australia in the deal, such as boosting the nation's security in a fragile, increasingly nuclear-armed world, and spin-offs for civilian uses of atomic energy in a country possessing large uranium resources. His duteous aid, Howard Beale, declared on 4 May 1955: 'The whole project is a striking example of inter-Commonwealth co-operation on the grand scale. England has the bomb and the knowhow; we have the open spaces, much technical skill and great willingness to help the Motherland'.[30] History has judged the legacy otherwise. One particularly acrid vilification came from Senator Peter Walsh who in 1984 denounced Menzies as 'the lickspittle Empire loyalist who regarded Australia as a colonial vassal of the British Crown … who invited the British to pollute Australia with nuclear fallout'.[31]

Menzies' appeasement of Britain contrasted with the Canadians' reluctance. Canada would have been a better partner for the UK in some ways, with its more advanced nuclear capabilities and, like Australia, large expanses of territory with few people. British officials had explored the possibility of establishing a testing programme in Canada, and surveyed potential sites, including at Churchill, in northern Manitoba. Yet the Canadian government declined any further cooperation once Britain's full intentions and the risks became clear.

Like Canada, Australia has Aboriginal populations who stood to be harmed by bomb testing. Commonwealth authorities had a cavalier attitude to the risks to them. The Maralinga lands covered part of the Central Aboriginal Reserve, which

[28] Treaty Banning Nuclear Weapon Tests in the Atmosphere, in Outer Space and Under Water (1963) 480 UNTS 3.

[29] Tynan (n 16) 72.

[30] McClelland, Fitch and Jonas (n 24) 15.

[31] Quoted in Tynan (n 16) 297.

Minister Beale falsely claimed was 'so arid and waterless' that Aboriginal people didn't use it.[32] In fact, about 1,000 Aboriginal people lived there. Nonetheless, the part of the reserve needed for the blasts – which was designated as Crown land rather than Aboriginal territory – was simply repealed by authorities in 1955, and the Maralinga Tjarutja people evicted, with most rehomed in a new settlement created at Yalata. Patrols by military personnel rounded up any who were found wandering in the no-go-zone; in one reported incident, after an unsuspecting family were found by soldiers to be camped in a bomb crater, the commanding officer warned his soldiers that 'the person who let this out to the papers, or press or Parliament, would be tried for treason' – punishable by firing squad or lengthy imprisonment.[33]

The general public was also kept in the dark about many aspects of the nuclear testing programme, and media releases were carefully vetted by authorities. As the McClelland Royal Commission in the 1980s summed up, 'the Australian Government had no intention of testing public reaction before deciding to agree to provide a permanent proving ground at Maralinga; no announcement was allowed until there was a formal commitment'.[34] The media generally toed the line. After the first bomb test, the press exclaimed: 'Echoes of the Monte Bello explosion are still reverberating round the world. Besides restoring Britain's prestige as a major Power, it has brought new hopes of closer Anglo-American cooperation in all phases of foreign policy'.[35]

Historian Elizabeth Tynan believes the government's issuance of so-called 'D-notices' helped to keep the press in line, as journalists were made privy to carefully-vetted information as a way to gain their sympathetic reporting rather than to seek alternate, unofficial sources that might be contrary or less favourable to the government's position.[36] In effect, the D-notices encouraged media self-censorship. A similar system operated in Britain. Much sensitive information was however quarantined from the media or other public scrutiny. Even when D-notices weren't issued, such as for the Vixen-B experiments, the media was docile and rarely asked troubling questions. The UK government was particularly keen to keep the Vixen-B programme under wraps because of tightening international controls in the lead-up to a treaty in 1963 to restrict nuclear testing. The Commonwealth itself was ignorant about many details of the British operations, with little sharing of the research data, even though Australia contributed cash and personnel for the tests so as to be perceived as a true partner, not to mention providing its territory.

[32] ibid 179.

[33] Quoted in C Gannon, 'The Legacy of Britain's Australian Nuclear Tests' (*Tribune*, 3 October 2021) tribunemag.co.uk/2021/10/the-long-legacy-of-britains-australian-nuclear-tests.

[34] McClelland, Fitch and Jonas (n 24) 8.

[35] 'Monte Bello Aids in Closing the Gap' (*News* (Adelaide), 8 October 1952) 12.

[36] Tynan (n 16) 205.

Great Britain believed it had concluded its responsibilities in regard to its tests when in 1968 it signed an agreement with Australia following decontamination of the site and removal of debris. The Commonwealth government accepted the UK's discharge however on the basis of a flawed survey to measure residual contamination after the clean-up operation. In subsequent years when the gravity of the toxic legacy became apparent, the UK either denied any risks remained or if they did they were no longer its responsibility – which this chapter will return to consider later.[37]

## III. Safety and Environmental Issues

The health and environmental legacies of the nuclear tests have been extensively written about, widely condemning both governments' handling of the tests, downplaying of the risks and subsequent cover-ups.[38] The most damming and methodical evidence came from the McClelland Royal Commission, reporting in 1985. Even by the rudimentary safety standards of the era, the Commission concluded: 'The measures taken before and at the time of the tests for protecting persons against exposure to the harmful effects of radiation … must be regarded as inadequate'.[39] An insouciant attitude prevailed that Maralinga was just a desert wasteland, whilst the few with grave doubts about the hazards of the nuclear weapons tests had little traction in government decision-making.

The Atomic Weapons Tests Safety Committee (AWTSC) was established in 1955 by the Commonwealth, ostensibly to monitor the environmental safety of the British testing programme, and to be a conduit for exchanging information between the UK and Australia. Although it established 60 monitoring stations around Australia, the committee was deferential to the advice of the British atomic scientists, and unwilling to seriously question their glib assurances about safety. The AWTSC was for much of its life (from 1957) headed by Professor Ernest Titterton who, affiliated with the UK atomic weapons elite, wasn't particularly mindful to look after Australia's interests. Indeed, the committee became 'more of a public relations mechanism than a true overseer of highly dangerous activities', according to one historian.[40] Justice James McClelland, who presided over the Royal Commission into the tests, would write: 'it would be hard to imagine anyone less suitable than Titterton to be entrusted with a task which called for disinterested concern for the safety of the Australian population from nuclear radiation'.[41] The other members of the AWTSC under Titterton's tenure were Leonard Dwyer,

[37] 'Monte Bello Aids in Closing Gap' (*News* (Adelaide), 8 October 1952) 12.

[38] See eg, J Smith, *Clouds of Deceit: The Deadly Legacy of Britain's Bomb Tests* (Faber, 1985); D Blakeway and S Lloyd-Roberts, *Fields of Thunder: Testing Britain's Bomb* (Allen and Unwin, 1985).

[39] McClelland, Fitch and Jonas (n 24) 12.

[40] Tynan (n 16) 140.

[41] Quoted in ibid 143.

director of the Commonwealth Bureau of Meteorology and Donald Stevens, director of the Commonwealth X-Ray and Radium Laboratory. They evidently did little to improve accountability. 'The AWTSC failed to carry out many of its tasks in a proper manner. At times it was deceitful and allowed unsafe firing to occur. It deviated from its charter by assuming responsibilities which properly belonged to the Australian Government', concluded the Royal Commission.[42]

The variable risks faced by military personnel, Aboriginal communities and the general public were acknowledged but downplayed by authorities. Though judged as most vulnerable, some servicemen were ordered to go to ground-zero immediately after bomb detonation or to fly in planes through the mushroom clouds, often without protective clothing. Curiously, UK scientists viewed the risk of exposure to radiation for air crew flying through detonation clouds to be negligible.[43] The next most vulnerable group were thought to be Aboriginal people. At the Maralinga tests, the McClelland inquiry found: 'Aborigines continued to move around and through the Prohibited Zone and inadequate resources were allocated … to ensuring their safety. The reporting of sightings of Aboriginal people was discouraged and ignored'.[44] Authorities sought to reassure the public that no Aboriginal communities or other groups would be harmed. When asked about the threat, the UK advised the bombs would not 'endanger the health of the Australian people'.[45] The media obsequiously concurred, reporting calmingly about safety precautions and 'harmless' dispersal of radioactive clouds.[46] Reflective of such insouciance, the *West Australian* proclaimed the 'atomic cloud will blow safely away … across uninhabited country'.[47]

The heightened dangers to Aboriginal people were only fully disclosed in the 1980s, via the McClelland inquiry. Some of the tests incurred sharp criticism: 'the attempts to ensure Aboriginal safety during the Buffalo series demonstrate ignorance, incompetence and cynicism on the part of those responsible for that safety'.[48] The Commission concluded that the lack of deaths or injuries to Aboriginal people 'was a matter of luck rather than adequate organisation, management and resources allocated to ensuring safety'.[49] The most controversial incident was the so-called 'black mist' that appeared after a test at Emu Field in October 1953. An ominous, large black haze allegedly descended around the settlements of Wallatinna and Mintabie, resulting in widespread vomiting, diarrhoea and skin

[42] McClelland, Fitch and Jonas (n 24) 11. In 1957 AWTSC's role was altered, being restricted to safety issues relating to weapons tests and to report only to the Prime Minister, whilst the task of examining radiation safety in the wider community, from all sources, was assigned to a new body, the National Radiation Advisory Committee.

[43] Tynan (n 16) 82.

[44] McClelland, Fitch and Jonas (n 24) 20.

[45] 'No Danger to Natives from Atomic Test' (*Warwick Daily News*, 3 May 1952) 6.

[46] See eg 'Atomic Blast Ends Wait at Maralinga' (*Canberra Times*, 28 September 1956) 1.

[47] 'Atomic Cloud Will Blow Safely Away' (*West Australian*, 29 September 1953) 1.

[48] McClelland, Fitch and Jonas (n 24) 20.

[49] ibid.

conditions, and seven deaths.[50] The Royal Commission found that the black mist story was credible but couldn't determine whether it was caused by a bomb test.

Many of the dangers had been known to authorities at the time but were kept secret or assuaged. Whistleblower Hedley Marston, an Australian agricultural scientist with the CSIRO, raised concerns about potential contamination of the food chain, as far away as livestock in North Queensland. But his warnings were rejected by the AWTSC.[51] Some press started to report on possible concerns from the mid-1950s, though they often had little evidence then to go on to allow more detailed coverage. On 8 March 1955 the headlined story of the *Sydney Morning Herald* conveyed the views of US and UK atomic experts expressing alarm at the risk of contamination from atmospheric tests, and calling on the United Nations to impose international controls.[52] The impacts of the tests in Australia also began to be scrutinised. One of these, in a 1958 edition of the *Tribune*, began: 'Facts about radioactive fallout in Australia after the 1956 atom bomb tests, now disclosed for the first time … make it essential that no nuclear weapon tests are ever again permitted in or around Australia'.[53] Elizabeth Tynan's detailed account of the British tests identifies 1956 as 'a watershed in media and public perception of the British tests' based on the government's own assessment of the situation, citing the emergence of an international peace campaign in the mid-1950s, a relaxation of Soviet aggression, and increased awareness of the dangers of atomic trials.[54] A Gallup poll in March 1956 after the Mosaic G2 test showed a majority of Australians opposed the tests.

Some media outlets became bolder in voicing concern, though the mainstream media from 1957 tended to abstain altogether from reporting on the tests. The *Argus* in 1956 decried 'there is no other country … where atomic vandalism is preceded and followed by such soothing, scientific lullabies'.[55] The same paper also asked, in relation to exploiting nuclear power, 'what protection has mankind got against the pollution of earth, sea and air … [and] it would be foolish to wait until millions have been spent and dangerous pollution has occurred before this matter has been examined from a global aspect'.[56] Some media reported on fallout from the tests: 'Atomic Cloud Pollutes Our Meat Country,' screamed the headline of one tabloid, referring to cattle in Alice Springs having to be slaughtered owing to being 'heavily affected by radioactivity',[57] and it went on to conclude that 'official

[50] L Arnold and M Smith, *Britain, Australia and the Bomb: The Nuclear Tests and Their Aftermath* (Palgrave MacMillan, 2006) 70–72.

[51] McClelland, Fitch and Jonas (n 24) 23.

[52] 'Atom Tests Alarm Scientists' (*Sydney Morning Herald*, 8 March 1955) 1.

[53] A Robertson, 'Alarming Revelations on Fallout' (*Tribune* (Sydney), 10 September 1958) 1.

[54] Tynan (n 16) 109.

[55] P Russo, 'Don't Fall for Atomic Lullabies' (*Argus* (Melbourne), 3 October 1956) 2.

[56] 'Give All and Now to the W.A. Natives' (*Argus* (Melbourne), 18 January 1957) 18.

[57] 'Atomic Cloud Pollutes Our Meat Country' (*Tribune* (Sydney), 10 October 1956) 1.

assurances about the "safety" of the Maralinga bomb test have been shown up as highly questionable'.[58]

Bipartisan political support for the tests also ended after Mosaic G2, with the Australian Labor Party (ALP) caucus voting in June 1956 to oppose further tests in Australia. Questions were increasingly asked in parliament questioning their safety. In May 1957, the ALP Leader of the Opposition, Herbert Evatt, observed, 'There has been a gradual change of public opinion concerning not only these tests but also the use of nuclear weapons in war', and he went on to criticise the Menzies' government in 'try[ing] to underrate the danger of the tests'.[59] Fellow ALP parliamentarian Robert Holt stressed: 'The recent and important statements which have been made on this subject by eminent nuclear scientists further emphasize the absolute urgency of the Australian Government taking a lead in banning further hydrogen bomb or atomic tests'.[60] In subsequent parliamentary sessions, questions were asked about specific risks associated with the tests. For instance, on 5 December 1957 the ALP's Edward Ward asked Minister Beale whether a 'mystery disease of epidemic proportions' that killed many Aboriginal children at a mission station in South Australia was 'attribut[able] to the effects of radio-active fall-out from atom bomb tests'.[61] Such increasing scrutiny unfortunately encouraged greater official secrecy, especially with the Vixen-B tests, which were innocuously labelled by UK authorities as 'minor trials'.

Peace activism against the nuclear arms race also emerged in the 1950s. Historian Robin Gerster argues that 'public unease at the testing never really developed into a widespread political activism', but there were shrill voices of dissent such as the Australian Peace Council established in 1949 and some trade unions, and by the late 1950s public opinion polls showed most Australians had shifted to an anti-nuclear sentiment.[62] The shift was global; for instance, the British-based Campaign for Nuclear Disarmament, led by Bertrand Russell, was launched in late 1957. Minor protests against nuclear weaponry and tests surfaced in Australia, such as small peace marches carrying 'Ban the bomb' placards, as well as some trade union opposition. The Newcastle Waterfront Group of Unions as early as 1954 declared 'such experiments would … endanger the aborigines, other civilians and animal life'.[63] By November 1957, the Melbourne Trades Hall Council had gathered 15,000 signatures for its petition opposing further atom bomb testing.[64] A 'Radial March' in 1962 involving protestors walking from Sydney's outer suburbs to the downtown was staged to signify the vast, outer reaches of devastation should

[58] ibid.
[59] Commonwealth, House of Representatives, Hansard, 15 May 1957, 1396.
[60] ibid 1386.
[61] Commonwealth House of Representatives, 'Answers to Questions', 5 December 1957, 992.
[62] R Gerster, *Hiroshima and Here: Reflections on Australian Atomic Culture* (Lexington Books, 2020) 85–86.
[63] 'Unions' Protest on Bomb Tests' (*Newcastle Sun*, 10 December 1954) 13.
[64] '"Ban the Bomb" Signs at Woomera' (*Tribune* (Sydney), 6 November 1957) 13.

the city ever be bombed. Yet, widespread anti-nuclear activism wouldn't become established in Australia until the 1970s, stirred by French testing in the South Pacific.

Aboriginal groups themselves began to agitate. In 1952 the President of the Australian Aborigines' League, Eric Onus, argued against planned bomb testing that would evict Aboriginal peoples from their homelands.[65] Henry Wardlaw, secretary of the Council for Aboriginal Rights, declared in the same year that 'atomic tests … would be the most barbarous of all the barbarous acts yet perpetrated against aborigines'.[66] The National Peace Conference held in Adelaide in October 1957 issued a statement acknowledging that the tests were causing 'Aboriginal peoples to be moved from their traditional hunting grounds … thereby seriously affecting their continued existence and exposing them to the dangers of radioactive fall-out'.[67] Minister Beale, denied the allegations.[68]

These dissenting voices were vindicated years later. Investigative journalist Brian Toohey in 1978 helped turn the tide, followed by the Commonwealth's establishment in 1984 of a public inquiry to investigate the legacies of Maralinga. It had to confront increasing scientific evidence and media scrutiny of illnesses and premature deaths of personnel involved in the atomic tests and in remote Aboriginal communities downwind of them. The Royal Commission into British Nuclear Tests in Australia was tasked with examining 'measures that were taken for protection of persons against the harmful effects of ionising radiation and dispersal of radioactive substances and toxic materials as judged against standards applicable at the time and with references to standards of today'.[69] The inquiry was led by Jim McClelland, a former Whitlam government minister and at the time he headed NSW's Land and Environment Court. Over approximately 12 months the Commission took evidence from 311 witnesses, including Aboriginal persons, scientists and military personnel, some of whom were from Great Britain. The Commission's principal recommendations were full remediation of Maralinga to allow the traditional Aboriginal owners to return, along with financial compensation to them, with such costs to be borne by Britain.

## IV. The Clean-up

The Australian and UK governments' agreement for the bomb tests included provision for clean-up afterwards, with the stipulation that the: 'United Kingdom

[65] 'Atomic Tests and Aborigines' (*Canberra Times*, 28 March 1952) 1.

[66] 'Aborigines and Atom Bomb' (*The West Australia*, 21 February 1952) 2.

[67] Quoted in 'Successful S.A. Peace Conference Declares Against Maralinga Tests' (*Tribune* (Sydney), 16 October 1957) 3.

[68] 'Maralinga Project Not Driving Aboriginals from Living, Says Beale' (*Canberra Times*, 19 January 1957) 6.

[69] Department of Resources and Energy, *Annual Report 1983–84* (Australian Government Publishing Service, 1984) 9.

Government accepts liability for such corrective measures as may be practicable in the event of radioactive contamination resulting from tests on the site'.[70] The agreement didn't detail how to conduct the clean-up.

The initial remediation was done by the British military from the mid to late 1960s with codenames such as Operation Clean-up (1963), Operation Hercules (1964) and Operation Brumby (1967). Contaminated building materials and vehicles were scrubbed, and discarded material buried in shallow pits. The clean-up of ground contaminated with plutonium included diluting the radioactive material by mixing and turning the soil and burying weapon fragments in concrete-covered holes. Surveys were conducted to assess any residual health risks, and areas identified as too hazardous were fenced off. Whilst the Maralinga site was the focus, Emu Field also received some attention, albeit of a cursory nature. The Monte Bello islands were not remediated until much later.

The clean-up effort was detailed in the Pearce Report, which for some years was assumed by authorities to be the final word on the adequacy of the remediation, but it was not made publicly available for independent scrutiny. Its author, Noah Pearce, worked for the UK Ministry of Supply's Atomic Weapons Research Establishment and oversaw the remediations in 1964 and 1967. The latter entity largely rubber-stamped the clean-up plan, evidently giving little thought to the risks to Aboriginal people. A report from the Maralinga Rehabilitation Technical Advisory Committee in 2003 concluded the efforts in the 1960s failed to rehabilitate the contaminated sites to a standard necessary for the protection of people and the environment, with hazardous radioactivity persisting in many areas.[71]

The Commonwealth nonetheless accepted the adequacy of the clean-up operation in an agreement signed with Great Britain on 23 September 1968, which released the UK 'from all liabilities and responsibilities'. The federal Department of Defence retained control of the former test sites. The agreement did not cover the Monte Bello islands, which underwent some remediation in 1979 by the Royal Australian Engineers, who found radioactive steel debris from the UK frigate the HMS *Plym* that had been detonated in one of the tests.

The shoddiness of the clean-up wouldn't become fully apparent until the Royal Commission in 1984. The majority of its recommendations related to the rehabilitation of the test sites, finding that the previous clean-up was 'based on wrong assumptions. It was planned in haste to meet political deadlines'.[72] Further, the Commission found 'the operation of ploughing and disc-harrowing was the wrong

[70] Clause 12, Memorandum of Arrangements of 7 March 1956 between the Government of the United Kingdom of Great Britain and Northern Ireland and the Government of Australia concerning the Atomic Weapons Proving Ground at Maralinga, 7 March 1956.

[71] Maralinga Rehabilitation Technical Advisory Committee, *Rehabilitation of Former Nuclear Test Sites at Emu and Maralinga* (Australia) (Department of Education, Science and Training, 2003).

[72] McClelland, Fitch and Jonas (n 24) 24.

procedure to control the radiological hazard' and 'large numbers of plutonium-contaminated fragments' were not remediated.[73] The biggest danger was posed by the plutonium residue from the Vixen tests, with Aboriginal people particularly vulnerable, such as their children digging and playing in the soil, or ingesting bush foods.

The Royal Commission's principal recommendation for much more extensive remediation, to be paid for by Britain, was rejected by the UK government either on the basis that no material health risks remained at the test sites or that it was no longer its responsibility owing to the 1968 agreement with Australia. Commonwealth negotiators cited evidence of British deceit, hiding important details about the tests and the resulting contamination. The UK government eventually paid £20 million (then about A$45 million), less than half the total $108 million estimated cost of the further clean-up needed. Further remediations were undertaken between 1995 and 2005, with the costs shared between Britain and Australia. By 2000 all but 120 km$^2$ of some 3200 km$^2$ of the former tests area had been remediated sufficiently, according to authorities, to allow Aboriginal people to return.

## V. Aftermath

The 1984–85 Royal Commission was the culmination of growing public unease and media scrutiny about who and what was affected by the bomb tests in the South Australian desert and on the Monte Bello islands. A more assertive, questioning media facilitated the shift, along with Aboriginal peoples themselves seeking land rights and compensation. Also relevant were the French nuclear weapons testing in the South Pacific during the 1970s and 1980s, which kept the issue alive and heightened public anxiety in Australia. Reports of ex-servicemen dying prematurely of cancer added to the public unease and resulting political pressure. Demands for a Royal Commission to get to the bottom of what happened began to surface in the 1970s, especially when journalist Brian Toohey, receiving a leaked federal Cabinet document, exposed Maralinga's toxic legacies in a story published on 5 October 1978.[74] His exposé also questioned whether Australia was compliant with the International Atomic Energy Agency's protocols for storage and safety of radioactive materials and the risk that terrorists might be able to retrieve some of the buried plutonium.

The saga has quietened, but might not be closed permanently. Some scientists still doubt the adequacy of the last clean-up operation. The nuclear engineer Alan Parkinson, who the chief adviser appointed for the Maralinga clean-up in the 1990s, was later sacked owing to his questioning the operation and cost-cutting.

[73] ibid.

[74] B Toohey, 'Killen Warns on Plutonium Pile' (*Australian Financial Review*, 5 October 1978) 1, 6.

Parkinson suggested the 'clean-up' was more akin to a 'cover-up' of cost-cutting short cuts such as dumping radioactive waste into shallow pits.[75] The official plan was to collect contaminated soil and bury it in deep trenches, and subject the debris to a process of *in situ* vitrification, which effectively turns the material into glass. The vitrification was aborted before completion owing to a fire, with the remaining trenches covered in concrete. Parkinson suggests that only 2 $km^2$ or less than 1 per cent of the contaminated land was adequately remediated. A cursory inspection might corroborate his scepticism, as even over 60 years since the major mushroom cloud blasts, the vegetation remains cleared within a one-kilometre radius, though kangaroos and other wildlife have started to return.

Long-lasting impacts on the Aboriginal community likely persist, as the McClelland Commission examined. Its findings included that the 'traditional owners of the Maralinga lands were denied effective access to these lands for over thirty years as a result of the British nuclear test programme. This denial bas contributed to their emotional, social and material distress and deprivation'.[76] The Commission recommended that financial compensation, which it believed would enable them 'to re-establish their links with the land as rapidly as possible and with as little hardship as possible'.[77] In 1995, the Commonwealth reached a compensation settlement, paying $13.5 million. In addition, in November 2009 it formally returned most of the Maralinga area to its traditional owners, now deemed safe to 'walk, camp, build and hunt'.[78] They now hold title to the Maralinga and Emu Field lands, totalling some 105,000 $km^2$ under South Australia's Maralinga Tjarutja Land Rights Act 1984.

Another simmering legacy is the health of the military personnel and their offspring. Many nuclear veterans have struggled for recognition that their maladies are owing to radioactive contamination, with only a minority receiving hard-fought compensation, often through resort to the courts. Some 35,000 servicemen participated in the tests, most wearing little more than shorts and sandals whilst only those considered to be at heightened risk received protective clothing. A study published in 1999 of the health outcomes of a sample of 2,500 nuclear servicemen found 30 per cent had already died, mostly in their fifties, and two-thirds of the deaths were due to cancers.[79]

The McClelland Commission concluded that their illnesses and diseases could not be discounted, and that the tests 'increased the risk of cancer to those participants who were exposed to radiation'.[80] Adding to their health burden,

[75] A Parkinson, *Maralinga: Australia's Nuclear Waste Cover-up* (ABC Books, 2007).

[76] McClelland, Fitch and Jonas (n 24) 28.

[77] ibid 29.

[78] 'Going Home to an Atomic Test Site' (*Sydney Morning Herald*, 30 January 2010).

[79] S Roff and D Holdstock, 'Mortality and Morbidity of Members of the British Nuclear Tests Veterans Association and the New Zealand Nuclear Tests Veterans Association and their Families' (1999) 15(Supp) *Medicine, Conflict and Survival* 1.

[80] McClelland, Fitch and Jonas (n 24) 347.

recent evidence suggests an unusually high number of children and grandchildren of ex-serviceman have severe deformities including Down syndrome and cerebral palsy.[81] A class action lawsuit brought for over 1,500 British and Australian veterans was unsuccessful after the UK Supreme Court ruled that because 60 years had passed it wouldn't be possible to prove the causes of their illnesses.

The nuclear weapons tests on Australian soil were the nadir for an era of limited environmental and public accountability 'before environmental law'. A swathe of the Outback was contaminated with long-lasting radioactive residues, and Aboriginal people were treated disdainfully. This case study exemplifies the worst connotations of nation-building and enlightened despotism, in which social justice and environmental caution were given just cursory recognition by lawmakers. Egregiously, scientific progress and a cult of expertise was used to stifle dissent and justify secrecy. Whilst today many look for national leadership using the best scientific knowledge to improve environmental decisions, the atomic bomb tests show how easily the same ingredients can cause much injury in the absence of the effective checks and balances of democratic governance. On the other hand, the establishment of the McClelland Royal Commission in 1984 exemplifies the power of polyarchal institutions in the form of the public inquiry to bring badly needed accountability, and whilst the Commission came too late to intervene, it at last enabled some justice to mitigate some of the legacies of the bomb tests.

[81] M Palin, 'New Generations of Australian Families Suffering Deformities and Early Deaths Because of "Genetic Transfer"' (News.com.au, 10 March 2016).

# PART III

# Defending a Continent

# 8

# The Furry and Feathered

## I. Valuing Wildlife

The struggle to defend Australia's natural heritage achieved some breakthroughs in the early twentieth century with the passage of bespoke laws to conserve wildlife. Whilst native species weren't all considered of equal value, over time the beneficiaries of conservation grew and their protection improved. This chapter tells the story. The first two sections trace the growing public appreciation of native wildlife, through the media and the curatorial practices of natural history museums, zoos and botanic gardens, along with concerns about animal cruelty. The legal analysis thereafter begins with reforms adopted in the states, and later the Commonwealth, in the first half of the twentieth century. The final two sections cover the second wave of wildlife conservation law, with comprehensive controls after World War II and even concerted efforts to save threatened species by translocation of populations to safe havens. The role of Aboriginal people as the continent's most experienced wildlife managers was ignored by lawmakers, however. Law reform was incremental and haphazard without proven blueprints to work from, and the advocates for change were outside the law profession, such as naturalists and bushwalking groups.

The motif of this chapter is that *beauty* leveraged the greatest law reform, favouring the most charismatic fauna and flora for protection, as likewise did laws conserving the most scenic landscapes (in the following chapter). This aesthetic turn was not codified in law, as beauty has an amorphous value that environmental law still struggles to formulate into standards,[1] but nonetheless it mattered, and was curated and shaped by several factors. Song birds, flowering plants and cuddly marsupials increasingly endeared Australians as writers and artists depicted them. This vicarious appreciation of the natural world was especially valuable for city dwellers remote from the untrammelled outdoors. The public's opportunities to roam outdoors increased when more leisure time ensued from adoption of the eight-hour working day and holiday leave, combined with easier transportation offered by trains and, later, motor vehicles (such transportation unfortunately also made it easier for poachers and traders in protected species).[2]

[1] BJ Richardson, *The Art of Environmental Law: Governing with Aesthetics* (Hart Publishing, 2019).
[2] 'Flower Destruction. Council Takes Action' (*Sun* (Sydney), 12 November 1916) 4.

Another influence on the law was emergent patriotism, expressed in coats of arms, flags, coinage and stamps that referenced native wildlife. Unlike earlier generations' trepidations of the bush as an alien or even forbidding world, even if mythologised as a place for building individuals' character, Australians in the twentieth century increasingly admired their continent and its fauna as sources of national pride and cultural fraternity. This nationalistic biophilia was nurtured by art and literature. The Heidelberg school of impressionist painters was influential in the lead-up to Federation in celebrating Australia's landscapes in a new perspective that relied less on European-like scenes. Involving painters such as Charles Conder, Arthur Streeton and Jane Sutherland working in the *en plein air* mode, the movement nourished the shifting perception of the continent's landscapes as a virtuous realm worthy of protection. The declaration of a 'Wattle Day' and 'Arbor Day' in the years following Federation harnessed this growing affection for Australian nature. However, Aboriginal people were not generally celebrated members of Australia's endowment in this era.[3]

The beauty of Australian wildlife could equally motivate hunting for their feathers or furs. During the NSW legislature's debates in 1918 over the Birds and Animals Protection Bill, one parliamentarian remarked: 'Not so many years ago many of our mountain valleys echoed to the liquid note of the lyre bird … a perfect feast of bird music, but today the same country is silent wilderness'.[4] From newspaper stories to learned societies' meetings, anxiety was increasingly voiced regarding gratuitous destruction of wildlife for fashion or sport.[5] The press frequently carried readers' letters expressing dismay, especially regarding harm to charismatic species such as koalas. Such sentiment was far from universal, however; South Australia's Act for the Protection of Birds 1900 was opposed by some because the 'closed season would interfere with Christmas holiday shooting and that the regulation of guns would deprive men of their livelihood'.[6]

Another, pragmatic case for wildlife conservation was farmers' recognition that *some* fauna could help control pest insects, rodents or reptiles. During a parliamentary debate in 1921 about Queensland's Bill to Protect Animals and Birds, the Secretary for Agriculture warned that 'nature's laws cannot be disobeyed with impunity', and he was 'sad to realise how bird life had been destroyed' by short-sighted practices that failed to recognise their economic value.[7] He cautioned

[3] On Aboriginal representation in John Glover's paintings, who preceded the Heidelberg school, see the interpretation by T Bonyhady and G Lehman, *The National Picture: The Art of Tasmania's Black War* (Tasmanian Museum and Art Gallery, 2018).

[4] PF Loughlin, NSW Legislative Assembly, Hansard, 15 August 1918, 833.

[5] J Barrett, *Save Australia: A Plea for the Right Use of our Flora and Fauna* (Macmillan, 1925).

[6] BC Newland, 'From Game Laws to Fauna Protection Acts in South Australia: The Evolution of an Attitude' (1961) 23 *South Australian Ornithologist* 52, 57.

[7] N Gillies, 'Animals and Birds Bill', Queensland, Legislative Assembly, Hansard, 9 September 1921, 658.

'we should not pass the death sentence on any bird until we are satisfied it is not doing useful work in the way of keeping down insect pests'.[8] Such views resonated with many. The *Cairns Post* in 1926 declared 'these ornithological specimens are friends of the sugar farmers, as they visit the fields and eat the grubs, etc, which attack the cane'.[9] Of course, such a utilitarian mentality also meant wildlife that farmers perceived as foes faced persecution, as chapter five examined. Thus, wildlife management law evolved in a dyadic fashion with some species classified as vermin, such as kangaroos, wombats and raptors, whilst some species of aesthetic and recreational value enjoyed protection.

There was also public distaste regarding cruelty to wild animals, especially the leg traps that condemned the unwary to an agonising death. Australian animal welfare law originated in British precedents. Kathryn Shevelow's account of this history identifies the world's first anti-cruelty law as the Act to Prevent the Cruel and Improper Treatment of Cattle,[10] passed by Westminster in 1822. It defied considerable opposition in a society where blood sports such as animal baiting, cockfighting and bull running were valorised for 'increase[ing] the vigor and manhood of Englishmen',[11] and a legal system that deemed animals mere chattels.[12] The motivations of law reformers were diverse, but Shevelow identified the growing popularity of household pets, making it 'increasingly difficult to think of animals as soulless machines or irrational bundles of appetites'.[13] The British law was soon followed by the founding of the Society for the Prevention of Cruelty to Animals in 1824. In Australia, the colony of NSW adopted bespoke animal protection legislation in 1850,[14] whilst the other colonies tended to include such provisions in police offences legislation, and societies to campaign against animal cruelty were established in tandem. Historian Steve White identifies a milestone in the evolution of such laws around Federation, when anti-cruelty measures began to extend to wild fauna, a shift associated with 'transforming an understanding of (some) native animals from "vermin" to "cute creatures" worthy of protection'.[15]

## II. Nature Museums, Zoos and Gardens

Wildlife governance cannot ignore the seminal role of institutions such as natural history museums and their scientists, often publicly funded, in shaping public attitudes and practices. The scientific community took a stance informing the

[8] ibid.
[9] 'Slaying the Birds' (*Cairns Post*, 2 July 1926) 5.
[10] The statute is reproduced in K Shevelow, *For the Love of Animals: The Rise of the Animal Protection Movement* (Henry Holt, 2008) 285–88.
[11] ibid 202–03.
[12] ibid 204.
[13] ibid 58.
[14] Act for the More Effectual Prevention of Cruelty to Animals 1850.
[15] S White, 'Animal Protection Law in Australia: Bound by History' in D Cao and S White (eds), *Animal Law and Welfare – International Perspectives* (Springer, 2016) 109, 123.

public and lawmakers about the distinctive values of the continent's endemic fauna and flora. The popularisation of natural history was advanced through organisations such as the Field Naturalists Club of Victoria (established in 1880), the Natural History Association of NSW (founded in 1887) and the Royal Australian Ornithologists' Union (created in 1901), whose importance was discussed in chapter two. They and other groups increasingly lobbied for laws to safeguard the wildlife they studied or cherished, and they engaged the wider public through natural history museums and zoos that offered not merely spectacle but education. Growing enclaves of natural scientists in Australian universities also contributed to this cultural shift. The collecting and curatorial practices of colonial-era natural history museums and affiliated bodies have been construed by historians such as Jack Ashby and Rebecca Machin as instruments of imperial power and mastery of nature,[16] as well as scientific racism in their ethnographic collections such as presentation of Aboriginal remains and relics, suggest Subhadra Das and Miranda Lowe.[17] Other scholars, such as Annie Coombes and Ruth Phillips, have also identified important shifts in recent times in these cathedrals of natural science that aid decolonisation by offering revisionist narratives and critical self-reflection on the foregoing ideologies and practices.[18]

Paralleling developments in Europe and North America traced by historian Susan Sheets-Pyenson,[19] natural history museums, as well as zoos and botanic gardens, were established in Australian colonies during the nineteenth century.[20] The first museum devoted to the country's natural history was the Australian Museum, established in 1827 in Sydney. The other colonies followed over the remainder of the nineteenth century but the Commonwealth's plans for its own collection, as envisioned by the Zoological Museum Agreement Act 1924, didn't materialise (like much of Canberra's stalled development). Museums offered a sanitised view of Australian nature that rarely acknowledged the exploitative side of the settlers' colonisation of the continent. Their acquisitive role itself, accumulating fauna skins and skeletons, has drawn comparisons with trophy hunting.[21] They invested in artistically created taxidermy and dioramas to bring to 'life' their specimens, with the Australian Museum installing dioramas from the early 1920s. This mission favoured the big, rare or bizarre – representing just a modicum of biodiversity. That bias began to change, thanks to efforts of the likes of Joyce Allan

[16] J Ashby and R Machin, 'Legacies of Colonial Violence in Natural History Collections' (2021) 8 *Journal of Nature Science Collections* 44.

[17] S Das and M Lowe, 'Nature Read in Black and White: Decolonial Approaches to Interpreting Natural History Collections' (2018) 6 *Journal of Nature Science Collections* 4.

[18] AE Coombes and RB Phillips, *Museum Transformations: Decolonization and Democratization* (Wiley, 2020).

[19] S Sheets-Pyenson, *Cathedrals of Science: The Development of Colonial Natural History Museums During the Late Nineteenth Century* (McGill-Queen's University Press, 1988).

[20] C Healy *From the Ruins of Colonialism: History as Social Memory* (Cambridge University Press, 1997) 86.

[21] L Robin, *How a Continent Created a Nation* (NewSouth Books, 2007) 77.

(depicted in Figure 8.1), a conchologist and illustrator who improved museum displays of invertebrates and other, lesser-known biota.

The Aboriginal people was also originally just as white-washed, where Aboriginal relics and body parts were sometimes displayed for public curiosity; one notorious example was Truganini, the supposedly last, full-blood Aboriginal from Tasmania who died in 1876. Her body was desecrated by the Royal Society of Tasmania, which had her body exhumed, and from 1904 to 1947 her skeleton was displayed in the Tasmanian Museum in Hobart.[22] Such practices were not uncommon, as explored by Paul Turnbull's history of the science of collecting.[23] Tom Griffiths contends this ethnographic curiosity in Aboriginal Australians was an extension of interest in nature rather than interest in their culture, a feature of the continent's 'natural history'.[24]

**Figure 8.1** Joyce Allan arranging bugs for the Australian Museum, 1933; National Library of Australia

[22] A Kühnast, 'The Utilization of Truganini's Human Remains in Colonial Tasmania' (2012) 39(1) *History of Anthropology Newsletter*, article 3: repository.upenn.edu/han/vol39/iss1/3.

[23] P Turnbull, *Science, Museums and Collecting the Indigenous Dead in Colonial Australia* (Springer, 2017).

[24] T Griffiths, *Hunters and Collectors: The Antiquarian Movement in Australia* (Cambridge University Press, 1996) 26.

Natural history museums gradually began to acknowledge the darker side of Australian settler history, and one means was their publications. From 1921 the Australian Museum launched a magazine, described in its inaugural edition as 'intended mainly for those who have no special knowledge … [and] will be written. so far as possible, in non-technical language'.[25] It gave a voice to nature conservation; one essay in 1921 by a curator from the American Museum of Natural History condemned the slaughter of Australian fauna: 'who would not rather see one kangaroo bounding tremendously over the plain than a hundred kangaroo skeletons or skins in a museum'.[26] In 1927 the magazine voiced 'keen regret' at the 'deplorable' hunting of koalas in Queensland.[27]

Zoos provided another outlet for the general public to engage with native wildlife, along with impressive exotic fauna. Like natural history museums, zoos could offer a highly distorted and problematic view of wildlife, many suffering wretched lives in cramped, concrete-floored cages. Film footage of a Tasmanian thylacine in a Hobart zoo in 1933, taken by zoologist David Fleay, shows a doomed creature pacing forlornly, an animal which died three years later of exposure after being locked out of his shelter overnight.[28] Melbourne Zoo, Australia's oldest, was established in 1857.[29] The most famous menagerie is arguably Sydney's Taronga Zoo, which opened in 1916 as a successor to the small collection established by the Zoological Society of NSW in 1884.

Some zoos consciously tried to challenge the status quo. One was Tasmania's Beaumaris Zoo, a private collection opened by Mary Roberts in 1895 at her spacious property in Hobart. She specialised in Tasmanian fauna, including the thylacine, quolls and devils that in her day were outlawed pests. Roberts was the first to breed Tasmanian devils in captivity, among many breeding successes she had, and sent their offspring to other zoos.[30] Her collection was popular with parties of school children, and even the Tasmanian Governor once visited.[31] Roberts also occasionally gave public lectures where she admonished authorities to do better; in 1918 she pleaded for 'the Royal Society of Tasmania bring to the urgent notice of the Government the urgent need for the better protection of native fauna, and the need for an amendment of the Game Protection Act'.[32] After her death in 1921, the Beaumaris collection was transferred to a zoo opened by the Hobart City Council, where the last thylacine died. In its final months the zoo was in a dishevelled state, described by one (rare) visitor as 'numerous empty cages [being]

[25] Editorial, 'The Objects of the Australian Museum Magazine' (1921) 1(1) *Australian Museum Magazine* 3, 3.

[26] WK Gregory, 'Australian Mammals and Why They Should be Protected' (1921) 1(3) *Australian Museum Magazine* 65, 73.

[27] Editorial, (1927) 3(4) *Australian Museum Magazine* 112.

[28] B Dibley, 'Capturing Spectral Beasts' (2020) 67 *Australian Humanities Review* 32.

[29] C de Courcy, *Evolution of a Zoo: History of Melbourne Zoo 1857–1900* (Quiddlers Press, 2003).

[30] 'Beaumaris Zoo' (*Mercury* (Hobart), 31 October 1910) 7.

[31] 'Beaumaris Zoo. The Governor on Treatment of Animals' (*Mercury* (Hobart), 6 March 1911) 2.

[32] 'The Royal Society. Protection of the Fauna of Tasmania' (*Mercury* (Hobart), 10 September 1918) 3.

about the most cheerful things there'.[33] It's no wonder that that Tasmania's Animals and Birds Protection Board in early 1937 refused permission for the Hobart City Council to attempt to acquire a wild thylacine to replenish the zoo's collection.

**Figure 8.2** Entrance to Hobart's former Beaumaris zoo, 2021, photograph by author

Although Australian zoos in the first half of the twentieth century catered primarily for public amusement, some like Roberts' one had the early markers of serious scientific and educational endeavours that could aid conservation. Another pioneer was zoologist David Fleay (1907–93), whose illustrious career began in Victoria.[34] In 1934 he was appointed by Melbourne Zoo to oversee its new Australian fauna collection, where he successfully bred a variety of birds and marsupials. He hoped to have done the same for the thylacine had he been able to collect a breeding pair during his searches in Tasmania in the 1940s. After a fallout with the Melbourne Zoo management, in 1937 Fleay became director of a wildlife sanctuary at Healesville, where he bred in captivity the first platypus. Fleay also engaged the public through radio broadcasts and newspaper writings, as well as penning essays and books such as *Gliders of the Gum Trees* (1947) and *Talking of Animals* (1956). After the Victorian government restricted private zoos, in 1951 Fleay moved to Queensland's Gold Coast where he opened a fauna reserve.

[33] 'Beaumaris Zoo: Unsatisfactory Conditions' (*Mercury* (Hobart), 13 March 1937) 14.

[34] See R Fleay-Thomson, *Animals First: The Story of Pioneer Australian Conservationist and Zoologist Dr David Fleay* (Petaurus Publishing, 2007).

He had a number of further firsts here, including breeding the powerful owl and wedge-tailed eagle. He earned much admiration, including an invitation to show his wildlife to the visiting Queen of England and Duke of Edinburgh in 1954.[35]

In many ways Fleay was out of step with, or ahead of, public opinion. Unfashionably, he denounced the hunting of wedge-tailed eagles and native rodents, arguing they assisted farmers by controlling rabbits and insects respectively.[36] Fleay also called for more wildlife sanctuaries and 'uniform game laws applied throughout Australia'.[37] He also voiced opposition to dichlorodiphenyltrichloroethane (DDT) and other pesticides that his research identified as harmful to platypuses. In 1962 he co-founded the Wildlife Preservation Society of Queensland, which would later fight against sand-mining and canal estates.

Like museums and zoos, botanic gardens also evolved to become more aligned with nature conservation, including propagation of native species, public education and academic study of horticulture, landscape gardening and other plant-related disciplines. Small botanic gardens in Australia were first established in the early nineteenth century in Sydney (1816) and Hobart (1818), and by Federation the country had 30. Today about 150 gardens are managed by public or private bodies.

Some botanic gardens had little affinity with Australian nature. Apart from favouring exotic plantings, their tidy aesthetics of closely trimmed lawns, clipped shrubs and pebbled paths, with a gentle summer jazz concert, were far removed from the rugged and remote aura of the Australian bush. Many gardens also paraded monuments to the British empire such as statutes of Royalty, World War canons and heroic explorers – but no acknowledgement of the continent's Aboriginal people. Changes to this mindset emerged, including the National Botanic Gardens established in Canberra in 1949 and devoted to showcasing native plants including species threatened in the wild. Another pioneer is this mould was Perth's Kings Park Botanic Garden, which in 1965 opened with a focus on Western Australian flora.

## III. Tentative Law Reforms

Wildlife conservation gained a tentative footing in Australia in the second half of the nineteenth century. The first generation of laws were enacted in Tasmania in 1860,[38] Victoria in 1862,[39] Queensland in 1863,[40] South Australia in 1864[41] and

[35] 'Queen Sees Native Animals, 2 Snakes' (*Daily Telegraph* (Sydney), 17 March 1954) 7.

[36] 'Wedgetail Eagle and Fat-tailed Mouse. Should Not be Killed' (*Argus* (Melbourne), 15 January 1936) 10.

[37] 'Some Animals "Dying Out"' (*News* (Adelaide), 3 March 1949) 2.

[38] Act to Provide for the Preservation of Native Game During the Breeding Season, 1860.

[39] Act to Provide for the Preservation of Imported Game, and During the Breeding Season, of Native Game, 1862.

[40] Act to Provide for the Protection of Imported Game, 1863.

[41] Act to Prevent the Wanton Destruction of Certain Wild and Acclimatized Animals, 1864.

NSW in 1866,[42] in which conservation served primarily to ensure the availability of hunters' quarry, especially imported game such as grouse, pheasants and other creatures that attracted gun-toting sportsmen and women. The first tranche of wildlife legislation usurped common law entitlements of landowners to take wildlife found on their properties,[43] by restricting when, where and how hunting could occur. The protection varied according to the species: some native birds enjoyed ongoing protection, primarily because of their beauty or pest-control benefits, whilst some animals were fair game anytime, anywhere.

More concerted efforts unfolded in the early twentieth century, although gaps and weaknesses in the law continued. Despite their enlightened titles, commonly the 'Birds and Animals Protection Act', these statutes didn't offer unadulterated protection. Their schedules differentiated species into the wholly protected, partly protected or unprotected, with licensing regimes for taking available species. Collecting specimens in the name of science also came under regulators' purview.[44] Interestingly, and unusual for an era of profound racism, this legislation sometimes explicitly allowed Aboriginal people to hunt, without a licence, for sustenance.[45]

Another characteristic of early wildlife regulation was its tenuous links to the science of conservation biology. Decisions about the listing or categorisation of species tended to reflect anecdotal observations or extraneous economic factors rather than careful scientific appraisal of species' conservation status. Furthermore, wildlife management generally occurred with little appreciation of species' habitat needs or of threats such as invasive species or pollution. Active programmes for recovery of threatened species or restoration of degraded environments were also lacking, other than translocation programmes for a few iconic species such as koalas and lyrebirds (a story told later in this chapter).

Designated 'vermin', as discussed in chapter five, were usually managed via separate legislation whilst wildlife conservation laws worked in tandem by excluding such animals from their oversight. Fauna protection laws of this era excluded many species, especially the ugly or dangerous. Snakes, unsurprisingly, were wholly unprotected virtually everywhere, including in most national parks, though curiously snake performers were popular entertainment for the public. Wildlife legislation also excluded species considered foes of farmers.[46] Consider NSW's Birds and Animals Protection Act 1918, which excluded the following animals (not including a similarly lengthy list of birds): rabbit, dingo, fox, fruit bat or flying fox, tiger cat, native cat, common kangaroo rat, Gaimard's

[42] Act to Provide for the Preservation of Imported Game and During the Breeding Season of Native Game, 1866.

[43] G Shyam, 'Is the Classification of Animals as Property Consistent with Modern Community Attitudes?' (2018) 41(4) *UNSW Law Journal* 1418, 1421.

[44] 'To Save Nature. Greater Public Interest Vital' (*Register* (Adelaide), 19 August 1921) 7.

[45] See eg South Australia's Act for the Protection of Birds 1900, s 4(g).

[46] Although curiously, NSW's Native Animals Protection Act 1903 prevailed over the Pastures Protection Act 1902, which contrariwise encouraged the destruction of any native fauna considered adverse to agriculture.

kangaroo rat, rufous kangaroo rat, hare wallaby, nail-tailed wallaby, white-throated wallaby, paddymelon, red-legged wallaby, black-stripped wallaby, wombat, long-nosed bandicoot, common bandicoot, and rabbit bandicoot (original spelling in the Act).[47] Some of these species are now extinct (eg the (eastern) hare wallaby) or severely depleted (eg tiger and native cats, known today as spotted-tail quoll and eastern quoll).

Some species benefited just from restricted hunting seasons designed to protect their breeding cycles and allow for periodic population recovery, such as NSW's Birds Protection Act 1901 which protected birds during an annual closed season from 1 August to 31 January. Yet unscrupulous hunters might keep active during the closed season and then simply claim that their quarry was bagged during the open months. This loophole probably also explains why in Queensland (with a similar law) five million possum skins were officially sold within a very short, two-month season in 1936.[48]

Hunting was by no means the only threat to native wildlife, yet law makers mostly ignored the wider perils. One growing menace was invasive species such as foxes, rabbits and feral cats; some of these invaders were subject to separate vermin control, albeit designed to assist agriculture rather than conserve native species. Interestingly, Prime Minister Billy Hughes' list of national research problems drawn up at a science and industry conference he convened in 1916 began with environmental pests such as prickly pear and rabbits.[49] The impact of feral cats was already being publicly discussed in this era, judging by newspaper accounts.[50]

The red fox (*Vulpes vulpes*) is southern Australia's worst invader. Introduced for game hunting in the mid-nineteenth century, it swarmed across the country from the 1870s after successful releases in Victoria near Ballart and Werribee Park. Historian Eric Rolls describes pastoralist Thomas Chirnside, responsible for the latter release, as a settler who 'tried to build a little England – with red deer and fallow deer, coursing, hunting, horse-racing and foxes'.[51] The omnivore feeds indiscriminately on small animals and by foraging on plants it spreads weeds. It didn't take long for authorities and landowners to realise the disaster that had been unleashed. From the 1880s newspapers increasingly shared correspondence about foxes' depredations. The *Ballarat Star* decried that 'if an effort is not made soon to cope with this growing evil, foxes will become as troublesome and as costly and difficult to exterminate as are the rabbits'.[52] Distressed landowners in the

[47] Second schedule of the Birds and Animals Protection Act 1918.

[48] Cited in B J Stubbs, 'From "Useless Brutes" to National Treasures: A Century of Evolving Attitudes Towards Native Fauna in New South Wales, 1860s to 1960s' (2001) 7(1) *Environment and History* 23, 45.

[49] 'Science and Industry. Prime Minister's Conference' (*Argus* (Melbourne), 6 January 1916) 8.

[50] 'Cats and Birds' (*Bundaberg Mail and Burnett Advertiser*, 16 August 1913) 6; Cats Versus Birds' (*Argus* (Melbourne), 16 August 1913) 8.

[51] E Rolls, *They All Ran Wild: The Animals and Plants that Plague Australia* (Angus and Robertson, 1969) 397.

[52] 'Foxes in Leighshire' (*Ballarat Star*, 22 May 1888) 4.

early 1880s began offering private bounties,[53] and in 1886 the Victorian Minister of Lands unveiled a government-paid bounty.[54] It was to no avail; by 1903 foxes had reached northern NSW, by 1905 they were in southern Queensland, as well as across much of South Australia, and in the 1920s they entered Western Australia. Only the far tropical north, with its unfavourable ecology, would ultimately remain fox-free, though it would later succumb to the cane toad. Today Australia has an estimated 1.7 million foxes, killing about 300 million native birds, mammals and reptiles annually.[55]

Wildlife legislation of this era was also typically blind to the habitat needs of protected species. Illustratively, Queensland's Animals and Birds Act 1921 defined the prohibited behaviour as: 'the hunting, shooting, destroying, poisoning, netting, snaring, spearing, pursuing, taking, disturbing, or injuring of any animal or bird, or the off- spring, young, or eggs thereof'.[56] Yet destruction or pollution of their habitat was outside the purview of Queensland's law. Other states' wildlife regulations of this era suffered similarly.[57] This gap in the law was critical, for land clearance has been one of the defining tropes of vanishing Australia, as documented in chapter four. The loss of native vegetation remains an ongoing problem in some areas of Australia.

Protection of native flora didn't go wholly unnoticed by lawmakers, but their focus was on the beautiful or rare rather than conserving ecosystems. The need for bespoke laws to protect highly coveted native plants was however justified. One complaint in 1918 about NSW's situation revealed: 'Sydney flower stalls and vendors at certain railway stations levy heavy toll of the flowering shrubs and trees of the State'.[58] The first ameliorating statutes were parsimonious. Western Australia's two-page Native Flora Protection Act adopted in 1912 covered just nine species, and only controlled their picking on Crown lands. In 1936 Western Australia's Premier personally announced more listed protected plants, with the press reporting favourably,[59] and the 1912 legislation was amended to cover private land albeit only against trespassers picking plants. Queensland's Native Plants Protection Act 1930 was similarly flawed, allowing landowners to do as they wished on their own estates. The selling of protected plants without lawful permission was penalised, however. Honorary rangers policed compliance, but being volunteers their commitment wasn't reliable. Similar governance regimes were provided by NSW's Wild Flowers and Native Plants Protection Act 1927, Victoria's Wild Flowers and Native Plants Protection Act 1930, Queensland's Native Plants

[53] 'The Fox Nuisance' (*Geelong Advertiser*, 15 June 1881) 3.

[54] 'Telegraphic Intelligence' (*Horsham Times*, 21 September 1886) 3.

[55] J Dielenberg, '1.7 Million Foxes, 300 Million Native Animals Killed Every Year' (*The Conversation*, 16 March 2022) theconversation.com.

[56] Section 2.

[57] See eg NSW's Birds and Animals Protection Act 1918, s 6(2).

[58] 'Our Fauna and Flora' (*Voice of the North*, 10 August 1922) 5.

[59] 'Guarding the Bush. List of Protected Flowers. Premier Appeals to the Public' (*Western Australian*, 23 September 1936) 21.

Protection Act 1930, and South Australia's Native Plants Protection Act 1939. Forestry legislation (see chapter eleven) suffered from a similar lacuna, in that controls on cutting trees tended to be confined to Crown lands, leaving freehold owners at liberty to do what they wanted.[60]

## IV. The Commonwealth Gets Involved

Although the Commonwealth possessed constitutional powers to intervene in environmental matters, as discussed in chapter two, it did so warily before the 1970s. The first major controversy it addressed was the international trade in fauna and their parts, following public pressure to curb the rapacious trade.

Facilitated by the tendrils of imperial empires, the global fashion and trophy collecting business levied a heavy burden on wildlife with alluring feathers, furs, skins, horns or tusks. The millinery industry, based in London, Paris and New York, expanded as traders' access to exotic feathers improved, reaching its apotheosis just before World War I.[61] Fashionable women flaunted hats adorned with not merely feathers but bird wings and even entire taxidermied specimens. Australia was a major supplier to the grisly trade; British bird protectionist James Buckland recorded in 1911 that 'over 400 lyre-birds were killed in one district in a single season to supply the London plumage market'.[62] Live specimens were also poached to appease pet lovers.[63] The Victorian-era penchant for souveniring eggs and feathers, and creating taxidermy trophies for natural history museums, was also responsible.[64]

Lawmakers worldwide began to protect birds and curb the trade. An International Convention for the Protection of Birds Useful to Agriculture was adopted by European governments in 1902. A British law proposed in 1908 to restrict commerce in bird feathers, dubbed the Plumage Bill, also generated much publicity, and although not enacted until 1921,[65] it emboldened reformists in other countries. The Australian media reported on the trade in increasingly critical language, blazing headlines of 'Spare the Birds'[66] and 'Birds Slaughtered

[60] See eg Tasmania's Forestry Act 1920, s 45.

[61] WT Hornaday, *Our Vanishing Wildlife: Its Extermination and Preservation* (Charles Scribner's Sons, 1913).

[62] J Buckland, *Pros and Cons of the Plumage Bill* (Racquet Court Press, 1911) 13.

[63] J Simons, 'The Scramble for Elephants: Exotic Animals and the Imperial Trade' in M Boyde (ed), *Captured: The Animal Within Culture* (Palgrave Macmillan, 2014) 26, 34.

[64] ST Asma, *Stuffed Animals and Pickled Heads: The Culture and Evolution of Natural History Museums* (Oxford University Press, 2003).

[65] Importation of Plumage (Prohibition) Act 1921.

[66] 'Spare the Birds' (*Herald* (Melbourne), 5 August 1908) 3.

for Fashion'.[67] The Royal Australasian Ornithologists' Union petitioned the Commonwealth to intervene.[68]

In March 1911 the Commonwealth Governor General issued a proclamation under the Customs Act banning the export of specified birds, including their plumage and eggs, except for approved educational or scientific purposes.[69] The protected birds included emus, cockatoos, kingfishers and lyrebirds, plus the government banned importation of the plumage and skins of some prized birds. Enforcement against importers who flouted the ban, however, unfortunately didn't result in destruction of their goods but a direction that they be returned to their source, principally traders in Europe. Australia's efforts to curb the trade were paralleled in the United States, where the Audubon Society, established in 1905 to promote bird conservation, helped secure landmark Congressional legislation, the Migratory Bird Act 1913, outlawing some of the commerce and hunting of native birds.[70]

The Commonwealth later extended export controls to other Australian fauna. The charismatic koala was one beneficiary, and although it wasn't the only marsupial to be slaughtered for its fur, it provoked the fiercest opposition. A Sydney newspaper described Queensland authorities' open season on koalas in the late 1920s as 'the greatest outcry of the kind ever known in Australia'.[71] Some 8,000 licensed hunters bagged nearly 600,000 koalas in the last open season, according to official figures.[72] Active in the campaign to stop the slaughter, the *Brisbane Courier* published numerous letters from concerned citizens, such as one who called for 'permanent protection of our sweet little "Teddy"'.[73] Yet some politicians continued to clamour for further open seasons, viewing them as helpful to the unemployed in hard times.[74] Following lobbying of the Prime Minister by the Wild Life Preservation Society and others, on 10 November 1927 the Commonwealth suspended permits altogether for the export of koala fur.[75] However, the Commonwealth has also approved the export of kangaroo and wallaby skins, and thus encouraged their slaughter: between 1950 and 1964, an average of 360 tonnes of macropod skins, representing half a million animals, were exported annually.[76]

[67] 'Birds Slaughtered for Fashion' (*Age* (Melbourne), 16 February 1907) 10.

[68] 'Eleventh Annual Report of the Royal Australasian Ornithologists' Union' (1911–12) 11 *The Emu* 166, 167.

[69] 'Protection of Australian Birds. Commonwealth Action' (*Morning Bulletin* (Rockhampton), 3 April 1911) 6.

[70] Ch 145, 37 Stat 828 (replaced in 1918).

[71] 'The Native Bear. Prosecution of a Sydney Firm Involves Inter-State Relations' (*Daily Telegraph* (Sydney), 27 September 1927) 21.

[72] WF Smith, Secretary for Agriculture and Stock, Queensland, Legislative Assembly, Hansard, 14 December 1927, 1720.

[73] 'Permanent Protection Wanted' (*Brisbane Courier*, 26 July 1927) 15.

[74] T Foley, Queensland, Legislative Assembly, Hansard, October 1928, 1165.

[75] 'Koala Skins. Export Ban Sought. Wild Life Preservation Society's Appeal' (*Brisbane Courier*, 4 August 1927) 10.

[76] D Whitelock, *A Dirty Story: Pollution in Australia* (Sun Books, 1971) 48.

**Figure 8.3** 3,600 koala skins, Claremont, Queensland, 1927; State Library of Queensland

The Commonwealth also had jurisdiction over wildlife in the territories it directly governed. After Australia took control of German-held New Guinea during World War I, it restricted the taking of and trade in birds of paradise, also being ravaged there. The German colonial administration, operating between 1884 and 1914, introduced ad hoc and largely ineffectual measures to conserve the birds but shied away from a complete ban.[77] The Commonwealth's injunction exempted takings for scientific research and museum collections.[78] Taking over responsibility for the Northern Territory from South Australia in 1911, the Commonwealth also began to enact nature conservation legislation in the Top End. The Protection of Birds Ordinance 1913 didn't afford complete protection however, with alternating closed and open seasons, exemptions for scientific research, and leaving wholly unprotected seemingly common or nuisance species. But progressive for its time, the Ordinance also exempted any 'aboriginal native killing birds or taking eggs on Crown lad (not being a bird protection district) for himself or his family'.[79] Whilst these regulations were periodically updated, the Commonwealth didn't create an equivalent ordinance for other fauna until 1962 and national parks legislation until 1955. Much wildlife in the Top End suffered from tardy oversight or lack of controls, especially crocodiles, which were decimated until their hunting was outlawed in 1964 (for the freshwater variety) and 1971 (for saltwater species).

[77] P Swalding, *Plumes from Paradise* (Sydney University Press, 2019) 254.
[78] Birds and Animals Protection Ordinance 1922, issued under the New Guinea Act 1922.
[79] Section 12(a).

The Commonwealth also legislated modest measures for the Australian Capital Territory (ACT), such as its Wild Flowers and Native Plants Protection Ordinance of 1936 that allowed the Minister to protect 'any tree, shrub, fern, creeper, vine, palm, or plant which is indigenous to the Territory'.[80] Today, 55 per cent of the ACT is protected, with the Namadgi National Park, the Crown jewels, created in 1984. Securing Namadgi owed to the efforts of the ACT National Parks Association, founded in 1960 with a vision to create a 'national park for the national capital'.[81]

The Commonwealth's constitutional jurisdiction over Australia's marine waters and their resources, including fisheries, also empowered federal authorities to deal with marine biodiversity. Whilst the state governments supervised near-shore fishing, the Commonwealth had control in deeper, offshore waters, and from the early 1950s it exerted control via the Fisheries Act 1952 and the Pearl Fisheries Act 1952, the latter regulating sedentary fisheries such as trochus, pearl shell and sea cucumber.[82]

Overall, the Commonwealth was relatively taciturn about exercising national leadership in wildlife conservation during the first two-thirds of the twentieth century, with virtually no oversight of the practices in the states. Even whilst the situation is ostensibly different today, owing to the Commonwealth's lodestar Environment Protection and Biodiversity Conservation Act 1999, recent federal governments have continued to be wary of stepping on the perceived prerogatives of the states, and administration of the latter legislation has been delegated in part to the states.

## V. Wildlife Conservation: From the Exception to the Ordinary

After World War I, improvements in wildlife conservation laws were typically incremental rather than revolutionary. New South Wales overhauled its legislation in 1918 with the Birds and Animals Protection Act. Sponsored by the Wild Life Preservation Society, the statute departed from the earlier principle of its predecessors that fauna was unprotected unless specifically listed for protection; now, all native species would be protected except those listed as noxious, as well as exclusion of reptiles and rodents en masse. The 'noxious' species initially included quolls, wombats and various species of wallabies and bandicoots to appease agriculturalists. The Act also recognised that any such species would not necessarily be deemed 'noxious' in all parts of NSW at all times, with options for customised,

[80] Sections 2 and 3.

[81] 'A National Park for the National Capital' *NPA Bulletin* 40th anniversary supplement (March 2000) 5.

[82] National Oceans Office, *Ocean Management: The Legal Framework* (National Oceans Office, 2002) 5–6.

district-level or seasonal controls.[83] Landowners under licence could also 'kill any bird or animal found on his land which may be destroying or injuring or be likely to become injurious to his property'[84] – a provision readily open to abuse. The NSW legislation, like its predecessors, also overlooked wildlife habitat. A tentative, remedial step was a curious statutory amendment in 1930 that enabled the Governor to proclaim wildlife sanctuaries within a one-mile radius of a public school.[85] This measure alone would hardly suffice of course, as recognised in earlier parliamentary debate when one sceptic explained: 'I want to know how you are going to preserve bird life while at the same time destroying Nature's shield for them by ringbarking trees'.[86]

Other governments followed NSW's example, although they were also far from perfect. South Australia's Animals and Birds Protection Act 1919 was critiqued by one newspaper as 'one of the greatest farces in legislation that Australia has seen'.[87] The main gripe, according to critic Robert Kaleski, an active commentator on environmental issues, was slack enforcement that rested on the 'already overburdened' police and honorary ranges. Interestingly for his depth of analysis on law reform, Kaleski recommended three key measures: 'It should be administered by one controlling authority, instead of half a dozen …; this controlling authority must have full power and means for enforcing the Act. Thirdly, this authority must be allowed ample funds for organising protective measures'.[88] South Australia's accompanying reform, the Fauna and Flora Reserve Act 1919, created a reserve on Kangaroo Island for their protection. The Act established a six-person board to oversee the reserve, including two members from the University of Adelaide and two from the Royal Society of South Australia. The board managed all Crown land assigned to it for fauna conservation as well (possibly problematically) for 'pleasure and health resort'.[89] The board's remit included to 'establish breeding grounds and places, and enclosures, reserves, and nurseries, for fauna and flora' – an innovative provision that suggested not merely the need to conserve nature but take active measures for its regeneration.[90] Related to this goal, the board could authorise the destruction of specified invasive species.[91] On paper, this was a progressive law for its era.

Tasmania's experience is also instructive about the increasing recognition lawmakers gave to institutional machinery to administer wildlife conservation. Tasmania's first Animals and Birds Protection Act, adopted in 1919, lacked a specialist administrative body to oversee its implementation, with enforcement

[83] Section 4.
[84] Section 18.
[85] Birds and Animals Protection (Amendment) Act 1930, s 5.
[86] BB O'Conor, NSW Legislative Assembly, Hansard, 17 October 1917, 1718–19.
[87] R Kaleski, 'Suggested Safeguards for Our Fauna and Flora' (*Daily Telegraph* (Sydney), 30 July 1926) 5.
[88] ibid.
[89] Section 16(1).
[90] Section 19(iii).
[91] Section 36(1)(f).

reposed in the Commissioner of Police. In this period, seasonal harvest quotas tended to be set on rather rudimentary estimates of target species' populations based on the advice of local police stations – entities hardly possessing such expertise.[92] Improvements came with creation of the Animals and Birds Protection Board, operative between 1929 and 1971 with dedicated members such as Clive Lord, who was Director of the Tasmanian Museum and secretary of the Tasmanian Field Naturalists' Club.[93] The Board however also had representatives from 'trappers and hunters', 'fur-skin merchants' and Tasmanian farmers[94] – interests hardly aligned with nature conservation, and the government favoured perpetuation of the fur industry because of the licence fees and royalties it collected.

A new phase of wildlife conservation emerged after World War II, led by NSW's Fauna Protection Act of 1948, and paralleling like-minded reforms in some other jurisdictions such as New Zealand's Wildlife Act 1953. The NSW reform ensued from the recommendations of the government's Fauna Protection Committee which consulted diverse stakeholders including nature conservation and scientific organisations. A breakthrough provided by the NSW legislation was recognition that wildlife habitat had to be protected. The Fauna Protection Act provided for 'nature reserves',[95] and 52 were gazetted under the 1948 legislation over the next two decades. Although various parcels of Crown land had been reserved before 1948 for nature conservation, notably national parks, they were not necessarily selected with fauna conservation as their main goal, and reserves created under the 1948 Act required parliamentary legislation for any change.[96] Each faunal reserve had to have a 'written scheme of operations' for the 'protection and care of fauna, the propagation of fauna and the promotion of the study of fauna on the faunal reserve'.[97] In today's terminology, that's a management plan.

The NSW lawmakers also recognised that fauna governance needed to be professionalised. The 1948 legislation created a Fauna Protection Panel, chaired by a Chief Guardian of Fauna,[98] with representatives from various NSW government bodies, other organisations concerned with the conservation or scientific study of fauna, and the agricultural industry. The panel was tasked with advising the Minister, educating the public about appreciation of wildlife, conducting scientific research, and managing faunal reserves.[99] Significantly, the panel could also reject any mining leases in such reserves.[100]

[92] N Haygarth and S Cubit, *A Peopled Frontier: The European Heritage of the Tarkine Area* (Circular Head Council, 2008) 54.
[93] M Sharland ('Peregrine'), *Tasmanian National Parks* (Mercury, 1972) 9.
[94] Section 7(3).
[95] Section 9.
[96] Section 9(4).
[97] Section 9(5)(c).
[98] Sections 5 and 7.
[99] Section 6.
[100] Section 10(2).

Native flora and fauna located outside the reserve system faced a precarious existence since their protection was limited to restrictions on taking individual specimens, and any conservation of their habitat depended on the goodwill of landholders. Moreover, the 1948 legislation didn't protect all fauna; wombats, flying foxes and a variety of raptors were unprotected either state-wide or in specified districts. Even protected species could be destroyed in specified purposes, including with a licence to remove animals 'injurious' to a landholder's property.[101]

Several state governments took notice of NSW's precedent, which illustrates the extent to which the Australian states copied one another's law reforms. Queensland's Fauna Protection Act 1952 expanded the number of protected species and created habitat reserves. Nonetheless, the legislation retained the epithet of 'pest fauna', such as raptors, as assessed according to their perceived impact on agricultural interests, as well as allowing open seasons for commercial harvesting of valuable fur or meat-bearing species such as kangaroos. The statutory prohibition on 'taking' protected fauna was defined narrowly and excluded indirect acts such as damaging wildlife habitat outside of dedicated reserves.[102]

Some concerns were voiced by the public about diminishing wildlife habitat[103] but it was the loss of picturesque landscapes that provoked the greatest angst. Urban sprawl and fringe development encroaching on green spaces were identified as a problem. The despoliation of the Dandenong Ranges (part of Melbourne's water catchment) due to messy sprawl and subdivision was publicly discussed in the 1950s.[104] Protecting their aesthetic values was a strong consideration, with one official report praising the area for 'some of the most beautiful hills and mountains in Australia'.[105] In South Australia, as early as the 1920s newspapers were reporting that the picturesque Adelaide Hills were suffering 'terrible defacement' by the 'scars' of ugly quarries and mines. The chairman of the South Australian Town Association called for legislative intervention to stop the 'outright vandalism'.[106]

## VI. The Long and Short Arm of the Law

The effectiveness of laws to protect wildlife so many decades ago is impossible to precisely ascertain now. We can't know how prevalent violations were, for instance. Yet, we can make educated guesses about some issues. One measure of the laws' overall efficacy is scientific evidence about Australia's biodiversity trends, such as species extinctions, contraction of species' ranges and reduced populations, which was unfavourable, as elaborated in the final chapter.

[101] Section 25.
[102] Section 5(1).
[103] LB Peacocke, 'Plea for Faunal Conservation' (*Land* (Sydney), 25 June 1954) 20.
[104] J Hetherington, 'Our Dandenongs are in Danger' (*Herald* (Melbourne), 11 October 1950) 4.
[105] 'Development Committee's Plan for Dandenongs' (*Mountain District Free Press*, 10 July 1952) 5.
[106] 'Disregarding the Beauty of the Hill. Defacement by Quarries' (*Mail* (Adelaide), 29 August 1925) 1.

Anecdotal evidence about policing practices and court cases suggests that even within the laws' modest goals they had limited traction. Just bringing a case to the attention of law enforcers was sometimes a tall order. The justices of the peace in rural areas often were local landowners who themselves typically enjoyed a bit of game hunting on the side, and who were prone to be unsympathetic to any zealous policing against others who did likewise.[107] There was also no prospect of third-party enforcement action, such as seen in contemporary environmental law practice where *locus standi* rules allow conservation groups to seek judicial review of executive decisions.

Media reports of the time shed some insight about the quality and outcome of enforcement, especially courts' decisions. An unlicensed hunter of a black swan in 1921 was fined £A5 (equivalent to A$460 in 2023).[108] A marsupial fur trader nabbed with 8,000 skins in 1929 had to pay £A1000 (equivalent to about $A90,000 in 2023).[109] A court in 1940 fined flower pickers in the Ku-ring-gai Chase bushland near Sydney between £A2 and £A3 each (about A$190–260 today).[110] Heavier fines were imposed in 1933 on three men busted for picking protected flowers, each fined £A3 and 10 shillings (about A$400 in 2023).[111] In 1929, an unlawful possum trapper was fined a relatively hefty £A155 (A$14,000 in 2023 money) or in default 12 months' hard labour.[112] Some offenders however got off lightly, according to press opinion; a poacher from Coolah, NSW, caught in 1931 with six kangaroo skins, received the 'light fine' of 12 shillings or just two days hard labour in default.[113]

The designation of alternating open and closed seasons for taking partially protected game created a loophole because it was difficult for authorities to verify that animal skins, feathers or other wildlife trophies offered for sale during the open season were in fact harvested during the allowed period. The Queensland press in 1938 complained: 'the official opening of the possum season had become more or less a joke, since by the time it was legally permissible for trappers and shooters to issue forth, most of them were on their way back to town with their consignments of skins all cured and ready for market'.[114]

Insufficient game wardens allowed for many abuses to go unchecked. For instance, in 1925 the Victorian Fisheries and Game Department had only four field inspectors to control poaching, and they struggled to adjust to the rise of

[107] G Bolton, *Spoils and Spoilers: Australians Make Their Environment 1788–1980* (Allen and Unwin, 1981) 102–03.

[108] P Gorrick, 'Our Fauna. Protecting Black Swans' (*Newcastle Sun*, 7 December 1921) 3.

[109] 'Our Birds and Animals' (*Voice of the North*, 11 November 1929) 5.

[110] 'Flower Pickers Fined' (*Sydney Morning Herald*, 8 September 1944) 4.

[111] 'Holiday Trip was Expensive: Picked Protected Flowers' (*Newcastle Sun*, 9 January 1933) 1.

[112] 'Opossum Killers. Heavy Fines Imposed' (*Australian Worker* (Sydney), 14 August 1929) 19.

[113] 'Coolah Police Court. Kangaroo Skins. Light Fine' (*Mudgee Guardian and North-Western Representative*, 3 August 1931) 8.

[114] 'A Law That Must be Observed' (*Evening News* (Rockhampton), 16 November 1938) 6.

mobile poaching gangs travelling in motor vehicles that were becoming increasingly affordable to the middle class.[115] Sheer insouciance by authorities to some practices also seems prevalent. The 1920 annual report of the Wild Life Preservation Society, mentioned: 'Bird traps are sold openly in the city and suburban shops in large numbers, boys wander through our suburbs … with pea rifles and traps, destroying the birds, and even discharge their firearms into private gardens'.[116]

Likewise, protected flora suffered from lax enforcement. Too few inspectors to uphold Western Australia's Native Flora Protection Act was reported by the press in 1940,[117] and ubiquitous picking of wildflowers was condemned in 1946 with a plea for tougher sanctions.[118] The pilfering of flowers from city parks made news in NSW in 1940.[119] The Queensland press in 1932 lamented how the Sunshine Coast needed 'drastic action … to preserve from vandalism the flora and fauna in the various mountain resorts and other national reserves'.[120] It suggested such action include stationing permanent rangers.[121] Such advice could apply to much environmental law, past and present.

## VII. Threatened Fauna: Translocation and Acclimatisation

Concerted intervention to save threatened species is sometimes necessary where just letting nature take its course will probably not suffice. One intervention is translocation of endangered wildlife to sanctuaries, such as offshore islands or fenced reserves, away from predators or other threats. The practice has become well documented by conservation biologists in Australia and other countries since the 1970s.[122] Species translocation may involve relocation of an entire population to an area its species does not inhabit naturally, or the restocking of an existing population in an area where it is naturally found with individuals from other areas to improve its reproductive success or overcome inbreeding.

It may be surprising to learn that such practices in Australia have a long history, although the earliest examples were adulterated with other motives. In 1870, the former Governor of New Zealand, George Grey, released five species of wallabies on Kawau Island, near Auckland. An avid fauna collector, Grey introduced

[115] C Barrett, 'War on Motor Poachers' (*Herald* (Melbourne), 20 June 1925) 15.

[116] Quoted in 'Save the Birds' (*Evening News* (Sydney), 7 August 1920) 4.

[117] 'Native Flora. More Protection Wanted' (*Western Australian*, 22 February 1940) 8.

[118] 'Prosecute Wildflower Vandals' (*Sunday Times* (Perth), 13 October 1946) 13.

[119] 'Council Officials' Opinion. Flower Beds Wrecked' (*Newcastle Sun*, 24 April 1940) 5.

[120] 'Flora and Fauna. Drastic Action for Protection' (*Nambour Chronicle and North Coast Advertiser*, 15 September 1933) 9.

[121] ibid.

[122] B Griffith et al, 'Translocation as a Species Conservation Tool; Status and Strategy' (1989) 245(4917) *Science* 477.

at least 30 animal species including zebras and monkeys to Kawau, which he purchased in 1862 to establish a grand estate with exotica. Fortuitously, Grey chose three species that later became threatened in Australia (the tammar, parma and brush-tailed rock wallabies), and these and other introduced macropods thrived, with 6,000 reportedly culled on Kawau in one year alone in the 1880s.[123] Whilst Grey wasn't driven by wildlife conservation in the manner contemporary translocations are, two examples in early last century were.

Decimation of koala populations a century ago owing to the fur trade, disease and habitat loss encouraged some enterprising individuals to relocate specimens to island refuges. Eighteen Victorian koalas were released between 1923 and 1925 on South Australia's Kangaroo Island, the country's third largest island at 4,405 $km^2$, but never with its own koalas. Professor Wood Jones of the University of Adelaide, who was highly critical of his state government's failure to save its own mainland population of koalas, was personally involved in the first releases on Kangaroo Island. The charismatic animal (*Phascolarctos cinereus*) was relatively common near Adelaide when European settlement began in the 1830s, but a century later they were virtually extirpated and received legal protection only from 1912. Without predators but abundant food, the koalas imported to Kangaroo Island thrived so well that by the 1960s some had to be relocated to the South Australian mainland.

Other koala relocations happened. Small numbers were introduced to the previously koala-free Phillip and French islands in Victoria in the late nineteenth century. In 1953 some koalas were shifted from the by then over-populated Phillip Island to Raymond Island, in Victoria's Gippsland region, where their numbers also grew, resulting in inbreeding and ill-health. Curiously, Phillip Island's own koalas are now also imperilled, with, in 2021, reportedly just 20 left in the wild due to 'disease, habitat loss and urbanisation', down from about 1,000 in the 1970s.[124]

Some superb lyrebirds (*Menura novaehollandiae*), one of the world's most glorious avian divas, with remarkable powers of mimicry and an elegant tail and courtship etiquette, were also relocated to safety. Although legally protected from feather-seeking hunters since the early 1900s, it was just notional for many birds; the Sydney press in 1912 exclaimed: 'the senseless slaughter still goes on. Our game laws are deplorably wanting in supervision and strict enforcement'.[125] Equally problematic, the law hardly buffered against the perilous threat from foxes and bush clearers. Plans to relocate the imperilled birds were first mooted in the 1920s.[126] From 1935 to 1949, 22 lyrebirds captured in Victoria were rehomed in Tasmania at Hastings Caves State Reserve and Mount Field National Park,

[123] 'Intercolonial' (*Leader* (Melbourne), 31 March 1888) 16.
[124] 'Phillip Island Koalas' Future Bleak' (*Phillip Island and San Remo Advertiser*, 14 February 2021) www.pisra.com.au/news/phillip-island-koalas-future-bleak.
[125] 'The Lyre Bird' (*Sydney Morning Herald*, 17 August 1912) 7.
[126] 'Protect the Lyrebird' (*Voice of the North*, 12 October 1925) 13.

with the aid of the Royal Australasian Ornithological Union.[127] The birds took readily to their new environs, with the local press reporting keenly on sightings by bushwalkers.[128] Today lyrebirds are common and still colonising more areas of Tasmania, and I have personally seen and heard them.

A variety of other wildlife relocations were undertaken for different purposes, more akin to the acclimatisation movement of the nineteenth century that imported species to Australia for utilitarian or ornamental purposes to aid settlers. The laughing kookaburra (*Dacelo novaeguineae*) was introduced to Tasmania in 1912 for its snake-catching prowess.[129] In 1944, however, the Tasmanian Animals and Birds Protection Board revoked the kookaburra's wholly protected status owing to its predation on smaller, native birds.[130] The laughing, long-beaked bird was also introduced to Western Australia in 1897 for similar reasons, and there too some disquiet emerged about its collateral damage.[131] In its native range the kookaburra has many admirers, and is NSW's official bird emblem. The rainbow lorikeet (*Trichoglossus moluccanus*), a brightly coloured parrot endemic to eastern Australia, was released in Perth during the 1960s, and their raucous flocks are now seen across a large swathe of the city. A variety of islands or remote sites around Australia were populated during the first half of the twentieth century with species of kangaroos and wallabies, sometimes to serve as tourist attractions, such as whiptail wallabies (*Macropus parryi*) brought to Queensland's Heron Island.[132]

[127] 'More Lyrebirds for Tasmania' (*Argus* (Melbourne), 3 September 1935) 7.
[128] 'Lyrebird Seen Outside National Park' (*Mercury* (Hobart), 4 March 1944) 7.
[129] 'Kookaburra in Tasmania' (*Examiner* (Launceston), 2 July 1924) 4.
[130] 'Plea for Kookaburra. Off the Protected List' (*Mercury* (Hobart), 28 February 1944) 3.
[131] 'Kookaburras' Defended. "Valuable Asset"' (*Western Australian*, 9 November 1937) 18.
[132] JL Long, *Introduced Mammals of the World: Their History, Distribution, and Influence* (CSIRO Publishing, 2003) 37.

# 9

# Scenic and Primitive Areas

## I. Wilderness

The notion of 'wilderness' has infused the history of nature conservation, of which its apotheosis is the national park. This chapter examines the evolution of the park movement in Australia, the values that have shaped their governance, and the complex and potentially problematic philosophical underpinnings of wilderness that to some represent another guise of coloniality. The chapter discusses case studies of conservation gains, in the NSW Blue Gum Forest in the 1930s, and losses, in the excision of forests from Tasmania's Mount Field National Park in 1950.

Wilderness as a realm for experiencing and protecting nature in its supposedly most untrammelled, authentic state has become problematised by contemporary researchers in a manner not so apparent before the 1970s, although the rhetoric of wilderness remains a potent and often uncritically interrogated ideal for environmentalists. Australian wilderness photography and film often evokes sublime imagery without traces of human presence,[1] juxtaposed to adulterated landscapes of farms, factories and freeways. An iconic example from the post-1960s conservation campaigns is Peter Dombrovskis' 1979 photograph, 'Morning Mist, Rock Island Bend', which the Wilderness Society displayed in prominent advertisements in Australian newspapers in the 1983 federal election to symbolise what would be lost if a hydropower project dammed Tasmania's Franklin River. The campaign to save, and now restore, Tasmania's Lake Pedder likewise draws heavily on the iconography of 'wilderness'.

The cult of wilderness in Australia began much earlier, though the language of 'primitive' area was originally used. In 1930, Earle Page, Leader of the Country Party, spoke in the federal parliament of the value of more national parks as a way to 'enable succeeding generations of Australians to realize what their country looked like in its primitive condition'.[2] He may have borrowed the term from the US Forestry Service, which used it in 1929 to denote large, relatively undisturbed natural areas.[3] Wilderness in Western societies was born from the desire not only to protect ecological values but provide people with places for spiritual

[1] T Bonyhady, 'The Art of Wilderness' in W Barton (ed), *Wilderness – The Future: Papers from the Fourth National Wilderness Conference* (Envirobook, 1993) 172.

[2] 'Forestry Bureau Bill', Third Reading, House of Representatives, Hansard, 3 July 1930, 3672.

[3] GW Williams, *The USDA Forest Service – The First Century* (US Department of Agriculture, 2005) 59.

and aesthetic appreciation.[4] Earlier generations of New World settlers readily disdained or feared wilderness as a profane and forbidding place harbouring dangerous beasts or malevolent supranatural forces.[5] Their successors denigrated wilderness as wasteland, better conquered by the axe or plough.[6] Such attitudes often coincided with the eviction of Indigenous people, which later helped cement the narrative of 'unpeopled' places.

A third attitudinal shift regarding wilderness is indebted to Western philosophers such as Americans John Muir and Aldo Leopold, and also Australia's Elyne Mitchell, who advocated a new human-nature relationship premised on the aesthetic and spiritual appreciation of 'untrammelled' nature.[7] This changing valuation of wilderness eventually influenced the law, changing such areas' status from lawless, beyond civilisation, to lawful. With the inauguration of national parks in the late nineteenth century, some areas considered unprofitable for resource extraction but valuable for aesthetic or scientific interest were legislated for protection without human settlement or other (significant) development pressures.[8] In 1964 the United States enacted the Wilderness Act, the world's first legislation explicitly designed to protect wilderness values. Australian governments followed suit, such as with NSW's Wilderness Act of 1987.

A fourth evolution of wilderness philosophy has sought to bring people back into the picture by depicting such areas as cultural landscapes with often a long history of Indigenous occupation. Val Plumwood argues that older views of wilderness wrongly mythologised her continent as historically unpeopled, aligned with the *terra nullius* doctrine that aided the legal dispossession of Aboriginal peoples.[9] She explains, 'Australian movements to protect such places from disturbance replaced the imperial concepts that denigrated wilderness with an American-centred concept that honoured it, but did not rethink its construction's absence, emptiness, or virginity'.[10] That rethinking, argues compatriot Deborah Bird Rose, should acknowledge the Aboriginal history that socialised these 'wild' areas, and the ongoing legitimate role for some human co-existence there.[11] Scholars of environmental law now also recognise that wilderness conservation cannot succeed in isolation to the interconnected ecological processes in both

[4] N Bauer, 'The Social Values of Wilderness' in K Bastmeijer (ed), *Wilderness Protection in Europe* (Cambridge University Press, 2016) 94.

[5] M Perrault, 'American Wilderness and First Contact' in M Lewis (ed), *American Wilderness: A New History* (Oxford University Press, 2007) 15.

[6] D Lowenthal, 'Empires and Ecologies: Reflections on Environmental History' in T Griffiths and L Robin (eds), *Ecology and Empire: Environmental History of Settler Societies* (Edinburgh University Press, 1997) 229.

[7] J Muir, *Our National Parks* (Houghton Mifflin, 1901); A Leopold, *A Sand County Almanac* (Oxford University Press, 1949); E Mitchell, *Soil and Civilization* (Angus and Robertson, 1946).

[8] R Poirier and D Ostergren, 'Evicting People from Nature: Indigenous Land Rights and National Parks in Australia, Russia, and the United States' (2002) 42 *Natural Resources Journal* 331.

[9] V Plumwood, 'Wilderness Scepticism and Wilderness Dualism' in JB Callicott and MP Nelson (eds), *The Great New Wilderness Debate* (University of Georgia Press, 1998) 655.

[10] ibid 658.

[11] DB Rose, *Reports from a Wild Country: Ethics for Decolonisation* (UNSW Press, 2004).

neighbouring and distant biospheres, and that human stewardship of wilderness is necessary to assist such areas in adapting to the upheavals of the Anthropocene.[12]

The foregoing philosophical evolutions have been paralleled by the Australian public's growing kinship with wilderness. The affinity has been aided by increasing access to the great outdoors. During the interwar period, increased leisure time and car ownership put the outdoors within easier reach of the substantial majority of city-dwelling Australians. Nature-based tourism wasn't just confined to the beaches and parks of the peri-urban hinterlands; 'The whole continent west of the Great Divide now proves to have an accessibility by car, camel, and plane, undreamt of by our fathers', observed conservationist Herbert Finlayson in 1936.[13] Before cars, Australians relied on trains, and some rail companies from the 1930s organised mystery bushwalks that took passengers to a surprise destination, like one depicted in Figure 9.1.[14] Yet rail travel offered nowhere near the flexibility of private vehicles for accessing remote wilderness. The motorisation of the Australian public evolved over many decades.[15] Passenger car and motorbike ownership grew from 136,850 vehicles in 1921, or one vehicle per 39.75 persons, to 1,483,811 cars and motorbikes in 1955, or one per 6.2 persons.[16]

**Figure 9.1** Mystery bush hike organised by railway service, 1932; Powerhouse Museum

[12] PC McCormack, BJ Richardson, D Takacs and K Bastmeijer, 'Wilderness Law in the Anthropocene: Pragmatism and Purism' (2021) 51 *Environmental Law* 383.

[13] HH Finlayson, *The Red Centre: Man and Beast in the Heart of Australia* (Angus and Robertson, 1936) 15.

[14] M Harper, *The Ways of the Bushwalker: On Foot in Australia* (NewSouth Books, 2020).

[15] JW Knott, 'The "Conquering Car": Technology, Symbolism and the Motorisation of Australia Before World War II' (2000) 31(114) *Australian Historical Studies* 1.

[16] Commonwealth Bureau and Census and Statistics, *Census of Motor Vehicles, 31 December 1955* (Commonwealth of Australia, 1956) 1; Australian Bureau of Statistics, *Australia's Motor Vehicle Fleet Since the 1920* (Year Book Australia, 2001) (the data excludes commercial vehicles).

Travel writers were also influential in enlightening the public to the continent's natural wonders.[17] They helped bring far-flung or exotic locations to a wide readership. Chronicles of epic road-trips were a popular format, and although they were not commonly devoted to the study of nature, many contained lively anecdotes about wildlife and natural scenery, as well as environmental degradation. One example is *Blue Coast Caravan: Queensland Road Trip 1930s Style*, narrating two couples' journey from Sydney to Cairns who valued 'unspoiled fragment of loveliness and its adjacent glories'.[18] Some of Australia's most untouched environments however were also derided by travel writers, such as William Hatfield who called the Outback a 'great frowning land'.[19]

Bush walking groups were also instrumental in these cultural shifts regarding wilderness. From the late nineteenth century, walking in the Australian bush began to emerge as a common pastime, especially for urban dwellers, and spurred demand for national parks. 'Bushwalking', as a term, entered Australian vernacular from the 1920s to describe walking in nature as a pastime, as opposed to a reference to someone just travelling through the bush. Mountaineering, closely affiliated, also gained popularity in Tasmania and the mainland's Great Dividing Range. Bushwalkers and mountaineers of the late nineteenth century were mainly middle class, often from white collar and professional occupations, a characteristic that perhaps reflected the financial costs and leisure time needed to indulge their hobbies. Historian Melissa Harper discerned that in the early twentieth century 'the appeal of walking expanded quite significantly' towards 'broader class and gender participation'.[20] As the Great Depression intensified in the 1930s and incomes shrank, Australians increasingly turned further to bushwalking as an inexpensive pastime.

Bushwalking also evolved into an organised pursuit through hiking clubs. Many were based in the Sydney region, including Myles Dunphy's Mountain Trails Club (established 1914), Sydney Bush Walkers (1927) and Coast and Mountain Walkers (1934). After the War, the Sydney University Bushwalking Club (1946) and the Canberra Walking Club (1947) were formed. Victoria acquired plenty of bushwalking groups at a similar time, though the first in the state were probably the Wallaby Club and the Melbourne Amateur Walking and Touring Club, dating from 1894. Pioneering Tasmanian bushwalking groups were the South-Western Expeditionary Club (established 1919), the Northern Tasmanian Alpine Club (1928) and the Hobart Walking Club (1929), the latter two still being active.[21] Numerous bushwalking fraternities were also established in the other states, though generally a bit later. They not only arranged walks but

[17] W Hatfield, *Australia Through the Windscreen* (Angus and Robertson, 1939) 208.

[18] FD Davison and B Nicholls, *Blue Coast Caravan* (Angus and Robertson, 1935) 275.

[19] Hatfield (n 17) 236.

[20] M Harper, *The Ways of the Bushwalker: Bushwalking in Australia, 1788–1940* (PhD thesis, University of Sydney, 2002) 215.

[21] See www.ntac.org.au; www.hobartwalkingclub.org.au.

held regular meetings, issued annual reports and some even published magazines. Unsurprisingly, Melissa Harper argues that 'bushwalkers were a significant force in developing and promoting an environmental consciousness' in Australia.[22] Some walkers also sought to safeguard the places they patronised, thereby becoming lobbyists for conservation of wildlife and creation of national parks, as discussed later in this chapter. They thereby became an important stakeholder in the early efforts to save Australia's vanishing nature. In turn, the needs of recreational walkers were increasingly recognised with provision of visitation infrastructure in parks. In sum, without bushwalking, the national park ideal would have struggled to take off in Australia in this era.

## II. National Parks

By 1967, Australia had about 85,000 km$^2$ or 1 per cent of its landmass reserved for conservation,[23] compared to in 2020 when 655,000 km$^2$ or 8.5 per cent of the continent was protected in government reserves, but 19.75 per cent of the continent when including reserves on Aboriginal and private lands.[24] The national park was the jewel in the crown, an ideal ostensibly born in Australia in 1879 when NSW designated a reserve just south of Sydney, known today as the Royal National Park. This milestone, and others to follow in the next few decades, were hardly what today would be regarded as a 'national park' – a sanctuary for natural values to thrive unmolested. Moreover, the areas selected for parks weren't representative of Australia's ecological and biological diversity, and there was little recognition that they might need active stewardship or restoration. Apart from the lack of alternate economic uses such as mining or agriculture, it was beautiful scenery, recreation and scientific curiosity that were the preeminent factors shaping the selection of areas for parks and reserves in this era.[25] Not until some decades into the twentieth century would the national park evolve into a form more recognisable today (though even today, park governance continues to improve).

The first areas designated for nature conservation, during the nineteenth century, were pockets of Crown estate reserved for their scenic values.[26] One was NSW's Jenolan Caves area, where 5,000 acres was reserved in 1866. Although the

[22] Harper (n 20) 11.

[23] Figures derived and clarified from JG Mosley, *National Parks and Equivalent Reserves in Australia: Guide to Legislation, Administration, and Areas* (Australian Conservation Foundation, 1968) 1; MF Day, 'The Role of National Parks and Reserves in Conservation' in AB Costin and HJ Firth (eds), *Conservation* (Penguin, 1971) 190, 190–92.

[24] Australian Government, 'Ownership of Protected Areas', www.dcceew.gov.au/environment/land/nrs/about-nrs/ownership.

[25] Mosley (n 23) 8; D Quarmby, 'Old Forests and Tasmania's Early National Parks Movement' in J Dargavel, D Gaughwin and B Libbis (eds), *Australia's Ever-changing Forests* (Centre for Resource and Environmental Studies, ANU, 2002) 197.

[26] G Bolton, *Spoils and Spoilers: Australians Make Their Environment 1788–1980* (Allen and Unwin, 1981) 104.

Yellowstone National Park was inaugurated in the United States in 1872, and is often touted as the world's first national park, the term 'national park' wasn't used by the US Congress when it reserved Yellowstone, and only retrospectively was it identified as such.[27] The Royal National Park, founded in 1879 and the first park to use that term, was established just south of Sydney to provide its residents with convenient access to scenic recreation. Many other parks or reserves (not necessarily with the 'national park' label) were likewise established around Australia on this precedent: in Melbourne's Dandenong Ranges (protected from 1882), the Belair foothills near Adelaide (in 1891), and Hobart's Mt Wellington/Kunanyi (in 1906). As some of these areas also yielded water catchments for city residents, their conservation had an additional justification.

The national park ideal took hold in Australia as an outcome of the growing popular affection for the continent's landscapes and their fauna that began in the colonial period.[28] The twentieth century saw such sentiments flourish, dovetailing with budding patriotism and national identity. Lacking the political revolutions or heroic wars that gave birth to other nations, and disinterested in protecting its Aboriginal heritage, Australians turned to the continent's cathedrals of nature to define their national character. Consider, for instance, the following description of the Grampians offered by the Victorian National Parks Association in the mid-1950s in soliciting public support for creation of a national park there:

> the people of Victoria have become increasingly aware that here, in the Grampians, is something remarkably spectacular-massifs of sandstone carved into grotesque shapes and effigies, faulted and eroded to startling chasms and precipices yet in season clothed in a harlequin mantle of wildflowers of a kind rarely seen elsewhere in such variety and profusion.[29]

Painters, poets, photographers and other artists were also instrumental in cultivating the aesthetic virtues of Australian nature that aided this cause. Nature photographers stirred Australians' affection for their country in unprecedented ways. With their images widely distributed via travel posters, postcards, travelling exhibitions and newspapers, they helped grow interest in nature-based tourism. Whilst they were evidently moved by Australian scenery and landscapes, that didn't mean they were necessarily challenging its colonisation. As Jarrod Hore's history of landscape photography of the late nineteenth and early twentieth centuries reveals, its practitioners were complicit in a new form of colonisation of the continent through their portrayal of unpeopled 'wilderness' that denied its Aboriginal history, and their evocation of a sensuous and sublime aesthetic framed in the Romantic tradition served to facilitate nature's possession and

[27] L Robin, 'Being First: Why the Americans Needed it, and Why Royal National Parks Didn't Stand in their Way' (2013) 36(3) *Zoologist* 321, 325.

[28] See T Bonyhady, *The Colonial Earth* (Megunyah Press, 2000).

[29] Quoted in B Wilkie, *Gariwerd: An Ecological History of the Grampians* (CSIRO Publishing, 2020) 108.

commodification for settlers' tourism and recreation.[30] A few examples can be given.

With its varied and spectacular scenery, Tasmania has long inspired landscape photographers schooled in the iconography of wilderness, most notably Olegas Truchanas (1923–72) and Peter Dombrovskis (1945–96), both of whom were active in seeking conservation of places imperiled by hydro-dams. They had an important forerunner who helped the national park ideal take hold in the island. He was John Watt Beattie (1859–1930), a Scottish immigrant, who learned his technical skills in wet-plate photography from his father who had a photography studio in Aberdeen. Arriving in Tasmania in 1878, Beattie junior found his element in the rugged terrain of western Tasmania, enamoured by its ancient gnarled trees, wild rivers, dramatic peaks and peaceful solitude.[31] He made a decent living selling images to the tourist industry, with whom he collaborated as a member of the board of the Tasmanian Tourist Association. Beattie's images of Tasmanian forests, mountain peaks and waterfalls were among the first to showcase the island's scenery to national and international audiences.[32] Beattie's talent enjoyed official patronage and media support. From 1896 he worked for the Tasmanian government as its official photographer, and postage stamps were adorned with his wilderness imagery. Publication in 1905 of Beattie's booklet *Beautiful Tasmania: The Garden Island*, won lavish praise, with Hobart's *Mercury* declaring: 'there can be no doubt that its sale and circulation will be the means of attracting a very large amount of attention to the beauties of the "garden island"'.[33]

A member of the Field Naturalists Club of Tasmania, and committed to conserving rather than just photographing nature, Beattie's evocative images cultivated political support for protecting some scenic places, most notably in 1916 when the Freycinet and Mount Field areas he admired became Tasmania's first national parks. Also, Beattie personally led a campaign in 1908 to expand a scenery preservation zone along the Gordon River in southwest Tasmania, then at risk from timber cutters. Making his case, Beattie gave an illustrated lecture to the Royal Society of Tasmania, coinciding with the opening of the state parliament, explaining: 'Apart from the aesthetic side of the Gordon's attractions, its scientific aspect, as contributing a unique display of our West Coast flora, must become apparent to all, and should alone warrant beyond question its rigid protection'.[34] With the media's backing, which recognised the benefits to tourism,[35] the area was saved.

[30] J Hore, *Visions of Nature: How Landscape Photography Shaped Settler Colonialism* (University of California Press, 2022).

[31] J Gato, *The Story of the Camera in Australia*, 2nd edn (Institute of Australian Photography, 1977) 80–83.

[32] See Beattie's photo archive: www.beattiesstudio.com.

[33] '"Beautiful Tasmania". Its Scenic Attractions' (*Examiner* (Launceston), 7 November 1905) 5.

[34] Quoted in 'The Gordon River. Forest Reservation Necessary' (*Zeehan and Dundas Herald*, 17 July 1908) 3.

[35] 'Gordon River Reserve' (*Examiner* (Launceston), 15 July 1908) 4.

Whilst we can admire Beattie for helping to promote the national parks ideal, he also (like other landscape photographers in Australia) fostered for the benefit of the leisured public an aesthetic of wilderness that was complicit in the erasing of Aboriginal history and presence. Curiously, though his nature photography promoted the vision of a wild, empty landscape, Beattie took an interest in photographing Aboriginal people. He made reproductions of portraits that Francis Nixon, Tasmania's first Anglican Bishop and amateur photographer, took in 1858 of the island's surviving Aboriginal people at Oyster Cove. Whilst Beattie could be construed as having a voyeuristic interest in documenting the so-called 'dying race', Beattie evidently had more sympathy. In a paper he read to the Tasmanian Royal Society in 1911, Beattie described the Aboriginal people as the 'original owners of the island of Tasmania' and then quoted approvingly of JF Calder's words: 'they held their ground bravely for 30 years against the invaders of their beautiful domain'.[36]

Another pioneer of Tasmania's national parks system was Gustav Weindorfer. Although not as handy with the camera, Weindorfer had a wide repertoire of bush skills and social acumen that helped him secure protection of Cradle Mountain. Born in 1874 in Austria, and emigrating to Australia in 1900, Weindorfer settled in Melbourne from where, whilst working in clerical jobs, be began to explore the Australian bush in his leisure. He became a member of the Victorian Field Naturalists' Club, which not only provided an outlet for his botanical interests, it's where he met his future wife Kate Cowle. Moving to a farm in northern Tasmania in 1906, they began frequent excursions to Cradle Mountain to marvel at its delicate alpine flora and glorious scenery. Gustav is credited as saying in 1910: 'This must be a national park for the people for all time. It is magnificent and people must know about it and enjoy it'.[37] Eager to share his passion, in 1912 Gustav began building at Cradle Mountain a hospitality retreat he called 'Waldheim', harvesting local timber to furnish rustic accommodation for his family, as well as visitors who would later include such dignitaries as the Danish Consul and the Tasmanian Attorney-General, not to mention occasional trespassing wildlife foraging for food scraps.

After the creation of Tasmania's first national parks in 1916, at Mount Field and Freycinet, Gustav began campaigning for similar protection to Cradle Mountain. He gave touring lectures with lantern slides to publicise its beauty and wilderness, and personally lobbied officialdom to act. His efforts were ultimately successful when on 16 May 1922 a scenic reserve was proclaimed over Cradle Mountain and adjacent lands south to Lake St. Clair, covering 64,000 hectares – though Gustav undoubtedly felt bittersweet that his wife Kate, who died in 1916, wasn't alive to share this success. Gustav himself didn't live to see the reserve

[36] JW Beattie, 'Out Straits Islands: Their Discovery and Early Occupation' (*Mercury* (Hobart), 17 June 1911) 10.

[37] M Giordano, *A Man and a Mountain: The Story of Gustav Weindorfer* (Regal Publications, 1987) 31.

eventually secure national park status. At age 58, on 5 May 1938, his ailing, overworked heart failed him, and Gustav was buried in front of his beloved forest retreat. The area won national park status in 1947 and World Heritage listing in 1982.

**Figure 9.2** Cradle Mountain, Lake Lilla, Gustav Weindorfer and his dog, 1922; National Library of Australia

Tasmania's first national parks legislation, the Scenery Preservation Act 1915, authorised the acquisition of land for conservation reserves and their governance by a Scenery Preservation. Board. The very name given to the Act and its principal agency conveys amply what motivated lawmakers, and a representative of the government's tourist department had a seat on the board. The Act remained in place until overhauled in 1970 in the midst of the Lake Pedder controversy. A similar trend unfolded in other Australian states but some modernised their laws more quickly. In 1959 Queensland's new Forestry Act, which also covered national parks, ambitiously provided, the 'cardinal principle to be observed in the management of National Parks and Scenic Areas shall be the permanent preservation, to the greatest extent, of their natural condition.'[38] Such an emphatic legislative statement in the environmental field was precocious for the era. Likewise, Victoria's National Parks Act 1956 prescribed explicit, pro-conservation objects that included

[38] Section 40.

'to protest and preserve indigenous plant and animal wild life and features of special scenic, scientific or historical interest in national parks' and 'to maintain the existing environment of national parks'.[39] It also established a bespoke National Parks Authority – a momentous innovation premised on the reality that effective conservation governance requires not just rules but an entity to manage parks.

The legal formation of national parks has sometimes proved insufficient to safeguard their environmental values. Apart from natural hazards such as bushfires and droughts, national parks were, and sometimes still are, vulnerable to other (economic) uses. With the longest history of any Australian park, the Royal National Park illustrates this vulnerability clearly.

Like many conservation areas, the Royal National Park was reserved on vacant Crown land and placed in the custody of a board of trustees. They approved a variety of commercial and recreational uses: the planting of exotic trees, hosting car races, conducting military exercises, quarrying gravel, and even some timber cutting to supply pit props for a nearby coal mine.[40] The latter concession, done to raise revenue for the park's administration, was particularly controversial, and David Stead of the Wild Life Preservation Society went to the media to protest. In one story headlined 'Trustee Vandals', the park's management were excoriated for having 'sold the birthright of our children' by allowing the coal miner to cut 'the most magnificent timber'.[41] The NSW Minister for Lands appeased the public outcry by replacing some of the trustees, though the underlying legislation remained flawed in that trustees retained discretion to make such problematic decisions.[42]

Unsurprisingly, this scandal wouldn't be the last for the Royal's management. In the inter-war years a proliferation of holiday cabins in and around the park became another. The Secretary of the NSW Federation of Bush Walking Clubs, Marie Byles, in 1937 stated 'keep that beauty unspoilt by unsightly hovels'.[43] Reflecting on this and other insensitivities, David Stead wrote in 1946 of the 'widespread … feeling of unrest and dissatisfaction with a method of Parks control and administration, which can have, ultimately, no other result but disaster for our great park lands'.[44] Such grievances stemmed from the governance of NSW national parks being tethered to a Public Parks Act, drafted in 1854, that emphasised public recreation rather than nature conservation. This bias was not seriously addressed until 1967 when NSW overhauled the legislation.

To challenge the debasing of the national parks ideal, Myles Dunphy and others in 1932 established the NSW National Parks and Primitive Areas Council.

[39] Section 3(1).

[40] G Mosley, *The First National Park: A Natural for World Heritage* (Envirobook, 2012) 33–40; C Pettigrew and M Lyons, 'Royal National Park: A History' (1979) 2(3–4) *Parks and Wildlife* 15.

[41] 'Trustee Vandals' (*Sydney Morning Herald*, 18 September 1922) 8.

[42] 'National Park. Reforming the Trust. Minister's Action' (*Sydney Morning Herald*, 2 November 1922) 8.

[43] MB Byles, 'Private Shacks in Public Lands' (*Sydney Morning Herald*, 23 September 1937) 5.

[44] DG Stead, 'The Tragic Story of National Park, New South Wales' (1946) 2 *Wild Life* 55.

It advocated three overarching goals for parks: that 'future generations may have the same beautiful and interesting fauna and flora as we have today', to maintain forest cover so as to prevent soil erosion and protect water supply and thirdly, to offer recreational opportunities including bushwalking.[45] Reflective of the settler colonial mindset that ignored the Aboriginal history unlike some contemporary Australia's protected areas,[46] the Council argued for prioritisation of conservation of 'primitive areas', which it described as 'real wildernesses of virgin country'.[47] The first NSW reserve dedicated explicitly under this guise was the 3,100 hectare Tallowa Primitive Reserve, established in 1934. The Council would advocate protecting more such reserves in the following decades, particularly in the Great Dividing Range.[48]

Articulating the purpose of national parks was much easier than implementing it. The paucity of parks and reserves created,[49] as well as disparities in the representation of different ecosystems in them, were publicly acknowledged.[50] The lack of visitation facilities in many parks was another grievance.[51] A milestone towards better park governance was the creation of specialist management agencies with full-time staff. In Victoria, a National Parks Authority was established in 1956, and NSW created an equivalent agency in 1967. The first jurisdiction to create state-wide oversight of its parks was Tasmania, with its Scenery Preservation Board in 1915. Yet, the latter had few resources and limited political clout, as made clear by the ignominious loss in 1950 of some majestic old growth forests in Mount Field National Park – a story worth telling later in this chapter, as it elucidates another dimension of the fragility of Australia's national park ideal.

## III. Saving the Blue Gum Forest

Some national parks were born from more contentious circumstances, a forerunner to the environmental clashes sweeping Australia in recent decades. The country's first major stoush concerned the Blue Gum Forest, a magnificent grove in the Grose Valley of NSW.[52] As a milestone in the struggle to save a vanishing continent, its story deserves telling. Now protected in the Blue Mountains National Park, the verdant enclave was a magnet for painters, photographers and writers from the 1870s. One admirer was the landscape painter William Piguenit,

[45] 'Parks and Primitive Areas' (*Katoomba Daily*, 5 December 1935) 4.

[46] T Bauman and D Smyth, *Indigenous Partnerships in Protected Area Management in Australia* (AIATSIS, 2007).

[47] 'Parks and Primitive Areas' (n 45).

[48] In 1968 the Council became known as the Colong Committee, and today is the Colong Foundation for Wilderness.

[49] See eg 'Survey Points to Need for More Reserves' (*Advertiser* (Adelaide), 19 September 1953) 2.

[50] 'Trees for Beauty and Utility' (*Land* (Sydney), 3 July 1953) 20, 48.

[51] 'Time to Develop Our National Parks' (*Age* (Melbourne), 11 January 1954) 2.

[52] See A Macqueen, *Back from the Brink: Blue Gum Forest and the Grose Wilderness* (Andy Macqueen, 2007).

who introduced the splendour of its towering blue gums to a wider public. This area in the Grose Valley was also recognised by the government of the time as scenically important, for in 1875 it was reserved as unavailable for sale: a government surveyor recommended 'no such selection of alienation in any form should be permitted. The Grose Valley is a national spectacle'.[53] Unfortunately, the Crown reservation prevented only the sale of the land but allowed its leasing, an omission that would be the genesis of the dispute over the future of the Blue Gum Forest in the 1930s.

**Figure 9.3** 'In the Valley of the Grose', oil on canvas, William Piguenit 1880; State Library of NSW

[53] ibid 239.

In the early 1930s a party of bush walkers encountered farmer Clarrie Hungerford who, holding a lease over the Blum Gum Forest, informed them he planned to clear its towering gums for his walnut tree plantation or to provide more grazing grass (the historical sources are unclear on his precise plans).[54] While other threats had loomed intermittently over this stupendous forest for several decades, including proposals for a railway, dam and mine, Hungerford's threat was the most palpable.

The conservation effort was led by Myles Dunphy (1891–1985), the most influential naturalist in NSW of his generation, and whose legacy was continued by his son Milo (1928–96). They exemplify how individuals can make a difference, and their motivation was tied to a growing sense of patriotism to defend their country's natural heritage, argues historian Williams Lines persuasively.[55] Myles' passion was seeded in his childhood days bush walking, and forming at age 15 the quaintly named Orizaba Tourist Club to promote sport and hiking. On some of these hikes around Sydney, before his environmental sensibilities had matured, Myles and his mates shot wildlife for fun; one trip recorded in his 1909 diary mentions they bagged 30 birds.[56] From 1910 Myles was venturing further afield to explore the Blue Mountains, and in 1914 he co-formed the Mountain Trails Club to pursue his passion for epic excursions, some of up to 300 kilometres.

**Figure 9.4** Blue Gum Forest, 1952, photograph by Max Dupain; State Library of NSW

[54] ibid 246.
[55] W Lines, *Patriots: Defending Australia's Natural Heritage* (University of Queensland Press, 2006).
[56] G Lalchere, 'Myles Dunphy' (Oxley Heritage and Historical Society, 2018) 7.

Myles' odysseys helped not only nurture his biophilic impulse but to appreciate the threat posed by those who didn't share it – a concern that morphed to define his noble vision to secure large national parks for NSW's dwindling wildernesses. These interests came to the fore with the Blue Gum Forest.

To protect it, Myles and his bushwalking friends launched a public appeal to raise funds to buy out Hungerford's lease. In 1931 they formed the Blue Gum Forest Committee – which also gave the name to the forest they sought to save – to coordinate action, thereby establishing what was probably Australia's first conservation lobby group. The campaign partnered several groups: Bush Walkers, Mountain Trails Club, Redgum League of Tree and Flower Lovers, Forest League, and the Wild Life Preservation Society. The media also became a stakeholder in the campaign. The influential *Sydney Morning Herald* covered the story closely, evocatively describing the coveted site 'a wondrous forest of tall trees, cathedral-like in its splendour. Mountain mists rise from it in the early morning … and in the evening, when the setting sun is reflected from an overtowering cliff-face, sunbeams filter through the trees in shafts of dancing gold'.[57] The newspaper thus queried: 'why destroy so much assured beauty and wealth of native timber on a gamble with walnuts'.[58]

With such evocative language, Myles' campaign raised through donations and loans the £130 that Hungerford sought (over $14,000 in 2023 money) – a considerable outlay during the Great Depression. The acquired land of 40 acres was then returned to the government for dedication as a public recreation reserve, which was created on 2 September 1932. A second, adjacent parcel held by another landholder, that was part of the same forest ecosystem, could not be acquired at the time by the Blue Gum Forest Trust – the successor organisation to the committee established in 1932 to manage the reserve. Further efforts over the years to acquire it were unsuccessful until 1969, when the owners could no longer afford the mounting municipal rates, and that land then too became a conservation reserve.[59]

Saving the forest fortified Myles' vision for a much larger reserve to secure in perpetuity the Blue Mountains – named after their blue haze. With the aid of the National Parks and Primitive Areas Council, which he founded in 1932, Myles publicised his proposal for what he called the 'Greater Blue Mountains National Park'; to safeguard nearly half a million hectares. In a letter to the press in 1934, Myles outlined his vision, utilising the language of 'primitive' area that had gained currency in the United States from the late 1920s:

> The thought that the country can never go wild again is positively appalling. It has resulted in this action: that all over the world forested and scenic areas have been set apart for the recreation purposes of mankind, where he can rid himself of the shackles of ordered existence. Hence the great national parks.

[57] 'Blue Gum Forest. Plea for Its Protection' (*Sydney Morning Herald*, 24 October 1931) 9.
[58] 'A Hundred Acres: Blue Gum' (*Sydney Morning Herald*, 19 November 1931) 10.
[59] Macqueen (n 52) 274–75.

> But more significant than this is the demand for really 'primitive areas' – great portions of huge national parks wherein no roads may be constructed, no buildings erected, and no fences or other "improvements" are allowed. …
>
> More and more people want back again the forested and mountainous wilderness which has been lost. … to have this wonderful palliative handy to preserve the natural balance of minds, strengthen the ordinary, comradely human nature, and perfect physique; also to preserve for the human race that connection things natural and wholesome which now is more than ever necessary, because of our remarkably artificial city and town environment.[60]

It wouldn't be until 1959 that tangible progress would accrue, with the official declaration of the Blue Mountains National Park. Whilst its 63,000 hectares was much smaller than Myles' plan, this national park would grow with substantial additions (the Blue Gum Forest itself was added in 1963). Myles Dunphy's idea for a 'primitive area' however was not explicitly acknowledged, and it would not be until 11 May 2011 that the area was officially designated a wilderness, the preferred terminology today for particularly wild areas, this one comprising 38,000 hectares of the Grose Valley.[61] The story of the Blue Gum Forest in growing the NSW national park system matters not just because of one individual's tenacity and vision, but because nature conservation was indebted to a generation of bushwalking enthusiasts without the benefit of specialist environmental lawyers who today play a seminal role in such causes.

## IV. Logging Tasmania's Mount Field

Tasmania's first national parks were created in 1916 at Mount Field and Freycinet. Conservation at Mount Field in fact began in 1885 when a pocket of 121 hectares around the beautiful Russell Falls was protected as a scenic reserve, ironically under the derogatorily named Waste Lands Act. The reserve's upgrading to national park, under the Scenery Preservation Act, expanded the protected enclave considerably to about 11,000 hectares.

In the 1940s the Australian Newsprint Mills (ANM) began to covet some of the park's towering swamp gums (*Eucalyptus regnans*), which would lead to the first major conservation struggle in Tasmania, and was a forerunner of the 'forestry wars' that would afflict the island's politics from the 1980s. The seeds of the confrontation were planted in 1932 when the Tasmanian parliament passed the Florentine Valley Wood Pulp and Paper Industry Act, which granted a timber concession over 124,000 hectares adjoining Mount Field National Park, a concession that

[60] B Thurat, 'Equilibrated Minds and Wilderness' (*Katoomba Daily*, 24 August 1934) 5 ('Barron Thurat' was a pseudonym occasionally used by Myles Dunphy).

[61] Macqueen (n 52) 313.

came under the control of the ANM in 1935. To supply Australia's newspapers, ANM and its partner in 1941 opened a paper mill in Boyer, just 50 km away.

The exploitation of the state's forests for the pulp and paper industry had been identified by the mid-1940s as problematic, when an inquiry into governance of Tasmania's forests, conducted by the Commonwealth Controller of Timber, observed:

> It is not easy to strike a balance between the advantages that have accrued to the State by the successful establishment of these important [pulp and paper] industries and the concessions that the Government found it necessary to grant to secure their location in Tasmania. It is very apparent that bargains made in this connection have been largely at the expense of the forests and the Forestry Department.[62]
>
> In Tasmania, Parliament has seen fit to grant very large concessions to the paper industry to encourage its establishment in the State which involved the use of species of timber not previously used for this purpose in any part of the world. These concessions have meant, virtually, that large areas of forest have passed out of the control of the Forestry Department and that good-quality forest can be exploited almost without restriction for conversion into pulp products.[63]

Requesting more big trees, the ANM in 1946 asked the state government to assign it some of the western slopes of Mount Field National Park in exchange for other lands from its timber concession. The Scenery Preservation Board rejected the ANM's request, including a revised proposal made to the Tasmanian Premier Robert Cosgrove, who was keen to support the industry, as was the State's Forestry Commission. The Board abhorred the proposed loss of 'first class heavily timbered virgin forest' for 'poor second and third class eucalypt and buttongrass country'.[64] Given the Board's objection, the only means of satisfying the ANM was to have the Board's authority overridden through an Act of Parliament. And that's what ensued.

A Joint Select Committee of the Tasmanian parliament investigated the controversy, giving time for conservation-focused groups, such as the Field Naturalists Club and the Hobart Walking Club, to lobby against the proposed land swap. However, the park excision enjoyed the backing of powerful political interests and the local press, which of course was a beneficiary of the newsprint industry. Tasmania's main newspaper, the *Mercury*, declared 'This strip is vital to the newsprint industry for logging operations', and 'The exchange of land between the company and the park would, in fact, improve the reserve'.[65] By contrast, the

[62] *Report on the Forests and Forestry Administration of Tasmania* (Journals and Printed Papers of Parliament, No.42, 1944–45) 8, quoted in D Quarmby, *The Politics of Parks: A History of Tasmania's National Parks 1885–2005* (PhD thesis, Murdoch University, 2006) 132.

[63] ibid 12; quoted in Quarmby, ibid.

[64] Quoted in L Mendel, *Scenery to Wilderness: National Park Development in Tasmania, 1916–1992* (PhD thesis, University of Tasmania, 1999) 99.

[65] 'Newsprint Industry Concession' (*Mercury* (Hobart), 21 March 1949) 3.

conservationists struggled to find political support or public sympathy in an era where nature conservation had little conscious support when stacked against jobs and revenue, especially where industry leaders enjoyed cosy relationships with politicians.

The result was that the Tasmanian parliament passed the National Park and Florentine Valley Act 1950 to excise approximately 1500 hectares of swamp gums from the national park, in exchange for a similar size area of mixed forest added to the park. The only positive outcome for conservationists was that the government agreed to the parliamentary inquiry's recommendation of a larger budget for the Scenery Preservation Board (but funded by increased timber royalties).[66]

This was not the first, nor the last time, the Tasmanian government excised part of a protected area for economic development. It did so in 1939, when nearly 1,300 hectares of the Cradle Mountain reserve was revoked under the Scenery Preservation Act 1915 to allow for the opening of the Wolfram mine. And in 1967, Lake Pedder in the southwest wilderness lost its national park protection for construction of a hydropower dam. Writing in the mid-1960s about her visit to Tasmania, British travel author Elspeth Young reflected caustically on the loss of the Florentine Valley's giants:

> some of them over 300 feet high, tall as the dome of St. Paul's, some no doubt to be put to good use but the pulp of others to be adorned with strip cartoons, with eulogies of soft drinks, nylons and carpets, with stale political accounts of murders, rape, theft, perversion and sports results; and finally to end as trampled litter down a dirty street.[67]

Despite the setback, historians believe the Mount Field controversy was 'a turning point for Tasmanian conservationists', a fillip for a more cohesive and better organised opposition to further assaults on the island's natural wonders.[68] Previously, Tasmanian conservationists comprised a medley of bushwalking clubs, nature scientists, artists and tourist operators. After the Mount Field blow, they established the Flora and Fauna Conservation Committee to be a permanent advocate for their causes. For instance, in March 1953 the Committee remonstrated against inadequate representation of environmental scientists on Tasmania's Animals and Birds Protection Board, then with just one such expert among its nine members.[69] They were successful here, with the government agreeing in 1954 to increase the number of scientists to three. The Committee would remain active over the next few decades until the emergence of a new generation of groups in the 1970s and 1980s that responded to the damming of Lake Pedder and the threat to dam the Franklin River.

[66] Quarmby (n 62) 137.
[67] E Huxley, *Their Shining Eldorado: A Journey through Australia* (Chatto and Windus, 1967) 172.
[68] Quarmby (n 62) 138.
[69] 'Displeased with Board Set-Up' (*Mercury* (Hobart), 2 March 1953) 7.

## V. Perth's Kings Park

The dispute over Mount Field National Park wasn't the only of its kind in Australia in this era. Another formative one concerned Perth's Kings Park, an inner-city patch of greenery along the Swan River. Part of the traditional territory of the Noongar Indigenous people, the Kings Park was the first of Western Australia's major bushland reserves, set aside in 1832 and officially gazetted in 1871 as a 'public park and recreation'.[70] The prime real estate received stronger legal protection under the Parks and Reserves Act in 1895, which introduced boards of management for reserves, and more protection under the Permanent Reserves Act 1899, which required, for the most important reserves ('Class A)') such as Kings Park, parliamentary consent for any alienation for other uses.

Described in 1929 as 'Perth's greatest treasure' by Western Australia's principal newspaper, the 400-hectare Kings Park impressed visitors with its 'delightful walks', spring flowers 'like the plumage of the cassowary', and 'entrancing glimpses of blue water',[71] along with the usual edifices commemorating Australia's colonial and military endeavours such as that depicted in Figure 9.5. Kings Park however might have had little natural bush had money been no objection, for the park's trustees were unable to develop the site into a European botanical garden like that found in Australia's other capital cities. Kings Park now provides a refuge for urban wildlife, with two-thirds of it comprising remnant banksia and tuart woodlands that are listed as threatened ecological communities under the Commonwealth's Environment Protection and Biodiversity Conservation Act 1999. Today, 92 bird species and 27 reptile species inhabit the park, along with six mammals, as well as at least 326 species of native plants.

Plans for a swimming centre at the park emerged publicly as early as 1950, with Perth's Lord Mayor backing the idea. The controversy took off in 1954 when the Perth City Council formally unveiled plans to build an aquatic centre for the 1962 Commonwealth Games. Occupying 20 acres, the development would comprise up to five swimming pools, car parks, tearooms and other visitor infrastructure. Supporters of the project, including the mainstream press and the park's governing board,[72] believed that the dedication of Kings Park as a reserve was never intended to keep the area wholly in a natural state for conservation of flora and fauna.[73]

The project's opponents formed the Society for the Preservation of Kings Park and Swan River, and at a conference convened in September 1956 resolved: 'to prepare a plan of action to preserve King's (sic) Park for the recreation and enjoyment of all citizens for all time without destroying in any way the beauty of its

[70] GE Rundle, 'History of Conservation Reserves in the South-west of Western Australia' (1996) 79 *Journal of the Royal Society of Western Australia* 225, 227.

[71] EH Pellee, 'King's Park Walks. Perth's Great Treasure House' (*Western Australian*, 24 August 1929) 17.

[72] V Serventy, 'Alienation of King's Park is Condemned' (*Western Australian*, 23 September 1954) 2.

[73] 'Some Misconceptions Have Arisen About King's Park' (*Western Australian*, 1 November 1954) 2.

natural growth and flora, which is indigenous to Western Australia'.[74] The Society allied some 20 metropolitan groups opposed to any tampering with Kings Park. Spearheaded by Bessie Rischbieth, a prominent feminist who enlisted the support of the Women's Service Guild, the campaign convened public meetings, lobbied legislators and wrote to the press. Olympic gold medallist Shirley Strickland, a well-known public figure and ally, was also recruited to boost publicity. Letters to the press suggested much grassroots opposition to the aquatic centre. One exclaimed: 'Most of our troubles in the world today are caused by the fact that we are getting farther and farther away from nature and seem intent on shutting ourselves upinside bricks and mortar'.[75] Another correspondent warned: 'There will soon be children in Perth who will never see bush flowers except in shop windows … Open spaces need to be zealously guarded'.[76] Appealing to children's future was also the pitch of another remonstrator: 'we would be failing un our duty to our children if we allowed this rare and valuable gift to posterity from the past to be whittled away'.[77]

**Figure 9.5** War Memorial, Kings Park, Perth, 1930; National Library of Australia

[74] Quoted in R Chapman, *Fighting for the Forests. A History of the Western Australian Forest Protest Movement 1895–2001* (PhD thesis, Murdoch University, 2008) 75.

[75] 'Letters to the Editor: "No Farther"' (*Western Australian*, 8 November 1954) 17.

[76] 'Letters to the Editor: Our Open Spaces' (*West Australian*, 9 November 1954) 13.

[77] W Kastner, 'King's Park' (*Western Australian*, 30 October 1954) 8.

The alliance between nature conservation and women's lobby groups, and recruitment of esteemed public figures, enabled the campaign to eventually succeed, although the aquatic centre was eventually built on another urban reserve, at Beatty Park in North Perth. The campaign's triumph, involving ordinary citizenry prevailing over Perth's political elites including the Lord Mayor, was a milestone in Western Australia's environmental activism even though the campaign's tactics were polite and non-confrontational compared to the belligerence to come in subsequent decades. Saving Kings Park also put a dent in the hegemony of modernist town planning, which during this era drove numerous urban 'renewal' projects, including highways, skyscrapers and 'slum' clearance, that fragmented communities and destroyed historic heritage.[78] The campaign thus revealed the limitations of the current polyarchal mechanisms in Perth's land use planning laws and the need for governance reform to give residents greater say in future plans and projects.

The Kings Park dispute also spurred the formation in 1956 of the Tree Society of Western Australia. According to its founding president, the group was necessary 'because a number of our citizens of this State felt so strongly about the growing despoliation of our countryside that they came together to present a united front to this national problem'.[79] The Tree Society flourished and formed numerous branches around Western Australia in the late 1950s to lobby for the protection of historic or aesthetically valuable trees, especially in Perth. Sadly, the Society had negligible impact on the massive land clearing in rural Western Australia during the 1950s and subsequent decades for agricultural settlement. The economic stakes were just too high there.

Yet there were isolated successes in Western Australia where high conservation values were jeopardised and influential lobbyists were involved. One of the best examples was at Two Peoples Bay, about 35 km east of Albany on the state's south coast, where in 1961 the noisy scrub-bird (*Atrichornis clamosus*) was rediscovered after being presumed extinct. The coastal heathland around the bay inhabited by the rare bird was however threatened by a proposal for a holiday resort. The campaign to save the area was boosted thanks to the intervention of Prince Philip, a bird lover, who lobbied the state government. Overtures from a variety of conservation groups and individuals continued until 1967 when Western Australian authorities capitulated, and designated Two Peoples Bay a nature reserve. The legal protection also ensured the conservation of Gilbert's Potoroo (*Potorous gilbertii*), which was presumed extinct since the nineteenth century but astonishingly also rediscovered at Two Peoples Bay, in 1994.[80]

[78] J Gregory and JL Grant, 'The Role of Emotions in Protests Against Modernist Urban Redevelopment in Perth and Halifax' (2014) 42(2) *Urban History Review* 44.

[79] Quoted in Chapman (n 74) 71.

[80] K Orr et al, *Two Peoples Bay Nature Reserve. Management Plan 1995–2005* (Department of Conservation and Land Management, 1995).

## VI. Reflections

The desire to conserve scenic and 'primitive' landscapes contributed to the creation of national parks and other conservation reserves. Other factors also played a role however that were not always consistent with such objectives. The national park ideal was nurtured by recreational values cultivated through bushwalking clubs and travel writings. The establishment of the Royal National Park particularly reflects this motivation, as a place for Sydney's working people to find convenient access to healthy recreation in a natural setting. Another crucial factor was that areas set aside for parks were often perceived to be economically 'worthless lands', unfit for agriculture, settlement or other productive uses, as examined by geographer Colin Michael Hall.[81] Queensland's first national park created on Tamborine Mountain in 1908 was on land judged by authorities to be 'unfit for any other purpose'.[82]

What might have been deemed 'worthless' when the park was created might change, as occurred when the forestry industry excised some of Tasmania's Mount Field National Park in 1950, and later when Tasmania's hydropower enthusiasts had Lake Pedder's national park status revoked in 1967. Even prestige conservation areas, such as Perth's Kings Park, were vulnerable to development projects. The successful campaign to safeguard Kings Park compared to the failure to save Mount Field shows that the outcome of disputes over conservation reserves could vary dramatically. Whilst dedicated nature conservation societies formed later in the twentieth century helped to broaden the criteria for national parks to include their ecological and biological characteristics, the creation or continuation of national parks has been a political battle, and continues today as pressure grows for reinstatement of Aboriginal custodianship of such places along with longstanding pressures for tourist development.[83]

Even at its best, the national park ideal represented an enclave model of conservation, in which it was assumed that designating environmental sanctuaries would suffice to meet all conservation goals while freeing the remaining, and much larger areas, for economic development and human settlement. It's a model of nature conservation fundamentally insufficient to conserve biological diversity. Although protected areas remain the flagship of biodiversity conservation, off-park conservation also matters to ensure wildlife can co-exist with human settlement and to enable movement of wildlife between parks. Moreover, the history of nature conservation in Australia last century shows that the designation of national parks was rarely sufficient for the enclaves themselves. They required enlightened and

[81] CH Hall, 'The "Worthless Lands Hypothesis" and Australia's National Parks and Reserves' in KJ Frawley and N Semple (eds), *Australia's Ever Changing Forests* (University of NSW, 1998) 441.

[82] W Wilkes, 'Down the Years with National Parks in Queensland' (Romeo Watkins Lahey Memorial Lecture, 1972) 3.

[83] E Lee and BJ Richardson, 'From Museum to Living Cultural Landscape: Governing Tasmania's Wilderness World Heritage' (2018) 20(1) *Australian Indigenous Law Review* 78.

competent management with adequate funding. This was rarely met; a study of the nation's conservation system by the ACF in 1968 found there 'is little formal planning of parks and reserves in Australia, and only in the last few years have a few authorities begun to prepare management plans for individual areas'.[84] Furthermore, too often, especially in the early twentieth century, parks prioritised recreational users at the expense of natural values.

As seen increasingly in the twenty-first century, national parks are also acutely vulnerable to the impacts of climate change. Significant bushfires have erupted at the Royal National Park periodically during the history covered by this book, including in 1913, 1916, 1928, 1933, 1939 1941 and 1951, according to newspaper reports. In January 1939 Australia suffered one of its worst ever bushfires, when the 'Black Friday' fires burnt nearly 2 million hectares in Victoria, including 800,000 of protected forest, following several years of drought.[85] Reflecting on the countless wildlife killed in the 1939 inferno, Melbourne's *Age* called for 'revolutionary changes in fire-prevention laws and penalties' to prevent another catastrophe.[86] This message could have been repeated after the 2019–20 bushfires of eastern Australia.

[84] Mosley (n 23) 11.

[85] Forest Fire Management Victoria, 'Past Bushfires'. www.ffm.vic.gov.au/history-and-incidents/past-bushfires.

[86] 'Wild Life Suffers in Bush Fires' (*Age* (Melbourne), 17 January 1939) 16.

# 10

# Town Planning and the Bush Capital

## I. Modernist Planning

Throughout the history of White settlement, the city and the bush supposedly have occupied 'separate moral universes' in Australian culture.[1] The bush infused the founding mythology of the settler society – a fulcrum for the cultivation of virtues of ruggedness and thrift, while the city, with its slums, festered with squalor and drudgery. For White environmentalists, another cleavage between the bush and city is that the former represents nature but the city does not, a distinction solidified in the early history of environmental law by its tendency to govern rural and urban areas as separate realms. Yet, ironically, the early lobbyists for nature conservation and environmental protection were typically based in the cities.

These tensions were promisingly lessened with Canberra, the national capital that carried the metonym the 'bush capital'. Until the 1960s this moniker was used sneeringly, dismissive of the city's isolation and rurality. The media's joke was that 'few members of Parliament live there except during the session. All who can shake the dust off their feet and make for their homes at the week-ends'.[2] The city's dishevelled appearance, suggested the *Sydney Morning Herald*, was epitomised by numerous 'temporary offices made of wood or fibrous material, of temporary hostels, of some whole districts of temporary prefabricated hostels'.[3] Such ridicule belied the unique planning of Canberra that sought to personify the nation's identity and landscapes. Unlike much of Australia where clearing the bush was a mark of progress, in Canberra the bush suffused the city's character.

Nature's ubiquitous shapes, shades and scents in Canberra's layout has mattered at several levels. At a utilitarian level, it conveys the importance of green

[1] G Davison, 'Sydney and the Bush: An Urban Context for the Australian Legend' (1973) 18(71) *Historical Studies* 191, 203.

[2] 'Occasional Notes. The Red Bill; The Bush Capital; State Govt' (*Goulburn Evening Post*, 23 November 1950) 4.

[3] 'A "Bush Capital" Grows Up. Canberra … The City Built by Federation' (*Sydney Morning Herald*, 10 May 1951) 2.

spaces for the amenity needs of the city's residents. Furthermore, it demonstrates a commitment not only to protect the aesthetic values of nature but to integrate them into the urban fabric. Finally, it symbolises the cultural salience of Australia's landscapes to the national identity, bringing the bush into the heart of the nation's capital and consciousness. This third dimension, to fashion a uniquely 'Australian city' in a post-colonial country, makes this chapter's focus on the building of Canberra valuable to illustrate the evolution in urban planning philosophies and techniques as a vital strand in the history of the nation's environmental law. This chapter begins by examining the history of land use planning governance in different Australian jurisdictions, and its international precedents, before turning to Canberra.

While any human settlement in Australia could through its architecture and planning evoke a certain cultural and environmental oeuvre, a capital city born out of the inception of a new nation can do so quite uniquely. This destiny for Canberra ensued from the aims of the city's designers as well as the site chosen for the capital. Instructions given to the Commonwealth's surveyor Charles Scrivener were to select an area for 'a beautiful city occupying a commanding position with extensive views, and embracing distinctive features … with a view to securing picturesqueness, and also with the object of beautification and expansion'.[4]

Canberra's destiny might seem improbable given the parlous state of town planning and amenity regulation in Australia in the early twentieth century. As large settlements were disparagingly associated with grime, infectious diseases and effluence, such as like that depicted in Figure 10.1, it isn't surprising that they were the targets of some of Australia's earliest regulations to improve conveniences, building standards and land use. All Australian states enacted laws to address these purposes, initially through omnibus local government ordinances and public health regulations, then later through specialist town-and-country planning regimes. Underpinning law reform was faith in the capacity of modernist planning to colonise the unruly, unsanitary or ugly elements of urban life, making it more orderly, functional and pleasant.[5]

With its rapid industrialisation and urbanisation in the nineteenth century, Great Britain led early reforms that set precedents for the empire's dominions. The UK's Nuisance Removal and Disease Prevention Act 1846 aimed primarily to control the spread of cholera, with controls on unsanitary situations such as houses that drained into open ditches. The Public Health Act 1848 authorised

[4] Instruction from Hugh Mahon, Minister for Home Affairs, to Charles Scrivener, 21 December 1908. National Archives of Australia.

[5] See K Lynch, *The Image of the City* (Technology Press and Harvard University Press, 1960); EP Mumford, *Designing the Modern City: Urbanism Since 1850* (Yale University Press, 2018).

local authorities to improve public health infrastructure through drainage, water supplies and street paving. These measures were supplemented by housing legislation, starting with the Artizans and Labourers Dwellings Act 1868, which allowed authorities to close unsanitary premises. Legal historian Ben Pontin has researched how the common law played a complementary role here through injunctions issued by courts to stop nuisances, especially from industrial sources.[6]

The early twentieth century saw a renaissance in land use planning, with new philosophies, the professionalisation of its practitioners and legislative reforms that included introduction of the concept of community 'amenity' as a seminal governance norm. North America and Great Britain furnished the most influential precedents for Australian cities, although other parts of the world such as Continental Europe were also innovating.[7] English planner Ebenezer Howard's vision of 'garden cities' was particularly influential from the 1890s, furnishing templates for greener town layouts spared from pollution and overcrowding.[8] From North America, the 'city beautiful' movement arose, accentuating monumental grandeur and beautification.[9] And owing to a recent worldwide economic slump, which in Australia saw real GDP dropping 17 per cent between 1892 and 1893,[10] planning philosophy also was conceived as a tool to help ameliorate economic stagnation and assuage social unrest. A cadre of planning professionals soon emerged. with the American Planning Association arising from a meeting in 1909 and the UK's Town Planning Institute forming in 1913–14.[11] The first Australian town planning conference was held in Adelaide in 1917, following the establishment of the country's town planning association, in NSW in 1913.[12] Of accompanying law reforms, in 1909 the UK enacted the Housing, Town Planning. Etc Act, with discretionary controls on sprawl in suburban areas and closer government oversight of housing construction.[13]

[6] B Pontin, *Nuisance Law and Environmental Protection: A Study of Nuisance Injunctions in Practice* (Lawtext, 2013).

[7] A Abarkan et al, *European Planning in the 20th Century: A Continent of Urban Planning* (Taylor and Francis, 2022).

[8] E Howard, *Tomorrow. A Peaceful Path to Real Reform* (Swan Sonnenschein, 1898); S Meacham, *Regaining Paradise: Englishness and the Early Garden City Movement* (Yale University Press, 1999).

[9] WH Wilson, *The City Beautiful Movement* (Johns Hopkins University Press, 1989).

[10] B Fitz-Gibbon and M Gizycki, *A History of Last-resort Lending and Other Support for Troubled Financial Institutions in Australia* (Reserve Bank of Australia, 2001) 21.

[11] JA Peterson, 'The Birth of Organized City Planning in the United States, 1909–1910' (2009) 75(2) *Journal of the American Planning Association* 123.

[12] R Freestone and M Park, 'The Limits to Nationalism: Moves Toward an Australian Town Planning Association 1913–1917' (2009) 40(1) *Australian Historical Studies* 32.

[13] P Booth and M Huxley, '1909 and All That: Reflections on the Housing, Town Planning, Etc. Act 1909' (2012) 27(2) *Planning Perspectives* 267.

**Figure 10.1** Slums, Ultimo (Sydney), 1933; State Library of NSW

Australian law reform and planning philosophy was influenced by international trends. From the 1890s many Australian towns and cities such as Sydney became greener, as government-supported botanic garden nurseries were sourced to provide trees to add 'shade and beauty to their streets', although exotic trees were more commonly used.[14] Negative factors were also targeted. The Public Health Act of NSW, adopted in 1896 and updated in 1902, empowered local authorities to abate nuisances from air and water pollution from factories and other premises.[15] Legislation constituting local authorities in NSW began in 1858,[16] and its Local Government Act 1906 specified the 'primary functions' of authorities to include mitigation of bushfire and flood risks, 'prevention of the pollution of natural watercourses;' management of water supply, and local parks, to plant trees and control noxious plants and animals.[17] Powers for land use planning were included in the next iteration, the Local Government Act 1919. Inspired by the UK's precedent, Part XII of the NSW law, entitled 'Town Planning', provided that local councils 'may control and regulate' the planning of 'new roads and subdivisions',

[14] J Frawley, 'Campaigning for Street Trees, Sydney Botanic Gardens, 1890s–1920s' (2009) 15 *Environment and History* 303, 318.

[15] See eg Public Health Act 1902, s 64.

[16] An Act for Establishing Municipalities Act 1858.

[17] Sections 73, 74, 84 and 112.

'the demolition, rearrangement, and reconstruction of buildings' and 'the improvement and embellishment of the area'.[18]

Still, problems with town governance persisted. Whilst such provisions allowed local councils to restrict undesirable development, the law had yet to plant the notion of zoning as a way to segregate incompatible land uses. Moreover, legislation gave local authorities discretionary powers but rarely *obliged* their exercise, and failed to furnish amenity standards to inform decisions. Municipal and planning governance had also yet to become democratically organised, as Ebenezer Howard championed, as the municipal franchise favoured property owners, and some areas of governance were controlled by government-appointed authorities without any elected representatives, such as under the Sydney Harbour Trust Act 1900.[19]

A further iteration of urban planning reform began in the interwar period. A milestone was the UK's Town and Country Planning Act 1932, enabling local authorities to prepare planning schemes for any land in England and Wales, not merely for suburban land as hitherto. However, the seminal Barlow inquiry 1937–40 appointed by the UK government highlighted the need for *mandatory* planning to curb the loss of prime agricultural land from urbanisation.[20] The transformative Town and Country Planning Act 1947 enshrined the principle that land use planning permission was necessary for land development, thereby ending the presumption that the right to develop was a natural incident of property ownership and shifting away from rigid and exclusive land use zones. Concomitantly, all municipal authorities were required by the 1947 Act to prepare comprehensive land use plans, overseed by a government Minister.[21]

An innovative breakthrough was the introduction of zoning. Despite some useful interventions, the common law proved insufficient to deal with rapid urbanisation and industrialisation as the torts of private and public nuisance couldn't leverage strategic planning for complex land use issues. Nor could common law property rights adequately assist. The landmark English case of *Tulk v Moxhay* in 1848,[22] concerning responsibility to maintain a garden, held that a covenant restricting a property to a specific use could only be enforced in Equity against a subsequent purchaser so long as the covenant is negative in orientation, it touches and concerns the land, and the subsequent purchaser had notice of it. With zoning, planning law could move beyond its focus on form and design, such as the layout of streets and controlling unsanitary premises, to include also land use, resulting in potentially far greater control over people's activities and thus the rights of property owners.

[18] Section 321.

[19] Y-F Ng et al, 'Democratic Representation and the Property Franchise in Australian Local Government' (2016) 76(2) *Australian Journal of Public Administration* 221.

[20] JH Jones, 'The Report of the Royal Commission on the Distribution of the Industrial Population' (1940) 103(3) *Journal of the Royal Statistical Society* 323.

[21] SA de Smith, 'Town and Country Planning Act, 1947' (1948) 11(1) *Modern Law Review* 72.

[22] (1848) 2 Ph 774.

Under zoning, incompatible land uses can be identified and separated from one another, and further that the structures allowed in given parcels of land can align with the purposes of the plan. Zoning thus offered the potential to produce settlements of harmonious land use and design. American and British legal precedents were important here. The first citywide zoning regime in the United States was New York City's zoning resolution of 1916, imposing setback and height controls and designating residential districts that excluded incompatible activities. In 1926, in the landmark US case of *Village of Euclid*, the nation's Supreme Court recognised local governments' right to regulate land use through zoning as a valid exercise of a state's police (regulatory) power.[23] Zoning however was insufficient to create attractive and functional cities where it focused on controlling development without envisioning a comprehensive plan to create communities with better amenities.

These international developments informed antipodean planning, where the need for reform was palpable. Murray Wilcox's account of the problem in NSW just after World War I likely reflected that afflicting many Australian towns: 'A council might now be able to avoid the worst evils of laissez-faire development, sub-standard buildings and inadequate sites, but it could do little to avoid buildings being thrust into disharmonious proximity.'[24] Researchers pinpoint South Australia's Planning and Housing Act 1916 and Subdivision of Land Act 1917 as major innovations for Australia.[25] Another was Western Australia's Town Planning and Development Act 1928, providing for 'town planning schemes' for 'improving and developing such land to the best possible advantage' as well as 'suitable provision for traffic, transportation, disposition of shops, residence, and factory areas, proper sanitary conditions and convenience, parks, gardens and reserves'.[26] Yet such legislative mandates, especially when only encouraging rather than mandating action, could result in sluggish progress, as occurred owing to obstructionist developers, conservative municipalities elected under systems that favoured property owners, and state legislatures dominated by rural interests unenthusiastic about expenditure on urban issues.[27] The promising start to town planning reform in the early twentieth century would have to wait until some decades after the post-war period to regain momentum.

## II. Post-War Planning Shifts

Further pressures to reform urban planning came after World War II with population boom in the capital cities; however law reform lagged, with one legal authority

[23] *Village of Euclid v Amber Realty Co* (1926) 272 US 365.

[24] MR Wilcox, *The Law of Land Development in New South Wales* (Law Book Company, 1967) 188.

[25] G Bolton, *Spoils and Spoilers. Australians Make Their Environment 1788–1980* (Allen and Unwin, 1981) 125–26; M Barker, 'How Planning and Environmental Law Has Shaped Our Cities' (Planning Institute of Australia National Congress, 2007).

[26] Section 6(1).

[27] Bolton (n 25) 126, 134.

in 1974 declaring that Australia's town planning laws remained 'much akin to the English pre-war planning system'.[28] The basic governance model in Australian settlements was to zone land with functionally incompatible uses, such as retail, housing, industry and parkland, segregated into discrete precincts. The criticisms of this approach were over reliance on rigid land-use classifications without sufficient flexibility to examine each development on its merits.[29] Furthermore, the vision of democratically governed cities was jeopardised by the professionalisation of town planning that had resulted in the growth of a culture of planning 'experts' taking control.[30]

Modernisation of cities and the soaring popularity of motor vehicles, explain urban historian Graeme Davison,[31] increasingly clashed with the need to safeguard green spaces, cultural heritage and community amenities.[32] It's a clash that unfolded in many other nations, often resulting in monotonous sprawl, behemoth malls and congested highways, as excoriated in Jane Jacobs' masterpiece, *The Death and Life of Great American Cities*.[33] Planning law struggled to resolve the tensions, leading to conflicts spilling beyond the legal system such as Sydney's 'Green Ban' movement of the 1970s, as discussed in chapter three. It's a story where the market and enlightened despotism prevailed over polyarchal processes in planning governance.

Sydney's ambitious County of Cumberland Planning Scheme of 1948 was the nation's first post-war, major metropolitan plan for accommodating a bigger city. Incorporating some of the garden city ideals, the Cumberland Scheme envisioned a 'Green Belt' and 'Harbour Scenic Protection Areas' in order to 'produce aesthetic harmony and improvement', as well as greater opportunities for 'outdoor recreation'.[34] Not only was horizontal growth to be better coordinated but vertical development as well, which became necessary as building-height limits were eased in 1957.[35] New South Wales pioneered the world's first, strata-title legislation, adopted in 1961 to enable community living especially in high-rises.[36] The model, allowing individual apartment owners within a shared, common property area, was adopted by many other countries from Canada to South Africa.

[28] S Fogg, *Australian Town Planning Law* (University of Queensland Press, 1974) 167.

[29] ibid 169–73.

[30] JM Powell, *Environmental Management in Australia 1788–1914* (Oxford University Press, 1976) 161, 166.

[31] G Davison, *Car Wars* (Allen and Unwin, 2004).

[32] R Freestone, 'Australian Environmental Planning Origins and Theories' in J Bryne, N Sipe and J Dodson (eds), *Australian Environmental Planning: Challenges and Future Prospects* (Routledge, 2014) 21, 25.

[33] (Random House, 1961). See also L Sandercock, 'Dreaming the Sustainable City: Organizing Hope, Negotiating Fear, and Mediating Memory' in BJ Eckstein and JA Throgmorton (eds), *Story and Sustainability: Planning, Practice and Possibility for American Cities* (MIT Press, 2003) 143.

[34] Cumberland County Council, *The Planning Scheme for the County of Cumberland, New South Wales* (1948) 204, 207.

[35] Height of Buildings (Amendment) Act 1957.

[36] Conveyancing (Strata Titles) Act 1961.

Sydney's post-war development deviated from the Cumberland plan as the economic and demographic pressures of the post-war boom intensified. The 1948 plan, described as 'visionary and radical' by one authority,[37] was overwhelmed by the surge in demand for new housing from the baby boom generation and leap in immigration, as the plan was based on a forecast population in the Sydney region of 2.3 million by 1980, a number reached 17 years earlier in 1963.[38] The drafters of the plan presumably had some inkling of this threat, given their acknowledgement that in some of the 91,620 acres supposedly earmarked for the Green Belt 'ex-servicemen and other prospective home builders have purchased home sites'.[39] Local councils increasingly ignored the Cumberland plan in opening up development, as was possible owing to the accessibility provided by a growing car-owning culture.[40] Eventually the NSW state government effectively overruled it when in 1963 it created a new State Planning Authority,[41] which in 1968 issued a new vision called the *Sydney Region Outline Plan*.[42]

As cities like Sydney grew upwards and outwards, historic buildings and intimate neighbourhoods were threatened.[43] One response was the establishment of national trusts at a state level, beginning with NSW in 1945, and culminating in the creation of a national, peak body in 1965. Modelled on the UK's National Trust founded in 1895, Australia's national trusts are community-based organisations that own and manage heritage places along with engaging with governments and other stakeholders to educate and advocate for conservation of significant heritage.[44] Many of the trusts' energies in their early history went to saving places threatened by 'progress' at a time where planning law undervalued 'old fashioned' architecture and ignored community opinion.

Additionally, grassroot, residential associations were establishing in Australian cities to challenge municipal planners and developers. Heather Goodall cites resident action campaigns from the mid-1940s battling against municipal authorities to protect the bush and mangroves around Sydney's Georges River.[45] In Hobart, the city council in the 1950s had little interest preserving or restoring the city's fine Georgian buildings, preferring instead to clear 'slums' to make way for wider roads and taller buildings that would increase property values and the municipality's coffers.

[37] R Bunker, 'In the Shadow of the City: The Fringe Around the Australian Metropolis in the 1950s' (2002) 17(1) *Planning Perspectives* 1.

[38] Cumberland County Council (n 34) 49; see also S Daniel, 'How a Post-war Population Explosion Put an End to Sydney's "Visionary" Green Belt Plan' (*ABC News*, 29 March 2018) www.abc.net.au/news/2018-03-29/curious-sydney-what-happened-to-sydneys-green-belt/9576144.

[39] ibid 215.

[40] I Boileau, D Hain and R Atkins, 'The Cumberland County Council 1945–64' (1964) 3(1) *Royal Australian Planning Institute Journal* 20.

[41] By the State Planning Authority Act 1963.

[42] State Planning Authority, *Sydney Region Outline Plan 1970–2000* (Government of NSW, 1968).

[43] See generally B Boer and G Wiffen, *Heritage Law in Australia* (Oxford University Press, 2006).

[44] J Lesh, *Values in Cities: Urban Heritage in Twentieth-Century Australia* (Routledge, 2022) ch 3.

[45] H Goodall, *Georges River Blues: Swamps, Mangroves and Resident Action, 1945–1980* (ANU Press, 2022).

The erection in 1967 of the conspicuous Empress Towers, depicted in Figure 10.2, in the historic enclave of Battery Point, was supposed to be the forerunner of the city's transformation. The Battery Point Community Association (founded 1948) successfully staved off most of the further threats to the neighbourhood's heritage.[46] A similar grassroots struggle unfolded in many inner-city communities in Australia in this era.

**Figure 10.2** Empress Towers, eye-sore erected in 1967 in historic Battery Point, Hobart; photograph by author

National trusts and residential groups represented some of the opposition to a planning system that associated sprawling suburbs, bulldozing old buildings and constructing freeways with 'progress'. British planning law scholar Patrick McAuslan argued that although an 'ideology' of public participation began to penetrate planning governance in the post-war era, especially from the 1960s, it had to compete against its two older ideologies, namely faith in the benevolent, expert public administrator (reflected in regulators' broad, discretionary powers) and protection of private property (reflected in policies to maximise land utility and give developers preferential rights in planning decisions).[47] Given these

[46] I Duckett, 'Battery Point: Engagement, Activism and Green Bans' (2015) 8(1) *Tasmanian Planner*.
[47] P McAuslan, *The Ideologies of Planning Law* (Pergamon, 1980) 1–6.

conflicting philosophies, planning law needed reform if it was to effectively give community stakeholders a greater say in town planning.

Whilst Australian planning legislation increasingly allowed for public rights to comment on proposed planning schemes, any rights to be notified about development applications or appeal against municipalities' decisions were slower to be liberalised. Victoria's Town and Country Planning Act 1961 marked a shift, allowing for public notices and third-party objector appeals in certain situations.[48] Until such reforms, the impacted wider community lacked limited recourse to the courts to challenge unwelcome developments. Standing to enforce provisions of municipal legislation and other types of administrative regulation was historically governed by the 1903 English precedent of *Boyce v Paddington Borough Council*,[49] where Judge Buckley confined *locus standi* in the following terms:

> A plaintiff can sue without joining the Attorney-General in two cases: first, where the interference with the public right is such as that some private right of his is at the same time interfered with … and, secondly, where no private right is interfered with, but the plaintiff, in respect of his public right, suffers special damage peculiar to himself from the interference with the public right.[50]

Whilst restricted standing rights supposedly discouraged meddlesome, unmerited litigation, and that the Attorney-General was better suited to enforce the government's own laws, it could be politically abused by governments to shield themselves from judicial accountability. One notorious example concerns Tasmania's Lake Pedder, discussed in chapter three. When environmentalists opposed to the damming of the lake sought a fiat from the state's Attorney-General to challenge the dam project's legality, the Attorney-General resigned after his Cabinet overruled his intention to grant the fiat, and thereupon the State Premier appointed himself as Attorney-General and refused a fiat. Thus, the Tasmanian courts were never able to rule on the legality of the dam in an area once designated a national park.[51]

Absent legislative reform, there was little scope under the common law for disgruntled citizens to bring public interest cases to the courts. For instance, in 1980 the High Court denied standing to the ACF, which it considered having only an emotional or intellectual concern in the environment, although the Court substituted 'special interest' for the 'special damage' limb of *Boyce* in recognition that a relevant interest need not be just economic in character.[52] Courts dealing with the related 'person aggrieved' test for standing for review of administrative decisions likewise showed a conservative bias.[53] NSW's Local Government Act 1919 allowed

[48] See eg s 18.
[49] (1903) 1 Ch 109.
[50] ibid 114.
[51] Australian Law Reform Commission, *Standing in Public Interest Litigation* (Commonwealth of Australia, 1985) 90.
[52] *Australian Conservation Foundation v Commonwealth* [1980] HCA 53.
[53] See eg *Mundy v Brisbane City Council* (1966) 13 LGRA 187.

persons aggrieved by decisions of a municipal authority to appeal, but courts held that this did not mean 'any person at all who may on any ground feel dissatisfied with what the Council has done' but rather 'the person who is dissatisfied in the sense that, having made application to the Council for its approval, he has either failed to secure it or secured it only on conditions with which he is dissatisfied'.[54] In recent decades courts in environmental cases have broadened standing to enable third-party challengers,[55] and legislative reform in some jurisdictions has gone further, offering open standing to 'any person'.[56]

The history and struggles of town planning in Australia last century can now be examined in detail through a case study of the nation's capital.

## III. Siting the National Capital

As plans for federation progressed, Australia's largest two cities vied to host the nation's capital. Yet as Melburnians and Sydneysiders could never agree to either claiming the spoils, a location elsewhere had to be found. This task had to respect that the new city would provide a tangible focus for expressing the identity and vitality of a young nation that would transcend regional or colonial parochialism, and engage Australians in a way that the passing of Australia's Constitution Act couldn't provide. The Constitution did not itself stipulate the site of the nation's seat of government other than decree, by section 125, that it shall be determined by the Commonwealth Parliament on the proviso that it be in NSW 'and not less than one hundred miles from Sydney'. Meantime, the federal government would operate from Melbourne. A protracted search and debate followed that took until 1909.

The mission for the country's lawmakers furnished an unprecedented opportunity to adapt the latest innovations in town planning to the national psyche. It was an era of progressive developments in planning theory as recognition grew of the importance of accommodating not only functional infrastructure such as roads and utilities but also the aesthetic ambience and health of urban living through green expanses and impressive civic spaces. Achieving these qualities would be easier where the host environment itself afforded a picturesque setting. Federal planners were evidently sensitive to such considerations, as the media reported on their goal to create a 'beautiful city' with 'panoramic value'.[57] As put by King O'Malley, the Commonwealth's Minister for Home Affairs at this formative stage, the new capital would be a place 'commensurate with the importance of this great Australian nation'.[58]

[54] *Greenberg v Sydney City Council* (1958) 3 LGRA 233, 225.

[55] See eg *Australian Conservation Foundation v Minister for Resources* (1989) 7 LGRA 200, 205.

[56] See eg Environmental Planning and Assessment Act 1979 (NSW); see also W Martin, 'The Importance of Town Planning Law' (State Administrative Tribunal Conference to Mark 80 Years of Town Planning Law in Western Australia, Perth, November 2009) 16–17.

[57] 'The Federal Capital' *Express and Telegraph* (Adelaide) 24 June 1909, 3.

[58] King O'Malley, House of Representatives Hansard, 1 November 1911, 2109.

Finding a suitable site was aided by a Royal Commission established in 1899 by NSW for 'obtaining information and reporting as to the most suitable site for the Federal Capital'. It considered criteria that included climate, accessibility, water availability and ownership of the land. Forty towns or districts made submissions to the Commission, many of which it inspected, with those offering a cooler climate being preferred as planners believed such conditions best suited European Australians.[59] Equally, aesthetics mattered. The hills overlooking Lake George – seemingly so promising after rains – lost contention when the rains didn't come; the visiting commissioner explained, 'the site itself commands an extensive view of Lake George, which would undoubtedly possess much charm if the lake were full of water … The site is wanting in picturesqueness'.[60] The Commission recommended the Eden-Monaro area as best meeting its criteria.[61]

The first federal parliamentarians had an opportunity to tour potential sites under the auspices of the Commonwealth's Capital Sites Enquiry Board established in 1902. Gostwyck Station near Armidale and my mother's farm at Orchardfield, was one of several sites they visited, being described by the *Australian Town and Country Journal* as a 'magnificent site … pleasant to the mind and sense'.[62] The Commonwealth also appointed its own Royal Commission in January 1903 to investigate further options, and it recommended that Albury or Tumut be chosen from 11 short-listed sites it evaluated.[63]

The parliamentary tours and royal commissions didn't settle the matter, however. In October 1903 the House of Representatives voted for a site 'at or near' Tumut, but the Senate wanted Bombala. Further investigations ensued, with Charles Scrivener, chief surveyor of the Department of Home Affairs, tasked with assessing more options in both these districts; he recommended Dalgety, on the Snowy River.[64] Then the newly elected government under Alfred Deakin in 1904 passed the Seat of Government Act, which stipulated that a site be chosen within 17 miles of Dalgety. This site however was fiercely opposed by the NSW government as being too far from Sydney and blighted by a sullen climate. Before the Commonwealth could press ahead with Dalgety, the government fell, and the tabled legislation didn't receive the necessary Royal Assent.

Further wrangling was thus necessary. Following a vote between the short-listed options of Dalgety and the Yass district, parliamentarians chose the latter, with a new Seat of Government Act passed in 1908 and nearly 1,000 square miles

[59] N Brown, *A History of Canberra* (Cambridge University Press, 2014) 39.

[60] NSW State Archives, 'Canberra – the Federal Capital Contest', www.records.nsw.gov.au/archives/magazine/galleries/canberra-the-federal-capital-contest.

[61] NSW Legislative Assembly, *Report of the Commissioner on Sites for the Seat of Government of the Commonwealth* (Government Printer, 1900).

[62] JC Neild, 'In Search of a National Capital' (*Australian Town and Country Journal*, 22 February 1902) 13.

[63] Royal Commission on Sites for the Seat of Government, *Report of the Commissioners* (Government Printer, 1903).

[64] TG Bates, 'From Riverina Water Shortage to Snowy Surplus: Charles Scrivener's Task to Locate a National Capital' (Proceedings of the 18th Association of Public Authority Surveyors Conference, Canberra, 12–14 March 2013).

of territory, including Jervis Bay for sea access, transferred by NSW to the Commonwealth. The Canberra valley was selected as the best site within the Yass region for building the bush capital, following further investigations in 1909 by Scrivener.[65] He favoured a site nested within a natural amphitheatre of gently forested hills overlooking a river floodplain, then occupied by pastoralists.

The home of the Ngunnawal people for thousands of years, the Canberra environs were first invaded by Europeans 200 years ago. Leading the way, explorer Charles Throsby and his nephew Charles Throsby Smith mounted expeditions in 1820 and 1821. From 1824 pastoralists began to establish permanent settlements and livestock ranches. By 1838, according to the official census, 1728 Europeans lived there, known then as the Limestone Plains because of its underlying geology.

The Aboriginal inhabitants were predictably soon dispossessed, with the dwindling survivors relegated to serving as farm labourers or domestic servants. In recent years Aboriginal people from various communities have returned to the area, with the 2021 national census recording 9,544 people who identify as Indigenous residing in the Australian Capital Territory.[66] An ACT government report in 2012 on the area's Aboriginal history observed that 'there appears to be no surviving traditional knowledge of lore, language, custom, kinship structures, oral history and genealogy associated directly with the ACT', although it confirms 'a distinct regional Aboriginal population that survived, resisted and adapted' to colonisation.[67]

When selected for the nation's future capital, Canberra's lowlands were predominantly treeless, sheep grazing country. Yet, its topography impressed surveyors, dotted with six high peaks, from 742 to 890 metres, clothed in extensive tracts of bushland, and dissected by the Molonglo River. To the west the larger Brindabella Ranges, often snow-capped in winter, add a picturesque backdrop. This verdant, natural amphitheatre would allow the Australian landscape to infuse the city's, and the nation's, identity.

## IV. Designing Canberra

Selecting the capital's site would prove less contentious than its actual design and construction. The Commonwealth's Seat of Government (Administration) Act 1910 said nothing about the town planning vision or standards for the capital's development other than stipulating that ordinances for administration of

[65] Quoted in J Horsfield, *Building a City: CS Daley and the Story of Canberra* (Ginninderra Press, 2015) 36.

[66] Australian Bureau of Statistics, 'Estimates of Aboriginal and Torres Strait Islander Australians' (ABS, 2022).

[67] Australian Capital Territory Government, *Our Kin Our Country* (Community Services Directorate, 2012) 24, 27.

the federal territory could be enacted by the Governor-General and that some NSW laws would continue to apply until thereby replaced. From 1911, a steady stream of such ordinances dealing with environmental matters was issued including, in the first decade, public health (1912), wildlife protection (1913), river pollution (1914), parks and gardens (1918), fish protection (1919), timber protection (1919), rabbit destruction (1919), and noxious weeds (1921).[68] Town planning itself wasn't specifically regulated, as it was then gradually improving in other Australian jurisdictions. Nonetheless, the city's planning was a priority of federal politicians, to address by another, novel means. In 1911 the Commonwealth launched an international competition to attract the best blueprint for Canberra, as it was officially called by 1913 – a name derived from the term for 'meeting place' in the Aboriginal vernacular.

The design competition coincided with some liberating shifts in town planning philosophy and governance, as earlier noted. The 'city beautiful' and 'garden city' movements glorified public access to open space and greenery – counteracting the legacies of the Industrial Revolution that blighted cities.[69] Although the town planning professions of the time jettisoned Ebenezer Howard's accompanying vision of organising urban life along communitarian or socialist ideals, his emphasis on public amenities and green spaces was embraced. The 'city beautiful' movement, led by Chicago architect Daniel Hudson Burnham,[70] idealised a metropolis centred on gracious, wide boulevards flanked by tidy parks and grand edifices. These innovations in city planning surely weighed on the Commonwealth's Minister for Home Affairs, King O'Malley, in launching the competition for Canberra's design, at that time envisioned as having 75,000 inhabitants living on 65 km$^2$. (By 2023, Canberra had 472,000 residents with an urban footprint of 814 km$^2$.) The competition rules stipulated two key conditions: the Commonwealth would own the chosen design, and its officers would determine its implementation.

Chicagoans Walter Burley Griffin (1876–1937) and Marion Mahony Griffin (1871–1961) were announced on 23 May 1912 as the competition winners, earning £1,750 prize money (equivalent to about $250,000 in 2023), from a field of 137 entries, including 42 from Australia. The potential pool of entrants was considerably reduced after the Royal Institute of British Architects and affiliated bodies in the empire boycotted the competition in protest against O'Malley's edict that he – without architectural training – be its final adjudicator, even though he convened an expert advisory panel to assess the entries. Ultimately, O'Malley did accept the panel's majority recommendation. On winning, Walter Griffin said in a lecture to business dignitaries that: 'We can all be interested in the Australian Federal Capital City … because of what it stands for, the best, I believe so far afforded for an expression of the democratic civic ideal and of all that means in accessibility,

[68] See ACT legislation archives of the Australasian Legal Information Institute, classic.austlii.edu.au.

[69] As recently as 1900, inner-city Sydney was afflicted by bubonic plague outbreaks in its crowded housing tenements.

[70] WH Wilson, *The City Beautiful Movement* (Johns Hopkins University Press, 1989).

freedom, wealth, comfort, conveniences, scale and splendor'.[71] O'Malley's apparent enthusiasm for Canberra's development was a dramatic turn from his earlier condemnation of 'a district which at times is so dry that a crow desiring to put in a weekend vacation there would have to carry its water-bag'.[72]

Marion Griffin's contribution to the winning design has sometimes been overlooked. She began working with Walter in his Chicago practice in 1910, where their romance began and marriage ensued the following year. An imaginative designer, Walter saw himself as a 'landscape architect' who accentuated the relationships between architecture and its natural settings, but he lacked his wife's flair for rendering the big picture into workable and eye-catching designs.[73] Canberra's topography radiated through the Griffins' design, despite relying on maps and a clay model of the environs that were made available to entrants. They and others also had access to a collection of panoramic paintings by Robert Charles Coulter, which revealed the site's varied and interesting terrain. The Griffins' entry included a 'design report', explaining the rationale for their plan, conveying their methodical analysis of the government's brief about the site's characteristics, and their architecture philosophy that 'form follows function'.

According to urban historian Robert Freestone, the 'city beautiful' oeuvre was more influential than Howard's garden city ideas in the Griffins' design, which 'conveyed a monumental city dominated by grand axes and vistas, ensembles of monolithic buildings, [and] terminal landmarks'.[74] Yet, the Canberra actually designed, arguably had much in common with Howard's schema. The Griffins' vision emphasised embellishment of Canberra's bush setting and incorporating 'the physical site itself as the new nation's enduring monument'.[75] Their design depicted a metropolis of elegant symmetry in its layout with abundant parks, tree-lined avenues and conservation of the surrounding bush-lad hills. A 'national triangle', comprising land and water axes aligned on the mountains and hills, was anchored on Capital Hill, which today is occupied by the new parliament house opened in 1988. It would be ringed by distinct enclaves for commerce, government and housing, interconnected by elegant boulevards flanked by the forested peaks of Mount Ainslie and Black Mountain. In an era before the motor car had become a planning issue, the Griffins' proposed a public transport network of trams, with the population housed predominantly in European-style, low-level apartments and compact terraces that wouldn't compete with the natural topography. A lake system, offering aesthetic, amenity and recreational benefits, was also fundamental to the Griffins' vision that would transform the meandering Molonglo River, a modest waterway that periodically flooded. The architects proposed damming the

[71] Quoted in R Willett, *The National Capital in the National Interest* (Self-published, 2019) 5.

[72] Quoted in Horsfield (n 65) 53.

[73] National Archives of Australia, *A Vision Splendid: How the Griffins Imagined Australia's Capital* (Commonwealth of Australia, 2013) 8.

[74] R Freestone, *Designing Australia's Cities: Culture, Commerce and the City Beautiful, 1900–1930* (Routledge, 2007) 99.

[75] National Archives of Australia (n 73), 7.

river to create a series of sculptured, interconnected water basins, enhanced with decorative foreshore parklands.

The Griffins also wished to embellish Canberra's greenery through reforestation and a national botanical garden. They saw contact with nature – light, water and plants – as vital for people's well-being; 'the basis of the architect's study', once wrote Walter, 'is nature itself – the beauty is where nature is allowed to work itself out'.[76] Australian trees in particular enamoured them, with Walter remarking: 'the gum-tree instead of being one continual monotony has strongly appealed to me. It is a poet's tree and ought to have a more dignified name. Gum tree! That does not fit at all. It's a wonderful tree – a decorator's tree'.[77] Canberra's extensive tree-clad landscape today would impress the Griffins, though much of it wouldn't, as the following section explains in revealing the difficulties a federal bureaucracy had in embracing visionary change, a story that also illustrates the larger problem of how government agencies often were an impediment to the more visionary ideals of environmental law reform in this book's history.

## V. Building Canberra

It's a myth that the Canberra of the twenty-first century faithfully reflects the Griffins' design. Parts of the utilitarian and symbolic vision of the Griffins' were implemented, but the Chicago architects would find much of the city doesn't resemble their plan. As the former head of Canberra's National Capital Development Commission once acknowledged: 'The impression given is that modern Canberra is Griffin's city, with a few changes necessitated by modern life, of which he would have approved' but 'the vitality of Griffin's proposed urban terraces and monuments has been replaced by quiet suburbs'.[78] While the planning bureaucrats embraced some of the environmental amenities and general layout of the Griffins' design, they rejected some crucial details including medium-density settlements and public transport – the result today being sprawling suburbia dissected with a labyrinth of roads, although a modest light rail system finally commenced in 2019.

The competition rules didn't stipulate that the winner would have any official role overseeing the building of the bush capital. Walter seemed to have a premonition of how city authorities might respond: 'I have planned [a city] not in a way that I expected any governmental authorities in the world would accept. I have planned an ideal city – a city that meets my ideal of the city of the future'.[79] It would

[76] Quoted in E Huxley, *Their Shining Eldorado: A Journey Through Australia* (Chatto and Windus, 1967) 35.

[77] Quoted in G Souter, *Lion and Kangaroo: The Initiation of Australia* (Collins, 1976) ch 9.

[78] P Reid, *Canberra Following Griffin – A Design History of Australia's National Capital* (National Archives of Australia, 2002) 4.

[79] Quoted in 'City Twenty-Five Miles Square to be Built Upon What is Now a Wilderness' (*New York Times*, 2 June 1912) SM3.

soon become apparent that his premonition was well founded, when Minister O'Malley and his staff discussed adopting a composite design from the best entries, with adjustments to accommodate financial constraints and the practicalities of building from scratch. A board of the Department of Home Affairs tasked with superintending Canberra's planning began formulating a revised design with these considerations, which William Kelly, the successor responsible Minister, accepted in 1913.

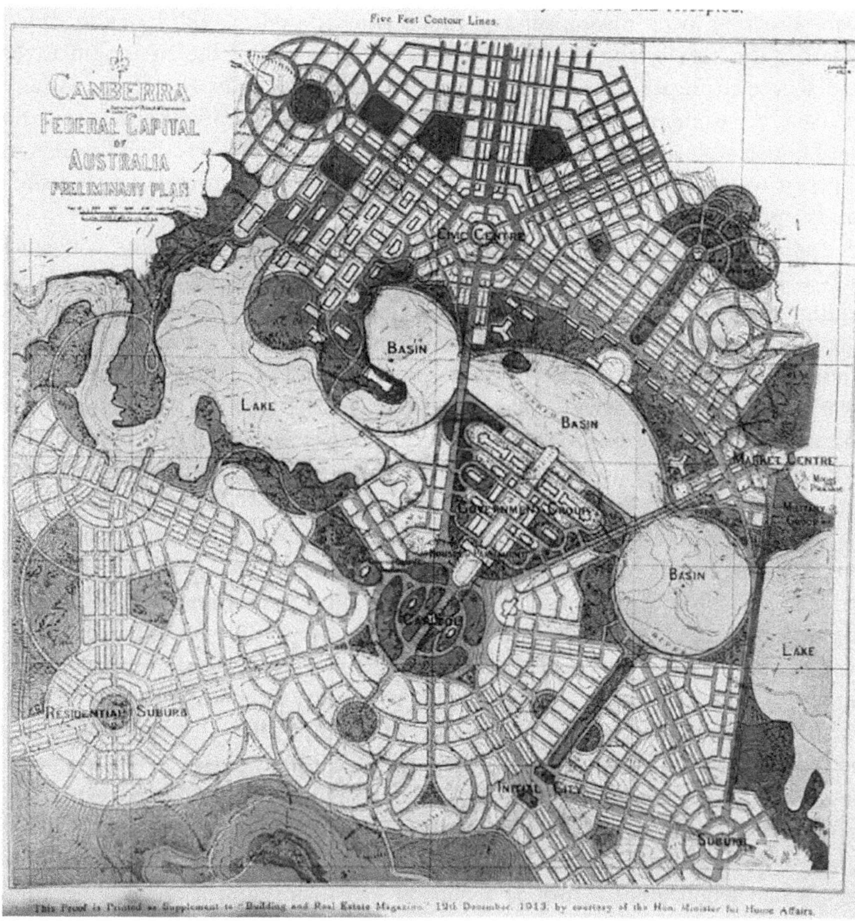


**Figure 10.3** Walter Burley Griffin's Plan of Canberra as finally revised and accepted, 1913, National Library of Australia

On learning of his snub, Walter came to Australia in August 1913 to seek reinstatement of his original plan. In a conciliatory move, the Commonwealth offered him the position of Federal Capital Director of Design and Construction, which Walter accepted, returning to Australia the following year with Marion. It proved a frustrating experience, for he found the government planners lacking a 'missionary sense of nation building'.[80] Moreover, Walter wasn't invited to design any of Canberra's flagship edifices, though he would later design buildings elsewhere in Australia.

Construction was slowed by the diversion of resources for World War I, and the growing rivalry between Walter and Department of Home Affairs staff, whose senior bureaucrats took umbrage at the appointment of an overseer from outside their ranks. The tensions between Walter and Canberra officialdom were also tied to philosophical and pragmatic differences. The latter included whether the core of the city should be north or south of the Molonglo River and where to locate the railway terminus. Philosophically, the Home Affairs bureaucrats' understanding of the 'garden city' differed from Walter's, favouring the English style of tidy bungalows in parklike settings and tree-lined streets in contrast to the Griffins' desire to accentuate the natural symmetry of the site's landscape.

Indicative of a broader trend in governance whereby governments' convened public inquiries to gather additional advice, quieten conflict and boost the legitimacy of their decisions, a Royal Commission was appointed by the Commonwealth in 1916 to review progress developing the national capital, and its findings generally corroborated Walter's criticisms of bureaucratic obstruction.[81] Sympathetically, Minister O'Malley formally approved putting the Griffins back in the picture, authorising Walter to oversee implementation of the capital's plan. With the revised 1918 city plan, Walter made some modifications aimed at making it less costly to build. But tensions still simmered.

By 1920 the Griffins had had enough of Canberra, leaving the city's future in the hands of the federal bureaucracy. When Walter returned briefly in May 1927 for the opening of the provisional parliament house, attending as a bystander, he would surely have been disappointed at what he saw.[82] Nonetheless, Walter had an eye for the long term, for in Melbourne's *Herald* he wrote that although Canberra wasn't yet a city, its 'natural attractiveness' exceeded that of other major capital cities around the world, an attractiveness he believed would eventually 'stimulate the Australian national sentiment' to complete the making of its capital.[83] Recognising his novelty, Walter explained he aimed 'to treat architecture as a democratic language of everyday life, not a language of an aristocratic, especially educated cult, as it has been since the year 1500, when architecture as a natural expression and a creative art died with the Renaissance'.[84]

[80] C Vernon, 'Australia's Lost Capitol' (2016) 70(2) *Journal of Architectural Education* 284, 296.

[81] Royal Commission on Federal Capital Administration, *Report of the Royal Commission on Issues Relating to Mr Griffin* (Parliament of the Commonwealth of Australia, 1917).

[82] 'Canberra Designer Ignored' (*Herald* (Melbourne), 3 May 1927) 4.

[83] WB Griffin, 'Canberra Founded on National Sentiment' (*Herald* (Melbourne), 7 May 1927) 17.

[84] WB Griffin, Untitled letter, 21 January 1913, to Minister for Home Affairs, King O'Malley, urbanplanning.library.cornell.edu/DOCS/grifltr.htm.

After his departure, the Federal Capital Advisory Committee under the auspices of the Minister of Home Affairs was tasked with the city's development. Walter declined an invitation to join it. His old foes hoped to use his absence to resurrect their own 1912 plan, yet the Committee lasted only until the end of 1924 when it was abolished because of the Minister's dissatisfaction with the sluggish progress. A new entity, the Federal Capital Commission, took over, vested by the Seat of Government (Administration) Act 1924 with wide-ranging town planning powers including 'forestry and afforestation, and the preservation of fauna and flora', and 'the destruction of vermin and noxious weeds'.[85]

Curiously, the Act omitted mentioning the Griffins' plan – instead, referring to the 'Minister's plan'.[86] That plan, issued in November 1925, was later characterised in 1955 by a Senate inquiry as 'the general plan as prepared by Burley Griffin with such modifications as had been approved up to that time'.[87] There was then some hesitation in the government however about creating the lake system, a cornerstone of the Griffins' design, as some believed it was unlikely to fill owing to insufficient water flow or, if it did fill, it would divide the city into twin towns.[88]

The Federal Capital Commission didn't long last either, closing in 1930. The Great Depression sapped the resources of the Commonwealth to fund Canberra's development, and thus the Commission was disbanded with its work apportioned among federal departments. At this time Canberra remained in a rudimentary state: it had just 9,000 residents, of whom one-third were construction workers. Visiting journalists from Melbourne and Sydney glumly observed that Canberra was 'the only illuminated cemetery in the world'.[89]

Further progress wouldn't occur over the next two decades owing to the national austerity engendered by World War II and its aftermath. By the mid-1940s, Canberra remained far from planners' original vision: buildings and sprawling suburbs were separated by extensive, open paddocks, public transport was limited, and the Molonglo River had yet to be transformed into the elegant lakes envisioned by the Griffins. They were not the first, however, to see the potential of flooding the Molonglo; government surveyor Charles Scrivener, who scouted for sites for the future national capital, recommended the site for reasons that included that its topography and river were conducive to store water 'for ornamental purposes at reasonable cost'.[90] Finally completed in 1964, and named Lake Burley Griffin, it embellished the capital with an elegant and recreational waterway of 6.6 $km^2$ with extensive lakeside parks.

[85] Section 14(1)).
[86] Section 14(3)).
[87] Australia, Senate, *Report of the Select Committee Appointed to Inquire and Report Upon the Development of Canberra* (Parliament of the Commonwealth of Australia, 1955) 7.
[88] Willett (n 71) 71.
[89] A Fitzgerald, *Canberra Engineering Heritage* (Institution of Engineers, 1983) 129.
[90] 'First Vision. Canberra's Beauty. Scrivener's Foresight' (*Canberra Times*, 3 June 1927) 8.

**Figure 10.4** Walter Burley Griffin and Marion Mahony Griffin, Castlecrag, 27 July 1930; National Library of Australia

Although too late for the Griffins, the 1955 Senate inquiry called for resurrection of their plan. It recommended a single authority to oversee the city's planning and development unlike the then 'system of divided departmental control' and the 'enormous waste of public convoys and lack of departmental efficiency by the carrying on of administration in the three cities of Canberra, Melbourne and Sydney'.[91] Further recommendations were made on some details of the federal capital's buildings that would have appealed to the Griffins, including that the 'pastoral or "garden" atmosphere of Canberra be kept' and that the 'tree patterns' and 'spacious parklands be recognised as important factors which must govern the future planning and development of the city'.[92] Greater population density in areas zoned for housing of 'highly qualified architects' for all government buildings, were other advice given. Like other Australian public inquiries however, the Senate's effort lacked regulatory authority and could only really help focus media attention and stir public debate on the issues.

## VI. Greening Canberra

When selected for the nation's capital, much of the 2,358 km$^2$ of the Federal Territory was heavily degraded. The lowlands presented a particularly barren, overgrazed landscape. One of the first tasks of the city's administrators was to rein in the rabbit plague by trapping, poisoning or other means of destruction. The greener parts of the Limestone Plains were graced with exotics planted by settlers, with the grandest estates furnished with oaks, elms and willows to remind their owners of their English or Scottish roots and make their residents feel 'at home'.

The Griffins appreciated the benefits of aesthetics to urban planning. Walter once counselled, 'city planning, as a fine art, will not come into existence until the populace has regained the natural viewpoint of primitive lovers of nature and of the outdoor life'.[93] The Griffins' vision for Canberra not only retained the existing bush but added much greenery including, as detailed in Walter's modified 1918 plan, an ambitious Continental Arboretum. It was to have embellished the slopes of Black Mountain, comprising five distinct clusters of plantings that corresponded in composition and relative location on a world map to all continents except Antarctica. Another unrealised lofty idea was to clothe the other high ground surrounding Canberra with trees of contrasting colours, such as yellow flowers on Mount Ainslie and red foliage on Red Hill. Progress towards his luminescent garden was made only on the latter site, where red bottlebrush survives today. Nonetheless, much of the Griffins' hope for a 'garden city' materialised, owing partly to the prevailing property tenure, in which Crown land or leasehold land enabled stricter controls than were it freehold, private property.

The implementation of the garden city also owed much to the enterprising horticulturalist Thomas Charles Weston. In May 1913 he was appointed Officer-in-Charge (Afforestation Branch), later as the Superintendent of Parks

[91] Australia, Senate, *Report of the Select Committee Appointed to Inquire into and Report Upon the Development of Canberra* (Parliament of the Commonwealth of Australia, 1955) 104.

[92] ibid 106.

[93] WB Griffin, 'Canberra: The Architectural and Developmental Possibilities of Australia's Capital City' (*Building*, 12 November 1913) 65, 68.

and Gardens. Besides horticulture, Weston was passionate about urban regeneration and was a member of the governing council of the NSW Town Planning Association. Although he shared the Griffins' interest in a *bush* capital, Weston had his own ideas about how to achieve it, and in fact, suggests one historian, 'the two men differed markedly in their approach to horticulture'.[94] Weston however worked under the auspices of Walter during his tenure as Federal Capital Director of Design and Construction.

Besides safeguarding uncleared hill-tops and regenerating native woodlands, Weston beautified Canberra with plantings along roadsides and its parks. He established two arboretums, at Acton and Yarralumla, nurturing both exotic and native species to test which would best adapt to the city's climate and soils. Over 200 species of trees were propagated in these nurseries, and saplings were offered to landholders on the city fringes, whose lease[95] included restrictions of ring-barking or lopping of trees for livestock fodder.[96] Weston's efforts were aided when the Timber Protection Ordinance was passed in 1919, unambiguously providing: 'any person who, without the permission of the Minister, cuts or damages growing trees on lands the property of the Commonwealth within the Territory shall be guilty of an offence'.[97] The prescribed penalty of the time was 10 pounds (about $900 in 2023 money).

In the 1920s the Federal Capital Advisory Committee, then overseeing Canberra's progress, endorsed Weston's advice to establish tree belts to buffer the city from violent winds that could rage across the Limestone Plains. Shelter belts were successfully established on several sites, including Yarralumla and Telopea. Weston also added greenery to Mount Majura and Mount Stromlo, among his priorities as he recognised it was important to restore tree cover here to keep dust down that could interfere with the new astronomical observatory.

The greening of Canberra had popular support. The media reported approvingly of a 'city of trees and birds'.[98] By the 1930s, much progress was becoming discernible, with the press declaring 'Canberra is indeed the very essence of a garden city' and 'probably nowhere in Australia is there such a display of wattle blossom to equal that to be seen in Canberra to-day'.[99] The *Canberra Annual*, a short-lived magazine of that period, remarked that 'in the city to-day Nature has played a part greater even than that of man. … [T]ree, shrub and flower have embellished the scene with beauty, dignity and character'.[100]

Wildlife followed, and in a move reminiscent of the acclimatisation societies of the previous century, some exotic fauna was imported to complement the city's gardens. In 1937 the Commonwealth Health Department approved importation

[94] Horsfield (n 65) 13.

[95] By virtue of the Seat of Government (Administration) Act 1910, stating: 'No Crown lands in the territory shall be sold or disposed of for any estate of freehold' (s 9).

[96] Under the Leases Ordinance 1918.

[97] Section 3.

[98] 'Good Work. Wild Life Preservation' (*Sun (Sydney)*, 22 March 1927) 9.

[99] 'Canberra Flowering Trees' (*Canberra Times*, 27 August 1932) 2.

[100] 'Canberra in 1934' (1934) 1 *Canberra Annual* 13, 147, quoted in J Regan, *National Landscapes* (PhD thesis, Australian National University, 2017) 147.

of 10 pairs of English thrushes for release in Canberra to control snails in the city's gardens and to cheer residents with their songs. The decision was opposed by the Royal Zoological Society of NSW and other natural history groups for fear that the imports would displace native birds.[101] A year later the birds were evidently thriving, with 'their mellow notes' heard in many parts of the city.[102]

Surrounding countryside also benefited from city greening. Walter had disapproved of talk to locate a government arsenal in Tuggeranong, complaining it 'would occupy the most attractive land of the Territory, land that is needed for a National Park.'[103] The arsenal plans were never realised, as World War I ended before they could be advanced. Today about 60 per cent of the ACT is protected for nature conservation and recreation, the crown jewel being the Namadgi National Park. These conservation areas protect the Territory's wildlife and aesthetic values, along with their original purpose of safeguarding the city's water catchment supply. The city's greenbelt is unrivalled for any Australian metropolis, and the national park's legal status is one reason, along with the unique political context, for this achievement.

**Figure 10.5** Planting trees near the first Parliament House, late 1920s; National Archives of Australia

[101] 'Thrushes. Imported to Canberra' (*Sydney Morning Herald*, 5 March 1937) 9.
[102] 'Grey Thrushes. Thrive in Canberra' (*Canberra Times*, 28 July 1938) 4.
[103] Quoted in Horsfield (n 65) 29.

Thomas Weston retired in 1926, and died in 1935. His legacy endures with the elegant tree-lined avenues, attractive nature strips and lush tree canopies gracing Canberra – many from among the original 2 million trees and shrubs planted during his tenure. Sadly, some of this urban forest may not survive because of climate change. Despite Weston's lasting contribution to Canberra – one historian describes him as 'more significant and more long-lasting than that of any other individual at the time'[104] – he was denied suitable professional recognition by the Commonwealth's Public Service Board, which didn't consider his work comparable to that of the city's architects and engineers.

Surprisingly, given the interest in bringing nature into Canberra's urban design, legislators didn't pay much attention to enacting measures to regulate other environmental issues that might affect that environmental vision. Under the Seat of Government (Acceptance) Act 1909, NSW assumed responsibility for controlling pollution in rivers flowing into the ACT.[105] Within federal territory itself several ordinances addressed pollution in a piecemeal manner without any overarching, statutory framework, including the Canberra Sewerage and Water Supply Regulations 1924, the Lake Burley Griffin Ordinance 1965, Motor Vehicle Traffic Act 1936, and the application of NSW's Smoke Nuisance Abatement Act 1902. Limited provisions to assist with conservation of wildlife were furnished by the Animals and Birds Protection Ordinance 1918 and Wild Flower and Native Plants Protection Ordinance 1936.

It was also a city planned with limited opportunities for lay persons' input, at odds with the direction of Australia's town planning law in recent decades. The inadequate scope for public input was clear in 1972 when the federal cabinet, in defiance of the National Capital Development Commission (which from 1958 to 1989 was responsible for coordinating the city's development) and numerous aggrieved submissions to the parliament's Public Works Committee which conducted an inquiry, approved a nearly 200-metre-high tower for telecommunications and tourism on Black Mountain overlooking Canberra.[106] The incoming Whitlam government's commission of an environmental impact study, an unprecedented measure, failed to turn the tide. A judicial challenge brought in 1973 by concerned citizens led by scientists and academics was ultimately dismissed, with the High Court rejecting the argument that alteration of the city's skyline or increased traffic through the nature reserve around the tower would constitute a public nuisance, and upholding that the Commonwealth had the executive power to perform works in the ACT without statutory authority.[107]

[104] ibid 74.
[105] First Schedule, cl 4.
[106] J Hotchin, 'Black Mountain as a Place of Protest' (Black Mountain Symposium, Paper 20, 2018) 401–10.
[107] *Johnson v Kent* [1975] HCA 4.

## VII. The Griffins' Final Ventures and Legacies

Tired of battling the federal bureaucracy, the Griffins turned their energies to new ventures. After a stint in Melbourne they moved to Sydney where they focused on designing an entire neighbourhood with acute environmental sensitivity. As nature enthusiasts, the Griffins had a particular fondness for Australian landscapes and their wildlife. In 1914 they joined the Field Naturalists' Society of NSW and enjoyed bushwalking. They named several Canberra suburbs, including Grevillea Park and Telopea Park, after Australian plants. Their most emphatic commitment to their adopted country's environment was in the Sydney foreshore suburb of Castlecrag, named after a soaring crag of rock overlooking this secluded finger of the harbour. Residing here from 1925 until 1935, Walter once explained: 'I want Castlecrag to be built … so that each individual can feel that the whole of the landscape is his. No fences, no red roofs to spoil the Australian landscape'.[108]

Their plans for this picturesque bush enclave included landscaping a natural amphitheatre as a hub for festivals and other community gatherings, and a network of meandering bushwalking trails in the 20 per cent of the area retained as public parkland, especially along the prized foreshore – well above the 2 per cent target set by municipal regulations. Walter also designed 19 houses, a refreshing change from his previous paucity of commissioned work to design Canberra's buildings. One architectural innovation was flat-roofed houses; he saw high-pitched roofs as superfluous in a city without snow. Flat-roofs, however, had drawbacks, as one writer recounted: 'A goldfish tank built into the ceiling … dripped disastrously on to a grand inaugural dinner. The wife of another rich client found bitumen oozing from above into her bath'.[109]

To coordinate his Castlecrag plans, Walter formed with several investors the Greater Sydney Development Association to purchase and develop 94 acres under a subdivision plan approved by Willoughby Council in 1921. The Association later purchased a further 650 acres in Castlecrag and neighbouring areas, mainly for conservation. To help preserve his legacy, Walter also placed covenants on the Castlecrag housing lots to ensure any building would remain sympathetic to the natural setting and community context. The covenants obliged property owners to pay a levy towards ongoing maintenance of the area including tree planting. In his article for *Australian Home Builder* in 1922, Walter called the Castlecrag estate 'an idealistic development' to 'conserve for the residents all the remarkable natural features of the place – its outlooks, monumental cliffs, caverns, ancient trees, fern glens, wild flower glades, waterfalls and foreshores'.[110] His efforts showed that with enough vision, resources and tenacity it was possible to create an eco-friendly

[108] Quoted in Walter Burley Griffin Society, www.griffinsociety.org/australia-sydney-castlecrag.
[109] Huxley (n 76) 36.
[110] Quoted in Federation House, 'Interwar Prairie Style', www.federation-house.com/interwar-prairie-style.

urban community in an era before town planning law had matured. Yet, that autonomy to design Castlecrag meant that their style of planning, with emphasis on preserving native bush and spacious housing lots, was considered by planners as too costly to replicate in many other urban areas, especially in working class suburbs where more frugal designs were needed.

The Griffins' most important legacy for the nation remains Canberra. Although some of their design for a stunning national capital wasn't realised, owing to the intransigence of officialdom, coupled with the fiscal austerity engendered by World Wars and the Great Depression, much of their vision of a garden city was achieved through retention of existing woodlands and regeneration of new greenery. Its creation is testament to the importance of environmental aesthetics in Australia's evolving national identity, and the role of planning governance in shaping that aesthetic character. The law itself played more of a backdrop to this story rather than being a direct regulatory instrument; the most important legal context was that all land was owned by the Commonwealth and thus it had the capacity to plan the bush capital without being concerned about existing uses or private property rights, as afflicted planning in other Australian settlements. The governance of Canberra's planning evolved with enlightened despotic touches, tightly controlled by federal politicians or their subordinates, with minimal public participation despite an open international design competition and subsequent commissions and public inquiries into the city's progress. The Aboriginal history of the site prior to Canberra also was hardly acknowledged in this era.

The monumental city envisioned by Canberra's planners, with grand public buildings and ornamental lakes, wouldn't begin to take shape until several decades after the Griffins left Canberra. Until then, life in the young bush capital had many detractors. One was diplomat Paul McGuire, who described Canberra in the late 1930s as 'a place of little scattered settlements, islands in the bush, with bitumen and concrete causeways'.[111] Equally derogatory, Charles Hawker, a federal parliamentarian from 1929–38, lampooned the capital as 'a good sheep station spoiled'. Emil Otto Hoppé, a seminal documentary photographer of his era, published the results of his 1930 sojourn in Australia in *The Fifth Continent*, and on Canberra he observed, 'The site selected, it cannot be gainsaid, is perfectly composed … but it is like a finely cut gem whose heart lacks fire, having as yet no background of human experience to give it atmosphere'.[112]

By the 1960s Canberra began to resemble the city that today's residents would more readily recognise. The Molonglo River was dammed in 1964, creating the most visible monument to the Griffins with the lake named after Walter. The National Library, with its elegant Corinthian columns, opened in 1968. Also by the lake, the nation's High Court building, designed in a modern Brutalist style, opened in 1980. And in 1988 the permanent Parliament House was established for

[111] P McGuire, *Australian Journey* (William Heinemann, 1942) 212.
[112] EO Hoppé, *The Fifth Continent* (Simpkin Marshall, 1931) ix.

Australia's bicentenary. There's not much beyond the lake that tangibly connects Canberra to its original designers., although its natural setting remains the city's timeless anchor. Australian journalist Kathleen Ussher, who in 1928 published *The Cities of Australia*, acknowledged the city's particularly striking setting in 'a bold semicircle of hills and distant mountains … [i]n winter these mountains are frequently snow-capped and present a striking feature'.[113]

After Australia, the Griffins established an architectural business in Lucknow, India, in 1935. It didn't last. Walter died of peritonitis at age 60 on 11 February 1937, and was buried there. Marion left India for Australia, but soon returned to the United States where she largely retired from architectural work but spent many years compiling a richly illustrated volume detailing her and Walter's careers. Marion lived until 1961, aged 90. Recently some Canberrans have proposed that Walter's remains be exhumed and reburied on the shores of the lake honouring him, so more people can remember his legacy for the national capital.

[113] K Ussher, *The Cities of Australia* (JM Dent and Sons, 1928) 78.

# 11

# Resource Users and Polluters

## I. Forestry Governance

Australia's history of regulating natural resource use and pollution in four areas, forests, soils, minerals and air and water quality, occupies this chapter. Some of these issues have already been canvassed in this book, including land degradation (chapter four), radioactive contamination from bomb tests (chapter seven) and logging of Tasmania's Mount Field National Park (chapter nine). As a big subject, where each topic could furnish a weighty tome, I prudently concentrate here on overarching governance themes and helpful anecdotes, beginning with forests.

Trees have occupied a dyadic place in the national consciousness, a symbol of nature's beauty and fecundity to some but an impediment to progress to others.[1] When conservationists discuss their pet causes, they often begin with forests, especially old growth, as the 'fate of trees is often emblematic of the wider environment'.[2] Forests though are just one genre of Australian 'bush', which includes woodlands, mallee and other lightly treed landscapes. Tom Griffiths, Stephen Pyne and Bill Gammage are among historians provoking awareness of the cultural lenses by which forests have been understood by Australians and the failure to acknowledge how these ecosystems were long socialised by Aboriginal people using fire to create more open landscapes than what contemporary environmentalist might regard as true 'forest'.[3] Whilst lighter treed landscapes have endeared some non-Aboriginal environmentalists, as showed in the 1967 campaign to save Victoria's Little Desert, forests with the grandest canopies still arouse the deepest sympathies, as fierce conflicts recently over Tasmania's Tarkine rainforests demonstrate.[4] 'Big forests' increasingly recognised role in sequestering carbon and mitigating climate change has fortified this bias.[5]

The natural sciences have seminally shaped the fate and understanding of Australia's forests. Influenced by Alexander von Humboldt, the pioneering

[1] J Dargavel, *Fashioning Australia's Forests* (Oxford University Press, 1995); LT Carron, *A History of Forestry in Australia* (ANU Press, 1985).

[2] O Jones and P Cloke, *Tree Cultures: The Place of Trees and Trees in Their Place* (Berg, 2002) 2.

[3] T Griffiths, 'How Many Trees Make a Forest?' (2002) 50(4) *Australian Journal of Botany* 375; SJ Pyne, *Burning Bush: A Fire History* (Holt, 1991); B Gammage, *The Biggest Estate on Earth: How Aborigines Made Australia* (Allen and Unwin, 2012).

[4] G Borschmann, 'After 20 Years of Uneasy Peace, the Forest Wars are Back' (*Guardian*, 20 March 2018) www.theguardian.com/environment/2018/mar/20.

[5] C Streck et al (eds), *Climate Change and Forests* (Brookings Institution Press, 2008).

German polymath,[6] the natural world came to be portrayed by the sciences as interdependent, where the loss or degradation of one part could reverberate through another. Understanding nature's interdependent properties, like how forests influence climate or soil, would become instrumental to improving environmental law. To protect forests' wildlife, it's necessary to protect where they dwell and feed, as well as protect even the smallest creatures, from bees to beetles, which help sustain ecosystems. Science would also come to directly reshape management of forests as a renewable resource to meet the people's economic needs. Conservation science thus helped shift the mentality of 'man versus nature' to 'man in nature', recognising that a vanishing continent had economic ramifications for people. As one prescient NSW politician recognised in 1933, 'unfortunately, we still destroy the trees upon which we should depend for the maintenance of our fertile lands'.[7] Yet the science of ecology, argues Libby Robin, has also been an ideology complicit in coloniality and subjugation of the natural world, such as used by the former acclimisatisation societies to reengineer Australia's biota,[8] and the value of Aboriginal traditional knowledge was long disregarded by ecologists.

Appreciation of nature's circle of life didn't come easily to Australia's first colonisers. As the colony expanded, settlers sanguinely viewed their 'big country' as blessed with vast timber reserves and other natural assets that didn't necessitate frugality or stewardship. The Western Australian media in 1894 praised the colony as 'splendidly timbered' and that the 'whole southwest … may be considered as one immense forest'.[9] Not so today, sadly, Despite the horrendous Federation Drought, the struthious belief persisted that even the arid interior was a land of opportunity, epitomised by the thrasonical Edwin Brady who claimed the Outback's 'red sandy soil … is everywhere proving, under correct treatment, the most fertile in the world'.[10]

Saner voices were making themselves heard, however. Geographer Stephen Legg has traced growing political agitation to save Victoria's forests from the late nineteenth century, as orchestrated through petitions, lobbying, public protest meetings and media campaigns.[11] As early as 1866 the Victorian press denounced the 'wholesale destruction of timber' from mining and farming, and warned 'the time will arrive, at no distant date, when the colony of Victoria will be even in a worse condition than parts of France if something be not done to conserve the magnificent forests'.[12] The NSW press in 1871 'warn[ed] of the destruction of timber resources [and] … there is a great danger in over-estimating the supply that these forests will afford the building trade twenty years hence'.[13] These prescient

[6] A Wulf, *The Invention of Nature. Alexander Von Humboldt's New World* (Alfred A Knopf, 2015).

[7] 'Soil Erosion. An Important Report' (*Yass Tribune-Courier*, 7 August 1933) 1.

[8] L Robin, 'Ecology: A Science of Empire?' in T Griffiths and L Robin (eds), *Ecology and Empire: Environmental History of Settler Societies* (Melbourne University Press, 1997) 63.

[9] 'Timber' (*Pictorial Australian*, 1 November 1894) 14.

[10] EJ Brady, *Australia Unlimited* (George Robertson and Company, 1918) 630.

[11] S Legg, 'Political Agitation for Forest Conservation: Victoria, 1860–1960' (2016) 2 *International Review of Environmental History* 7.

[12] 'Thursday Morning' (*Geelong Advertiser*, 30 August 1866) 2.

[13] 'Preservation of Timber' (*Maitland Mercury*, 15 July 1871) 4.

voices however didn't stop the onslaught, gauging by the distress still expressed the following century. Civil engineer and explorer Sydney Upton in the 1930s lambasted that in 'the last thirty years no less than 35,000 square miles of forest and scrub have been cut down by white men'.[14] Poet Dorothea Mackellar captured the deforested landscape's ugliness in her stanza: 'The stark white ring-barked forests, all tragic to the moon'.[15] William Hatfield's odyssey in the 1930s through swathes of ring-barked country behoved him to plea: 'a law should be passed compelling every occupier of ringbarked forest land to clear away every bit of dead timber and replant a little belt of trees'.[16]

Some individuals went beyond bemoaning about the losses to taking personal action. One was North Queenslander Hugo Flecker (1884–1957), a medical practitioner fascinated by venomous snakes, scorpions and jellyfish. In the 1930s he founded the North Queensland Naturalists' Club, edited its magazine *The North Queensland Naturalist*, and penned a nature column in the *Cairns Post*. Flecker personally campaigned in the early 1950s to save a 300-year-old giant fig tree (*Ficus infectoia*) in downtown Cairns, which he called 'the best-known advertisement for tourists in Cairns'.[17] In an era before environmental decision-making routinely allowed community participation, Flecker's plea for a popular referendum to decide the tree's fate went unheeded, and it was eventually felled by an unmoved Cairns Council citing the tree's allegedly costly upkeep.

Forests conservation grew as officialdom found economic motives for the cause. Besides setting aside land for nature parks, the principal alternative to agriculture was to 'save' it for forestry – although sometimes Australian lawmakers revoked conservation reserves where their trees were found to have more value as timber.[18] The visible denudation of the Australian woodlands from ring-barking and fire, along with recognition that the country's treed areas were not inexhaustible, spurred efforts to safeguard the dwindling remnants. These efforts were influenced by the American prophet of conservation, George Perkins Marsh (1801–82), who counselled for managing natural resources scientifically to rectify the wasteful plundering he observed in his homeland and elsewhere.[19] Marsh favoured not just preservation of nature but its improvement through introduction of 'superior' foreign species – and thereby some historians suggest his ideas dovetailed with the acclimatisation societies.[20] His legacy was extended by Gifford Pinchot (1865–1946), who professionalised American forestry governance and headed the

[14] S Upton, *Australia's Empty Spaces* (George Allen and Unwin, 1938) 190.

[15] D Mackellar, 'My Country' in *The Closed Door and Other Verses* (Australian Authors' Agency, 1911).

[16] W Hatfield, *Australian Through the Windscreen* (Angus and Robertson, 1939) 301.

[17] 'Destruction of Historic Fig Tree in Cairns: Public Meeting Asks Council to Rescind Decision' (*Cairns Post*, 13 July 1951) 1.

[18] GE Rundle, 'History of Conservation Reserves in the South-west of Western Australia' (1996) 79 *Journal of the Royal Society of Western Australia* 225.

[19] GP Marsh, *Man and Nature* (Charles Scribner, 1864).

[20] I Tyrrell, 'Acclimatisation and Environmental Renovation: Australian Perspectives on George Perkins Marsh' (2004) 10(2) *Environment and History* 153.

**Figure 11.1** Parade passing big fig tree in Abbott Street, Cairns, which Dr Hugo Flecker sought to save, 1940s, Cairns Libraries and State Library of Queensland

US Forest Service.[21] Pragmatists rather than sentimentalists, Marsh and Pinchot's environmentalism differed from compatriot John Muir who admired nature for its aesthetic and spiritual values. A seminal intellectual driver of the national park movement, Muir spoke with lofty prose: 'The clearest way into the Universe is through a forest wilderness'.[22]

The decimation of Australia's timber country eased as authorities established forestry reserves and required licences to log. Sawmillers were early lobbyists for action, fearing their investments would disappear if agriculture prevailed. Rudimentary forestry legislation emerged in the late nineteenth century, notably South Australia's Forest Trees Act 1873 and in 1882 its government founded a department to oversee forestry. Victoria followed suit, with its own Forests Act in 1876 and appointment of a Conservator of Forests in 1888. More comprehensive legislation and professionally trained foresters in the twentieth century helped plant a stronger voice for saving forests. The Australian Forest League, with chapters in each state, was formed in 1912, to promote public awareness of the value of

[21] C Miller, *G Pinchot and the Making of Modern Environmentalism* (Island Press, 2013); G Pinchot, *The Fight for Conservation* (Doubleday, Page and Co, 1910).

[22] Quoted in United States Department of Interior, '10 John Muir Quotes That'll Inspire You to Explore America's Great Outdoors', www.doi.gov/blog/10-john-muir-quotes-that-ll-inspire-you-explore-america-s-great-outdoors.

timber wealth and to modernise forest management.[23] Forestry commissions were created in each state in the early decades of last century, but they tended to see forests as stands of timber rather than complex ecosystems holding other values, a mindset that would eventually see forestry and nature conservation struggle to find common ground. One nasty rupture occurred over Tasmania's Mount Field National Park, which in 1950 lost a slice of its finest swamp gums to the pulp and paper industry, an ignominious episode discussed in chapter nine.

The ascendancy of the forestry sector was still hindered, explains John Dargavel, a leading historian here, because it had to compete 'against the ethos of agricultural development firmly held by the large, well-entrenched Lands Departments'.[24] They continued to allocate Crown land, often with conditions that it be cleared and farmed, such as occurred under Tasmania's Crown Lands Act 1903.[25] The Australian Forest League tried to mitigate such policies by educating farmers on the value of trees, such as the commercial value of softwood plantations as an alternate revenue stream, and to furnish wind breaks and shelter for livestock.[26]

The struggles within the state governments over different visions of the country's forests are epitomised by the story of Edward HF Swain (1883–1970). An autodidact who published widely on the subject,[27] Swain visited the United States during World War I to observe its forestry practices that were then well ahead of Australia's owing to Gifford Pinchot's leadership. Between 1918 and 1924 Swain was Queensland's Director of Forests and thereafter Chairman of its Forestry Board until 1932. Moving to NSW he became Chief Commissioner of its Forestry Commission from 1935 to 1948. Swain helped secure sizeable forest reserves for the industry and establish plantations with introduced species. He also modernised forestry management, including the introduction of forest assessment surveys, train staff and setting more realistic pricing of timber products.

Yet Swain's outspokenness against the enormous transfer of forested public lands to private farmers – what he called the 'forest disaster of first magnitude'[28] – alienated his superiors. His conflicts with the Queensland Lands Department contributed to formation of a public inquiry in 1931 to investigate such issues in the north of the state, where the tensions were palpable. The Royal Commission on the Development of North Queensland, whose official name betrayed its purpose, was, in one historian's analysis, 'a forum for advocates of the expansion of

[23] WR Grimwade, 'The Australian Forest League' (1922) 1(1) *Empire Forestry Journal* 66.

[24] J Dargavel, 'Forestry' in J Dargavel (ed), *Australia and New Zealand Forest Histories* (Australian Forest History Society, 2005) 25, 26.

[25] R Onfray, 'A Land Reborn: "Lorina Over the Bridge"' in ibid 184, 189–90.

[26] S Petrpw, 'Save the Forests: Forest Reform in Tasmania, 1912–1920' in J Dargavel, D Gaughwin and B Libbis (eds), *Australia's Ever-changing Forests* (Centre for Resource and Environmental Studies, ANU, 2002) 163, 170.

[27] See eg EHF Swain, *Reafforestation and the Hardwood Supply in Relation to North Coast Forests* (Government Printer, 1911).

[28] Quoted in I Frazer, *Conservationism and Farming in North Queensland, 1861–1970* (James Cook University. 2003) 32.

**Figure 11.2** Edward HF Swain, 1902; State Library of Queensland

what the commissioners described as the "largely vacant" North'.[29] Although the inquiry recommended more land be set aside for forestry and national parks, up from 971,000 to 1.3 million acres in the region, the status quo was hardly altered.

In Western Australia a similar struggle unfolded between the pro-forestry faction, in the minority, and the land-clearing zealots. In 1896 John Ednie-Brown was appointed the state's first Conservator of Forests, but his untimely death just three years later, and the lack of his replacement for several years, stalled the state's institutionalisation of forestry management. An articulate writer, Ednie-Brown keenly discerned the economic value of forests: '[they] are nature's gift … an inestimable inheritance of great commercial and climatic value … To destroy it

[29] ibid 31, citing WL Payne et al, *Report of the Royal Commission on the Development of North Queensland (Land Settlement and Forestry)*, volume II (Government Printer, 1931).

therefore, for the sake of a few more blades of grass, is suicidal and reprehensible in the extreme'.[30] As in Queensland, his state government appointed public inquiries to investigate land use conflicts. The 1904 report of the Royal Commission on Forestry gave blunt advice: 'State acquiescence in the destruction of good timber, only because the export trade demands it, is a crime against coming generations'.[31]

A breakthrough, of sorts, in Western Australia came in 1916 with the appointment of Charles Lane Poole as the new Conservator of Forests.[32] An internationally trained forester, Lane Poole began by surveying the state's forests and reorganising his portfolio. On finding far fewer timber resources than assumed, owing to rapacious clearing, Lane Poole pushed for a tougher Forests Act, which was adopted in 1918. In discussing the Bill in the Legislative Assembly, the Attorney General and Minister for Woods and Forests excoriated previous authorities for 'exploit[ing] as much as timber as possible in the shortest possible period',[33] and failing to establish a competent forestry authority. The Minister went on to describe (like the 1904 Royal Commission) the state's forests in language more familiar to contemporary green activists: they are 'the heritage of our children' and 'the mining of timber is a crime against future generations'.[34] He summarised the main goals of the 1918 legislation as 'permanent reservation of all prime timber country'; 'restriction of the cutting of timber to that quantity which the forest will reproduce naturally', and implementing 'sylvicultural operations in the cut-over areas in order to assure the regeneration of the best species'.[35] Despite the law reform, Lane Poole's efforts to implement it weren't particularly successful without enough political backing, and he resigned in 1921.

He was followed by Kim (Stephen Lackey) Kessel, who as Western Australia's Conservator of Forests in the 1920s had more success, pioneering innovative forestry practices that were adopted in whole or part across the continent. He also was the inaugural president of the Institute of Foresters of Australia (a professional association of forest managers and scientists, established in 1935), and helped redraft forestry legislation to challenge unsustainable practices. In evidence tendered to a 1943 Commonwealth inquiry, Kessell gave this colourful opinion: 'The Anglo-Saxon settlers who populated Australia brought with them no tradition of forestry … the forests were looked upon as the enemy of progress to be slaughtered. … Even the forests which have been retained have been regarded as mines to be worked out'.[36] Kessell's counsel influenced the formation in 1946 of the

[30] Quoted in MA Fraser, *Notes on the Natural History, etc. of Western Australia, Being Extracts from the Western Australian Year Book for 1900–1901* (Government Printer, 1903).

[31] Western Australia Royal Commission on Forestry, *Final Report* (Government Printer, 1904) 10.

[32] J Dargavel, *The Zealous Conservator: A Life of Charles Land Poole* (UWA Publishing, 2008).

[33] RT Robinson, 'Bill – Forests. Second Reading', Western Australia Legislative Assembly, Hansard, 17 September 1918, 343, 346.

[34] ibid 344–45.

[35] ibid 346.

[36] Evidence to the Commonwealth Rural Reconstruction Commission, File No. 1943/638, Australian Archives, quoted in PH MacFie, *'The Newsprint'. A Social and Forestry History of Maydena* (Peter MacFie, 2020) 90.

Tasmanian Forestry Commission, controlling some of Australia's richest timber stands. Yet, it would not be long before this state's modernised forestry sector would itself be embroiled in environmental controversy. Like its counterparts in Australia, the Tasmanian Forestry Commission had a conflicted, dual mandate – promote the industry's commercial success whilst being a 'watch-dog' in the public interest, and too often it prioritised the former. The tension arose in the Florentine Valley. Following the Florentine Valley Paper Industry Act 1935, a pulp mill opened in the early 1940s, and its demand for more wood would necessitate special legislation in 1950 to excise some 1,500 hectares of old growth trees from the Mount Field National Park. (This episode was examined in chapter nine.) Ironically, during this controversy Kessell assumed a senior role in the Australian Newsprint Mill that operated the responsible pulp mill.[37]

Over cutting hasn't been the only environmental grievance with forestry governance. Other controversial practices include copious use of strychnine and 1080 poisons to reduce native herbivores' pressure on regrowth in logged coupes, replanting practices that promote forest monocultures (sometimes comprising exotic plantations), and fire suppression.[38] In his analysis of the massive 1939 wild fires in Victoria, which burnt an area more than 10 times the state's annual bushfire average, David Lindenmayer suggests blame may lay with forest disturbances by logging, such as 'creation of spatially extensive, even-aged stands with limited structural complexity'.[39] Even larger bushfires in 2019–20, one of the most brutal of nature's backlashes seen in Australia, have reignited debates about the complicity of forestry governance. The solution, suggest Bill Gammage and Bruce Pascoe, is to apply Aboriginal fire management, involving more frequent but less intense firing of wooded landscapes.[40]

Though believing it lacked constitutional powers to regulate forestry, the Commonwealth wasn't entirely marginalised from the foregoing history. It established and funded an Australian Forestry School which operated in Canberra from 1927 until 1964 for training students in the science of forests management. It was led by Charles Lane Poole for much of this period, who after his disappointing experience in Western Australia saw a need for a national forestry policy and Commonwealth governance of the industry, as did some other federal officials in submissions to the 1927 Royal Commission on the Constitution of the Commonwealth.[41] The Commonwealth also established a Forestry Bureau (1927–45) and its successor the Forestry and Timber Bureau (1946–78) for

[37] MacFie, ibid 90–92.

[38] ibid 245–46.

[39] DB Lindenmayer, 'Using Environmental History and Ecological Evidence to Appraise Management Regimes in Forests' in S Dovers (ed), *Environmental History and Policy: Still Settling Australia* (Oxford University Press, 2001) 74, 88.

[40] B Gammage and B Pascoe, *Country: Future Fire, Future Farming* (Thames and Hudson, 2021).

[41] B Bennett, 'An Imperial, National and State Debate: The Rise and Near Fall of the Australian Forestry School, 1927–1945' (2009) 15(2) *Environment and History* 217, 229.

conducting research in silviculture and forest management. It would not be until the 1980s that the federal government became more directly involved in governance as the nation's legendary 'forestry wars' took off, but that's a story for another book.

## II. Soil Conservation

Like the dithering over forests protection, conserving soils was slow to take off despite farmers' palpable self-interest in safeguarding their lands' productivity. Soil has numerous life-sustaining benefits, including 'acting as a carbon store; hosting biodiversity; producing biomass; storing and filtering water; storing and cycling nutrients'.[42] The complex aetiology of soil erosion, a telling sign of nature's backlash in rural Australia, challenged landholders and lawmakers in the early twentieth century to identify what threats to prioritise: rabbits were a major scourge but ring-barking and pastoralists' overstocking were also to blame in drought-prone landscapes.

The nation was born in the midst of the worst drought its settlers had ever experienced. The 'Federation Drought' fluctuated in intensity for seven years until 1903, the last phase being the severest when much of the parched continent received less than 40 per cent of typical rainfall. Huge dust storms over the vegetation-stripped land, fanned by high winds, engulfed many towns, like the example in Figure 11.3. The Melbourne media reported a 'furious dust storm that stopped trains, interfered with telephone services and caused shops to close',[43] and 'a vast curtain of murky brown, flecked with yellow, and angry red where the setting sun struck through'.[44] In later decades, such frightful events were rightly more often attributed to people rather than acts of God; readers of the *Argus* in 1949 were reminded that 'erosion of soil … has very tragically been the child of white settlement'.[45]

Australia has a long history governing soils but a much shorter history of governing them well.[46] Its first such regulation dates from 1803,[47] and further ad hoc legal measures came in the nineteenth century such as Western Australia's Sand Drift Act 1889, and establishment of government departments of agriculture and agricultural colleges to inculcate better land management. In the early decades of the next century incremental reforms continued. In NSW, the Western Lands Act 1901 was available to lessen soil erosion through inclusion of land management conditions on Crown leases – though degradation continued as insouciance set in

[42] J Williams, 'Soil Governance in Australia: Challenges of Cooperative Federalism' (2015) (special issue) *International Journal of Rural Land and Policy* 1, 1.

[43] 'Furious Dust Storm' (*Weekly Times* (Melbourne), 15 November 1902) 19.

[44] 'Storm and Heat. A Record Dust Storm' (*Age* (Melbourne), 9 February 1901) 6.

[45] P Knox, 'Fights Against Erosion Must be Unceasing' (*Argus* (Melbourne), 29 January 1949) 3.

[46] A Chisholm and R Dumsday, *Land Degradation: Problems and Policies* (Cambridge University Press, 2012).

[47] Williams (n 42) 5.

**Figure 11.3** Broken Hill dust storm, c. 1907; State Library of South Australia

after the drought passed, as documented by a public inquiry in the early 1930s.[48] Another reformer, South Australia's Sand Drift Act 1923 obliged landholders to control wind erosion, and penalised practices that created a nuisance. Soil law specialist John Bradsen (son of the famous cricketer Don Bradman) characterises these measures as asserting the primacy of the public interest in maintaining productive landscapes over the hitherto belief that a 'man's home is his castle'.[49] Yet, law on the books wasn't the same as law in practice.[50] In the 1930s, warnings about dire land degradation from the Victorian government's premier soil conservation expert, Harold Hanslow, were ignored by his superiors.[51] Yet authorities had an altogether different view of rabbits, obliging landowners to control the legally designated 'vermin', though rabbits weren't solely blameworthy and didn't inhabit the continent's top third.

The delays owed partly to the distractions of World War I, and possibly also the nationalist fervour of a young country confident of its abilities to tame nature's backlash. In 1905 one newspaper ebulliently declared: 'There is not a flower that

[48] Royal Commission into Administration of the Western Division, *Report of the Royal Commission of Inquiry into Administration of the Western Division of New South Wales*, (Government of NSW, 1931).
[49] J Bradsen, 'Soil Conservation: History, Law and Learning' in Dovers (n 39) 273.
[50] 'Soil Salinity. Agricultural Outlook' (*Daily News* (Perth), 14 September 1929) 8.
[51] 'Sir Albert Dunstan Attacked. Neglect Charges on Soil Erosion' (*Argus* (Melbourne), 7 February 1949) 1.

blooms, a fruit that ripens, a tree or shrub or a plant that grows to perfection in any other part of the world that does not, or cannot, find congenial soil in some part of Australia'.[52] Another rapturous endorsement of Australia's prospects boasted of 'Exceptionally rich quality of the soils of the "desert-like" Western areas'.[53]

By the 1930s and 1940s such irrational exuberance was waning. Nature writers such as Elyne Mitchell warned that soil erosion posed an existential threat: 'Erosion could decide the future of the human race. A Judgement Day is much more likely to come in annihilating dust-storms or muddy floods caused by man's misuse of soil, than in any decision of God's to end the human race'.[54] Some politicians also remonstrated. William McKell, the NSW Premier in the 1940s and a rural landowner himself, wrote: 'The Government of this State is, despite wartime difficulty, resolutely proceeding with its plan to at once assist the man on the land and save the common heritage of its people from its greatest enemy – soil erosion'.[55]

Science became indispensable to turning the tide.[56] British pedologist Francis Ratcliffe was brought to Australia by the CSIR in the 1930s to investigate, in his words, 'the problem of Erosion and Soil Drift, which had assumed threatening proportions in the more arid pastoral districts'.[57] He reported graphically: 'I saw paddocks with the bush completely stripped – "black as the ace of spades"' [and] 'deserted homesteads with the drift sand piled to the tops of the windows, of stockyards buried, and even of river-beds which had disappeared under sand-dunes'.[58]

A new generation of laws to tackle Australia's menace were influenced by the US' response to its infamous 'Dust Bowl'. In 1935 President Franklin Roosevelt approved the Soil Erosion Control Act that created a new agency, the Soil Conservation Service, tasked to control 'preserve natural resources, control floods, prevent impairment of reservoirs, and maintain the navigability of rivers and harbors, protect public health, public lands and relieve unemployment'.[59] In 1936 this legislation was revised, under the renamed Soil Conservation and Domestic Allotment Act, to encourage farmers to plant grasses and legumes to improve soil fertility. The US experience would become not just a precedent for Australia but a number of other nations whose experiences Australian lawmakers would later also learn from, such as New Zealand's Soil Conservation and Rivers Control Act 1941

[52] LJ Brient, 'Australia's Destiny. If It Only Had Population' (*Daily Telegraph* (Sydney), 18 September 1950) 8.

[53] 'Our Untapped Riches' (*Sunday Times* (Sydney), 13 August 1905) 1.

[54] E Mitchell, *Speak to the Earth* (Angus and Robertson, 1945) 105.

[55] WJ McKell, 'Tragedy of Soil Erosion. Government Active in Control Measures' (*Western Herald* (Bourke), 2 July 1943) 6.

[56] L Robin, 'Ecology: A Science of Empire?' in T Griffiths and L Robin (eds), *Ecology and Empire: Environmental History of Settler Societies* (Melbourne University Press, 1997) 70.

[57] F Ratcliffe, *Flying Fox and Drifting Sand: The Adventures of a Biologist in Australia* (Chatto and Windus, 1938) 191.

[58] ibid 213 and 245.

[59] 16 US Code, s 590a.

that shifted emphasis from damage control to *prevention* by inter alia enabling catchment boards to prevent or mitigate damage from land degradation.[60]

The new generation of laws emphasised building institutional capacity and cooperation with landholders, which Bradsen argues gave farmers too much freedom of action that ultimately proved to undermine soil conservation governance.[61] Reform took off from the mid-1930s, following establishment of an Australian Agricultural Council as an advisory body for representatives of the Commonwealth and state governments to consult on agricultural problems and governance solutions.[62] In 1938 New South Wales created a Soil Conservation Service under the Soil Conservation Act, the first of the new wave of reforms. The NSW regime targeted river catchments and other areas prone to soil erosion, implemented controls via agreements between the Soil Conservation Service and landowners or, failing agreement, for the Service to undertake necessary measures at the landowners' expense. Additionally, the NSW statute created Catchment Areas Protection Boards to regulate the disposal of Crown lands in areas subject to serious erosion, to advise on soil protection and to survey terrain. Success however would be gradual in a regime where landholders were under little compulsion; for instance, a 1954 survey of the New England district found that 58.3 per cent still suffered at least moderate soil erosion.[63]

The other states followed NSW's lead, albeit with variable ambition. Queensland's Land and Water Resources Development Act 1943 provided for supervision and coordination of soil conservation via a Bureau of Land Investigation. In Victoria, where the semi-arid, mallee lands had withered considerably,[64] legislation was adopted in 1940 that created a Soil Conservation Board to oversee action, with the responsible overseeing Minister being the Premier of Victoria. Having first enacted legislation to combat 'sand drift' in 1923, South Australia in 1939 introduced a new Soil Conservation Act, created an advisory Soil Conservation Committee with representation from pastoral and government interests, and empowered authorities to acquire land for soil conservation reserves. Amendments to this legislation in the mid-1940s gave it more regulatory teeth. Western Australia followed a similar trajectory with its Soil Conservation Act 1945.

The Commonwealth didn't get directly involved in soil conservation but participated in meetings of the Australian Agricultural Council. In the early 1940s the Curtin government contemplated seeking a constitutional amendment to extend Commonwealth powers for post-war recovery, including authority over soil conservation. In language that environmentalists would frequently use from the 1970s, the official rationale was: 'soil erosion is a classic example of a

[60] NR Wheen, 'A Natural Flow – A History of Water Law in New Zealand' (1997) 9(1) *Otago Law Review* 71. 81 and 97.

[61] Bradsen (n 49).281–83.

[62] KO Campbell, 'The Development of Soil Conservation Programmes in Australia' (1948) 24(1) *Land Economics* 63, 64.

[63] RW Bloch, 'Soil Formation and Erosion in the New England Plateau' (1954) 10(3) *Journal of the Soil Conservation Service of NSW* 141, 145.

[64] Sand Drift Committee, *Report on Sand Drift Problems in Mallee Area* (Government Printer, 1933) 5.

problem which can only be solved by an integrated governmental and administrative machinery directed from top to bottom by a common policy'.[65] The popular referendum held in August 1944, to approve the transfer to the Commonwealth of 14 powers including over 'national works' (a term envisioned to cover soil protection measures) for five years after the war, failed to win enough electoral support to pass.[66]

Unlike many environmental laws of the era, soil conservation emphasised carrots rather than sticks in the hope of inducing compliance. After World War II, the NSW Soil Conservation Service established five research stations to study soil erosion mitigation, and on selected private lands it convened demonstration sites to showcase best practice. From the late 1940s, the Service provided concessional loans and technical assistance to landholders,[67] and assisted the soldier resettlement schemes by assessing allocated lands and advising on soil management. That the NSW Soil Conservation Service still operates in 2023 is perhaps testament to the success of its collaborative approach,[68] but that does not necessarily mean the scourge of land degradation has gone (the nation's 2021 *State of the Environment* report found 'land and soil condition is generally poor … as a result of land clearing, unsustainable agricultural practices and erosion').[69] This history also suggests that polyarchal governance, emphasising collaboration with stakeholders, may not assure optimal environmental outcomes where resource users face conflicting, short-term market pressures to maximise yields from the land.

Another trend in soil governance has been the movement away from chemical-laden, industrial farming. A variety of greener approaches have developed under the rubric of organic farming, biodynamic farming and other names, which in the Western world were stimulated by the teachings of Austrian Rudolf Steiner, who founded the Experimental Circle of Anthroposophic Farmers and Gardeners in 1924. It attracted some Australian members who helped transplant Steiner's ideas.

The Australian Organic Farming and Gardening Society (AOFGS), established in Sydney in October 1944, marked the first agricultural body in this country to use the 'organic' label.[70] Its official purpose enunciated in a ten-paragraph statement began: 'overstocking, overcropping, monoculture and the excessive use of chemical fertilisers, poisonous sprays and dusts have resulted in erosion and serious loss of soil fertility in Australia', which 'the Society associates with these unwise land practices, the destruction of bird life, the denuding of forests by over-exploitation and bushfires, and the pollution of rivers and streams'.[71]

[65] Attorney-General's Department, *Post War Reconstruction – A Case for Greater Commonwealth Powers*, prepared for Constitutional Convention at Canberra (Government Printer, 1942), 64 (footnote).

[66] Constitution Alteration (Post-war Reconstruction) Act 1944.

[67] Soil Conservation (Amendment) Act 1947.

[68] For its current activities, see www.scs.nsw.gov.au.

[69] ID Cresswell et al, *Australia State of the Environment 2021* (Commonwealth of Australia, 2021) 26.

[70] R Jones, 'Soil: A Real and Imagined Environment for Australian Organic Farmers and Gardeners in the 1940s' (2008) 14(2) *Environment and History* 205.

[71] 'The Purpose and Objectives of the Australian Organic Farming and Gardening Society' (AOFGS, 1952) 39–40, orgprints.org/15089/1/15089new.pdf.

Besides opposing agri-chemicals, the AOFGS endorsed 'large-scale tree-planting operations to temper the natural aridity, conserve moisture, foster bird-life, and provide wind breaks'.[72]

Such values were extraordinarily progressive for the era, at odds with the then (and often still) prevailing norms in Australian agriculture, including those on my mother's ancestral farm at Orchardfield. In the late 1940s the Society warned against DDT (or Dichlorodiphenyltrichloroethane) when its spraying was widely considered prudent farming practice. The toxic insecticide was not banned in Australia until 1987. Government regulations of the mid-twentieth century were not directed to limiting the risks to human health or the environment but to set standards for the labelling and retailing of insecticides to protect farmers from purchasing 'worthless and ineffective' products.[73] From the late 1940s the Australian media began to acknowledge their health and environmental risks, particularly as in light of overseas reports.[74] Equally, however, voices to the contrary found a ready outlet in the press, praising how agri-chemicals boost yields by controlling insects.[75]

Over the next decade the AOFGS published the quarterly *Organic Farming Digest* (later renamed *Farm and Garden Digest*) to spread its gospel and bring readers the latest international news on 'wise farming'.[76] The AOFGS also published in 1952 a guide to organic agriculture, the first of its kind for Australia. Yet although the Society's work gained some favourable publicity,[77] it folded in 1955 owing to insufficient funds and support from the mainstream farming community. Another Sydney-based organisation, Men of the Land, was formed in late 1954 with aspirations to continue the legacy of the AOFGS, and lasted until 1984 under the name Conservation Society of NSW.[78]

Efforts to develop eco-friendly agriculture also sprung up at the grassroots in Australian cities and towns as middle- and working-class households took to domestic food production in their backyards and community gardens. Historian Andrea Gaynor's landmark study of this practice identifies a number of influences on the growth of urban agriculture, including residents' response to poverty, the Great Depression, concerns about food quality and Scottish reformist Samuel Smiles' ideas about self-help through patience and fortitude.[79] Planning and municipal law were also important in the early twentieth century for this practice, especially local by-laws allowing city dwellers to keep a variety of animals (eg poultry and even cows) and stipulating minimum lot sizes in subdivisions that made possible the space around houses to grow produce.[80] Gaynor cites a 1941 study

[72] ibid.

[73] 'Legislation to Control Insecticides' (*Land* (Sydney), 23 March 1945) 20.

[74] 'Insecticide Drift: Large Scale Problems Could Arise' (*Gloucester Advocate*, 9 March 1948) 1.

[75] See eg 'Chemicals are Key to Growth' (*Maryborough Chronicle*, 7 November 1952) 2.

[76] Quoted in J Paull, 'The Lost History of Organic Farming in Australia' (2008) 3(2) *Journal of Organic Systems* 2, 6.

[77] E Jeremy, 'Nation's Health Depends on Soil Health' (*Advocate* (Tasmania), 14 October 1944) 6.

[78] 'Men of the Land' (*West Wyalong Advocate*, 9 September 1954) 10.

[79] A Gaynor, *Harvest of the Suburbs: An Environmental History of Growing Food in Australian Cities* (UWA Press, 2006).

[80] ibid 6, 59.

in Melbourne that '48% of sampled households produced food of some kind'.[81] Urban backyard agriculture didn't however translate into a model for large-scale agriculture in rural Australia, and it would take inter alia the impact of Rachel Carson's watershed *Silent Spring*, published in 1962, to galvanise broader interest in challenging industrial agriculture.

## III. Mining Regulation

Extraction of minerals has been one of Australia's most environmentally degrading activities. Known to some as the 'mining nation', Australia's extractive industries are an indelible part of the continent's colonisation.[82] Gold discoveries in 1851 helped transform a 'convict dumping ground and pastoral backwater into a liberated new nation', trumpeted one historian on mining's economic and cultural significance.[83] The goldrushes sparked an economic and immigration boom: by 1871 Australia's population had quadrupled from 430,000 to 1.7 million people.[84] Entire townships became synonymous with mining, like Kalgoorlie and Broken Hill, the latter where Australia's largest company, Broken Hill Proprietary (BHP), was founded. My great, great grandfather Franklin Jackes was one of many immigrants enticed by the gold rushes, but like many novices he eventually found better prospects (establishing Orchardfield). By 1901 mining comprised 10 per cent of national GDP, yet afterwards 'mining descended into the doldrums', explains one historian, amounting to about 3 per cent GDP by the mid-1960s.[85] By 2021 it had rebounded to its glory days.[86] Other economic metrics of mining industry's salience include jobs and export earnings (in 2021, mining generated two-thirds of the nation's export revenue, according to its industry proponents).[87]

Such economic influence translates into political influence, enabling miners to trespass Aboriginal land rights,[88] avoid environmental responsibility and, in recent years, impede action on climate change.[89] Mining creates pollution including discharge of tailings and sludge, and release of dust and noise, and these impacts can linger long after the mine closed.[90] Open cut mines are typically the most

[81] ibid 100.

[82] G Blainey, *The Rush That Never Ended: A History of Australian Mining* (Melbourne University Press, 1963).

[83] K McQueen, 'The Importance and Future of Mining History: An Australian Perspective' (2012) 31(2) *Earth Sciences History* 316, 317.

[84] L Carpenter and L Fraser (eds), *Rushing for Gold* (Otago University Press, 2016).

[85] D Lee, *The Second Rush: Mining and the Transformation of Australia* (Connor Court Publishing, 2016) preface.

[86] Commonwealth Treasury, *Economic Roundup Centenary Edition* (Commonwealth of Australia, 2001) 59.

[87] Minerals Council of Australia, 'Record High for Resources Export Revenue' (3 February 2022) www.minerals.org.au/news.

[88] C Jennett, 'Aborigines, Land Rights and Mining' in EL Wheelwright and K Buckley (eds), *Essays in the Political Economy of Australian Capitalism*, vol 5 (Australia and New Zealand Book Company, 1983) 119.

[89] M Beeson and M McDonald, 'The Politics of Climate Change in Australia' (2013) 59(3) *Australian Journal of Politics and History* 331.

[90] R Jain, *Environmental Impact of Mining and Mineral Processing* (Elsevier Science, 2015).

aesthetically and ecologically injurious, drastically altering and breaking landscapes that cannot recover even when mining ceases (as in the Tasmanian example depicted in Figure 11.4). Mining also consumes forests, not only to make room for open-cut quarries but to supply pit props, square sets and railway lines servicing mines. Some operations also once needed a lot of firewood, such as the 47,000 tonnes per month in 1902 at the Kalgoorlie mines to fuel their machinery.[91] Interestingly, miners' dependence on timber assisted those seeking conservation of forests from land clearing agriculturalists.[92] In Victoria in the early twentieth century the Miners' Association sought to cooperate with the Forests Protection League to challenge the Lands Department's alienation of Crown timber reserves to farmers.[93] Another environmental impact comes from dredging waterways and mining sand dunes that can erode rivers and beaches. The processing of minerals in smelters can also discharge harmful air and water pollution. Mining workers themselves can directly suffer; the most lethal were the explosion in 1902 at the Mount Kembla coal mine in NSW that killed 96 workers, and Queensland's Mount Mulligan mine disaster in 1921 that claimed 75 lives.

**Figure 11.4** Scarred landscape of Mt Lyell mine; Tasmania; 2022; photograph by author

[91] G Bolton, *Spoils and Spoilers: Australians Make their Environment 1788–1880* (Allen and Unwin, 1981) 45.
[92] 'Preserving Pit Props' (*Newcastle Morning Herald*, 18 December 1926) 10.
[93] 'Our Timber Resources' (*Bendigo Independent*, 23 June 1904) 1.

Mining regulation centred on bespoke legislation, providing for issuance of licences or leases for prospecting and extracting, and although mining laws historically contained rudimentary environmental provisions, other legislation including for water management and land use planning could in theory mitigate some of mining's environmental impacts. The law rested on colonial administrations' (and their state successors) reservation of minerals for the Crown. The common law traditionally affirmed the Crown's monopoly over gold and silver deposits, but ownership of other minerals belonged to the owner of the soil.[94] The change to the law was legitimated under the guise that 'mineral deposits are a fortuitous "gift of nature" and that any net benefits flowing from their exploitation should accrue to the community as a whole'.[95] Under the Offshore Constitutional Settlement negotiated in the late 1970s, the Commonwealth gained control of minerals on the seabed in coastal waters three nautical miles from shore, although long before then it supported the onshore industry by soft means, such as forming in 1946 the Bureau of Mineral Resources, Geology and Geophysics to map the continent's mineral deposits.

The Crown has rarely itself undertaken mining, instead allocating rights to private parties, mostly large corporations today. Traditionally, such acquired rights were governed by special Mining Acts, integrating property law and development regulation, but from the 1950s big mining ventures sometimes have been regulated via bespoke agreements with government, sometimes providing more lenient environmental standards and other concessions.[96] The country's earliest, recognisable mining laws were enacted in the mid-nineteenth century in each of the colonies. Federation did not explicitly disturb their control of minerals although the Constitution gave the Commonwealth powers to indirectly regulate, such as via the corporations and trade and commerce powers, and from 1911 it controlled the Northern Territory. With Federation most of the states updated their mining laws, such as Western Australia's Mining Act 1904, NSW's Mining Act 1906 and Tasmania's Mining Act 1905. These laws were accompanied by dedicated mining departments to supervise governance and specialist mining warden's courts to adjudicate disputes.

Some environmental impacts could be mitigated through conditional mining approvals, such as to use specific pollution control technologies and rehabilitate sites, but lawmakers have been cautious because of their conflicts-of-interest in maximising the industry's economic success including royalty earnings. Researchers have called this stance the 'absent presence of the state', where ostensible official oversight belies the reality of perfunctory or even corrupt regulation.[97]

[94] AJ Bradbrook, 'The Relevance of the Cujus Est Solum Doctrine to the Surface Landowner's Claims to Natural Resources Located Above and Beneath the Land' (1988) 11 *Adelaide Law Review* 462.

[95] Industry Commission, *Mining and Mineral Processing in Australia*, vol 3 (Commonwealth Government Printer, 1991) 7.

[96] D Mercer, *A Question of Balance: Natural Resources Conflict Issues in Australia* (Federation Press, 2000) 210–11.

[97] EE Skrzypek and NA Bainton, *The Absent Presence of the State in Large-Scale Resource Extraction Projects* (ANU Press, 2021).

Consider Tasmania's huge Mt Lyell copper mine (see Figure 11.4) which operated for most of the twentieth century discharging toxic sludge and sulphur fumes into its catchment with the acquiescence of regulators who could have intervened given powers under the state's mining legislation.[98] Historically, mines were approved without any formal environmental impact assessments, as is now commonly done (albeit with limitations in practice), and the day-to-day environmental regulation of mining was rudimentary. Typical of the parsimonious approach, Western Australia's Mining Act 1904 authorised the Governor to make regulations 'for preventing the accumulation of, and for the removal to some convenient place of sludge tailings and other waste' and 'for the prevention of nuisances' from mining tenements.[99] The Department of Mines' annual report of 1960 doesn't give much confidence that authorities took much interest in this mandate beyond some limited environmental monitoring.[100] This Act remained in place, with no significant relevant amendments, until 1978 when Western Australia introduced a new Mining Act.

Mining sludge, the muddy, viscous mixture of waste and water, is one of the industry's most conspicuous forms of pollution. As the home to Australia's first goldrushes, it's no surprise that Victoria was an early mover in (ostensibly) tackling the problem with its bespoke Sludge Act, adopted in 1885 with further iterations in following decades. Enforcement was patchy, in part due to careless legislative drafting. A case heard in 1909 by Victoria's Sludge Abatement Board, which had ordered a miner to stop discharging into a creek and change its operations, resulted in the defendant convincing the court that the Board lacked power to do so owing to fatal loopholes in the legislation.[101]

Law makers' deference to the mining industry's environmental sequelae showed also by allowing mining in conservation reserves or excising areas in such reserves for mining. Western Australia's Mining Act 1904 allowed the state's Governor to declare certain public reserves open to mining.[102] Whilst NSW's Kosciusko State Park Act 1944 revoked previously issued extractive rights, this wasn't particularly controversial given the 'few, tiny, isolated mining ventures' in the alpine region, explains researcher Monica McDonald,[103] and the Act authorised the park's board of trustees to allow new mining 'subject to such conditions and restrictions as it may impose'.[104] In Tasmania, the Mining Act 1929 exempted land in a public reserve but allowed the Governor by proclamation to authorise otherwise.[105] In 1938 Tasmania's parliament amended its Scenery Protection

[98] RN Singh, 'Environmental Catastrophes in the Mining Industry in Australia and the Development of Current Management Practices' (International Mine Water Association Congress Proceedings, 1999) 737, 738.

[99] Subsections 308(16) and (21).

[100] Department of Mines Western Australia, *Report for the Year 1960* (Government Printer, 1961).

[101] *Bremner v Victoria United* (1909) Argus LR 15, 36.

[102] Sections 3 and 30.

[103] M McDonald, *The Influence of the National Park Concept on Kosciusko National Park* (Master dissertation, ANU, 1981) 22.

[104] Section 8(1)–(2).

[105] Section 6(1).

Act 1915 to require the Act's governing Board to consent to such authorisations, and interestingly stipulated that it 'shall not consent' unless 'satisfied that the advantages of making the relevant land available for mining purposes materially outweigh the disadvantages'.[106] Despite such a procedural obstacle, this legal aperture was exploited by a truculent Mines Department to have 1,324 hectares of Cradle Mountain National Park revoked in 1939 for the Wolfram mine.[107] Another way mining could override conservation goals, where mineral deposits were assumed, was to stop proposed protected areas being created, as researchers have documented in many instances.[108]

One institution that offered some accountability was mining warden's courts, established as arbiters of local disputes between miners about mining matters.[109] In an era when, as environmental lawyer Rob Fowler explains, there was 'no other readily available forum or avenue of expression for public comment on proposed mining operations',[110] the warden courts occasionally were petitioned to consider environmental concerns, as in the example considered in chapter three where Queensland's Innisfail warden court in 1967 rebuffed a request to mine a coral reef. Environmental issues were most commonly brought to mining wardens where local property owners were affected. Because of gaps in their expertise, mining wardens weren't well qualified to assess allegations of pollution. For instance, a mining warden in East Maitland (NSW) in 1946 declined to issue an injunction against a colliery alleged to have polluted a river used by a nearby dairy farmer 'as it had not been definitely established that the pollution was caused by the defendant company'.[111] These courts sometimes also heard complaints brought by governments, such as a 1952 Queensland case in which the Herberton mining warden sanctioned a tin miner who had breached an environmental condition attached to its dredging operations.[112]

Mining has also grievously affected Aboriginal peoples.[113] Illustratively, the Queensland government in 1957 enacted the Commonwealth Aluminium Corporation Pty Ltd Agreement Act to allow a huge bauxite mining operation over Aboriginal lands in Cape York, along with conceding privileges that bypassed environmental regulations. Excisions of Aboriginal land were sometimes rationalised on the assumption that affected communities had no legitimate proprietary interest or they would benefit economically through job opportunities that would

[106] Section 10(4).

[107] L Mendel, *Scenery to Wilderness, National Park Development in Tasmania, 1916–1992* (PhD thesis, University of Tasmania, 1999) 95–96.

[108] O Pouliquen-Young, 'Evolution of the System of Protected Areas in Western Australia' (1997) 24(2) *Environmental Conservation* 168, 174.

[109] CW O'Hare, 'A History of Mining Law in Australia' (1971) 45 *Australian Law Journal* 281.

[110] RJ Fowler, 'Environmental Law – A Review of Legislative Controls Applicable to the Minerals Industry' (1978) 1(2) *Australian Mining and Petroleum Law Journal* 533, 543.

[111] 'Black Creek Pollution' (*Newcastle Morning Herald*, 1 August 1946) 9.

[112] 'Court's Decision on Alleged River Pollution' (*Townsville Daily Bulletin*, 28 February 1952) 2.

[113] L Behrendt and L Strelein, 'Old Habits Die Hard: Indigenous Land Rights and Mining in Australia' (2001) 25(1) *Cultural Survival*, www.culturalsurvival.org/publications/cultural-survival-quarterly/25-1-mining-indigenous-lands.

offset any losses.[114] The injustice attracted little public scrutiny before the 1960s. A watershed, discussed in chapter four, concerned the *Gove* land rights case, when in 1963 the Yolngu people of Arnhem Land sent a bark petition to the Commonwealth's House of Representatives to protest against planned bauxite quarrying of their homelands. A Select Committee established to inquire into their grievance recommended protection of their sacred sites and hunting grounds, plus financial compensation.[115] It would not be until the Aboriginal Land Rights (Northern Territory) Act 1976 that the Commonwealth gave communities like the Yolngu better rights to deal with miners, and later the Native Title Act 1993 extended Aboriginal rights to many others.

In recent decades mining governance has also had to consider legacy issues from ecologically degraded areas. The need for restoration was recognised many decades ago, and sometimes positive actions were taken beyond any legal requirements. In the NSW mining town of Broken Hill, with rich silver, lead and zinc deposits nearby, the surrounding terrain had by the 1930s become severely barren from overgrazing and wood cutting, leading to Broken Hill itself being engulfed by sand drift and dust storms (see Figure 11.3). Regeneration in the late 1930s was led by the enlightened Albert Morris, a metallurgist at one of the mines and self-taught botanist, with his wife Margaret. The regeneration is told in Horace Webber's *The Greening of the Hill*, which described the region as originally 'clothed in vegetation'.[116] Morris and others established the Barrier Field Naturalists' Club to assist the regeneration, and funding was secured from the mining companies. Although Albert died in 1939 before his vision was complete, the Club continued the effort and the regenerated areas were protected by the Broken Hill Council. The NSW Soil Conservation Service also took a keen interest in the regeneration project, seeing it as a guide for soil erosion projects elsewhere.[117] The value of ecological restoration in reversing the vanishing continent is explored further in this book's closing chapter.

Ecological restoration remains a pressing regulatory challenge. Whilst environmental regulation of the site-based impacts of mining has improved considerably since 1901, the continent remains littered with legacy or orphan mines from historic mining where no responsible operator remains to pay for rehabilitation. One is BHP's former sulphur mine at Brukunga east of Adelaide, which operated from 1955 to 1972 and left an 'environmental nightmare' for South Australian authorities to cleanup.[118] With some legacy mines no one assumes liability for

[114] J Roberts, *From Massacres to Mining: The Colonization of Aboriginal Australia* (War on Want, 1978) 100.

[115] House of Representatives, *Report from the Select Committee on Grievances of Yirrkala Aborigines, Arnhem Land Reserve* (Government of the Commonwealth of Australia, 1963).

[116] H Webber, *The Greening of the Hill: Revegetation Around Broken Hill in the 1930s* (Hyland House, 1992) 14.

[117] PJ Ardill 'Albert Morris and the Broken Hill Regeneration Area: Time, Landscape and Renewal (2017) 35–36, aabr.org.au/_upload/Articles/morris-broken-hill/Ardill-3rd-ed-Broken-Hill.pdf.

[118] Mercer (n 96) 207.

the remediation as, for instance, cites Kenneth Walker, with the toxic waste from a Queensland gold mine that ceased in 1955 that's now home to a suburban community in outer Brisbane.[119] At least 50,000 such sites have been identified in Australia, and some sites may never be fully remediated because (apart from the enormous financial expense) they contain features such as old mine shafts that authorities have designated as cultural heritage.[120]

## IV. Pollution Control

Mining of course isn't the only source of pollution. It was far more palpable to Australians before 1967 than today, though not necessarily more dangerous, as a new generation of pollution hazards from climate change to plastic waste now confronts everyone. In the early years of the new nation, smoke-belching factories, putrid rivers and rubbish-strewn streets were common, especially wherever people congregated. In 1889, poet Banjo Paterson wrote these lines, probably referring to Sydney where he then lived:

> I am sitting in my dingy little office, where a stingy
> Ray of sunlight struggles feebly down between the houses tall,
>
> And the fetid air and gritty of the dusty, dirty city
> Through the open window floating, spreads its foulness over all.[121]

Rural localities could also suffer, especially those hosting intensive agricultural facilities like piggeries, and mines too.

Early pollution control was shaped by threats to public health rather than natural values. A rough barometer of the salience and public concern about pollution can be gleaned from the popular media. 'Foul odors' from an abattoir in Sydney's Rozelle Bay in 1904 attracted condemnation, with a plea for authorities to take sterner action availing powers under the Sydney Harbour Trust Act 1900.[122] The Hobart media reported in 1932 that ships' discharges in the Derwent River caused 'a greasy scum over wide expanses of water, killing fish and fouling the sides of other ships', and grumbled that the penalties 'do not seem to be high enough to act as an effective deterrent'.[123] River pollution from upstream mining operations in 1911 soiled the water supply of the NSW town of Wagga Wagga, rendering it 'so discoloured and so heavily charged … that it is quite unfit for domestic use', and as with adulteration of Hobart's waterway, the affected residents reportedly had little

[119] KJ Walker, *The Political Economy of Environmental Policy: An Australian Introduction* (UNSW Press, 1994) 9–18.

[120] C Roche and S Judd, *Ground Truths: Taking Responsibility for Australia's Mining Legacies* (Mineral Policy Institute, 2016) 7.

[121] A Barton 'Banjo' Paterson, 'Clancy of the Overflow' *Bulletin* (21 December 1889).

[122] 'Whence Comes the Foul Odors of Rozelle Bay' (*Balmain Observer*, 24 December 1904) 5.

[123] 'Harbour Pollution' (*Mercury* (Hobart), 18 November 1932) 8.

assistance from authorities.[124] The media could also condone pollution however: public agitation about fumes from Hobart's zinc works, one paper observed, had to be balanced with the facility furnishing 'considerable employment' and being 'a large taxpayer'.[125] In some cases, pollution from 'essential services' such as power stations had to be tolerated, such as that from the New Farm Power House located on the edge of Brisbane's downtown (see Figure 11.5).

**Figure 11.5** Smoke from New Farm Power House, 1952; State Library of Queensland

[124] 'On the Land. Fam and Station. River Pollution' (*Sydney Morning Herald*, 2 October 1911) 7.
[125] 'Air Pollution' (*Mercury (*Hobart), 28 September 1923) 6.

Pollution control in Australia began during its colonial era when municipalities began enacting ordinances to counter the most abominable waste and degradation, supplementing common law mechanisms such as the tort of private nuisance which Ben Pontin argues provided some checks on industrial pollution in industrialising Britain.[126] Australia's early regulations often had little effect. Efforts to protect Melbourne's Yarra River were described in one account in 1887 as follows: 'despite the fact that a law was passed exactly 32 years ago prohibiting pollution by fellmongeries and tanneries, the stream continues to be defiled by manufactories … and by the foul sewage which flows into it'.[127] By the early twentieth century, control was theoretically more possible albeit via a hodgepodge of municipal by-laws (eg NSW's Local Government Act 1919) and public health statutes (eg NSW's Public Health Act 1902) and laws governing specific land uses such as mining (eg Victoria's Mines Act 1928). Yet these were limited by their narrow mandate to safeguard human health or property rights rather than the natural environment at large. Illustratively, Western Australia's Health Act 1911 authorised authorities to intervene when pollution to water would 'become injurious to health'.[128] Municipal legislation could also tackle pollution nuisances; Tasmania's Local Government Act 1906 authorised by-laws for 'preventing by any means whatsoever the contamination of any water which contributes to or constitutes a public water supply for domestic purposes'.[129] Though without scientifically set pollution standards and systematic environmental monitoring, such provisions had little traction. When the courts occasionally heard prosecutions brought under such laws, they had to rely on imprecise colloquial knowledge of what constituted pollution, such as a case from NSW in 1929 involving deposition of night soil near a river bank, the outcome of which hinged on the phrase 'polluting matter' under the Local Government Act 1919.[130]

Municipal planning legislation offered another tool for pollution control. Land use plans and subdivision schemes could facilitate proper disposal of sewage and management of other wastes, and to separate (more polluting) industrial and residential areas into different precincts. The efficacy of town planning, as already discussed, only began to materialise from the 1950s when a new generation of planning legislation put the principles of land use zoning into practice, coupled with more attention to the siting and design of developments within zones. Sydney's Cumberland plan of 1948 envisioned zoning 'special industrial areas' where industries 'require a wide degree of segregation due to atmospheric pollution',[131] and although the plan ultimately was superseded it helped to plant

[126] B Pontin, 'Nuisance Law and the Industrial Revolution: A Reinterpretation of Doctrine and Institutional Competence' (2012) 75 *Modern Law Review* 1010.

[127] 'The Pollution of the Yarra' (*Argus* (Melbourne), 30 April 1987) 13.

[128] Sections 110 and 111.

[129] Section 205(15.1).

[130] *Winterton v Wilson* (1929) 29 NSWSR 187.

[131] Cumberland County Council, *The Planning Scheme for the County of Cumberland, New South Wales* (Cumberland County Council, 1948) 97.

the idea that zoning should at least segregate sources of pollution from human residences. Local communities in this era became increasingly vocal in challenging municipalities' decisions to allow industrial uses near their homes, such as complaints in the 1950s in Wollongong and Muswellbrook, NSW.[132]

Water supply legislation also could address pollution, though rarely with any detail. The Water Act 1912 of NSW contained only one relevant clause, prohibiting any person from polluting water under the control of a trust (an entity managing works for water conservation and supply).[133] Because of authorities' discretion to enforce such provisions, with no corresponding *obligation* to achieve a specific water quality standard, such laws tended to create only the *appearance* of pollution control. A study of Queensland water pollution regulation after World War II found that it was implemented with an attitude of 'compromises' with the polluters in which, absent a major threat to public health, waste emissions were considered a 'legitimate use' of the state's waterways.[134]

A few specialist laws dealt directly with pollution, often focusing on industrial smoke or effluent that was palpably odorous or unsightly – a threshold that naturally overlooked hidden or incremental contamination. Such laws not only lacked underpinning environmental standards, they had cumbersome enforcement machinery, and sloppy legislative drafting could thwart prosecution of offenders. Illustratively, NSW's Smoke Nuisance Abatement Act 1902, adapted from English legislation in 1821, sounded promising yet in practice was window dressing. According to a Sydney Health Officer interviewed in 1908, the legislation is a 'dead letter' as, in order to prosecute, 'it has to be proved that the furnaces have not been so constructed as to prevent, as far as possible, the formation of smoke therein, or that the owner … has negligently used them'.[135]

Australia's first generation of modern air pollution legislation was also modelled on international precedents, explains Alan Gilpin's history of law reform.[136] Victoria's Clean Air Act 1957 (replaced in 1958),[137] was modelled on British 1956 legislation adopted in response to lethal smogs in London, and it focused on smoke, dust and grit from various fixed and non-stationary sources. New South Wales followed in 1961 with its Clean Air Act, which became the template for much of Australia, with Queensland and Western Australia legislating similarly in 1963 and 1964 respectively.[138] (The other states modernised their legislation later). These controls sometimes only applied to specific areas; for instance, Queensland's

[132] 'Woonona Industrial Area Protest' (*Illawarra Daily Mercury*, 3 April 1951) 4; '103 Names on Petition to Council. Little Hope of Easing of Ash Problem' (*Muswellbrook Chronicle*, 15 July 1955) 10.

[133] Section 71(e)–(f).

[134] J Wegner, 'Queensland's First Water Pollution Legislation, 1944–1985' (2009) 15(2) *Environment and History* 199, 211.

[135] 'A Smokeless City. Interview with Health Officer' (*Sydney Morning Herald*, 15 May 1908) 5.

[136] A Gilpin, *Air Pollution* (University of Queensland Press, 1971) 23–25.

[137] A private member's Bill in 1957 established Victoria's first Clean Air Act, but the state government adopted its own version in 1958.

[138] JL Sullivan, 'Australian Air Pollution Legislation' (1965) 15(9) *Journal of the Air Pollution Control Association* 429.

Clear Air Act 1963 initially only covered the highly urbanised Brisbane–Ipswich area until 1970 when it was extended state-wide.[139]

The NSW legislation drew more closely on the UK's Alkali, &c. Works Regulation Act 1906, which established a licensing regime for registration, control and inspection of major industrial plants, where limits on noxious emissions were set. Unlike Victoria's, the NSW legislation also adopted the 'best practicable means' standard, as a catch-all requirement for occupiers of registered premises, numbering about 700 in the mid-1960s, where specific emission limits were not yet set by regulations. A specialist Air Pollution Control Branch, within the NSW Department of Public Health, administered the legislation, in conjunction with local councils. All scheduled (registered) premises had to be licensed, an important technique of modern environmental law for creating a quasi, contractual relationship between regulatees and regulators.

Overall, Australian pollution control historically was patchy and ineffective, compounded by lacklustre implementation. Prevalent problems included: the fragmented statutory framework; case-by-case setting of environmental standards through the licensing system, which overlooked the cumulative and synergistic effects of numerous pollution sources; statutory exemptions or concessions to important businesses; overriding powers of the Minister; limited grounds for recourse to the courts; insufficient penalties for statutory violations; insufficient environmental monitoring; and undue faith in the assimilative capacity of airsheds, waterways and other environmental media to cope with pollutants. Given the bias to minimise the regulatory on burden on business, the solution to pollution was typically to dilute and disperse, such as by reliance on tall smokestacks. Thus, a perception of a cleaner environment could be illusionary.

The efficacy of the Victorian and NSW regimes – supposedly embodying Australia's best legal regimes – was reviewed in the late 1960s by the Commonwealth's Senate Select Committee on Air Pollution. Its report, tabled on 10 September 1969, found in NSW an 'improvement in the overall picture',[140] and in Victoria 'a slight decrease in levels … in some areas' but static in some other areas and in a 'few areas' the 'position worsened'.[141] The Committee recommended 'urgent co-ordinated action' to address air pollution, and for the Commonwealth to enact such legislation for its own territories and to coordinate a 'more uniform approach' across Australia.[142] The federal government had already started in another domain; its Pollution of Sea by Oil Act 1960 gave effect to the International Convention for the Prevention of Pollution of the Sea by Oil.[143]

[139] Public Interest Research Group, *Legalized Pollution: The PIRG Report on Pollution Control Laws in Queensland* (University of Queensland Press, 1973) 16.

[140] Parliament of the Commonwealth of Australia, *Report from the Senate Select Committee on Air Pollution* (Commonwealth Government Printing Office, 1969) 45.

[141] ibid 47.

[142] ibid 65.

[143] (1959) 4714 UNTS 4.

Independent researchers corroborated the foregoing concerns. Don Whittington's national survey of water pollution, published in 1970, highlighted the fragmentary nature of legislative regimes, and he too recommended national leadership.[144] Further revelations of serious regulatory failures were made the following year in Derek Whitelock's *A Dirty Story*.[145] Another analysis published in 1971 identified low statutory penalties as ineffective deterrents to polluters.[146] A 1973 report by Queensland's Public Interest Group was bluntly titled *Legalized Pollution*.[147]

Given these deficits, aggrieved persons sometimes had to pursue justice privately using the common law. It wasn't an adequate substitute for public regulation given that remedies for the torts of private nuisance, trespass or negligence are available only to protect personal injury or property damage rather than public amenities.[148] Thus, pollution of the sea by a ship's discharges would probably not allow an action by these mechanisms. The tort of public nuisance had broader scope but was still restricted by requirements that include for a plaintiff to show 'special damage' above that suffered by the public in general, and that the balance of convenience favoured controlling pollution over the economic benefits of the polluting activity. The costs of litigating were also considerable for the average plaintiff. Case law history shows Australian courts occasionally considered pollution-related torts. Illustratively, in 1948 the Supreme Court of Victoria heard a complaint brought by a couple of artists about the noise, dust and fumes from a neighbour's sawmill in the bush-clad Dandenong Ranges near Melbourne.[149] In granting injunctive relief, the court concluded that the noisy sawmill was a 'serious inconvenience' to the plaintiffs' 'reasonable comfort' and that it was relevant that the 'locality has the character of a quiet countryside' rather an a 'city or industrial area'.[150] Sometimes such complaints were brought against governments themselves, such as a case in 1916 brought by a NSW farmer against the Bega Municipal Council alleging nuisance and negligence over its careless management of a nearby odorous night-soil depot.[151]

Public laws, such as town planning and pollution control statutes, were difficult to enforce by aggrieved citizens via recourse to the courts because of the narrow criteria of standing, as earlier discussed in this book. The reluctance to widen public interest standing persisted into the late twentieth century, such as when the High Court denied *locus standi* to the Australian Conservation Foundation (a national body) on the basis of a 'mere intellectual or emotional concern' in an environment threatened by a decision under the Commonwealth's Environment

[144] D Whittington, *The Effluent Society: Pollution in Australia* (Thomas Nelson, 1970).
[145] D Whitelock, *A Dirty Story: Pollution in Australia* (Sun Book, 1971).
[146] A Lanteri, 'Clean Air Legislation in Australia' (1971) 8 *Melbourne University Law Review* 253, 273.
[147] See n 139 above.
[148] M Lunney, *A History of Australian Tort Law 1901–1945 England's Obedient Servant*? (Cambridge University Press, 2017).
[149] *Dunstan v King* [1948] VLR 269, 269.
[150] ibid 272–73.
[151] *Howard v Bega Municipal Council* (1916) 16 NSWSR 138.

Protection (Impact of Proposals) Act 1974.[152] Citizens were likely only to have standing to challenge government decisions when they are directly and personally impacted, such as a neighbouring landowner allowed to challenge a municipality's planning decisions that would unreasonably interfere with her land.[153]

Compounding the inadequacies of pollution regulation, offending businesses might unscrupulously avail corporate law structures to insulate themselves from liability. One notorious example was Australian asbestos manufacturer James Hardie Industries, which likely had known of the health risks many decades before claims arose. It created under-capitalised subsidiaries from the 1930s to which it assigned the riskier side of its business, which were later exposed to negligence claims from victims of mesothelioma or pleural disease.[154] A 2004 NSW government inquiry into the corporate restructuring of James Hardie found that the health risks of asbestos were clearly established by 1960, and yet funds the parent company had made available to asbestos injured claimants were grossly inadequate.[155]

[152] *ACF v Commonwealth* [1980] HCA 53.

[153] See eg *Day v Pinglen Pty Ltd* [1981] HCA 23 (involving obstruction of views from the plaintiff's property by a building proposed by adjoining landowner).

[154] PV Nessen and A Herzberg, 'James Hardie's Asbestos Liability Legacy in Australia' (2011) 26(1) *Australian Journal of Corporate Law* 55.

[155] DF Jackson, *Report of the Special Commission of Inquiry into the Medical Research and Compensation Foundation* (NSW Government, 2004).

# 12

# Looking South: Icy Lands and Stormy Seas

## I. Australia's Final Frontier

At a time when many of Australia's natural resources and ecosystems were vanishing, the young nation began looking south. More than any issue in this book's history, Australia's engagement with Antarctica and its waters elevated the role of the Commonwealth, with unprecedented opportunity for national leadership in environmental governance. Although in recent decades the Commonwealth has stepped up, such as supporting the mining ban under the 1991 Madrid Protocol on Environmental Protection to the Antarctic Treaty,[1] and in 2010 taking Japan to the International Court of Justice to stop its whaling,[2] Australia was previously more pre-occupied with legally securing its place in the scramble for the region's resources.

This chapter examines the governance history of Australia's ambitions in Antarctica to exploit, and later conserve, its natural resources. This history matters to this book because although Antarctica is a separate continent, Australia has claimed sovereignty over much of it, and environmental issues including marine life have dominated its political and legal chronicle. Originating from Great Britain, Australia's claim to nearly half the icy continent rested on the assumption that it was *terra nullius*, literally without pre-existing human habitation. It's a curious contrast to the earlier, reprehensible invocation of the same doctrine to justify annexation of the Australian mainland that was already occupied by an 'uncivilised' Aboriginal people. Unlike other case studies in this book showing the efficacy of the law in aiding the exploitative colonisation of the environment, the history of Australia's engagement with Antarctica and the Southern Ocean reveals a more muted impact owing not only to the region's remoteness and technological challenges but that the geopolitical rivalries among nations claiming the spoils led to a unique legal solution that brought an environment-saving truce. From that truce has evolved the idea advocated by some that Antarctica forms part of the common heritage of humankind, or at least part of the global commons – international principles that challenge the norms of colonisation and exploitation of nature.[3]

[1] (1991) 30 ILM 1461.

[2] CR Payne, 'ICJ Halts Antarctic Whaling – Japan Starts Again' (2015) 4(1) *Transnational Environmental Law* 181.

[3] CC Joyner, *Governing the Frozen Commons: The Antarctic Regime and Environmental Protection* (University of South Carolina Press, 2008).

The region is inhospitable. As historian Tom Griffiths wrote from his first-hand excursion in the summer of 2002–03, Antarctica 'is Earth's only true wilderness' and remorselessly inhospitable to human life – the world's coldest, driest and most mountainous continent.[4] So too its surrounding Southern Ocean is intimidating with its gale-force winds and tempestuous seas, reflected in the menacing names given to its circumpolar latitudes – the roaring forties, the furious fifties, etc. To reach Antarctica through them requires five days travel by ship across 3,500 km from Hobart, Australia's closest port. The polar mass, covering some 14 million km$^2$ – about twice the size of Australia – has long been mythologised as the final frontier of discovery and conquest.[5] Legends from Antiquity presumed a 'Great Southern Land' counterweighting the northern hemisphere's large landmasses. The first cartographic depictions of this mysterious continent, during the Renaissance, showing a single landmass cusping the bottom of the planet although then without documented evidence of its existence or dimensions. The name Antarctica is the Romanised version of the Greek word *antarktiké*, meaning 'opposite to the Arctic', which Aristotle wrote about in *Meteorology*.

No person, however, came close to visiting Antarctica for about 2,000 years. In the 1700s, European explorers began to dispatch ships, as detailed in Joy McCann's fascinating history of the Southern Ocean's climate, wildlife and exploitation.[6] In 1772 Captain James Cook ventured close, encountering icebergs but not sighting the continent's shoreline. The first to see it (but not set foot on it) was a Russian expedition in 1819–21. By the mid-nineteenth century, brief landings had begun by intrepid sealers and whalers – a forerunner to the international scramble that was eventually checked only by a unique treaty that asserted a vision of peaceful scientific research and cooperation.

It wasn't until the late nineteenth century that the continent's deep inland was penetrated.[7] The first pioneers were sponsored by the Belgian Geographical Society in 1897, with 17 expeditions mounted by other nations and groups to follow until 1922, which historians concur marked the closure of the 'Heroic Age' of Antarctic exploration. The expeditions served geographic mapping, scientific research and, most controversially, to stake territorial claims. The 'heroic' character of these expeditions reflected individuals' personal sacrifice and lethal hazards, such as the five who perished in 1912 during the British Antarctic Expedition to reach the South Pole, and because explorers were competing to claim territory for their nations.

Australia's interest in Antarctica grew in the late nineteenth century, explain Marie Kawaja and Tom Griffiths, a notable milestone being formation in 1886 of the Australian Antarctic Exploration Committee to promote scientific research.[8]

[4] T Griffiths, *Slicing the Silence: Voyaging to Antarctica* (Harvard University Press, 2007) 4.

[5] S Martin, *A History of Antarctica* (Rosenberg Publishing, 2013).

[6] J. McCann, *Wild Sea: A History of the South Ocean* (University of Chicago Press, 2019).

[7] EJ Larson, *An Empire of Ice. Scott, Shackleton, and the Heroic Age of Antarctic Science* (Yale University Press, 2011).

[8] M Kawaja and T Griffiths, '"Our Great Frozen Neighbour" Australia and Antarctica Before the Treaty, 1880–1945' in M Haward and T Griffiths (eds), *Australia and the Antarctic Treaty System* (UNSW Press, 2011) 9, 30.

From 1898, Australians began to join UK expeditions to the continent. The most important for Australia were those involving Douglas Mawson, who visited in 1907–09, 1911–14 and 1929–31. Mawson's was undertaken not just out of fidelity to Britain's imperial ambitions but also Australia's emerging nationalism and desire to secure its place in the southern hemisphere. Since 1933 Australia has claimed sovereignty over 42 per cent of Antarctica – the largest share asserted by any of the seven claimant nations – along with claiming adjacent marine waters and some subantarctic islands. Australia has also had long-standing interests in exploiting the Southern Ocean's fish and cetaceans. The Australian Antarctic Territory, as this huge wedge of some 6 million $km^2$ is known, presently hosts three year-round stations – Casey, Davis and Mawson. They are administered by the Australian Antarctic Division, established by the Commonwealth in 1948 to provide administrative and logistical support for the nation's research expeditions.

Well before Antarctica acquired national interest, the coastal waters of the Australian mainland were exploited for their riches. Although the world's second driest continent, after Antarctica itself, Australia has vast waters of the salty variety – some 8.2 million $km^2$, the third largest coastal waters held by any nation. Australia's maritime zone was vastly smaller in the early twentieth century, when international law generally limited a coastal state's marine space to a belt of three nautical miles (5.6 km) seaward.[9] Enlargement of maritime zones pursuant to the United Nations Convention on the Law of the Sea 1982,[10] which consolidated legal changes initiated over several decades, brought immense marine resources and territory under Commonwealth jurisdiction, including fisheries and offshore energy projects. One resource no longer exploited today, which had been an indelible part of Australian maritime history, is whales.

Like that on the mainland, this history began with an exploitative ideology. Prized for their pelts and oil, seals were harvested in the Bass Strait islands and other coastal areas of southeast Australia from the late eighteenth century.[11] It was an unregulated, brutal industry, and the indiscriminate slaughter quickly led to its implosion.[12] A similar story of greed and excess unfolded with the penal colony's exploitation of whales. Sealing and whaling then became profitable only further afield, into international waters including around Antarctica. This insouciance regarding nature's seeming bounty started to wane in the mid-twentieth century, dovetailing with Australian policy-makers' growing awareness of the *international* context to stewardship of natural resources, an awareness elevated as the nation looked southward. The following section traces the story of Australian whaling and its governance in the twentieth century.

[9] HSK Kent, 'The Historical Origins of the Three-Mile Limit' (1954) 48(4) *American Journal of International Law* 537.

[10] (1992) 21 ILM 1261.

[11] JCH Gill, 'Notes on the Sealing Industry of Early Australia' (1967) 8(2) *Journal of the Royal Historical Society of Queensland* 218.

[12] J Robertson, *Sealed Souls* (Sealed Souls, 2022) 1–46.

## II. Rise and Fall of Whaling

Unlike today's fervent anti-whaling sentiment, a century ago whaling had few detractors. Newspapers could discuss its grisly practices without discomfort or disapproval.[13] Consider one Australian journalist's account on a whaling ship in 1953:

> I saw the harpoon rope streak out and heard a second muffed boom as the harpoon head exploded in the whale's body. … The whale was drawn right up under the bows and a second show quickly stopped its feeble struggles. … The chief flenser begins with an incision under the whale's jaw and a triangular flap of blubber is soon laid back. A cable is made fast and to this, as the winch winds, the flensers move along the length of the body, cutting off the blubber in three huge strips. Then the head of the whale is further dissected.[14]

Australia's profitable, shore-based whaling industry ended around the mid-nineteenth century when, without harvesting regulations, the accessible whales became depleted. Early in the following century, whaling in Australian waters modestly revived when new explosive harpoons allowed the taking of larger species, and interest in extending whaling to the whale-rich Southern Ocean emerged from the 1920s. Increased whaling by other seafaring nations, especially Japan, created anxiety in Australia that its whalers might be out-competed internationally: 'Of the 40,000 whales taken in Antarctica in 1931', remarked one concerned reporter, 'not one was taken by an Australian company'.[15] Nonetheless, any Australian whaling was governed by the UK's Whaling Regulation Act 1934, which extended to ships registered in Australia.[16]

World War II put the industry into abeyance; but the reprieve for cetaceans didn't last long, as a post-war global shortage of fats and oils boosted the price of whale products and, coupled with some recovery in whale populations, the industry appeared again to offer lucrative returns. Shore-based whaling was re-established in Australia in the 1950s in the wake of the Whaling Industry Act that was enacted in 1949 to establish an Australian Whaling Commission tasked to 'engage in whaling in Australian waters' and be 'an aid to the economic and stable operation of its whaling activities in Australian waters'.[17] Until 1956 the Commission managed a whaling station at Babbage Island off Western Australia, but it never ventured into Antarctic waters. The Babbage facility was the most modern of the whaling stations in Australia (other whaling facilities were at Albany and Port Cloates in Western Australia, Moreton Island in Queensland, and Byron Bay and Eden in NSW, plus one on Norfolk Island). By the early 1960s whale stocks accessible to these facilities were near exhaustion and several stations closed. Albany's was the

[13] K McC, 'Hunting Blue Whales the Modern Way' (*Cairns Post*, 20 January 1952) 8.
[14] 'Whaling off Western Australia' (*Daily Examiner*, 15 January 1953) 2.
[15] 'Whaling' (*Sydney Morning Herald*, 12 June 1937) 16.
[16] Section 15(2).
[17] Section 15.

last to go, on 21 November 1978. A similar history unfolded with Australia's closest allies. New Zealand closed its last shore-based facility, the Perano Whaling Station, in 1965, as whale numbers crashed. Great Britain ended its whaling industry in the mid-1960s.[18]

**Figure 12.1** Whale skeleton, Albany Whaling Station, Western Australia, 2022 photograph by author

Although Australia never exploited whales in Antarctic waters it had contemplated this, and scrutinised other nations' whaling there. In the 1930s the region's waters yielded the bulk of whales caught globally: of 32,008 whales taken in the 1933–34 season, 26,087 came from the Southern Ocean.[19] During this antebellum period, Commonwealth ministers mooted support for a private-sector-led whaling industry in the area, an idea backed by Douglas Mawson, Australia's preeminent Antarctic explorer.[20] An active Australian-affiliated whaling industry, reasoned proponents, would help consolidate the country's asserted sovereignty in Antarctica, which few nations had accepted.[21] The Commonwealth ultimately shunned the idea due to the high financial outlays, insufficient ships, concerns

[18] See whalinghistory.org.

[19] Citing the Statistical Year Book of the League of Nations, in 'Whaling Industry. Antarctica's Predominance' (*Western Australian*, 10 September 1935) 17.

[20] 'Whaling Industry' (*Daily Mercury* (Mackay), 31 March 1938) 3.

[21] 'Whaling in Antarctic. Australia's Chances' (*Advertiser* (Adelaide), 11 April 1946) 6.

about the long-term viability of market demand, and risks that future international conservation measures might undermine the industry.

Nonetheless, Australia didn't wish to be entirely a bystander, and like some other nations including New Zealand and Norway, it wished to limit Japan's whaling.[22] The United States, without whaling operations in Antarctica, was however willing to appease the Japanese because it would boost food aid in the aftermath of the war when millions of Japanese faced starvation. Moreover, by the late 1940s Japan was identified by the United States as a potential ally in containing the spread of communism.

Whilst Australian opposition to the resumption of Japanese whaling owed to the symbolic threat it posed to Australia's territorial interests in Antarctica, and that Japan's whaling vessels might be adapted for military purposes, another concern, shared with some nations, was Japan's chronic failures to adhere to conservation stipulations under the Convention for the Regulation of Whaling 1931, and the Agreement for the Regulation of Whaling 1937.[23] By ignoring them, Japan had enlarged its share of the global whale catch from 2 per cent in 1935 to 12 per cent in 1937. After the War, US authorities agreed to improve monitoring of Japan's whaling when Australian officials complained that it was violating international accords including by catching under-sized specimens.

A more far-reaching whaling treaty was adopted in 1946 that established the International Whaling Commission (IWC), with the aim 'to provide for the proper conservation of whale stocks and thus make possible the orderly development of the whaling industry'.[24] Japan joined the IWC in 1951 but left in 2019 after losing a stoush with Australia in the International Court of Justice, which found that Japan's so-called 'scientific research' whaling was subterfuge for unlawful, commercial harvesting contrary to the IWC's ban since 1986.[25]

## III. Scramble for Antarctica

In 1929 the Australian press broadcast 'A Scramble for Antarctica'.[26] Before the 1950s the continent lacked permanent human habitation, hosting only occasional expeditions and seasonal camps. Despite the fleeting human presence and sparse geographical mapping, the continent attracted territorial claims by Norway, Great Britain, France and others. Control over natural resources, primarily whales then, but potentially other riches in the future, was a motivating factor. The first to move was Britain, in 1908 claiming part of the Antarctic Peninsula and

[22] See K Dorsey, *Whales and Nations: Environmental Diplomacy on the High Seas* (University of Washington Press, 2013).

[23] N Sellheim, *International Marine Mammal Law* (Springer, 2020) 86.

[24] Preamble.

[25] *Whaling in the Antarctic (Australia v Japan; New Zealand intervening)*, ICJ Reports (2014), 226.

[26] 'A Scramble for Antarctica' (*Advertiser* (Adelaide), 8 April 1929) 8.

some offshore islands. Evolving international legal norms in the early twentieth century prescribed that sovereignty claims had to be backed by more than mere ceremonial flag-raising; some level of continuous, effective occupation, such as economic activity, physical presence and/or administrative oversight were additional elements expected to 'perfect' a putative title.[27] Yet a ruling of the Permanent Court of International Justice in 1933 on the status of Eastern Greenland furnished an important legal precedent: for uninhabitable land, symbolic possession (*animus occupandi*) indicative of a state's intention was sufficient for territorial annexation without the need additionally to show effective occupation (*corpus possesionis*).[28] Thus, the legal question for Antarctica was would it be considered 'uninhabitable' to justify the claims of Australia and others or, if not, what additional steps would claimant nations need to make?

Thereby, UK authorities came to recognise the strategic value of the empire's dominions in furnishing a better territorial nexus as well as logistical access to the continent. In the 1920s and 1930s both Australia and New Zealand collaborated with Britain to support its claim, including participation in discovery explorations. The need for allies grew as any hopes of Britain's total imperial control of Antarctica ended when France made a claim in 1924 and Norway in 1939, whilst Chile and Argentina cited fifteenth-century papal decrees to define the Antarctic Peninsula as an extension of their Latin American domain.

Great Britain's claim to 42 per cent of Antarctica was transferred to Australia in 1933, a decision motivated by Australia's better geographical position to manage the territory, to shift the financial burden of administering it, and as a reward for Douglas Mawson's expeditions that assisted the UK.[29] In 1911–14, Mawson led the Australasian Antarctic Expedition and in 1929–31 led the British Australian and New Zealand Antarctic Research Expedition (BANZARE), which received some financial and in-kind support from the governments. Mawson was not merely a curious scientist but actively lobbied for the Australian and British governments to formalise territorial claims to Antarctica.[30] Accepting the UK's offer was attractive to Australia, suggested the country's then Minister for External Affairs, John Latham, because of the prospect of economic riches including whaling and 'that embarrassing circumstances would arise if any other power assumed the control and administration of the area'.[31] A rival claim by France to a wedge of the territory claimed by Australia, based on its own sponsored explorations of the area,

[27] FAP von der Heydte, 'Discovery, Symbolic Annexation and Virtual Effectiveness in International Law' (1935) 29 *American Journal of International Law* 448.

[28] *Legal Status of Eastern Greenland (Norway v Denmark)* [1933] PCIJ A/B, No. 53; L Preuss, 'The Dispute Between Denmark and Norway Over the Sovereignty of Eastern Greenland' (1932) 26 *American Journal of International Law* 469.

[29] PJ Beck, 'Securing the Dominant "Place in the Wan Antarctic Sun" for the British Empire: The Policy of Extending British Control Over Antarctica' (1983) 29(3) *Australian Journal of Politics and History* 448.

[30] Kawaja and Griffiths (n 8) 22.

[31] 'Australian Antarctic Territory Acceptance Bill', Second Reading, House of Representatives, Hansard, 26 May 1933, 1951.

was reluctantly accepted by Australia for fear of undermining the rationale for its own title, then based only on the rituals of surveying, reading proclamations and raising flags. The Australian Antarctic Territory Acceptance Act 1933 covered: 'all the islands and territories, other than Adelie Land, situated south of the 60th degree south latitude and lying between the 160th degree east longitude and the 45th degree east longitude'.[32] Whilst the Australian assertion of sovereignty at the time was only contested by Norway, which withdrew its objection in 1939,[33] the Commonwealth was unable until 1954 to establish a station on Antarctica, to demonstrate any actual settlement, as some nations including the US believed was necessary to give claims any credence.

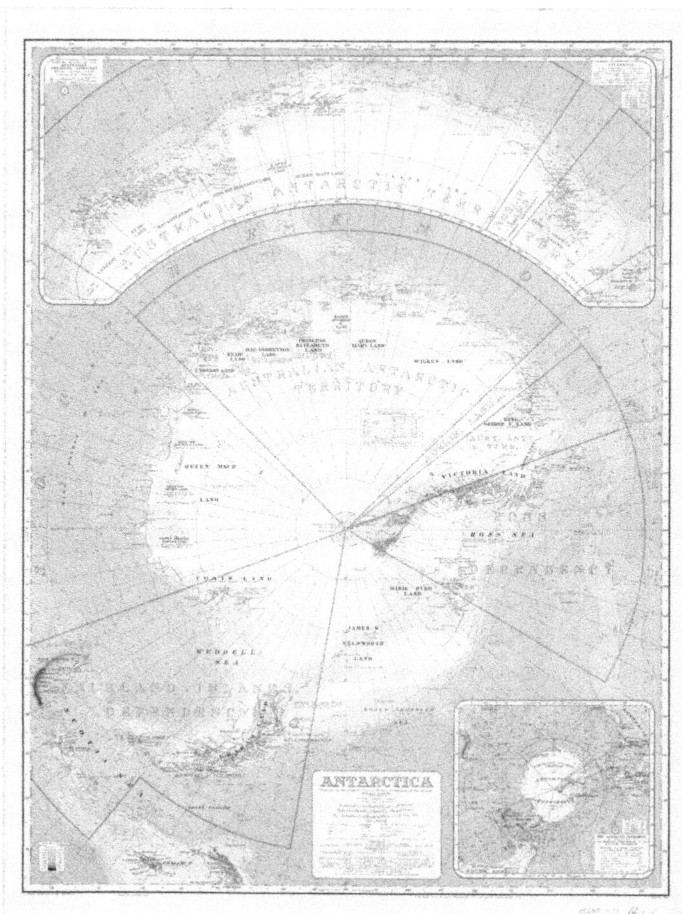


**Figure 12.2** Antarctica and Australia's territory, Commonwealth Department of the Interior, 1939; National Library of Australia

[32] Section 2.
[33] DR Rothwell and A Jackson, 'Sovereignty' in Haward and Griffiths (n 8) 48, 52.

The United States and Soviet Union rejected existing national sovereignty claims, rationalising that Antarctica belonged to no one. Yet they also reserved the right to possibly make their own claims one day, including to areas Australia claimed. In its interpretation of international law, the US maintained that discovery and exploration of new territories without subsequent effective control or occupation didn't make annexation valid.[34]

A counterweight to this rivalry were efforts by the global community to promote scientific collaboration. Its apotheosis was the International Geophysical Year (IGY), a watershed for galvanising scientific interest in Antarctica. Lasting from 1 July 1957 to 31 December 1958, the IGY mobilised 60,000 scientists from 67 countries gathering, analysing and sharing data, particularly regarding the polar regions from which new understandings about Antarctica's climate and ice sheets were generated. The memorable IGY logo depicted a revolving Earth partially in shadow, hinting at its relationship to the wider universe, and a satellite orbiting the planet to symbolise the connection between humankind and science. Relevantly, the logo also gives prominence to the South Pole.[35]

The IGY advanced the norm that scientific research in such realms for peaceful purposes should be open to everyone. During the IGY the participating nations agreed to put aside their sovereignty claims to Antarctica, whilst the United States convened international meetings to explore how to resolve its contested and ambiguous legal status. From such goodwill ensued the Antarctic Treaty,[36] with one of its core pillars being that the region should be dedicated to peaceful, international scientific cooperation.

## IV. Antarctic Treaty

Over six weeks in late 1959, invited representatives from 12 nations met in Washington DC to finalise an agreement for governance of Antarctica, which they had been negotiating for the last 18 months.[37] The Antarctic Treaty, adopted on 1 December 1959 and operative from 23 June 1961, has been remarkably successful in forging international cooperation and peace on the world's fifth largest continent, covering 9.2 per cent of the Earth's land area. Its principal achievements have been to reduce environmental exploitation and to forestall geo-political tensions by freezing territorial claims to any part of the continent as they existed in 1959. Seven nations had made different and sometimes overlapping territorial claims: Australia, Argentina, Chile, France, New Zealand,

[34] For a recent legal interpretation that discounts the US position, see SV Scott, 'The Irrelevance of Non-recognition to Australia's Antarctic Territory Title' (2021) 70(2) *International and Comparative Law Journal* 491.

[35] H Odishaw, 'International Geophysical Year Symbol' (1956) 123 *Science* 722.

[36] Antarctic Treaty (1961) 402 UNTS 71.

[37] R Hall and M Kawaja, 'Australia and the Negotiation of the Antarctic Treaty' in Haward and Griffiths (n 8) 68, 83.

Norway, and the UK. The treaty puts them in abeyance, whilst no other nations may initiate new claims.[38]

To properly understand governance of Antarctica, we must foremostly appreciate its unique geography, with 98 per cent of its surface entombed under a gigantic frozen mantle. Until the mid-1950s, the human presence there was ephemeral, as explorers occasionally planted flags, took photographs or erected makeshift huts. That changed in 1954 when Australia established its year-round Mawson station, and extended its domestic laws to its southern territory, thereby consolidating the Commonwealth's territorial ambitions. Other nations soon emulated Australia's example, with 42 permanent stations, and at least double that number of summer bases, by 2022.

Negotiating the Antarctica treaty at the height of the Cold War is remarkable.[39] The IGY nurtured interest in securing the area as a global common. At one pole in the treaty negotiations was the option to partition the continent into state-controlled sovereign realms. With the largest claim, Australia's position was clear: Antarctica wasn't a communal space to share.[40] Australian negotiators thus favoured minimal international governance, in which Antarctica would be reserved for scientific cooperation and other peaceful purposes with little international oversight. Argentina and Chile's positions were broadly similar to Australia's. At the other pole in the negotiations was the proposal from India, supported by New Zealand, to collectively hold the continent under the auspices of an international entity, such as a United Nations. trusteeship. The negotiated outcome sits between these options.

The Antarctic Treaty applies to south of latitude 60° S, including all ice shelves but not the high seas.[41] Three core principles anchor its governance: peaceful use, international scientific cooperation and suspension of sovereignty claims without necessarily invalidating them along with barring assertion of new territorial claims. The prospect of economic exploitation of the region was omitted from the treaty, which helped to secure agreement in the absence of any finality on the sovereignty claims. The principle of peaceful use wasn't defined but the treaty elaborates that 'There shall be prohibited, inter alia, any measure of a military nature'.[42] The principle of freedom of scientific investigation in Antarctica was established in light of international arrangements arising from the IGY.

Another tenet of the treaty is consensus decision-making: key decisions of the parties require unanimous agreement, though, apart from informal diplomatic pressure, the treaty itself lacks specific sanctions to move an uncooperative party.

[38] Article IV. No nation has claimed Marie Byrd Land, in West Antarctica.

[39] J Hanessian, 'The Antarctic Treaty 1959' (1960) 9 *International and Comparative Law Quarterly* 436, 436–50.

[40] RG Casey, 'Address by the Australian Minister for External Affairs at the Opening Session, October 15 1959' (Conference on Antarctica, Washington DC, 15 October 1959).

[41] Although, it remains legally unclear whether water under ice sheets should be defined as part of the high seas.

[42] Article I.

Whilst the treaty freezes existing territorial claims in Antarctica, which would be unlikely to be recognised given the need for consensus, a claimant state could withdraw from the treaty (though that in itself wouldn't have any legal consequence for other states in regard to that sovereignty claim). There's also nothing in the law to prevent any state not party to the treaty to claim territory or conduct activities in Antarctica, such as mining, contrary to the treaty – though implementation of any such act would be altogether a different matter, and quite improbable at this time.

Whilst Australia advocated for a limited, exclusive club of nations to manage Antarctica's governance, the Soviet Union and Japan favoured opening it to all interested nations, a stance closer to that adopted in the negotiations. Its administrative machinery, detailed in article IX, deems the 12 original signatories (including Australia) the 'Consultative Parties', with authority to consult together on matters of common interest and to formulate, consider and recommend measures (by consensus, as required by Article IX(4)) to their governments. The Antarctic Treaty Consultative Meeting, which is the assembly of treaty parties, was first held in 1961 in Canberra and has met annually since 1994. Fifty-six nations have as of 2023 acceded to the treaty, and those that demonstrate their interest in 'conducting substantial research activity'[43] in the continent are entitled to participate in meetings of the Consultative Parties (29 states at present).

The international community has also wrestled with the legal status of the waters around Antarctica, and other oceans, under increasing exploration and development. The evolution of the United Nations Convention on the Law of the Sea (UNCLOS) progressed with four agreements adopted in 1958 governing coastal states' maritime jurisdiction, the freedom of the high seas, and the conservation and management of marine living resources.[44] The 1958 agreements didn't settle all legal issues, and many nations declined to ratify them, yet this milestone assisted the Antarctic Treaty by affirming the right of innocent passage for foreign ships through any marine waters.

The final UNCLOS concluded in 1982,[45] which effectively superseded the 1958 agreements, resolved many legal issues, some with implications for Antarctica claimant states. Australia was one to use UNCLOS's provisions to declare an Exclusive Economic Zone (EEZ), extending 200 nautical miles offshore from the Australian Antarctica Territory, and thus injected, explain Donald Rothwell and Andrew Jackson, a bit of geopolitical rivalry into the continent that the 1959 treaty had sought to suspend or resolve.[46] The EEZ gave Australia potential control over vast fisheries.

The Antarctica Treaty didn't mark the beginning of any utopian, post-colonial future for the continent. The treaty channelled and neutralised some international

[43] Article IX(2).

[44] AH Dean, 'The Geneva Conference on the Law of the Sea: What was Accomplished' (1958) 52(4) *American Journal of International Law* 607.

[45] (1992) 31 ILM 841.

[46] Rothwell and Jackson (n 33) 59–61.

rivalry, which still simmers, such as the prospect of opening Antarctic to mining after the review of the ban scheduled in 2048. The International Court of Justice has never been asked to rule on the validity of any state's claim to Antarctica, and geopolitical tensions have grown in recent years as China asserts its presence and likely interest in future mining.[47]

## V. Australia in Antarctica: Governance at a Distance

Just four nations recognise Australia's claim to part of Antarctica – France, Norway, New Zealand and Great Britain – yet the Commonwealth has all along acted as though Australian law applies to the Australian Antarctica Territory (AAT). Australia's 1933 legislation that created the AAT however 'did nothing to support the administration of law in the AAT' explain Stuart Kaye and others,[48] and no ordinances that could have been enacted under the 1933 Act to guide the ATT's governance were enacted. That lacuna lasted until 1954 when the Commonwealth decided that the laws of the Australian Capital Territory were deemed by the Commonwealth to apply to the AAT, by virtue of the Australian Antarctic Territory Act, though given that environmental laws in the Australian Capital Territory, such as tree-clearing regulations, were unlikely to be relevant to the AAT, this extension of the Territory's laws to Antarctica had little practical effect on environmental decision making.

Although the 1959 Antarctic Treaty doesn't represent Australia's preferred negotiation position, by at least participating in the treaty the Commonwealth believed it could best protect Australia's territorial claim and collateral interests in the continent from rival states. The Commonwealth has also since maintained an active role in polar science, including hosting three research stations, to demonstrate its assertion as a major stakeholder in Antarctica's future. The nation's presence is also bolstered by its management of marine resources, such as its pro-conservation stance in the implementation of the Convention on the Conservation of Antarctic Marine Living Resources, adopted in 1980,[49] whose administering Commission sits in Hobart.

Australia's three bases furnish its most tangible presence in Antarctica. The Mawson base was the first established, in February 1955, comprising a tiny colony of prefabricated, wooden huts and a few caravans. The huts have acquired the status of national heritage, an Australian marker in its last frontier.[50] A replica of one of Mawson's huts used for the 1911–14 expedition was erected on the Hobart waterfront, a stone's throw from where Mawson's team departed.

[47] AM Brady, *China as a Polar Great Power* (Cambridge University Press, 2017).
[48] S Kaye, M Johnson and R Baird, 'Law' in Haward and Griffiths (n 8) 97, 106.
[49] (1980) 19 ILM 841.
[50] C Collis, 'Mawson's Hut: Emptying Post-colonial Antarctica' (1999) 23 *Journal of Australian Studies* 22.

Mawson first ventured to Antarctica as a member of Ernest Shackleton's 1907–09 'Nimrod' expedition, sponsored by the UK government, in search of the South Pole. Born in 1882 in England, Mawson emigrated to Australia as an infant, and trained as a geologist and mining engineer at the University of Sydney. After Shackleton's expedition, Mawson headed the Australasian Antarctic Expedition, which from 1911 to 1914 surveyed thousands of kilometres of hitherto unknown terrain, collecting geological samples and making other scientific observations. On 30 January 1912, Mawson raised the British and Australian flags from the apex of the hut his expedition assembled, claiming possession of a huge wedge of the continent in the name of the British Empire.

Mawson's 1930 expedition even more explicitly was associated with colonisation. A poignant moment was when Mawson chose a small rocky island, home to a large penguin rookery. Climbing to the island's 245-metre summit, Mawson read an official proclamation of territorial annexation, and placed the Union Jack in a cairn of stones gathered on the site. The ceremony had a momentary mishap when Mawson, about to read the proclamation, discovered that his fellow expeditioners had placed the document in a canister and buried it under the cairn. But he was able to recite the proclamation from near-memory: 'the full sovereignty of the territory of Enderby Land, Kemp Land, MacRobertson Land' and all islands between 73° E and 47° E.[51] One of his men hammered a wooden plaque to the pole: it read, 'The British Flag was hoisted and British Sovereignty asserted on 13th January, 1930'. Frank Hurley, a renowned Australian photographer who accompanied several expeditions to Antarctica, took a commemorative picture (see Figure 12.3). The BANZARE expeditioners couldn't land on the continent itself, owing to adjoining thick pack-ice, but from this nearby island they felt sufficiently close to assert a continental claim (and similar proclamations of annexation were made at other coastal sites). Annexation of this 1,000 km labyrinth of coastline and its hinterland was solidified as Mawson named landforms observed from his ship *Discovery*, with the island just mentioned becoming Proclamation Island, and various sighted inland mountains given names honouring his fellow expeditioners. The crew also collected biological specimens and geological samples, albeit likely to facilitate future economic exploitation rather than nature conservation.

Mawson's 1929–31 expedition was memorialised by video footage taken by Hurley, who created *Siege of the South* that was exhibited around Australian cinemas. The film's most memorable scene is at Proclamation Island, beginning with imagery of an empty land, a *terra nullius*, into which Mawson's expedition enters to discover and claim with pomp and ceremony as he read the proclamation, then raises a flag, singing 'God Save the King'.[52] These rituals along with their documentation through Hurley's film and photography, as well as maps, helped render the uninhabited, continent into an Australian national possession in their interpretation of international law.

[51] Kawaja and Griffiths (n 8) 34; see further D Mawson, 'The Antarctic Cruise of the "Discovery", 1929–30' (1930 20(4) *Geographical Review* 535.

[52] C Collis, 'The Proclamation Island Moment: Making Antarctica Australian' (2004) 9 *Law Text Culture* 47.

**Figure 12.3** British Australian and New Zealand Antarctic Expedition (BANZARE) 1929–31, Proclamation ceremony on Proclamation Island: photographer Frank Hurley; National Archives of Australia

This aestheticised claim to Antarctica was cultivated in the national consciousness through other means as well. Since 1957 the Commonwealth has issued Antarctic-themed stamps for the AAT, which can be validly used for mail anywhere under Australian jurisdiction. The first post office in the AAT opened in 1947 at Heard Island, in the southern Indian Ocean, and in 1954 the first post office on the Antarctica continent opened at Mawson station. The Antarctica postage elucidated a cartographic representation of the territory as Australian space – an act of a sovereign state asserting its spatial possession.

**Figure 12.4** Australian Antarctic Territory stamp, 1959; Australia Post

When Australia took over Britain's Antarctica stake pursuant to the Australian Antarctic Treaty Acceptance Act 1933, commentators suggested that Australia's supervision might bring environmental protection benefits including 'to check the indiscriminate slaughter which threatened whales within extinction in these waters'.[53] Mawson himself however wasn't taciturn about opening Antarctica to economic development. Given his professional training, it's not surprising that he eyed the prospects for mining. In 1935 the Sydney press reported: 'Sir Douglas Mawson … emphasised the value to Australia of the resources of the Antarctic continent. He said the day was fast approaching when prospecting for mineral wealth would be carried out on a big scale'.[54] Like his compatriots, Mawson also supported whaling. In 1930 he counselled: 'Australia may think the Antarctic difficult of access … but I recommend Australia to go with the job. There is money in whaling'.[55] Addressing the Australian and New Zealand Association for the Advancement of Science in 1935, Mawson advised: 'The immediate prospects of commercial development in Antarctica are centered on the fisheries, and whaling is ascendant just now. … This unique and rich industry could be perpetuated for all time were more adequate international control established'.[56]

Mawson's hopes for Australian-led whaling and mining never materialised; instead, the AAT, like other parts of the continent, became a realm for scientific research shared with other nations. Most visibly, the Territory hosts a variety of stations of other nations, including several from Russia, long resolutely opposed to Australia's sovereignty claims. One of its stations, Mirny, was established by the Soviet Union in 1956, just 24 months after the Mawson station, and at the time was substantially more modern and larger. Surely named not without reference to its significance, Mirny was one of the ships of the Imperial Russian Expedition of 1819–21 to Antarctica, thus implying Russia's own historical precedent and legal claim to Antarctic space.

## VI. Environmental Governance in Antarctica

Conservation of Antarctica's environmental values, in the world's largest remaining wilderness, received little attention in the negotiation of the Antarctic Treaty even though nature conservation was subsequently discussed during the earliest meetings of the treaty parties.[57] Until the late 1950s, nature protection in Antarctica was of limited scope, confined to conserving cetaceans and seals for ongoing resource exploitation. The governments of Australia, Britain, France, New Zealand and Norway passed regulations for such purposes from the early twentieth century.

[53] 'Australia and Antarctica' (*Sydney Morning Herald*, 16 February 1933) 8.

[54] 'Antarctica. Evidence of Mineral Wealth' (*Sydney Morning Herald*, 1 February 1935) 10.

[55] 'Antarctica. Wealth in Whaling' (*Sydney Morning Herald*, 2 April 1930) 13.

[56] 'Future of Antarctica. Use to Humanity' (*Sydney Morning Herald*, 17 January 1935) 12.

[57] A Antonello, 'Nature Conservation and Antarctic Diplomacy, 1959–1964' (2014) 4(2) *Polar Journal* 335, 338.

These regulations also served to demonstrate 'occupation' of the region. In more recent decades the concerns have broadened, including waste from the increasing base stations on the continent.

The earliest conservation reserves were established in subantarctic islands. In 1910, New Zealand established a Reserve for the Preservation of Fauna on Adams Island in the Auckland Islands. In 1924, France declared a conservation reserve on the Kerguelen Islands, whose elephant seals were being heavily slaughtered, at a time when France sought to increase its presence there and part of the polar continent itself known as Adélie Land that it claimed.[58]

Although Australia didn't establish an Antarctic whaling industry, it sought to regulate other nations' whaling there. The Commonwealth's Whaling Act 1935 was intended to give effect to the Convention for the Regulation of Whaling of 1931, requiring whalers in Australian coastal and Antarctic waters to obtain a licence from the Commonwealth, and it prohibited taking certain species of whales in such waters including 'any calf or suckling whale or immature whale'.[59] The Act extended to ships registered in Australia wherever they operated. After World War II, which had curtailed economic activities in the southern pole, Australia used the newly established International Whaling Commission, set up under the 1946 International Convention for the Regulation of Whaling, to try to curb Japanese Antarctic whaling.[60] However, its stance was compromised by the fact that Australia itself had re-established its own whaling industry in the 1950s, and in any event the Whaling Commission did not embrace a strong anti-whaling position until the 1980s.

Another seminal international development before the Antarctic Treaty was the International Geophysical Year (IGY). By promoting scientific research into Antarctica, the IGY helped to conceptualise the polar continent's geography and how it should be used. Yet in its focus on geophysical processes rather than living biodiversity, the IGY perhaps inadvertently implied that the continent is generally lifeless. Concomitantly, however, the belief of the time that Antarctica lacked viable mineral resources to exploit contributed to the perception that it lacked economic value. These views helped to inculcate the view that Antarctica's terrestrial environment lacked significance, either for conservation or resource exploitation – but it would not be long before this perception would be challenged.

Science would soon play a more decisive role, as it had in shaping some of Australia's earliest environmental governance, by directly informing the first regulations for nature conservation in Antarctica. Biologists Robert Falla (New Zealand), Carl Eklund (US), Jean Prevost (France), Brian Roberts (UK) and WJL Sladen (US) were influential via international conferences and scientific groups

[58] Kawaja and Griffiths (n 8) 24.

[59] Section 6(1)(b).

[60] SV Scott and LM Oriana, 'The History of Australian Legal Opposition to Japanese Antarctic Whaling' (2019) 73(5) *Australian Journal of International Affairs* 466, 471.

in advocating for action in Antarctica. A symposium convened in 1959 by the International Union of Geology and Geophysics in Buenos Aires, passed a resolution that recognised that Antarctic birds and mammals were vulnerable to disturbance from scientific expeditions, such as from rogue dogs, air flights over rookeries, and ships' waste discharges. The 1960 conference of the International Council for Bird Preservation called for the protection of birds in Antarctica.[61] That year the International Union for Conservation of Nature (IUCN), the world's premier body of its kind, passed a resolution at its annual assembly calling for protection of Antarctic fauna and flora.[62]

A leading Australian biologist in this formative phase was Robert Carrick, with the CSIRO's Wildlife Division. He submitted a paper to the 1959 IUGG symposium of the International Union of Geology and Geophysics, presciently spelling out three grounds for conservation: the region's unique scientific values associated with life forms adapted to extreme climatic conditions; the aesthetic values, such as spectacular penguin and seal colonies; and thirdly, the economic value of conserving whale and seal populations for possible future exploitation.[63] Carrick championed a scientific approach to nature conservation that acknowledged the complex ecological and biological relationships as opposed to just focusing on individual species. Ahead of his time, Carrick also believed that polar wildlife belonged to the common heritage of humankind – a concept later formally acknowledged in international environmental law – when he exclaimed that 'political boundaries have no significance for migrating animals, and rare and interesting species are, in a very real sense, the property of the whole world'.[64]

Environmental issues cropped up in the negotiations to draft the Antarctica Treaty. The United States wanted explicit acknowledgment of the need to regulate use of natural resources and conservation of biodiversity. Australia wished to exclude such provisions, believing they might jeopardise the integrity of its sovereignty claim. When the official conference to adopt the treaty opened on 15 October 1959, the draft text omitted the foregoing issues. The US delegates again advocated for their inclusion, suggesting: 'certainly one of the objects of scientific investigation in Antarctica is investigation of living things there. And if we don't conserve them, there will be nothing to investigate'.[65]

Ultimately, the Antarctic Treaty included just one brief but seminal clause on nature conservation. Article IX, which establishes the meetings of the 'Consultative Parties' and the subjects for which they should take further action, includes within its agenda the 'preservation and conservation of living resources'.[66] This pithy clause has evolved to become one of the backbones of Antarctic governance, giving

[61] Antonello (n 57) 340.
[62] IUCN Resolution: Antarctic Fauna and Flora (1960), portals.iucn.org/library/node/43456.
[63] R Carrick, 'Conservation of Nature in the Antarctic' (1960) 6 *SCAR Bulletin* 299.
[64] Quoted in Antonello (n 57) 340.
[65] Quoted in A Antonello, *The Greening of Antarctica* (Oxford University Press, 2019) 36.
[66] Article IX.1(f).

imprimatur to regulations and policies over the following decades on a variety of environmental concerns.

Shortly before the treaty was adopted, a Scientific Committee on Antarctic Research (SCAR), with Australian representation, was formed by the International Science Council, a committee that would evolve to shape the scientific underpinnings of the continent's environmental governance. At its first meeting in February 1958, SCAR identified its task as to 'prepare a plan for the scientific exploration of Antarctica in the years following the completion of the International Geophysical Year programme'.[67] It has collaborated and exchanged scientific information through a variety of international meetings. At SCAR's fourth meeting, in 1961, a statement on 'Conservation of Nature in Antarctica' was prepared by its Working Group on Biology, in consultation with national governments, declaring: 'Antarctic flora and fauna are of outstanding scientific importance and every effort should be made to minimize interference by man' and that the region 'merits preservation as a world heritage'.[68] Since then, SCAR has worked to identify and promote understanding of Antarctic and Southern Ocean environmental issues for policy makers, using conduits such as its observer status at the Antarctic Treaty Consultative Meetings, and tendering advice to other international bodies including the Intergovernmental Panel on Climate Change.

At the inaugural Antarctic Treaty Consultative Meeting, in Canberra in July 1961, nature conservation was also on the agenda. Great Britain took the lead in promoting the subject in light of advice tabled from SCAR. The delegates agreed to a recommendation to recognise the importance of conservation of living resources, to promote scientific research on the Antarctic environment, and to develop interim and long-term protection measures.[69] In 1962, the UK moved plans for a separate international agreement for such purposes, including provisions to prohibit injury to or disturbance of wildlife without permission, and creation of nature sanctuaries. Other treaty parties were sympathetic to this proposal but some disagreed on whether to incorporate such measures in the existing treaty or via a separate convention, and whether to extend such measures beyond the Antarctic landmass to its extensive marine pack ice.

The 'Agreed Measures for the Conservation of Antarctic Fauna and Flora' adopted in June 1964[70] designated all of Antarctica a 'Special Conservation Area' with a variety of obligations on the treaty parties. The measures specifically require governments to 'minimize harmful interference' with the living conditions of fauna, and to restrict the taking of any wildlife only with permits granted for such eligible purposes as feeding people or dogs and for scientific collecting, taking into account the ability of species to 'normally be replaced by natural reproduction'[71]

[67] SCAR, www.scar.org/about-us/history.
[68] 'Conservation of Nature in Antarctica' (1961) 8 *SCAR Bulletin* 103, 105.
[69] Recommendation I–VIII, in 'Report of First Consultative Meeting, Canberra', 1961.
[70] Agreed Measures for the Conservation of Antarctic Fauna and Flora, Brussels, 2 June 1964.
[71] ibid art VI(4a).

and for the maintenance of 'the variety of species and the balance of the natural ecological systems'.[72] Some wildlife could also be designated 'Specially Protected Species', thereby receiving higher legal safeguards, and some areas of high conservation value could be designated 'Specially Protected Areas' in 'order to preserve their unique natural ecological system'. Although it would take 18 years, until November 1982, for the Agreed Measures to come into legal force because of the requirement of unanimous support, all parties including Australia behaved during this interval as though the measures were operative.[73] During this interval the Treaty's Consultative Meetings passed a wide variety of recommendations relating to nature conservation, including regulating tourist visitations (1966)[74] that would become significant environmental governance concern in the following century. In 1991 the Agreed Measures were subsumed within the Madrid Protocol on Environmental Protection in the Antarctic Treaty,[75] which after entering into legal force in 1998 offered a more comprehensive regime of environmental governance for Antarctica.

## VII. Australia's Subantarctic Islands

Australia's southern dominions include the subantarctic Macquarie Island and the Heard and McDonald Island group. Unlike its territorial claim in Antarctica, Australia's sovereignty to them isn't contested. These islands have an environmental history that shifted from plundering to cautious conservation. Both are administered by the Australian Antarctic Division (AAD) – part of the Commonwealth's foreign affairs portfolio.

Located 1,500 km from Hobart, Macquarie Island is half way between Tasmania and Antarctica, and far closer to the Australian mainland than the Heard and McDonald Islands, some 4,100 km from the closest major city, Perth. The small size of Macquarie Island, at just 128 km$^2$, belies its significance to the ecology and history of the Southern Ocean. The island was sighted by Captain Frederick Hasselborough on 11 July 1810, who claimed it for Great Britain, which assigned it to the colony of NSW that year, and then in 1825 it came under the auspices of Van Diemen's Land, as Tasmania was then known. Under international law today, Australia enjoys sovereign rights also over the 200 nautical miles seaward EEZ around Macquarie island totalling a whopping 471,000 km$^2$ of marine waters. An elevated patch of seafloor on the cusp of two tectonic plates, Macquarie Island has unique geological properties that earned its inscription on the World Heritage List in 1997.[76]

[72] ibid art VI(4b).

[73] BB Roberts, 'Conservation in the Antarctic' (1977) 279(963) *Philosophical Transactions of the Royal Society of London:* Series B, Biological Sciences 97.

[74] Recommendation IV-27 (1966): Effects of Antarctic Tourism, in B Saul and T Stephens (eds), *Antarctica in International Law* (Hart Publishing, 2016) 189.

[75] (1991) 30 ILM 1455.

[76] A Dermer and D Wood, *A Hostile Beauty. Life on Macquarie Island* (Melbourne University Publishing, 2011).

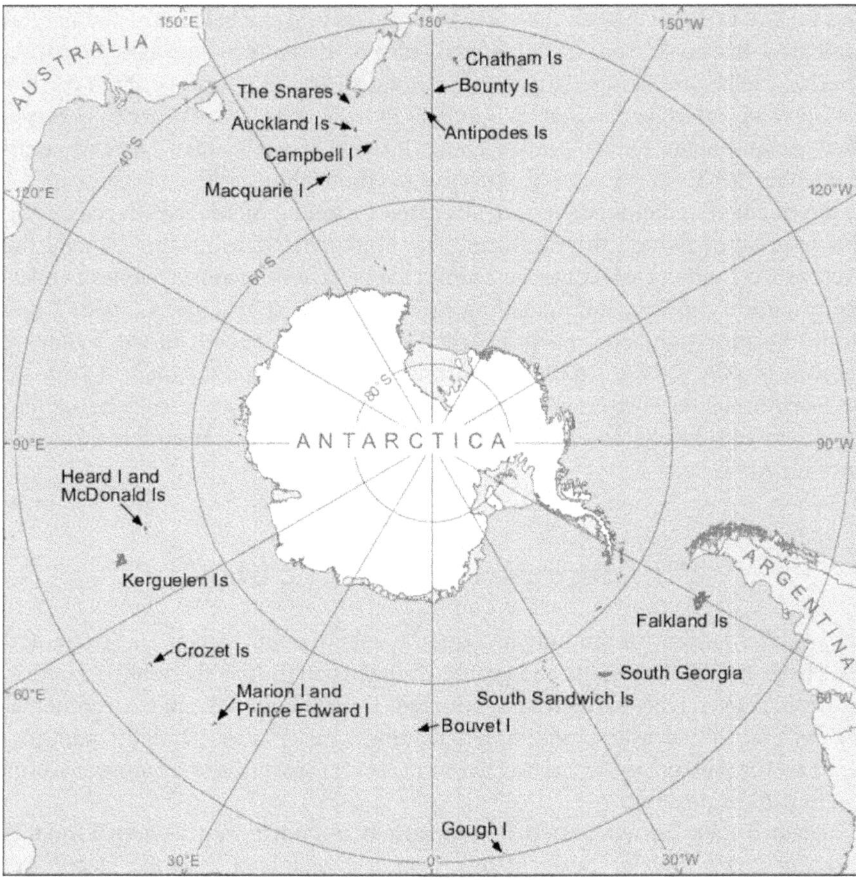


**Figure 12.5** World's subantarctic islands; Australian Antarctic Data Centre

The island hosts huge colonies of birds and mammals, which once attracted merchants and businessmen interested in their blubber and oil to power machinery and lights. The fur and elephant seals were the first to bear the brunt of the barbarous industry, which virtually exterminated the population by 1830. The sealers enjoyed a modest revival towards the end of that century despite an edict from Tasmanian authorities in 1891 prohibiting harvests on Macquarie Island, an edict generally ignored because authorities then had little capacity to enforce it.

Penguins, of which there are four species on the island, were next to be targeted, with the industry ostensibly licensed by the Tasmanian government. The slaughter of their behemoth colonies, once some three million birds, intensified from the 1880s with the aid of better technology. Penguins were either herded into enclosures to be clubbed to death or driven along ramps where they would fall into a steam cooker called the 'digester' that would extract fats from the penguins' bodies. A New Zealand team was processing about 3,500 penguins a day by 1905. The slaughter was 'necessary' to generate viable commercial returns, as each penguin produced a measly 400 ml of oil; so two-and-a-half penguin lives would yield just one litre.

During the closing years of the unsustainable industry, a journalist in 1913 observed 'the beaches of Macquarie Island present a somewhat gruesome appearance, being strewn with skeletons'.[77] Yet the reporter reassured readers that the penguins would survive because they numbered 'countless thousands'.[78] Likewise, the paper insouciantly suggested that elephant seals, inhabiting remoter enclaves of the island, were safe with 'little likelihood of extermination within the next century'.[79]

Other anecdotal evidence was less sanguine. In 1905 the International Ornithological Association wrote to the Australian Prime Minister requesting urgent action to safeguard the island's penguin and petrel populations from the barbarity.[80] One news report in 1910 began: 'A terrible slaughter of penguins by gangs of men … is causing indignation', and it suggested the Tasmanian authorities might cancel the lease held by the responsible party, Southern Isles Company.[81] By 1915, Mawson and other members of the Australasian Antarctic Expedition, who had begun investigating Macquarie Island since 1911, started campaigning against the slaughter, and proposed a wildlife sanctuary. In a lecture he gave in 1930, Mawson stated:

> The wild life of this island was threatened with extinction until the Tasmanian Government, which controls the island, decided in 1916 to discontinue leasing it to sealers … For some years now, the island has been maintained as a sanctuary for Australian sub-Antarctic life. Our observations indicate that as the result of this commendable action, penguins and seals are slowly recovering.[82]

Credit for this accomplishment also has been attributed to the Wild Life Preservation Society, which 'agitated for several years for the setting aside of Macquarie Island as a permanent sanctuary for the penguins and seals', with 'valuable assistance from Captain Hurley's vivid pictures of the penguins'.[83]

Despite a century of slaughter, Macquarie Island's seals and penguins rebounded and today thrive. In 1933 the island was declared a sanctuary under the Tasmanian Animals and Birds Protection Act 1928, with enduring protection since which culminated in 1997 in its protection under the World Heritage Convention (albeit for its geological values rather than wildlife populations). The cessation of the wildlife slaughter however wasn't sufficient to ensure complete ecological recovery, for rats, mice, cats and rabbits that were introduced intentionally or inadvertently by sealers remained on the island, and they had disastrous effects on some native biota until eradicated by 2014 by the Tasmanian Parks and Wildlife Service.[84]

[77] E Waite, 'Macquarie Island' (*Leader* (Melbourne), 20 September 1913) 46.
[78] ibid.
[79] ibid.
[80] 'Slaughter of Sea Birds' (*Observer* (Adelaide), 16 September 1905) 45.
[81] 'The Macquarie Island Penguins' (*Evening Telegraph* (Charters Towers), 18 October 1910) 2.
[82] 'Mawson Party on Macquarie Island' (*Sydney Morning Herald*, 16 December 1930) 11.
[83] "Macquarie Island. To the Editor of the Herald' (*Sydney Morning Herald*, 6 August 1931) 6.
[84] The pest eradication success is recounted in M Anderson, *Feral Dilemma: The Life of a Ranger on Sub-Antarctic Macquarie Island* (Forty South Publishing, 2014).

Australia's other subantarctic islands, Heard and McDonald Islands, have likewise become outposts of valuable nature conservation. Near neighbours in the Indian Ocean, the islands occupy 372 km$^2$ of land plus yield 410,000 km$^2$ of Exclusive Economic Zone waters under Australian auspices. Heard Island, by far the larger of the two, with 368 km$^2$, has Australia's largest mountain, Big Ben, an active volcano of 2,745 metres (9,006 ft). The tiny McDonald islands, comprising three rocky outcrops, cover less than 4 km$^2$. Being more remote, explain researchers, these islands didn't suffer as great an environmental pressure as Macquarie had, due to having far fewer invasive species.[85]

Both are named after their sightings by seafarers John Heard, in 1853, and William McDonald, in 1854.[86] Like the fate of Macquarie Island, sealers soon arrived and decimated the elephant seal population. Sporadic harvesting continued until 1910, when Britain formally added them to its empire, marked by the raising of the Union Flag and the erection of a beacon by Anton Evensen, captain of a whaling vessel. Scientific research began in the 1870s, but even well into the twentieth century visits by scientists were infrequent because of the remote and treacherous conditions. Australian research expeditions began in 1947, when Britain transferred the islands to Australia. To ensure protection of its natural values and address other administrative needs, the Heard Island and McDonald Islands Act was passed in 1953, and its current formulation provides for the application of the laws of the ACT, though administered by the Hobart-based Australian Antarctic Division. The islands are also subject to some national and international laws. Relics of the sealing sites on Heard Island are now considered to be of historic significance and legally protected. The islands also won World Heritage status in 1997.

The history of the exploitation or conservation of Australia's subantarctic islands is a microcosm of the larger fate of Antarctica and the Southern Ocean – exploration, acquisition, exploitation and finally conservation. Improvements in environmental governance came from advances in scientific research coupled with the weakening economic gains as natural resources such as whale and penguin populations crashed from lack of regulation. Conservation, in other words, ensued not from prescient safeguarding of natural wonders but rather from belated awareness of their increasingly scarcity or degradation. Nature had agency in its changing conservation status, from unprotected when abundantly rich in wildlife to protected as fauna disappeared. The international context to this history is particularly important, both in driving unsustainable exploitation owing to global demand for animal products such as whale meat and oil, as well as building awareness and peer pressure for nature conservation, as shown in the evolution of the Antarctic Treaty. No part of the history of Australia's vanishing nature has owed more to the international context than this polar region.

[85] LK Kriwoken and N Holmes, 'Emerging Issues of Australia's Sub-Antarctic Islands' in LK Kriwoken, J Jabour and AD Hemmings (eds), *Looking South: Australia's Antarctic Agenda* (Federation Press, 2007), 159.

[86] B Roberts, 'Historical Notes on Heard and McDonald Islands' (1950) 5 *Polar Record* 580.

# PART IV

# The Future's Past

# 13

# Restoring a Continent

## I. A New Agenda

So then, what should we make of the nation's environmental law history for the future? Whilst I haven't sought to explicitly compare Australia's past and current laws, I hope that by unveiling the period 'before' environmental law, that we can better appreciate where today's laws originated and why governance problems endure. History matters particularly in the Australian context because an ancient land and culture were trespassed on by a colonising society. That society however was not wholly destructive, for the green activism unleashed in late 1960s, explain Martin Mulligan and Stuart Hill, 'had roots within Australia going back many decades'.[1]

I'm not going to discuss recent Australian environmental law, as abundant literature already exists.[2] Instead, I wish to comment briefly on three major headwinds that blunt its future prospects, and all relate to this book's history: the trajectory of diminishing returns, systemic barriers to change, and thirdly, the impact of legacies.

Precedents or circumstances born in the nation's earlier history shape how the environment is governed today. A smorgasbord of environmental laws arose well before the late 1960s, steered via governance mechanisms associated with science, polyarchy, markets and enlightened despotism. However, their focus on *means* rather than ends restricted what could be achieved. They were embellished by emerging policy norms, such as 'wise use' (eg resource use), 'amenity' (eg town planning) and 'conservation' (eg national parks) but applied without a coherent normative direction and laws often worked at cross-purposes. Environmental law from 1901 to 1967 at least helped mitigate the extent and gravity of the vanishing continent's losses; more would have gone without laws for soil conservation, wildlife protection and other subjects this book covers. These early gains accrued because they were the low-hanging fruit for regulators – the easy pickings with low political, economic or technological barriers to overcome, such as parks being created on what were perceived as economically 'worthless lands', as Colin Michael Hall puts it.[3] They were also relatively easy pickings as they ensued with a degree of

[1] M Mulligan and S Hill, *Ecological Pioneers: A Social History of Australian Ecological Thought and Action* (Cambridge University Press, 2001) 9.

[2] Useful sources are the *Environmental and Planning Law Journal*, published since 1984, and the reports of the former Australian Panel of Experts on Environmental Law, available at www.edo.org.au/publication/australian-panel-of-experts-in-environmental-blueprint-and-technical-reports.

[3] CH Hall, 'The "Worthless Lands Hypothesis" and Australia's National Parks and Reserves' in KJ Frawley and N Semple (eds), *Australia's Ever Changing Forests* (University of NSW, 1998) 441.

path dependency that built on prior institutions and practices without disrupting the basic fabric of Australia's settler society.

Increasingly, however, this path has faced its own 'law' of diminishing returns, as existing tools and strategies become relatively less effective in tackling new problems or making further gains with old ones, as historian Joseph Tainter has conceptualised in regard to the downfall of ever-more complex societies.[4] Whilst the first generation of law reforms sometimes yielded impressive dividends (consider air quality regulations ridding cities of smog),[5] the more intractable environmental challenges in the twenty-first century require greater resources, knowledge and sacrifice to resolve, including climate change, plastic pollution, nitrogen overload, and more invasive species. The ostensibly dramatic legal reforms over the past half century, emboldened with ambitious targets such as to limit global warming to 1.5°C and protect 30 per cent of the continent's landmass by 2030,[6] face far more burdensome challenges than their predecessors. Governance interventions are accruing ever-meagre results to the point where the costs of governance become economically and politically unsustainable for society.[7]

The second headwind is that further environmental improvements won't easily ensue from just cranking out more laws that are grafted into an anthroparchic nation. Environmental law continues to function within, rather than transform, the colonising politico-economic system embedded in Australia's history. As Stephen Dovers distils, the country's environmental problems have 'causes rooted deeply in patterns of production, consumption, settlement, and governance'.[8] Furthermore, because Australia's environmental problems are increasingly entangled in other nations' practices, notably carbon emissions, homegrown laws can no longer (if ever they could) furnish a complete solution. These systemic factors are associated with capitalism and the nation-state itself, and manifest in their enabling legal architecture including property tenure, corporate governance and trade law. We cannot avert the crisis of the Anthropocene if the structural factors in its creation remain unaltered.[9] Activist protest movements such as Extinction Rebellion (see Figure 13.1) are among voices targeting these structural obstacles, and the reaction of authorities via harsh, anti-protest laws, which have led to the imprisonment of some activists, underscore the hostility of business and political elites to systemic change.[10]

[4] JA Tainter, *The Collapse of Complex Societies* (Cambridge University Press, 1988).

[5] See eg, G Nagle, *Hazards* (Oxford University Press, 1998) 117 (discussing the UK's Clean Air Act 1956, which helped reduce the sources of smog that had killed hundreds of Londoners shortly before its passage).

[6] Commonwealth Government, *Nature Positive Plan* (AGPS, 2022).

[7] Tainter (n 4) 92, 115 and 122.

[8] S Dovers, 'Still Settling Australia' in S Dovers (ed), *Environmental History and Policy: Still Settling Australia* (Oxford University Press 2000) 2, 3.

[9] See eg D Stuart, R Gunderson and B Petersen, *The Degrowth Alternative. A Path to Address Our Environmental Crisis?* (Taylor and Francis, 2020); A Grear, *The Great Awakening: New Modes of Life Amidst Capitalist Ruins* (Punctum Books, 2020).

[10] BJ Richardson (ed), *From Student Strikes to the Extinction Rebellion: New Protest Movements Shaping our Future* (Edward Elgar, 2020).

**Figure 13.1** Environmental protest calling for radical change, Hobart, Tasmania, October 2020; photo by author

The third big hindrance to environmental law is its reforms haven't proceeded from a blank slate but applied to a continent already severely degraded – the problem of cumulative environmental damage, or what David Mercer calls the 'legacy of history'.[11] Legislative stipulations to promote 'sustainability' or conserve biodiversity are disingenuous where the current ecologies and biota are already grievously impoverished, for what exactly are we now meant to be 'sustaining'? Had Australia (and other nations) adopted robust environmental laws before the Industrial Revolution, the recent catch-up therapies might have been superfluous. Environmental law of our era has been swimming against the tide, working against the compounding interest of an Earth debt incurred by a long history of colonisation, of which climate change is the denouement.

Addressing the history of the vanishing continent can help respond to the foregoing headwinds. The history that particularly matters is the continent's pre-colonial era – its ancient lands and cultures. The growing disquiet around celebrating Australia Day (26 January) illustrates the problem with the mainstream conception of the nation's past, a date now ignominiously known to many as 'Invasion Day'. Recent debates about constitutional reform to plant an 'Indigenous Voice' in the Commonwealth parliament and negotiate a treaty with First Nations

[11] D Mercer, *A Question of Balance: Natural Resources Conflict Issues in Australia* (Federation Press, 2000) 10–12.

could facilitate the direction needed, building on the native title reform of the past 30 years. It provides the well-spring for a new co-existence with nature radically unlike the colonial impost, breaking away from the tunnel vision of path dependency. It taps into new resources and ideas to help counter the law of diminishing returns. And it provides a focus for environmental and cultural restoration to unwind some of the legacies of a vanishing continent.

In the following pages I discuss ideas and strategies for restoration governance. Reversing the continent's losses and injuries no doubt presents daunting scientific and economic challenges, as well as legal difficulties given temporal inertia in the legal system such as the grandfathering of existing land uses and the deadweight of legal precedent. To succeed, it must go beyond the technical, piecemeal approaches to environmental restoration accommodated in existing law.

## II. Orchardfield and the Vanishing Continent: Epilogue

Before examining this new agenda, let's return briefly to Orchardfield, my mother's ancestral home in northern NSW, whose more recent history reveals many shards of a vanishing Australia so that we can better understand what can and should be restored.

After the property in 1950 passed to new owners, Charles W Allbut and his progeny, it continued as an orchard for about 20 years. Its proximity to the Armidale aerodrome however cast a shadow over its future; during World War II a grove of eucalyptus trees along Orchardfield's northern boundary, then retained to shield grazing sheep, was felled to provide a better approach gradient for the airport, and by 1953 rumours began that the property might one day be expropriated for expansion of the airport.[12] When the Dumaresq Shire (as the Armidale Regional Council was then known) acquired the property in the 1970s, they installed a caretaker who resided at the original homestead, but according to my uncle Edward Jackes, who documented Orchardfield's history, 'evidently he knew very little about orcharding and especially about the essential spraying and pruning, so in the end the Shire bulldozed the orchard, probably to guard against fruit fly and codling moth'.[13] Then, in the early 1980s, in the ultimate ignominy, the historic homestead itself ended under a bulldozer's blade. The Shire allegedly arranged for a late-night demolition to pre-empt the homestead's nomination to the Register of the National Estate,[14] perhaps fearing the property would have been too costly to upkeep or that it would interfere with its airport plans.

[12] 'Armidale Drome to be Extended?' (*Inverell Times*, 12 June 1953) 1.

[13] Edward Jackes, personal communication, 31 December 2012.

[14] See archived Australian Heritage Database, 'Orchardfield, New England Hwy, Armidale', Indicative Place ID 13924.

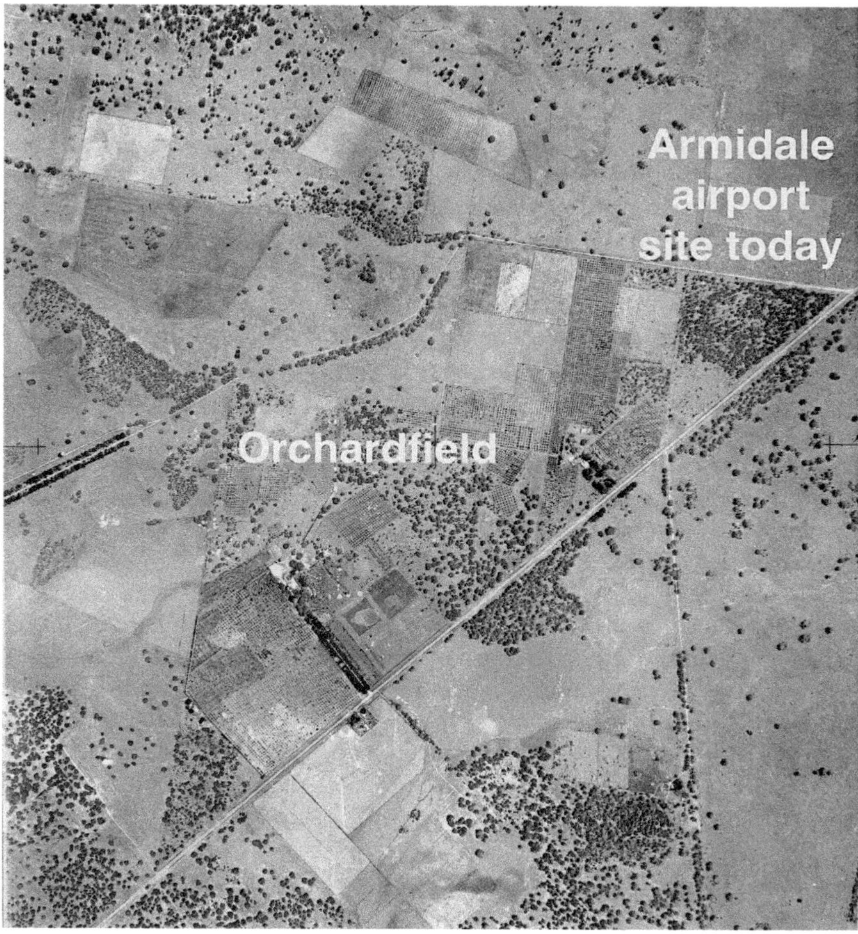


**Figure 13.2** Orchardfield environs in 1943; already extensively cleared, and showing location of Armidale airport today; photograph from author's family archives

The forlorn, empty property as of 2023 remains partly with the municipality, earmarked for the airport's business precinct and industrial estate.[15] If it is like others dotted around Australian cities, it will feature bleak warehouses and big-box retailers in over-sized, windowless, concrete monoliths adjoining sprawling carparks. These eye sores devour acres of greenery, not to mention their wider eco-footprint from their business suppliers and customers. Contrary to the insouciance of then Armidale Mayor and cattle grazier Simon Murray that the business park 'site was assessed by ecologists as highly degraded, from years of grazing and

[15] Armidale Regional Airport, *Master Plan* (June 2016) 17.

invasion by perennial weeds',[16] environmentalists pointed out that it had pockets of Yellow Box-Blakely's Red Gum Grassy Woodland, a threatened vegetation community listed under environmental legislation.[17] Remonstrating against the business park isn't to imply that Orchardfield in its heyday was environmentally innocuous. As Figure 13.2 above shows, the landscape had already been substantially deforested by the early 1940s.

The wider New England Tableland suffers from years of environmental neglect and injury, and any belief that the modernisation of environmental law might have transformed its fortunes seems unverified. In 1954 the NSW Soil Conservation Service touted that 'the age of indifference to that fate of the soil appears to be over for most landholders in the area'.[18] Yet 30 years later, the Service characterised New England as in 'crisis' owing to 'more land … being cleared for cropping'.[19] A 2003 official bioregional assessment found 'numbers of grassland and ground-feeding insectivorous birds have declined in the bioregion, as have some temperate woodland and forest species, mainly due to changes caused by agriculture'.[20] A 2020 study, when 10.39 per cent of the region was under conservation tenure,[21] found it retained just 36 per cent of its extant ecological carrying capacity before White settlement.[22]

Climate change is exacerbating such stresses. In 2010 the Commonwealth's former Climate Commission warned 'the bushfire season may become longer and fires more intensive' in New England along with 'more severe droughts' [and] the 'resulting poorer growing conditions would reduce vegetation cover and increase soil erosion'.[23] One didn't have to wait long to experience such prophesies. By October 2019 a protracted drought had pushed Armidale to the brink, nearly running out of water. Massive bushfires raged across southeast Australia that summer, scorching 310,000 hectares in the Armidale hinterland, mostly national parks.[24] The NSW government's inquiry into the inferno, which burnt an unprecedented 5.5 million hectares state-wide, concluded 'climate change … clearly played a role in the conditions that led up to the fires and in the unrelenting

[16] 'Armidale Regional Council's Ecologically Friendly Business Park' (*Armidale Express*, 23 August 2019) www.armidaleexpress.com.au/story/6345856/armidale-regional-council-business-park-ecologically-friendly.

[17] New England Greens, Submission to EPBC Amendment (Streamlining Environmental Approvals) Bill 2020, submission 113 (2020) 12.

[18] RW Bloch, 'Soil Formation and Erosion in the New England Plateau' (1954) 19(3) *Journal of the Soil Conservation Service of NSW* 141, 147–48.

[19] Soil Conservation Service of NSW, *The Northern Crisis – Soil Erosion* (Land and Water Conservation, 1984) 4.

[20] NSW National Parks and Wildlife Service (NPWS), *Bioregions of NSW* (NPWS, 2003) 159.

[21] Commonwealth Department of Agriculture, Water and Environment, 'Terrestrial Protected Area Data' (2020) www.awe.gov.au/agriculture-land/land/nrs/science/capad/2020.

[22] NSW Department of Planning, Industry and Environment, *NSW Biodiversity Outlook Report* (NSW Government, 2020) 41.

[23] Climate Commission, 'The Critical Decade: Consequences for the New England/Northwest NSW Region', www.climatecouncil.org.au/uploads/bd3683de02d94ab5c6c2231cd74ef877.pdf.

[24] D Owens and M O'Kane, *Final Report of the NSW Bushfire Inquiry* (NSW Government, 2020) 24.

conditions that supported the fires to spread'.[25] A similar verdict could be reached for many parts of Australia which burnt that summer. Then in 2022, during an intense La Niña season, eastern Australia, including around Armidale, suffered successive drenching and flooding that submerged houses, damaged critical infrastructure, disrupted businesses and even claimed some human lives – described by Australia's Climate Council as one of the nation's worst natural disasters.[26] One can only speculate about the vast but unquantifiable wildlife casualties.[27]

This is also a story about nature's backlash. Ecosystems and their biota aren't mere passive recipients of anthropogenic pressure but have agency, and their often, unpredictable permutations can inflict grave harm including economic costs, public health impacts and aesthetic and cultural losses. Whilst climate change most starkly epitomises nature's backlash, many other environmental upheavals have had costly repercussions. The COVID-19 pandemic has been described by ecologists as another backlash, as humankind's trespassing on nature's domain has spawned environmental conditions that expose people to additional threats from zoonotic diseases.[28]

The lands and waters of Australia today are not as they were over two centuries ago or indeed even in 1901. No longer can we refer just to the 'vanishing' continent; sometimes it's more accurate to acknowledge that which has already vanished. We can quantify some of the vanished biodiversity. Australia has lost 34 terrestrial mammal species since 1788, or more than 10 per cent of its 320 known land mammals.[29] Another 56 of its land mammals are near extinction, according to the Red List of the International Union for Conservation of Nature.[30] Nine bird species endemic to Australia have also disappeared since colonisation. Numerous invertebrates, likely many unrecorded in science, have gone. Thirty-seven species of plants are recorded as extinct and 1,374 species and subspecies are officially threatened.[31]

Habitat destruction, invasive species and Aboriginal dispossession explain why much has vanished, with habitat losses the most visible sign of nature's trauma. Many of Australia's forests have gone, a particularly grievous loss given that they were never extensive, like the vast boreal forests of Canada or the jungles of the Amazon, owing to the continent's desiccated soils and unfavourable climate.

[25] ibid iv.

[26] J Putrill, 'NSW, Queensland Floods on Track to be Among Country's Worst-ever Natural Disasters, Climate Council Says' (*ABC News*, 10 March 2022) www.abc.net.au/news/science/2022-03-10/floods-nsw-queensland-climate-change-worst-ever-natural-disaster/100894956.

[27] L Chung, 'True Impact of Floods on Animal Populations Remains Unknown' (*Sydney Morning Herald*, 27 March 2022) www.smh.com.au.

[28] D Carrington, 'Coronavirus: "Nature is Sending Us a Message", Says UN Environment Chief' (*Guardian*, 25 March 2022) www.theguardian.com/world/2020/mar/25.

[29] A Morton, 'Australia Confirms Extinction of 13 More Species, Including First Reptile Since Colonisation' (*Guardian*, 3 March 2021) www.theguardian.com/science/2021/mar/03.

[30] JZ Woinarski et al, 'Ongoing Unraveling of a Continental Fauna: Decline and Extinction of Australian Mammals Since European Settlement' (2015) 112(15) *PNAS* 4531.

[31] As of February 2023, see www.environment.gov.au/cgi-bin/sprat/public/publicthreatenedlist.pl?wanted=flora.

Today, 38 per cent of Australia's forests before colonisation have gone, and overall 70 per cent of native vegetation is degraded or fragmented.[32] Most of this land clearing, especially in southeast Australia, occurred from the late nineteenth to mid-twentieth centuries.[33] The depilation of the landscape persists, mostly in agricultural areas, condoned by lax regulation.

The continent is also inundated with exotic fauna, flora, parasites and disease-causing organisms, which according to the Threatened Species Recovery Hub 'are a problem for 1,257 threatened species in Australia, or about four out of five species'.[34] Foxes, feral cats, rabbits and rogue pigs are among the worst scourges. Australia is also burdened with over 2,700 naturalised weeds, comprising about 12 per cent of its flora.[35] Despite national and state laws intended to save threatened species, their plight has generally worsened. The Commonwealth's Environment Protection and Biodiversity Conservation Act 1999 provides for recovery plans for listed threatened species but in 2018 about 60 per cent of species lacked these plans.[36] Even Australia's remote Antarctic territory has intruders; thus far, 11 non-native invertebrate species, including mites and an earthworm, have established thanks to human visitors, and likely further interlopers have invaded the marine waters.[37]

These environmental losses may seem trivial against climate change. Australia's 2021 *State of the Climate* report reveals the country's climate has already warmed by an average of 1.47 ± 0.24°C since national records began in 1910, that Australia's coastal waters are acidifying and have warmed by slightly over 1°C since 1900, and rainfall has decreased in the southwest and southeast of the continent.[38] Scientists blame such changes for the collapse of 19 marine and terrestrial ecosystems in Australia over the last 30 years.[39] Record-breaking, brutal marine heatwaves bleached vast coral reefs in Queensland and contributed to the decimation of Tasmania's kelp forests and tracts of mangroves along the Gulf of Carpentaria. The Murray-Darling Basin lurches towards irreparable damage from greedy withdrawals for agriculture, damage that's also associated with siltation and eutrophication. Australia's Antarctic territory also shows evidence of climate change. Since the

[32] CJA Bradshaw, 'Little Left to Lose: Deforestation and Forest Degradation in Australia Since European Colonization' (2012) 5(1) *Journal of Plant Ecology* 109; Department of the Environment, Sport and Territories, *1996 Australia State of the Environment* (CSIRO Publishing, 1996) 4–5.

[33] ibid (Bradshaw).

[34] Threatened Species Recovery Hub, 'Australia's 10 Worst Invasive Species, Study' (2019).

[35] AJ Dodds et al, 'The Changing Patterns of Plant Naturalization in Australia' (2015) 21(9) *Diversity and Distributions* 1038.

[36] L Cox, '"Fantasy Documents": Recovery Plans Failing Australia's Endangered Species' (*Guardian*, 19 February 2018) www.theguardian.com/environment/2018/feb/20.

[37] DM Bergstrom and S Donoghue, 'Invasive Species are Threatening Antarctica's Fragile Ecosystems as Human Activity Grows and the World Warm' (*The Conversation*, 20 November 2021) theconversation.com.

[38] See www.csiro.au/en/research/environmental-impacts/climate-change/state-of-the-climate.

[39] DM Bergstrom et al, 'Combating Ecosystem Collapse from the Tropics to the Antarctic' (2021) 27(9) *Global Change Biology* 1692.

mid-1950s, the Antarctic Peninsula has recorded an average 1°C temperature rise, and the melting snow packs and ice-sheets on coastal fringes have opened niches for plants to colonise. Decline in krill populations, a crucial food-web resource, is also likely having ripple effects on marine life.[40]

## III. Environmental Restoration

Nature's vanished past engenders three governance challenges for Australia's future.[41] First, people's memories of the natural world, its landscapes and wildlife, fade with the passage of time, and as successive generations pass and further losses accumulate, firsthand knowledge of the nature's former condition world may disappear, leaving posterity with only the means to know about it vicariously through history books, museums or other records. Imprints of nature's erstwhile riches can be encountered by the general public even without necessarily looking for them, such as the toponyms recorded on Australian maps – the place names indicating or memorialising the former presence of wildlife or other environmental features. In Sydney, the suburb of Woolloomooloo is likely derived from a related Aboriginal word for kangaroo, but long gone from there. Tasmania's Emu Bay was named after an early explorer found the bird's footprints on the bay's beach, but the emu was extirpated from the island by the 1870s. Recent renaming of geographical places with their original Indigenous language – treating the landscape as an ongoing palimpsest in which place-names are erased, replaced or reinstated – has also been an important means of acknowledging Australia's past. For, instance, Hobart's towering peak Mt Wellington now carries the dual name of 'kunanyi', meaning mountain in the palawa kani, a reconstructed language of Aboriginal Tasmanians.

The second challenge for governance is that the lengthening of history beyond people's lifetimes can obscure their knowledge of the extent and causes of the attritional vanishment of nature. If one notices, the fewer quolls or quokkas might seem disquieting from the vantage of recent decades but disastrous if measured over a century, beyond living memories. The environmental loss or decline might also, from recent history, be attributed to the wrong factors – to clearing native vegetation, for instance, when long-term climatic shifts might be the underlying driver. Scientific research can correct such misapprehensions but it may have limited impact on understandings held by lay people or law makers. History amply shows how the advice of scientists has been ignored, especially when there were countervailing economic considerations, as with the introduction of cane toads or destruction of the thylacine.

[40] A Znój et al, 'Rapid Environmental Changes in the Western Antarctic Peninsula Region Due to Climate Change and Human Activity' (2017) 15(4) *Applied Ecology and Environment Research* 525.

[41] See further BJ Richardson, *Time and Environmental Law: Telling Nature's Time* (Cambridge University Press, 2017).

As anthropogenic changes have intensified and their legacies become normalised over time, a third governance challenge is not only losing sight of nature's past but becoming habituated to the altered landscapes of farms, factories and freeways. This scourge, explains biologist Daniel Pauly, leads to 'shifting environmental baselines' in which successive human generations accept the inferior condition of their environs due to lack of memory or knowledge of its past ecological richness and diversity.[42] Such lowered expectations in turn can diminish the ambitiousness of environmental laws. The leitmotif of 'sustainability' that permeates contemporary legislation[43] – the notion of sustaining the condition of *existing* biodiversity and ecosystems – thus becomes susceptible to just *maintaining* current (inferior) environmental conditions.

To counter such unambitiousness we must strive to *improve* rather than just maintain the status quo.[44] If pollution is not removed, soil erosion reversed, or fisheries replenished, then progress towards sustainability will be measured against a baseline much inferior to that enjoyed by previous generations, and working from a fragile environmental baseline that may itself be insufficiently resilient to last. Environmental restoration, as such improvements are called, should be prioritised in Australia as part of a strategy to address a vanishing continent, and when done with community participation it should also improve the public's ecological literacy to help counter further shifting baselines.

Globally, restoration is in vogue, with the United Nations sponsoring a Decade on Ecosystem Restoration for 2021–30 to catalyse international cooperation and national action to restore worldwide an area nearly the size of India.[45] Few laws have yet been modernised for this mandate[46] but progress has begun, such as the European Commission's incoming nature restoration regulation.[47] International law still furnishes few obligations or inducements for governments to practice restoration; the clearest stipulation is in the Convention on Biological Diversity 1992 to 'rehabilitate and restore degraded ecosystems and promote the recovery of threatened species', albeit without defining what might be acceptable rehabilitation or restoration.[48]

Meeting this vision challenges environmental law, given this book's history shows Australian governments have tended to be far more effective at unleashing

[42] D Pauly, 'Anecdotes and the Shifting Baseline Syndrome of Fisheries' (1995) 10 *Trends in Ecology and Evolution* 430.

[43] See eg Commonwealth's Environment Protection and Biodiversity Conservation Act 1999, s 3(1).

[44] Society for Ecological Restoration (SER), International Science and Policy Working Group, *The SER International Primer on Ecological Restoration* (SER, 2004).

[45] See www.decadeonrestoration.org.

[46] A Telesetsky, 'Ecoscapes: The Future of Place-based Ecological Restoration' (2013) 14(4) *Vermont Journal of Environmental Law* 493; MA Palmer and JB Ruhl, 'Aligning Restoration Science and the Future of Law to Sustain Ecological Infrastructure for the Future' (2015) 3(9) *Frontiers in Ecology and the Environment* 512.

[47] European Commission, *Proposal for a Regulation of the European Parliament and of the Council on Nature Restoration*, COM(2022) 304 final.

[48] (1982) 31 ILM 818, article 8(f).

environmental destruction than constraining it. The complexities and costs of restoration of vast degraded landscapes would place additional, onerous demands on governance. And the continent's ecological and biological systems have been so warped and disturbed by past exploitation that reinstating nature to its original condition might be unfeasible. There's also the question of how to address seemingly positive changes. Consider macropods, for instance: despite extensive commercial culling, the populations and range of the largest species, the red and grey kangaroos, have grown in many areas since 1788, taking advantage of waterholes established by farmers, the opening of more grazing land, and the removal of the dingo, their natural predator.[49]

A crucial decision for restoration governance is whether to calibrate recovery against an historical baseline. Restoring Australia to circa 1788 or other colonial-era markers is unrealistic for many reasons including extinct species, 'novel ecosystems' engendered by colonisation to their former condition, and the permutations introduced by global warming. Some discrete restoration projects however target distant baselines; Western Australia's Dirk Hartog Island is being restored to its condition in 1616 when the first Europeans arrived.[50] When addressing recent damage, such as with post-mining rehabilitation and clean-up of pollution spills, specific time baselines may be feasible where the aim is to return a site to its condition immediately prior to the impacting event. The Society for Ecological Restoration Australasia (SERA), which sets national standards for best practice, recommends identifying a 'reference ecosystem to guide project targets' rather than a specific past baseline.[51]

The law itself hinders recovery of baselines because of the temporal inertia embedded in the legal landscape. Environmental law does not operate on a blank slate but rather functions within existing, previously authorised land uses plus societal expectations of stability and certainty of legal rules. Many environmental uses are 'grandfathered', meaning that their impacting activities are shielded indefinitely or temporarily from transitions to stricter legal standards.[52] Some of these affected areas, such as in cities and intensive farmlands, will have become 'novel ecosystems', meaning irreparably changed places due to extensive environmental transformation.[53]

Ecosystem restoration may also not always be feasible because of financial costs and community opposition. The financial outlays may be prohibitive, and both governments and the private sector may oppose the steep upfront costs such

[49] On the impact of settlers' perceptions of animal populations, see N Cushing and J Frawley (eds), *Animals Count: How Population Size Matters in Human-Animal Relations* (Routledge, 2018).

[50] See www.sharkbay.org/restoration/dirk-hartog-island-return-1616.

[51] ASER Standards Reference Group, *National Standards for the Practice of Ecological Restoration in Australia* (ASER, 2017) 4.

[52] J Nash and R Revesz, 'Grandfathering and Environmental Regulation: The Law and Economics of New Source Review' (2007) 101 *Northwestern University Law Review* 1677.

[53] RJ Hobbs, E Higgs and C Hall (eds), *Novel Ecosystems: Intervening in the New Ecological World Order* (Wiley-Blackwell, 2013).

as acquisition of properties, decontamination work, reforestation and pest control, along with years of ongoing maintenance. Affected communities hosting a restoration project may be uncooperative, especially if economic development is curtailed and existing landholders burdened with restoration obligations. Thus, not everything gone can return, but what can be restored requires lawmakers' concerted coordination of the scientific, community and financial issues.

Respecting these financial and social constraints dovetails with the need to work with the agency of nature, for restoration projects are probably unsustainable if they require indefinite human intervention and support. Restoration will best succeed when it works with, rather than against, ecological and biological processes. As SERA's definition of restoration recognises: 'the process of assisting the recovery of an ecosystem that has been degraded damaged or destroyed' and can be considered achieved 'when the ecosystem's attributes are on a secure trajectory … without further restoration-phase interventions being needed'.[54] Hence, we can consider restoration a success when nature re-establishes its agency, becoming decolonised.

Where restoration can't reinstate deep historical baselines, a few options exist. One is what Michael Rosenzweig coins 'ecological reconciliation', a form of restoration intended for human-dominated ecosystems that improves biodiversity and furnishes social benefits without precisely reinstating former ecologies.[55] In limited places of high conservation significance, the law could unseat grandfathered uses to provide this reconciliation: one example is the Victorian government's intervention in the 1980s to compulsorily acquire and close the entire town of Summerland in order to safeguard and restore a threatened population of penguins that couldn't co-exist with people.[56] Another strategy is 'renewal ecology', which David Bowman and others describe as promoting adaptation to climate change by creating new ecosystems into which threatened species can be relocated or migrate by themselves.[57]

## IV. Existing and Proposed Restorations

Government leadership in restoring Australia has been patchy. The 2020 Samuel Review of the Commonwealth's Environment Protection and Biodiversity Conservation Act 1999 found it 'cannot mobilise the large-scale restoration

[54] Standards Reference Group, *National Standards for the Practice of Ecological Restoration in Australia, Edition 2.2* (Society for Ecological Restoration Australasia, 2021) 2.

[55] M Rosenzweig, *Win–Win Ecology* (Oxford University Press, 2003).

[56] F Pepper, 'When Phillip Island Penguins Won, and Land Owners Lost' (*ABC Radio National*, 8 April 2018) www.abc.net.au/news/2018-04-08/phillip-island-when-penguins-won-and-land-owners-lost/9464698.

[57] D Bowman et al, 'Renewal Ecology: Conservation for the Anthropocene' (2017) 25(5) *Restoration Ecology* 674.

needed'.[58] Australian law thus far has typically required ecological restoration just in discrete situations, including remediation of former mines and contaminated brownfields, often tied to the aim of returning such places to economic use. The truncated spatial and temporal scope of such interventions, while locally beneficial, does not regenerate ecosystems on the scale Australia needs. Another legal fulcrum for restoration is the biodiversity offset, where a degraded area is restored to compensate for new losses at another site from a project such as a mine.[59] In 2022 the Commonwealth proposed a 'nature repair' mechanism, utilising offsets as part of its modernisation of the above legislation.[60] Yet offsets are controversial because of difficulties comparing the ecological values at different sites, the long interval between the impacting development and any offsetting gains, and risks that the offset (eg regrown forest) will never accrue given the presence of threats such as fires or floods.[61]

Environmental restoration in Australia, or other countries, isn't unprecedented. Laura Martin's new book unveils a long history of environmental restoration projects in the United States since the early twentieth century.[62] In Australia too, the movement began to take hold in a similar era, but in an ad hoc manner. Illustratively, community groups and municipal authorities were restoring coastal teatree forests along Victoria's Port Phillip Bay in the 1920s and 1930s.[63] The Commonwealth's and UK's remediation of Maralinga is one of the nation's largest and most expensive restoration projects, though some critics suggest the clean-up is incomplete.[64] Regardless, it isn't a particularly useful precedent for addressing the problems covered in this book including invasive species and tree loss, or the compounding effects of climate change. Perhaps a better model is the nation's 'bush capital' whose forests have been regenerated and protected.

Today, private and community sector initiatives in Australia are underway, as in other countries.[65] Some have ensued with limited official support or direction, which constrains their capacity to be replicated elsewhere where the financial and social pre-conditions are lacking. One approach to intensive restoration is extensive fencing of areas to exclude pests. This was the model for Earth Sanctuaries, established in 1988, which at its peak managed 11 sanctuaries totalling 100,000 hectares where extirpated wildlife was reintroduced and flourished.[66] Despite winning awards, Earth Sanctuaries, a public company, went bankrupt in 2005

[58] G Samuel, *Independent Review of the EPBC Act: Final Report* (Commonwealth of Australia, 2020) 126.

[59] See eg Queensland's Environmental Offsets Act 2014.

[60] Department of Climate Change, Energy, the Environment and Water, *Nature Positive Plan* (Australian Government, 2022) 22.

[61] P Gibbons and D Lindenmayer, 'Offsets for Land Clearing: No Net Loss or the Tail Wagging the Dog?' (2007) 8(1) *Ecological Management and Restoration* 26.

[62] LJ Martin, *Wild by Design: The Rise of Ecological Restoration* (Harvard University Press. 2022).

[63] P Ardill, 'Innovative Federation and Inter-war Period Repair of Degraded Natural Areas and Their Ecosystems' (Ecological Restoration History, 2021).

[64] A Parkinson, *Maralinga: Australia's Nuclear Cover-up* (HarperCollins, 2007).

[65] C Fraser, *Rewilding the World* (Picador, 2009).

[66] B Aretino et al, *Creating Markets for Biodiversity: A Case Study of Earth Sanctuaries Ltd* (Australian Productivity Commission, 2001) 26.

after being unable to earn enough revenue from its assets. The federal Productivity Commission's inquiry into its history observed: 'the market value of native flora and fauna is difficult to establish, … [a]n inability to trade and hence establish the value of the assets could limit a firm's ability to borrow, raise funds and generate revenue'.[67]

Despite this setback, this 'enclave' model of restoration has adherents, albeit supported via philanthropic tutelage rather than profit-making. One success is in Canberra itself, where endangered fauna at the ACT government-owned Mulligans Flat's reserve thrive in a fenced 1,300 hectares sanctuary.[68] Another effort is Arid Recovery, a 123 km$^2$ enclosed sanctuary in the South Australian desert where reintroduced, endangered wildlife thrive unmolested.[69] A multi-stakeholder partnership supports Arid Recovery, including the South Australian government, University of Adelaide and several community groups, as well as BHP. A more ambitious 'exclosure', as some call such reserves, is the Australian Wildlife Conservancy's Newhaven property, in the Northern Territory, which aims to conserve 100,000 hectares for endangered wildlife.[70] The exclosure model helps biodiversity hot spots but it's financially expensive and thus unlikely to be replicated everywhere we need biodiversity restoration.

Another restoration model creates 'wildlife corridors' across landscapes. and their large size often requires numerous landholders' cooperation. A pioneer is Gondwana Link in Western Australia, acclaimed by an international commentator as 'one of the most concerted efforts to resurrect nature ever attempted'.[71] Established in 2002, Gondwana Link is reconnecting habitat across a 1,000 km corridor of southwest Australia through tree plantings, pest control and other measures to revive a heavily degraded landscape.[72] The philanthropic-funded project purchases land for rehabilitation or places conservation covenants on unpurchased properties, as well as engages with the local community including Aboriginal groups and promotes new business models for farmers to achieve win-win outcomes for nature conservation and economic success.[73] A variety of smaller versions of Gondwana Link are underway, such as in the Tasmanian Midlands, where artists have assisted as depicted in Figure 13.3.[74]

[67] ibid 31.

[68] K Burgess, 'Mulligan's Flat Sanctuary to Triple in Size' (*Canberra Times*, 5 June 2017) www.canberratimes.com.au/story/6032256/mulligans-flat-sanctuary-to-triple-in-size.

[69] See www.aridrecovery.org.au.

[70] N Zhou, 'Australia Completes the World's Largest Cat-proof Fence to Protect Endangered Marsupials' (*Guardian*, 24 May 2018) www.theguardian.com/environment/2018/may/24.

[71] Fraser (n 65) 327.

[72] See www.gondwanalink.org.

[73] K Bradby, A Keesing and G Wardell-Johnson, 'Gondwana Link: Connecting People, Landscapes, and Livelihoods Across Southwestern Australia' (2016) 24(6) *Restoration Ecology* 827.

[74] BJ Richardson and N Davidson, 'Financing and Governing Ecological Restoration Projects: The Tasmanian Island Ark Project' (2021) 22(52)(special issue) *Ecological Management and Restoration* (2021) 36.

**Figure 13.3** Artworks serving as bird nest sites, Tasmanian Midlands project, 2021; photograph by author

Some proposed restorations face ominous political obstacles. Tasmania's Lake Pedder, whose flooding for a hydropower scheme was identified in chapter three as one of the late 1960s' turning points in Australia's environmental governance, has this problem. Despite the passage of over half a century since this ignominious act, the campaign for its restoration grows.[75] In 1973, literally as Lake Pedder was being impounded, the recently elected Whitlam government appointed a committee to report on circumstances surrounding the dam and its future, including possible restoration.[76] The behemoth reservoir was later included in the Tasmanian Wilderness World Heritage Area, with the IUCN report to the World Heritage Committee acknowledging that 'long term restoration of the natural lake should be considered'.[77]

By 1995 the call for Pedder's restoration had stirred enough public debate and earned political legitimacy to induce the federal House of Representatives to commission an inquiry. It concluded that 'technically it is feasible to drain the

[75] C Sharples (ed), *Lake Pedder: Values and Restoration* (University of Tasmania, 2001) 51.

[76] Lake Pedder Committee of Enquiry, *Final Report, April 1974, the Flooding of Lake Pedder* (Department of Environment and Conservation, 1974).

[77] IUCN, *World Heritage Nomination – IUCN Summary. Tasmanian Wilderness (Australia)* (IUCN, April 1989) 16.

present impoundment and restore the original lake'.[78] Yet, because of the alleged economic costs of a reduction in the capacity of the hydro-electricity system, the inquiry led to nothing. An increasingly ebullient campaign has grown for Pedder's restoration, currently led by former Australian Greens leader Christine Milne.[79] She argues the '57MW from Lake Pedder can easily be replaced from existing wind and demand management'.[80] Furthermore, Milne suggests the timing is auspicious: 'with the launch of the United Nations Decade of Ecosystem Restoration coinciding with the 50th Anniversary of the inundation of Lake Pedder'.[81] I have personally participated in several events convened by the Lake Pedder Restoration campaign, and believe its reinstatement could be a beacon for a new environmental vision for a beleaguered continent.

Environmental restoration of the scale needed cannot rest on community altruism and volunteerism alone. The solution to current governance deficits isn't enlightened despotism either. Restoration needs far better governance frameworks to help identify and prioritise areas for restoration, to create financial incentives to mobilise needed economic and technical resources, and to enhance collaboration among key stakeholders. Legal reforms are thus needed across multiple domains including property law (relating to the responsibilities of landholders), regional land use planning (to coordinate restoration on a landscape scale) and the social responsibilities of business (to undertake more social and environmental leadership). I have written about some of these legal issues in more detail already.[82] Corporate sector initiative will be most plausible where degraded environments can be attributed to specific companies, such as BHP's leadership in financing the massive Hunter River Remediation Project in NSW that was launched in 2009 by the nation's largest company which was responsible for much of the pollution from its steel works that operated from 1915 to 1999.[83]

The history of a vanishing continent is fundamentally intertwined with dispossession of its Aboriginal people, an injustice accompanied by violence, population decline and cultural devastation, and resulting in dissipation of Indigenous environmental knowhow.[84] From the late 1960s, the tide began to shift. The watershed 1967 constitutional referendum empowered Commonwealth lawmaking in regard to Aboriginal people, a mandate that would begin to be exercised in the 1970s by the Whitlam government under a philosophy of Aboriginal self-determination,

[78] House of Representatives Standing Committee on Environment, Recreation and the Arts, *Inquiry into the Proposal to Drain and Restore Lake Pedder* (Parliament of the Commonwealth of Australia, 1995) xiii.

[79] Lake Pedder Restoration Committee, www.lakepedder.org.

[80] Lake Pedder Restoration Inc, 'Spend the $65M Restoring Lake Pedder Not Propping Up Dams' (Media release, 23 April 2021).

[81] ibid.

[82] See eg A Akhtar-Khavari and BJ Richardson (eds), *Ecological Restoration Law: Concepts and Case Studies* (Routledge, 2019); BJ Richardson and T Lefroy, 'Restoration Dialogues: Improving the Governance of Ecological Restoration' (2016) 24(5) *Restoration Ecology* 668.

[83] Ventia, 'Hunter River Remediation Project', www.ventia.com/projects/australia-s-largest-remediation-project.

[84] B Gammage, *The Biggest Estate on Earth. How Aborigines Made Australia* (Allen and Unwin, 2011).

later morphing into the reconciliation agenda. The return of Aboriginal land has been the main legacy. Approximately 50 per cent of Australia's landmass as of 2023 is under some Aboriginal proprietary control (exclusive or nonexclusive possession).[85] These land rights include areas in South Australia formerly used for bomb testing.

Returning land has helped reinstate Aboriginal environmental stewardship, or 'caring for country' as it is commonly labelled. One fillip is the federal Native Title Act's provisions for negotiating Indigenous Land Use Agreements (ILUAs), which allow native title claimants or holders to negotiate, among other things, for environmental management and restoration of their territory.[86] Some 1,400 ILUAs had been concluded by early 2023. For instance, two IULAs negotiated in the Cape York Peninsula covering Rio Tinto mines have helped shape post-mining restoration.[87] Indigenous Protected Areas (IPAs) can also leverage cultural and environmental restoration. Aboriginal-owned territories that are voluntarily included in IPAs comprise almost 7 per cent of the continent and 49.6 per cent of Australia's overall conservation reserve system as of early 2023.[88] Through protocols such as 'Healthy Country Planning', the IPAs facilitate restoring Aboriginal relationships to the land and harnessing Aboriginal knowledge and custom in culturally appropriate ways for ecological restoration and other management.[89] For instance, in northern NSW near Wardell, the Jali Aboriginal Land Council has restored areas in the Ngunya Jargoon IPA with financial aid from the NSW Environmental Trust. These and other efforts illustrate the intertwined and often inseparable ecological and cultural dimensions of restoration. Though, regaining Indigenous control does not necessarily allow for any simple return to traditional ways because of possible irreparable environmental damage and the need to negotiate with non-Aboriginal actors who may wish to remain.[90] There are also urban Aboriginal communities, domiciled away from their traditional homelands, seeking to manage and restore environments, such as those researched by Heather Goodall and Allison Cadzow in Sydney's Georges River area.[91] Margaret Cook and others' recent book on Australian cities also argues Aboriginal knowledge and stewardship will be crucial for sustaining Australia's cities.[92]

[85] National Indigenous Australians Agency, 'Land and Housing', www.niaa.gov.au/indigenous-affairs.

[86] DG Craig, 'Native Title and Environmental Planning: Indigenous Land Use Agreements' (2000) 17 *Environmental and Planning Law Journal* 440.

[87] M Annandale, J Meadows and P Erskine, 'Indigenous Forest Livelihoods and Bauxite Mining: A Case-study From Northern Australia' (2021) 294 *Journal of Environmental Management* 1, 5.

[88] National Indigenous Australians Agency, 'Indigenous Protected Areas', www.niaa.gov.au/indigenous-affairs/environment/indigenous-protected-areas-ipas. See L Godden and S Cowell, 'Conservation Planning and Indigenous Governance in Australia's Indigenous Protected Areas' (2016) 24 *Restoration Ecology* 692.

[89] ibid.

[90] H Goodall, 'Renewing Country: Aboriginal People and their Lands in Rangeland Environments' (2001) 23(1) *Rangeland Journal* 99.

[91] H Goodall and A Cadzow, *Rivers and Resilience: Aboriginal People on Sydney's Georges River* (UNSW Press, 2009) 248–77.

[92] M Cook et al, *Cities in a Sunburnt Country* (Cambridge University Press, 2022).

# V. Revisiting the 'Before' Environmental Law Mythology

I began this book quoting some leading thinkers of environmental law in Australia and abroad who espouse the narrative that there was an era 'before' environmental law – a time before the late 1960s when there wasn't any environmental law, or nothing of merit. It's a view that has become mythologised, questioned by just a few among the now large community of scholars and practitioners specialising in environmental law. I haven't surveyed my peers but wish to close this book with reflections on why this uncritical view of legal history persists.

One plausible reason is that before the 1970s there weren't specialist practitioners or scholars of environmental law, giving rise to the inference that hence there was no body of environmental law. I won't comment on other jurisdictions but in Australia there was a discernible shift in the 1970s as a small cadre of scholars in its law schools began teaching and writing about environmental law, such as Douglas Fisher in Queensland and Robert Fowler in South Australia,[93] along with growing interest among practitioners.[94] There was sporadic scholarly literature on the subject before then but without the dedicated focus that these and other academics forged. Susan Bartie at the Australian National University is writing a history of this subject and I keenly await her findings.

The field undoubtedly took off during the following decade. The nation's (and world's) first specialist environmental judicial body, the Land and Environmental Court, was established in NSW in 1980.[95] A national academic and practitioner network was launched in 1982 with the National Environmental Law Association.[96] In 1983, Macquarie University's Ben Boer and Donna Craig established a Centre for Environmental Law, a trail-blazing research hub where I worked as a research assistant whilst completing my law studies at Macquarie. The Environmental and Planning Law Journal was launched in 1984 and remains a magnet for scholarship in this field. The Environmental Defenders Office (EDO) was launched in NSW in 1985 (now a national network),[97] spearheading public interest litigation and advocacy. I had the pleasure also of volunteering at the EDO in its formative years. This isn't a complete dossier of major milestones and personalities in this era but amply indicates the surge in consciousness of a distinct field of environmental law. Yet, it doesn't excuse the amnesia about Australia's environmental law history.

A second reason for the mythology might be a perception that laws dealing with environmental issues before the late 1960s were too primitive to qualify as

[93] See eg DE Fisher, 'Overview of Environmental Law in Australia' (1977) 3 *Earth Law Journal* 47; RJ Fowler, 'The Prospects of Judicial Review in Relation to Federal Environmental Impact Statement Legislation' (1977) 11 *Melbourne University Law Review* 1.

[94] LD Bowden, 'Evolution of Involvement of Lawyers in Environmental Problems' (1975) 49 *Australian Law Journal* 399.

[95] See www.lec.nsw.gov.au.

[96] See www.nela.org.au.

[97] EDO, 'About', www.edo.org.au/about.

'environmental law'. No doubt, there was much that disappointed. Yet, plenty of today's environmental laws originated in vital precedents from early last century and some of those precedents remain on the books, such as NSW's Soil Conservation Act 1938. Moreover, whilst it would be hard to disagree that environmental law has often improved in the past half century, the natural world overall has continued to wither, as the nation's 2021 State of the Environment report disclosed. That environmental regulators could as recently as 2019 approve such monstrosities as Adani's behemoth Carmichael coal mine during the global climate crisis attests to grave failings in the nation's environmental laws that continue to be complicit in a vanishing continent.[98] Thus, if efficacy is the yardstick of what qualifies as environmental law, it fails miserably to justify ignoring its past.

Another final possible reason for the insouciance about environmental law's history might be that some believe it simply doesn't matter, for reasons that the country is now beset by unprecedented, new environmental challenges, from global warming to plastic pollution. Such an argument overlooks how the past can teach us about the present, such as why past environmental laws failed or succeeded, and thereby to help contribute to better solutions today. Often the governance issues are generically similar, such as how to give a voice to affected communities or improve law enforcement. Moreover, to address the growing intersection between Aboriginal rights and environmental law, Australian law makers must take into account the continent's history.

In closing, we must accept that this 'before' phase wasn't a dull recess in the chronologies of environmental law. The law's dyadic and mercurial temperament, articulated through modes of governance – enlightened despotism, scientific expertise, polyarchy and market mechanisms – unfolded as the young nation wrestled with its natural endowment. Australia's official decolonisation in 1901, a step towards independence, didn't equate to the decolonisation of the continent's ecologies or original First Nations. Yet this book's history also shows that the forms of environmental law and its broader governance did evolve during the twentieth century. The uptake of these changes understandably varied in a federal system where each state had considerable autonomy, but with a national government and interjurisdictional connections there was more convergence than divergence.

I hope that future scholarly accounts of Australian environmental law will now better appreciate its history. To help, I finish here with the following statement suggested for inclusion in the literature:

> Environmental law has a long history in Australia, dating from the earliest years of the young nation and its antecedents, and vastly longer with the continent's Indigenous First Nations. Although environmental lawmaking has evolved with changes in its methods, goals and subject matter, especially since the late 1960s, the continent's nature has continued to vanish. Environmental law has sometimes lessened these losses but a comprehensive and effective system to protect and restore the ancient continent remains to be achieved.

[98] 'Adani Gets Final Environmental Approval for Carmichael Mine' (*ABC News*, 13 June 2019) www.abc.net.au/news/2019-06-13/adani-carmichael-coal-mine-approved-water-management-galilee/11203208.

# INDEX

**Aboriginal people** 4, 43–4, 61–2, 81–6 *see also* **land rights of Aboriginal people**
Aboriginal Progressive Association 82–3
advocacy/community groups 82–4, 168
Anēwan people 27
art 176
assimilation 27
botanic gardens 182
*Bropho* case 46
Canberra's parliament house, gatecrashing opening of 83
children 82, 96, 167
coercive measures 27, 96
'caring for country' 15, 67, 85, 313
citizenship 82
colonisation 4–5, 51, 63, 81–2, 299–300, 315
Commonwealth
concurrent legislative power 19
legislation 19, 32, 84–6
Parliament, representation in 82–3, 299–300
power to legislation on Aboriginal affairs 32, 67, 84–6
Constitution, referendum on amendment of 84–6, 312
Crown immunity 46
Crown land, designation of Aboriginal land as 163
cultural identity 27, 82
'dying race', aboriginals seen as a 36, 82–3, 204
Gurindji people 84
hunting 92, 183, 188
legal traditions, sweeping aside 31
legislate on Aboriginal affairs, Commonwealth power to 32, 67, 84–6, 312
museums, remains and relics in 178, 179
nationalism 50–1, 57
Noongar people 106, 214
Orchardfield 22, 27–8
photographers 57, 204
political life, exclusion from 12
protests and advocacy 82–4
public awareness 85–6
racial equality 82, 178
scientific racism 178
sedentism 95
stamps 53
strikes 84
surveillance 11, 96
Tasmania, desecration of skeleton of Truganini of last Aboriginal in 179
treaty with Aboriginal people, proposal for 85, 299–300
unpeopled places narrative 198, 199, 202
urban areas 67, 313
Wallumedegal people 69
White families, placement of children in 82
wilderness 198, 199–200
**access to courts** 12–13; *see also* **standing**
**acclimatisation societies** 6, 30, 112–14, 134, 247, 248
**accountability** 32, 68, 164–5, 169, 171–2, 228, 264, 272
**activism** *see* **advocacy groups, activism, campaigns and protests; community groups**
**Adelaide, South Australia**
Aboriginal people 83
Adelaide Hills 192
artists 156
dust storms 107
Green Bans 70
koalas, slaughter of 195
Maralinga 161, 162–3, 165, 170–1
mining 192, 265
national parks 202
planning 221
urban sprawl 192
**Adélie Land, Antarctica** 288
**administrative state, creation of an** 139
**adverse possession** 95
**advocacy groups, activism, campaigns and protests** 19, 32, 59, 64–8, 175, 297
Aboriginal people 66–7, 82–4
anti-protest laws 298

atomic weapons testing 65, 166, 167–8
Blue Gum Forest, NSW, saving the 14, 74, 197, 207–11
climate change 298–9
Colong Caves, NSW, protests against limestone mining in 19, 74–6
cruelty to animals 177
Empress Towers, Hobart, campaign against 227
fashion, campaigns against trade in fur and feathers for 60
Franklin River, Tasmania, damming of 213
forestry governance 247
Georges River, Sydney, opposition to development around 226
Georgian buildings, residential associations' campaigns to save 226–7
Great Barrier Reef, protests against mining in 19, 79–81
Kings Park in Perth, campaign to save 214–16, 217
Lake Pedder hydropower project, Tasmania 65, 71–4, 197, 213
Little Desert, Victoria, protests against agriculture in 19, 46, 65, 66, 76–9, 103, 146
Melbourne, protests against Transportation Plan 1969 in 68
Mount Field, Tasmania, campaign to stop logging in 197, 207, 211–13, 252
New Zealand, Lake Manapouri in 65
peace activism 166, 167
public interest litigation 65, 314
restoration 307–8
Royal National Park, NSW 206
subantarctic islands, slaughter of wildlife in 293
Sydney, Kelly's Bush dispute in 65, 68–71
Tasmania 65, 71–4, 197, 211–13, 252
Victoria, opposition to alienation of Crown timber reserves to farmers in 261
women's lobby groups 215–16

**aesthetics and scenery** 32, 197–218
acclimatisation societies 30
Antarctica 289
artists 57, 73, 156, 175–6, 202, 207–8
Blue Gum Forest, NSW, campaign to save the 197, 207–11
Canberra 220, 229–30, 239, 241, 244
consciousness, promotion of an environmental 201
Kings Park, Perth 214–16, 217
national parks 59–60, 201–7, 214–18
nature conservation 175, 183, 185
Outback 155–6
photography 56–7, 73, 156–7, 197, 202–4
public opinion 192
Scenery Protection Act 1915, Tasmania 205, 213, 263–4
spiritual values 29, 58, 110, 146, 156, 197–8, 249
Tasmania 153, 197, 205, 207, 211–13, 217, 263–4
wilderness 197–201

**agriculture**
Australian Agricultural Council 257–8
Australian Organic Farming and Gardening Society (AOFGS) 258–9
backyard gardens and community gardens 6, 259–60
banks, state-run 102
bush, taming the 91–2, 102, 108
chemical-laden, industrial farming, move away from 258–60
clearing 91, 103–7, 304
climate change 304
closer settlement schemes 92, 98–9, 137
cooperative federalism 41
corporations 16
Crown lands, controls on 25
degradation of landscape 67, 103, 107, 304
emus 130–2
engineering mania 136–8, 140
forestry governance 10, 250–1
grazing leases 141
herbicides 110–11
insecticides 111, 182, 259
International Convention for the Protection of Birds Useful to Agriculture 1902 186
invasive species 112–13, 116, 125, 133–4
irrigated agriculture 136–8, 140
kangaroos 130, 133
Little Desert, Victoria, protests against agriculture in 19, 46, 76–9, 103, 146
livestock, increase in 29
mining 261
nature conservation 177, 189–90, 191–2
new business models 310
Orchardfield 22
organic and biodynamic farming 258–60
Outback, introduction of cattle into the 156–7
pesticides 10, 110–11

planning 259–60
ring-barking 106–7
Snowy Mountains Scheme 141
soil erosion 257–60
soldier settlement schemes 92
sugarcane plantations, protection of 10, 120–5, 134–5
thylacines 133–4
Tree Society of Western Australia 216
vermin control 130–3
**air pollution** 45, 222, 261, 269–70
**Albrecht, Glenn** 109
**Allan, Joyce** 178–9
**Allbut, Charles W** 300
**amenities** 5, 221, 223, 232, 233–4, 297
**Anderson, Benedict** 50
**Anēwan people** 27
**animals** *see* **wildlife**
**Antarctica** *see* **Southern Ocean and Antarctica**
**Aristotle** 274
**Armidale, NSW** 21–3, 25–6, 114, 230, 300–2
**artists and art** 57, 73, 156, 175–6, 202, 207–8
**asbestos** 272
**Ashby, Jack** 178
**Ashfield, JW** 80
**atomic weapons testing in the Outback** 10–11, 18, 155–72
Aboriginal people 15, 159, 161, 162–3, 165, 167–8, 170–2
compensation 170–1
deaths of children 167
restoration 168–70, 313
accountability 164–5, 169, 171–2
aftermath 170–2
Atomic Weapons Test Safety Committee (AWTSC) 161, 164–6
birth defects 172
black mist after test at Emu Field 165–6
Buffalo series 165
cancer, risks from 171–2
class action in UK Supreme Court on behalf of veterans, failure of 172
CND in Australia, launch of 167
Cold War politics 162, 165
colonisation 32, 162
Commonwealth 11, 42, 159–61, 164, 168–9, 171
compensation 170–1
D-notices, issue of 163
defence, Commonwealth's power over 159–60
Defence (Special Undertakings) Act 1952 159
Emu Field 165–6, 169, 171
enlightened despotism 11, 42, 159, 172
food chain, contamination of the 166–7, 170
French nuclear testing in South Pacific, concerns over 168, 170
Great Victoria Desert, South Australia 160
Labor Party, opposition from 167
Maralinga, South Australia 160–3, 165–71, 309
McClelland Royal Commission 161, 163–6, 168–72
media/public relations 159–60, 163–7, 170
military personnel, risks faced by 165, 170–2
cancer and birth defects, risks of 171–2
class action in UK Supreme Court on behalf of veterans, failure of 172
compensation 171
minor trials 161–2, 163, 167, 170
monitoring stations 164
Monte Bello Islands, Western Australia 159–62, 163, 169
nation-building 159, 172
official secrecy 167, 169, 172
Operation Hurricane 160
Operation Mosaic 161
opposition 65, 166–8
peace activism 166, 167
political support, ending of bipartisan 167
protests 65, 167–8
public opinion 163, 166–8, 170
radioactive fallout 161–2, 165–72
restoration/clean-up 168–71, 309
Aboriginal people 168–70, 313
costs 309
cover-up, as 171
residual contamination, measurement of 164
safety and environmental issues 164–8
scientific progress 31, 159, 172
South Australia 15, 159–71
terrorism, risks of 170
trade union opposition 167
Treaty Banning Nuclear Weapon Tests in the Atmosphere 1963 162
United Kingdom's nuclear programme 159–72
decontamination of sites and debris removal 164

responsibility for toxic legacy, denial of 164
Vixen A and B experiments 161–2, 163, 167, 170
Western Australia 159–62, 163, 169
whistleblowing 166
Woomera, South Australia, rocket testing in 159–60
**Attenborough, David** 64
**Attlee, Clement** 162
**Attwood, Bain** 84
**Audubon Society** 187
**Austin, Thomas** 126
**Australian Academy of Science** 9, 146
**Australian Capital Territory (ACT),** *see also* **Canberra**
Aboriginal people 84, 231
Antarctic, application of ACT laws to 40
Commonwealth 189, 284
Namadgi National Park 189, 241
urban planning 17
**Australian Conservation Foundation (ACF)** 19, 65, 217, 271–2
**Australia Day** 82, 299
**authoritarianism** 4, 7–11, 14, 137

**backlash, nature's** 6–7, 92–3, 107–11, 133–5, 303
**bandicoots** 158, 184, 189
**banknotes and coins** 54, 176
**Barrett, Charles** 61–2
**Bartie, Susan** 314
**Barwick, Garfield** 19
**Beale, Howard** 162, 167–8
**Beattie, John Watt** 56–7, 203–4
**Beaumaris Zoo, Tasmania** 132, 180–1
**Bell, Arthur** 122
**Bergmann, Michael** 144
**best practicable means (BPMs) standards** 45, 270
**biodiversity conservation,** *see also* ***nature conservation***
Aboriginal people 85, 303
Antarctica 289
Biodiversity Convention 306
Environment Protection and Biodiversity Conservation Act 1999 (Cth) 304, 308–9
national parks 217
scientific evidence 192
**biological control** 119–20, 128–9, 134–5 *see also* **cane toads**
**birds** 4, 102 *see also* **emus; lyrebirds; kookaburras**
acclimatisation societies 113, 241
Antarctica 289, 292–3
birds of paradise in New Guinea, protection of 188
black swans 53, 193
Canberra, greening 241
Commonwealth 186–7
crows and magpies, open season on 119
eggs 60, 119, 185–8
English birds, release of 26–7, 113, 240–1
exports 18, 62–3, 187
Gilbert's Potoroo, re-discovery of 216
International Convention for the Protection of Birds Useful to Agriculture 1902 186
invasive species 113, 241
kookaburras 53, 196
legislation, effectiveness and enforcement of 193–4
lyrebirds 17–18, 53, 61, 176, 183, 186, 195–6
malleefowl, protection of 76
media 186–7
nature conservation 60, 176–7, 181–91, 194–5, 214
organic farming 258
penguins 292–3, 294, 308
pests 24–5, 111–13, 119, 130, 176–7, 190, 194
pets 62
Plumage Bill 1921 186
rainbow lorikeet 196
soil erosion 302
threatened species 59, 107–8, 176, 195–6, 216, 302–3
translocation 183, 196
Two People's Bay, re-discovery of noisy scrub-bird in 216
wedge-tailed eagles 102, 182
writers 57, 59, 175
**Bjelke-Petersen, Joh** 65, 80
**Black Mountain, Canberra** 233, 239, 242
**black swans** 53, 193
**Blackstone, William** 49
**Blue Gum Forest, NSW, campaign to save the** 14, 74, 197, 207–11
Blue Gum Forest Committee 210
Blue Gum Forest Trust 210
Blue Mountains National Park 207, 211
lawyers, use of specialist environmental 211

leasing 208–10
national parks 74, 197, 207–11
wilderness, designation as a 211
**Boer, Ben** 314
**Bolton, Geoffrey** 28–9, 113
**Bonyhady, Tim** 4, 17, 30
**botanic gardens** 175, 177–82
Aboriginal people 182
Canberra 182, 234
planning 222
**Bouddi Natural Park, NSW** 13, 66
**Bowen, Howard** 16
**Bowman, David** 308
**Boyd, David** 46–7
**Bradfield, John JC** 137–8, 140
**Bradsen, John** 255, 257
**Brady, Edwin** 59, 90–2, 114–15, 149, 241
**Brindabella Ranges** 231
**Brisbane, Queensland** 123, 187, 266–7, 270
**British Empire Expedition** 54–5
**Broken Hill, NSW, mining in**
Barrier Fields Naturalists' Club 265
Broken Hill Proprietary (BHP) 16, 260, 265, 310, 312
Hunter River Remediation Project, BHP leadership of 312
regeneration 265, 310
soil erosion projects 265
**Broome, Richard** 77–8
**Bruce, Stanley** 14, 91–2
**Buckland, James** 186
**Bureau of Sugar Experiment Stations (BSES)** 121–2, 125
**Burnham, Daniel Hudson** 232
**the bush** *see also* **atomic weapons testing in the Outback**
**bush** *see* **bush settlement schemes; bush, taming the; Outback; wilderness**
**bush settlement schemes** 98–103
agricultural banks, state-run 102
closer settlement schemes 98–100, 115
conditional purchase schemes 99, 106
soldier settlement schemes 14, 30, 78, 92, 96, 100–3
tax on unimproved land 99–100
**bush, taming the** 89–111 *see also* **Outback; wilderness**
Aboriginal people 32, 89, 92, 109
agriculture 91–2, 102, 108
backlash, nature's 92–3, 107–11, 303
bush, definition of 89
bushrangers 89
Canberra 219–20, 231, 233–4
civilisation 90, 92
clearing 32, 90–1, 99–100, 103–7
colonisation 32, 90, 108–9
culture 89
desert myth 90
droughts 107–9
floods 108–9
land degradation 107–11
poetry 59
property tenure 93–8
remaking the land 89–93
rural life, reverence for 89–90, 107, 176
soldier settlement schemes 100–3
**bushfires**
climate change 7, 218, 302–3
drought 108, 218, 302–3
flooding 303
forestry governance 253
national parks 218, 302–3
Orchardfield 302–3
planning 222
**bushwalking** 13–14, 54, 72, 175, 199–201, 206–13, 217, 243
**Busst, John** 79–80
**Butters, John** 149
**Byles, Marie** 13, 66, 206

***Cactoblastis* moths, importation of** 119–20, 121–2, 124, *see also* **cane toads**
**Cadzow, Allison** 313
**Calder, JF** 204
**Calwell, Arthur** 41
**camels** 112, 156, 199
**campaigns** *see* **advocacy groups, activism, campaigns and protests**
**Campbell, Archibald James** 52
**Canada**
atomic bomb test sites for UK, exploration of 162
city beautiful movement 221
compulsory purchase, protection of native land from 98
**Jackes family history** 22, 114
traditional property rights of First Nations, recognition of 97–98
**Canberra** *see* **Canberra, construction of; Canberra, greening; Canberra, planning of the**
**Canberra, construction of** 231, 234–9
amenities 234
austerity following World War II 237, 244

Australian Forestry School 253
Department of Home Affairs 235–7
English style 236
Federal Capital Advisory Committee 237
Federal Capital Commission 237
funding 237
garden city movement 31, 236, 244
Griffin, Walter and Marion, plans of 234–8
Department of Home Affairs 236
modifications 236–7
official role, lack of 234–7
partial rejection 234
reinstatement of original plan 235–6, 238–9
tensions 236
Lake Burley Griffin 237, 244
media 237, 239
Molonglo River 236
National Capital Development Commission 234
parliament, opening 83
public inquiry 238–9
public transport, limited 234, 237
rail system 234, 236
Royal Commission 236
Seat of Government (Administration) Act 1924 237
suburbs 234, 237
zoned areas for housing 239

**Canberra, greening** 219–20, 232, 239–45
aesthetics, importance of 239, 241, 244
arboretums 239–40
birds, introduction of 241
Black Mountain 239, 242
botanical garden, 182, 234
bush capital, as the 29, 240, 309
climate change 242
design 238–42
enclave model of restoration 310
English trees by settlers, planting of 239
exotic fauna, import of 240–1
garden city movement 239–40
greenbelt 241
Griffins, plans of 234, 239–40
horticulture 239–40
Mulligans Flat's reserve, fencing of 310
Namadgi National Park 189, 241
National Botanic Gardens 182
National Capital Development Commission 242
national identity 29
nature conservation and recreation, land reserved for 241
plantings along roadsides and parks 240
property tenure 239
rabbits, dealing with 239
reforestation 234
suburbs, naming of 243
telecommunications tower on Black Mountain, approval of 242
thrushes, introduction of 241
Timber Protection Ordinance 1919 240
trees 234, 240, 242
water catchment supply 241
Wild Flower and Native Plants Protection Ordinance 1936 242
wildlife 240–3

**Canberra, planning** 17, 219, 229–45
Aboriginal people 82–3, 231, 244, 299–300
administration ordinances 231–2
aesthetic value 220, 229–30
amenities 232, 233
Black Mountain 233
Brindabella Ranges 231
bush capital, as 219–20, 244
bushland 219–20, 231, 233
Capital Hill 232
Capital Sites Enquiry Board 230
choice of capital 229
city beautiful movement 31, 232, 233
climate 230
colonisation 229, 231
Commonwealth 228–34, 244
competition 232–3
Constitution Act 229
construction of Canberra 231, 234–9
criticism of Canberra 244
Dalgety area 230–1
design 31, 231–4, 238–42, 244–5
finding a site 229–30
garden city movement 31, 232, 233, 240
Governor-General, ordinances enacted by 232
greening 219–20, 232, 234, 239–45
Griffin, Walter and Marion
final ventures and legacies 243–5
plan 232–4, 243–5
lake system 233–4, 244–5
layout 219–20
media 219, 229, 240
Molonglo River 231, 233–4, 244
Mount Ainslie 233
national identity 219–20, 229, 231, 235

National Library 244
New South Wales (NSW) laws, application of 232
Ngunnawal people, dispossession of 231
Parliament House 83, 232, 244–5
pastoralists, occupation of Canberra environs by 231
public inquiries 244
public transport 233
royal commissions 229, 230, 244
Seat of Government Acts 230–1
Seat of Government (Administration) Act 1910 231
short-list 230–1
siting the 229–31
Yass district 230–1
**cane toads** 112, 116, 120–5, 185, 305
Bureau of Sugar Experiment Stations (BSES) 121–2, 125
Council for Scientific and Industrial Research (CSIR) 123
moths, importation of *Cactoblastis* 124
opposition to introduction 10, 123–5
research, lack of 122, 134–5
sugarcane plantations from beetles, protection of 10, 120–5, 134–5
**canines** 25, 54, 125, 129, 131, 133–4, 183, 290, 307
**capital city** *see* **Canberra, construction of; Canberra, greening; Canberra, planning of the**
**Capital Hill, Canberra** 232
**'caring for country'** 15, 67, 85, 313
**Carle, Susan** 14
**Carmichael coal mine, Queensland, approval of** 315
**Carrick, Robert** 289
**Carson, Rachel** 10, 64, 110–11, 260
**Cass, Moss** 42–3
**Castlecrag, Sydney** 243–4
**cats** 26, 54, 112, 128, 133, 184, 293, 204
**celebrating nature** 57–63
**cetaceans** 275–6, 287 *see also* **whaling**
**Chandler, Leslie Gordon** 102
**charismatic/iconic flora and fauna** 17, 29, 175, 176, 183, 187–8, 195
**Chifley, Ben** 141–3
**children's books** 57–8
**China** 3, 284
**Chirnside, Thomas** 184
**Chisholm, Alec** 57
**cities** *see* **urban areas**
**city beautiful movement** 44, 222, 232, 233
**civilisation** 58, 82, 90, 92, 110, 113, 155, 198, 273
**Clarke, William** 105
**Clayton-Dixon, Callum** 22
**clearing of land** *see* **land clearing**
**Cleghorn, William** 26
**Clements, Jimmy** 83
**climate change**
Aboriginal people 109
acidification of coastal waters 304
activism and protests 298–9
Antarctic Territory 304–5
bushfires 7, 218, 302–3
Carmichael coal mine, approval of 315
degradation of landscape 67, 108
floods 7
forestry governance 146
heatwaves 304
marine and terrestrial ecosystems, collapse of 304
mining 260
national parks 218
rainfall, decrease in 304
renewal ecology 308
restoration 298, 307–8
Snowy Mountains Scheme 148–9
**Clode, Danielle** 62
**closer settlement schemes** 92, 98–100, 115, 137
**cloud seeding** 148–9
**Clutha Development Pty Ltd Agreement Act 1970, public opposition to** 45
**coats of arms and emblems** 50–1, 52, 54, 176
**Coleman, Edith** 62–3
**Coleman, William** 18
**Collier, James** 90
**Collins, Robert Martin** 6
**Collis, Brad** 136
**Colloff, Matthew** 28, 86
**coloniality** 3–7, 47, 53, 197, 247
**colonisation** 3–7, 16, 28, 32, 297–8, 304
150th anniversary, opposition to 82
Aboriginal people 4–5, 50–1, 57, 63, 81–2, 299–300
acclimatisation societies 6, 30, 112–14, 134, 247, 248
Antarctica 273, 285
atomic weapons testing 32, 162
Australian Colonies Government Act 1850 17

botanic gardens 178, 182
bush, taming the 32, 90, 108–9
Canberra, planning 229, 231
clearing 103, 304
climate change 299
coats of arms 50–1
Colonial Laws Validity Act 1865 49
coloniality 3–7, 47, 53, 197, 247
common law 31, 49
Commonwealth 53
Constitution 5, 35–6, 47–8
Crown land 93
decolonisation 5, 178, 308, 315
English property tenure system 5, 32, 93, 94–5
federalism 36, 47
forestry governance 6, 106, 247, 252, 304
invasive species 32, 112–16, 125–6, 133–4
legal system 31–2
mining 260, 262
museums 178–80
national parks 202–3, 207
nationalism 17
nature science writing 61–2
Orchardfield 22, 26, 302
Outback 155–6, 159
penal colony, Australia's origins as a 10
photography 56–7
planning 219
pollution control 268
post-colonialism 220
property rights 14–15, 93–6
restoration 307
settler triumphalism 90
statues to colonial figures 51
*terra nullius* doctrine 14–15, 49–50, 81–2, 199, 273
vermin control 6–7, 129, 134
wilderness 66, 197–8
zoos 178

**Colong Caves, NSW, protests against limestone mining in** 19, 74–6
Associated Portland Cement Manufacturers Australia (APCMA) 75–6
AGM, purchase of shares in order to attend 75–6
relinquishment of licences 76
Colong Committee 75–6
Labor Party candidates, protestors standing as 76
media 75–6

**common heritage of mankind** 273, 289–90

**common law**
colonisation 31, 49
English traditions 48, 93, 224
nature conservation 183
native title 50, 97–8
nuisances, use of injunctions to stop 221, 268
planning 221, 223
pollution control 268, 271
property tenure 93–4, 117, 183, 224
riparian rights 94
standing 228
states 43, 262
statutory regimes, supplementation with 5
torts, exemption of liability from 45

**Commonwealth** 17–18, 302
Aboriginal people 82–5, 299–300
concurrent legislative power 19
Gurindji people, confiscation of lands of 84
Parliament, representation in 82–3, 299–300
power to legislate on Aboriginal affairs 32, 67, 84–6
air pollution 270
Antarctica 17, 273, 275, 284, 286
atomic weapons testing 42, 159–61, 164, 168–9, 171
banknotes and coins 54
Canberra, planning 228–34, 244
colonisation 53
Constitution, amendment of
Aboriginal affairs, power to legislate on 32, 67, 84–6
atomic weapons testing 160
defence, power over 41–2, 143, 159–60
Environment Protection and Biodiversity Conservation Act 1999 40, 189, 214, 304, 308–9
federalism 36–40
film units, documentaries commissioned by Commonwealth 55–6
financial assistance to states 39–40
fisheries 37, 189, 275
Forestry and Timber Bureau 253–4
Franklin Dam case 38
legislative powers 19, 32, 36–7, 84–6, 93
mining 262
Murray-Darling Basin, allocation of water of 17
nature conservation 186–9
Northern Territory (NT), control of 262

oil pollution 270
property tenure 93
public inquiries 42–3
seabed, minerals on the 262
Snowy Mountains Scheme 41–2, 142–6
soil erosion 257–8
stamps 52–3
states
cooperation 38
financial assistance 39–40
priority of Commonwealth law over state laws 36
reservation of powers 39
Tasmania, Lake Pedder hydropower project in 71, 73–4
taxation, concurrent power over 39–40
territorial sea 81
territories, environmental law for 40
water management 37–8
whaling 277–8, 288
**Commonwealth Games, Perth, 1962** 214–15, 217
**Commonwealth Institute of Science and Technology (CISI)** 128–9
**Commonwealth Scientific and Industrial Research Organisation (CSIRO)** 9, 39, 78, 129, 166, 289
**Communist Party, attempts to outlaw the** 11, 42
**community groups**, *see also* **public participation and engagement**
Aboriginal people 82–3, 168
birds 102
Commonwealth 42
exports 42
field naturalist associations 9, 14, 60, 62, 102, 178, 191, 203–4, 212, 243, 265
governance 7
Kings Park, Perth, campaign to save 215
Little Desert, Victoria, protests against agriculture in 78
national parks 60, 79, 202
natural history 57, 59–60, 102, 178, 241
nature conservation 12, 60, 64–7, 78–9, 141, 178, 193, 210–16, 293
professional groups 60, 252
residential associations 226–7
restoration 74, 309–10
Snowy Mountains Scheme 141–2
standing 193
Sydney, Kelly's Bush dispute in 68, 70
Tasmania 46, 74, 213
urban development 19, 68, 227, 243
walking groups/clubs 13–14, 175, 199–201, 206–7, 212–13, 217
women's lobby groups 215–16
**compensation** 98, 104–5, 153, 168, 170–1
**compulsory acquisition** 98, 308
**Conder, Charles** 176
**conditional purchase schemes** 99, 106
**Connell, Daniel** 41
**Connor, Joseph** 127
**Connors, Libby** 76
**conservation** *see* **nature conservation**
**Constitution** 5, 47–9
Aboriginal affairs
Commonwealth power to legislate on 32, 84–6, 312
stewardship 66
voice in parliament 299
amendments 11, 32, 66, 67, 84–5, 160
atomic weapons testing 160
colonisation 5, 35–6, 47–8
Constitution Act 17, 47–9, 229
English law 5, 35, 47–9
federalism 17, 32, 35–8, 40–1, 43, 46–7, 63
forestry 253
legislative powers 11, 36–9, 47, 81, 160
location of Canberra 229–30
marine environment 81, 189, 262
mining 262
monarchy 31
national identity 63
Snowy Mountains Scheme 142
soil erosion 11, 257
structure 32, 35
water management 37–8, 41
**construction of Canberra** *see* **Canberra, construction of**
**Cook, James** 274
**Cook, Margaret** 313
**Coombes, Annie** 178
**coral reefs** 61, 264, 304 *see also* **Great Barrier Reef, protests against mining in**
**corporations**
accountability, restructuring to avoid 272
agriculture 16
Commonwealth jurisdiction 36, 38, 136–37
corporate governance 14, 76, 298
corporate social responsibility 16
Crown corporation 8
dams and sell electricity, establishment of companies to 136
economic growth 15–16

English law 15
incorporation 16
limited liability 15–16, 272
mining companies 15–16, 262, 264
property rights 15–16
restoration 312
social accountability in corporate law, lack of 68, 76, 272
**Cosgrove, Robert** 212
**Costin, Alec** 146
**Coulter, Robert Charles** 233
**Council for Scientific and Industrial Research (CSIR) 9, 41,** 123, 128, 256
**covenants** 95, 223, 243, 310
**Covid-19** 10, 139, 303
**Cowle, Kate** 204–5
**Cradle Mountain, Tasmania, protection of** 204–5, 213, 264
**Craig, Donna** 314
**cropping** 22–3, 28, 99, 302
**Crosbie Morrison, Philip** 63
**Crown immunity** 11, 46
**Crown land**
agriculture, controls on 25, 250
atomic bomb testing areas 163
common law 262
forestry governance 105, 250
gold discoveries 262
leases 94, 118, 254–5
mining 14, 94, 262
nature conservation 130, 185–6, 190–1, 206
New South Wales (NSW) 99, 254–5
prickly pear 117–18
property tenure 94–6, 99, 239
rabbits 127
Victoria, opposition to alienation of Crown timber reserves to farmers in 261
Western Australia 99
**cruelty to animals** 62, 175, 177
**culture**
1960s, social and cultural change in 18–19
Aboriginal people 27, 82, 89, 106, 313
bush, taming the 89
celebrating nature 32
forestry governance 246
mining 260, 266
museums 178
national identity 235
wilderness 198, 200
**Curtin, John** 257–8
**dams**
Canberra, planning 233–4, 244
Franklin River, Tasmania 20, 38, 71, 136–7, 154, 197, 213
New Zealand, Lake Manapouri in 65
Ord River, Western Australia 137
scientific knowledge 31
Snowy Mountains Scheme 141, 144, 147
Tasmania 16, 19, 137, 139, 152, 154
**Dandenong Ranges, Victoria** 192, 202, 271
**Dargavel, John** 250
**Das, Subhadra** 178
**Davison, Graeme** 93, 225
**DDT, use of** 111, 182, 259
**Deakin, Alfred** 230
**Decade of Ecosystem Restoration 2021–30 (UN)** 33, 74, 306, 312
**degradation of landscape** 6, 11, 30, 247 *see also* **soil erosion**
agriculture 41, 105, 304
artists 156
bush, clearing the 107–11
Canberra 239
clearing land 67, 103, 107
climate change 67, 108
conditional purchase schemes 99
droughts 107–8
industrial pollution control 268
invasive species 67, 113, 119
mining 260, 265
Orchardfield 28, 301–2
Outback 156–7
scientific expertise 31
Southern Ocean and Antarctica 294
writing 58–9, 61, 200
**Derwent river, Tasmania, ship discharges into** 266
**desert myth** 90
**desert rat-kangaroos (oolacunta), extinction of** 158
**despotism** *see* **enlightened despotism**
**Dexter, Raquel** 122
**Dirk Hartog Island, Western Australia** 307
**dingoes** 25, 129, 133–4, 183, 307
**dioramas** 178–9
**disaster relief** 108
**Dixon, Owen** 48
**documentaries (film)** 55–6, 155
**dogs** 25, 54, 125, 129, 131, 133–4, 183, 290, 307, *see also* **dingoes**
**Dombrovskis, Peter** 197, 203
**Douglas, James** 105

**Dovers, Stephen** 298
**Drake-Brockman, Henrietta** 137
**drought** 107–9, 127, 140
bushfires 108, 218, 302–3
dust storms 107, 254, 256
Federation Drought 107–8, 247, 254
irrigation schemes 108
National Drought Policy 108
Orchardfield 302–3
public inquiry 255
rainfall records 107–8, 254
soil erosion 254–6
**Drysdale, Russell** 156
**Dunlap, Thomas** 8, 59
**Dunphy, Milo** 75, 209
**Dunphy, Myles** 14, 75, 200, 206–7, 209–11
**dust storms** 31, 107, 110, 254, 256, 265
**Dwyer, Leonard** 164–5

**Earth Sanctuaries** 309–10
**Eastick, Jennifer** 36
**economic interests**
celebrating nature 32
degradation of landscape 6, 67
growth 14, 15–16
national parks 12, 59, 74, 76, 207–11
nature conservation 183
politics 6, 105–6, 212–13, 260–1
pollution control 270
property tenure 95
protests 64, 66
regulatory capture 12
states 43
**Ednie-Brown, John** 251–2
**Ehrlich, Paul** 64
**Eklund, Carl** 288
**El Niño-Southern Oscillation** 108, 303
**Elizabeth II, Queen** 54, 182
**Else-Mitchell, Rae** 13
**emblems and coats of arms** 29, 50–1, 52, 54, 133, 176
**Emu Bay, Tasmania** 305
**Emu Field, South Australia** 160, 165–6, 169, 171
**emus**
agriculture 130–2
coats of arms and emblems 52
bounties 119
emu wars 52, 131–2
export ban 187
fencing 127, 131–2, 134
open season 119, 132
protected 187
prickly pears, as spreading 119, 132
slaughter and persecution 52, 119, 129–32, 134, 305
stamps 53
vermin control 131–2, 134
**enclaves/fencing** 66, 127, 129, 131–4, 309–10
**engineered landscapes** 32, 136–54
environmental engineering mania 136–40
Snowy Mountains scheme 141–9
Tasmanian economy, powering the 149–54
**engineering mania** 136–40
**England** *see* **English landscape, emulation of; English law**
**English landscape, emulation of**
acclimatisation societies 6, 30, 112–14, 134, 247, 248
birds, release of English 26–7, 113, 240–1
Canberra, construction of 236
Orchardfield 26–7, 28, 114–15
trees, planting English 27, 113–15, 239
**English law** 15, 47–50 *see also* **common law; town and land use planning in United Kingdom**
Aboriginal people 47, 49–50
Australia Acts 1986 49
Clean Air Act 1956 269
Colonial Laws Validity Act 1865 49
Constitution 5, 35, 47–9
Crown immunity 46
cruelty to animals 177
extraterritoriality 49
federalism 35
independent legislative powers 48–9
judicial activism 48
nuisance 220–1, 268
planning 220–1, 223–4
precedents, following English 47–8
Privy Council 47–9, 96
property tenure 5, 32, 93, 94–5
shadow of English law 47–50
Statute of Westminster Act 1931 48–9
textbooks 48
**enlightened despotism** 4, 7–8, 10–11, 136, 152
atomic weapons testing 11, 42, 159, 172
authoritarianism 4, 7–8, 10–11
Canberra, planning 244
governance 4, 7–8, 10–11, 297, 315
planning 225
property rights, interference with 11
restoration 312
states 11, 44–5

**Environmental and Planning Law Journal, launch of** 314
**environmental assessments** 68, 70, 72, 136, 143–4, 263
**environmental engineering mania** 136–40
**environmental law, narrative of an era before** 3–4, 314–15
**Evatt, Herbert** 167
**Evensen, Anton** 294
**Exclusive Economic Zones (EEZs)** 283, 291, 294
**expeditions** 56, 274–5, 278–9, 282, 284–5, 289
**experts** *see* **scientific expertise**
**exports/international trade** 186–8
- birds 18, 62–3, 186–7
- Commonwealth 17–18
- kangaroos 180, 187, 192–3
- koalas 187–8
- mining 20, 39, 260
- nature conservation 186–7
- pet industry 186
- public opinion 42, 186
- restrictions 42
- taxidermy trophies 186
- timber 252

**Extinction Rebellion** 298

**Fadden, Arthur** 161
**Falla, Robert** 288
**fauna** *see* **wildlife**
**federalism** 17–20, 35–43; *see also* **Constitution; Federation**
- colonisation 35–6, 47
- Commonwealth 36–40
- Constitution 32, 35–8, 40, 46–7
- cooperative federalism 40–1
- external affairs power 38
- nationhood and nature 35–6
- state governments and laws 36

**Federation** 17–20, 31, 50–1
- botanic gardens 182
- Federation Drought 107–8, 247, 254
- mining 262
- nature conservation 176, 177
- property tenure 93, 96
- Red Centre, populating the 137

**fencing/enclaves** 66, 127, 129, 131–4, 309–10
**Ferrier, Grant** 76
**field naturalist groups** 9, 14, 60, 62, 102, 178, 191, 203–4, 212, 243, 265
**films and television** 33, 55–6, 64, 132, 155, 180, 197, 285
**Finlayson, Herbert** 59–60, 92, 126, 156–8, 199
**fire** *see also* **bushfires**
- Aboriginal people, use by 66, 90, 253
- clearing 103–4
- forestry governance 66, 90, 248, 253

**First Nations** *see* **Aboriginal people**
**Fisher, Andrew** 52
**Fisher, Douglas** 314
**fish and fisheries**
- Aboriginal people 98, 109
- Antarctica 275, 283, 287
- British Empire Expedition 54
- Commonwealth 37, 189, 232, 275, 283
- invasive species 113, 114
- Lake Pedder 72
- licensing 43
- restoration 306

**FitzSimons, Trish** 56
**flags** 53, 176, 280, 282, 285
**Fleay, David** 14, 180–2
**Flecker, Hugo** 248
**flooding** 7, 42, 46, 71–74, 108–9, 148, 152, 222, 237, 303, 311
**flora** *see* **forestry, trees and plants**
**flying foxes** 23, 129–30, 133, 183, 192
**folklore** 4, 89
**Fogg, AS** 44
**foreign species** *see* **invasive/foreign species**
**forestry, trees and plants** 246–54 *see also* **prickly pear; ring-barking**
- Aboriginal people 246–7, 253
- acclimatisation societies 247, 248
- aesthetic and spiritual values 249
- agriculture 10, 250–1, 261
- Australian Forest League 249–50
- Australian Forestry School 253
- botanic gardens 175, 178, 182
- bushfires 7, 108, 218, 222, 253, 302–3
- Canberra 219–20, 232, 234, 239–45
- climate change 146, 304
- colonisation 6, 106, 247, 252, 304
- Crown Land 250, 185–6
- deforestation 22, 26, 29, 30, 302, 304
- English trees, planting 27, 113–15, 239
- fire 66, 90, 248, 253
- foreign species, improvement through 248–9
- Forestry and Timber Bureau (Commonwealth) 253–4
- forestry wars 211, 254
- golden wattle 52–3, 58, 60, 176
- governance 246–54

herbicides 110–11
interdependence of nature 246–7
invasive species 113–14
kelp forests, effect of climate change on 304
licences for logging 43, 249
livestock, shelter for 250
mining 206, 261
modernisation 250
national park movement 249, 252
nature conservation 185–6, 189
New South Wales (NSW) 22, 26, 29, 52, 243, 247
noxious weeds 26, 100, 112–13, 117, 120, 129–30, 222, 232, 237
Orchardfield 22, 26, 302
professionalization 8–9
public awareness 249–50
public inquiries 250, 252
Queensland 248–9, 250–1
rainforests 6, 59, 246
reforestation 234, 308
roadsides and parks, planting alongside 240
scientific expertise 10, 246–7
soil, water and forestry management, coordination of 43
South Australia 249
strychnine and poisons, use of 253
swamp gums 211, 213, 250
Tasmania 45, 197, 207, 211–13, 246, 250, 252–3
Timber Protection Ordinance 1919 240
Tree Society of Western Australia 216
Victoria 246–7, 249, 253, 261, 309
waratah 52
Western Australia 29, 251–3
windcover, trees as 240, 250
**Fowler, Robert** 264, 314
**Foxcroft, Edmund** 50
**foxes** 21, 25, 77, 112, 114, 133, 158, 184–5, 195
**France**
Adélie Land, claim to 288
Antarctic claims 278–9, 281, 284
Kerguelen Islands, Antarctica, establishment of a conservation reserve on 288
nuclear protests 65
'nuclear testing in South Pacific 168, 170
**franchise** 12
**Franklin River, Tasmania, proposal to flood** 71, 154, 197, 213
**Fraser Island beaches, Queensland, protection of** 39
**Frawley, Jodi** 112–13, 119
**Frazer, Charles** 52
**Freestone, Robert** 233
**freeways and roads** 44, 78, 141, 144–7, 197, 222–3, 226–9, 234, 306
**French Island, Victoria** 195
**Froggatt, Walter** 10, 123–4
**Frost, Warrick** 6

**Gallipoli landings** 4
**game wardens, lack of** 193–4
**Gammage, Bill** 28, 58, 86, 246, 253
**garden city movement** 44, 221, 232, 233, 236, 239–40, 244
**gardens** *see* **botanic gardens**
**Gaynor, Andrea** 6, 107, 259–60
**Georgian buildings, residential associations' campaigns to save** 226–7
**Germany** 65, 71, 156, 188
**Gerster, Robin** 167
**Gibbs, May** 57–8
**Gilbert's Potoroo, re-discovery of** 216
**Gilpin, Alan** 269
**Gippsland and Atherton Tablelands** 6
**global commons** 273
**gold mining** 22, 28, 54, 260, 262–3, 266
**golden wattle** 52–3, 58, 60, 176, 240
**Gondwana Link (Western Australia)** 33, 310
**Goodall, Heather** 67, 96, 99, 226, 313
**Gordon River, Tasmania** 154
**Gorton, John** 81
**Gould, John and Elizabeth** 60
**Gould League of Bird Lovers** 60
**governance** 7–16, 297–8
Aboriginal people 12, 13, 14–15
access to the courts 12–13
Antarctica 40, 273, 284–91
authoritarianism 7, 8, 14
enlightened despotism 4, 7–8, 10–11, 42, 297, 315
exploitation versus protection 7–8
forestry, trees and plants 246–54
legal system 31–2, 36
non-government actors 7
market mechanisms 4, 7–8, 14–16, 297, 315
museums 177–8
nongovernmental constituencies 13
petitions to elected representatives to express grievances 12
political life, exclusion of Aboriginal people and women from 12
polyarchy 4, 7–8, 11–12, 14, 297, 315

public participation 12–14, 67–8
resource development 44–5
restoration 305–7, 311–12
scientific expertise 4, 7–10, 13, 297, 315
whaling 276–8
**government**, *see also* **enlightened despotism**
agencies 9–10, 12, 139, 234
Australian Colonies Government Act 1850 17
big government 11, 139
bush, taming the 92, 106, 108–10
corporations 16, 72
environmental disputes 64
executive agencies 12
federalism 36
film units 55–6
growth 139
intergovernmental relations 40–1, 84, 192, 257, 315
local government 12, 44, 70, 223–4, 268
market mechanisms 8, 14
museums 57
non-government institutions, collaboration with 33
science, sponsorship 9–10
Seat of Government Acts 230–1
Seat of Government (Administration) Act 1910 231
Seat of Government (Administration) Act 1924 237
Westminster system of responsible government 35
**Goyder's Line** 90
**Grampians, Victoria** 202
**Great Barrier Reef, protests against mining in** 19, 79–81
Commonwealth, intervention by the 81
Great Barrier Reef Marine Park Act 1975 (Cth) 81
lobbying 80
oil exploration 65, 79–81
protests 65, 66
public opinion and publicity 80–1
Save the Reef campaign 79, 80–1
World Heritage listing 79, 81
**Great Britain** *see* **United Kingdom**
**Great Dividing Range** 22, 116, 200, 207
**Great Lake Power Scheme, Tasmania** 149–51
**Green Bans** 19, 65, 70–1, 225, 270
**green belt** 225, 241
**Gregory, Walter** 156
**Grey, George** 194–5
**Griffin, Marion Mahony** 31, 232–4, 237–9, 243–5
**Griffin, Walter Burley** 31, 232–9, 241, 243–5
**Griffiths, Tom** 61–2, 90, 140, 179, 246, 274–5
**Group Settlement Schemes** 99
**Gulf of Carpentaria, mangrove tracts along the** 304
**Gurindji people** 84

**habitat destruction**
clearing 133, 185
flooding 152
invasive species 303
koalas 195
legislation 129, 185, 190–2
public opinion 192
Snowy Mountains Scheme 147
urban sprawl 192–3
**Hall, Colin Michael** 217, 297
**Hall, Guy** 112
**Hallam, Sylvia** 66
**Hanslow, Harold** 255
**Hardin, Garrett** 93
**Harper, Melissa** 200–1
**Hasselborough, Frederick** 291
**Hatfield, William** 58–9, 105, 126, 200
**Hattah-Kulkyne National Park, Victoria** 103
**Hawker, Charles** 244
**Haynes, Roslynn** 155
**Hean, Brenda** 74
**Heard Island** 291, 294
**Heard, John** 294
**heatwaves** 304
**Heidelberg school of impressionist painters** 176
**herbicides** 110–11
**Heron Island, Queensland, wallabies on** 186
**Heyer, John** 155
**Heysen, Hans** 156–7
**high modernism** 10–11
**High Tops, dispute over use of** 146–7
**Hill, Stuart** 57, 297
**Hirst, John** 36
**historic buildings and intimate neighbourhoods, threats to** 226–7
**Hobart, Tasmania**
Aboriginal people displayed in the Tasmanian museum, relics of 179
Battery Point Community Association 227
Beaumaris Zoo 132, 180–1
botanic garden, establishment of 182
bushwalking clubs 200, 212

Derwent river, ship discharges into the 266
Empress Towers, campaign against 227
Georgian buildings, residential associations' campaigns to save 226–7
hydropower 152
Mount Wellington/Kunanyi 202, 305
photography 203
planning 226–7
pollution control 266
slums 226–7
thylacine, death of last known 132, 180–1
zinc works, air pollution from 266
**Hobbes, Thomas** 10, 11
**Holmes, John** 99
**Holt, Robert** 167
**Hoppé, Emil Otto** 244
**Hore, Jarrod** 56–7, 202
**housing**
Canberra 239
flat-roofed houses 243
Georgian buildings, residential associations' campaigns to save 226–7
Green Bans 19, 65, 70–1, 225, 270
residential areas, industrial pollution near 268–9
residential associations 226–7
slums 89, 216, 219, 222, 226–7
Sydney 69, 226, 243
zoning 239
**Howard, Ebenezer** 44, 221, 223, 232–3
**Hughes, Billy** 9, 184
**Humboldt, Alexander von** 246–7
**Hungerford, Clarrie** 209–10
**Hunter River Remediation Project, BHP leadership of** 312
**hunting**
Aboriginal people 92, 183, 188
breeding cycles 184
crocodiles 188
licensing 25, 183, 187, 191, 193, 288
loopholes on restrictions 184, 188
lyrebirds 195
magistrates in rural areas, by 193
museums 180
nature conservation 176–7, 183–5, 188
nature science writing 62
open seasons 24, 119, 184, 188, 193
pest control, shooting of birds useful for 176–7
rabbits 124–6
trophies 54–5, 178–9
unlicensed hunting, prosecutions of 25, 193
zoos 182
**Hurley, Frank** 56, 285, 293
**Hutton, Drew** 76
**Huxley, Elspeth** 105, 110, 147
**hydropower** 136, 138–9, 152 *see also* **Snowy Mountains Scheme; Tasmania, hydropower in**

**identity** *see* **national identity**
**Idriess, Ion** 137
**immigration policy** 41, 226, 260
**indenture legislation** 44–5
**India** 65, 245, 282, 306
**indigenous people** *see* **Aboriginal people; land rights of Aboriginal people**
**inquiries** *see* **public inquiries**
**insects**
birds 176–7, 182, 302
cane toads 120–3, 125
herbicides 110–11
insecticides 111, 182, 259
moths, importation of *Cactoblastis* 119–20, 121–2, 124
pesticides 10, 23, 25, 110–11
Prickly Pear, control of 119–20, 121–2, 124
**intergenerational equity** 157, 207, 252
**International Geophysical Year (IGY)** 281, 282, 288, 290
**international law** 3, 275, 281, 285, 289, 291, 294, 306
**international trade** *see* **exports/international trade**
**International Whaling Commission (IWC)** 278, 288
**invasive/foreign species** 112–35, 248–9, 303–4 *see also* **cane toads; prickly pear; rabbits; pest control; vermin control**
acclimatisation societies 6, 30, 112–14, 134, 247, 248
agriculture 112–13, 116, 133–4
Antarctica 293–4, 304
closer settlement schemes 115
colonisation 32, 112–13, 133–4
degradation of landscape 67, 113, 119
English species 26–7, 113–15, 239–41
nature conservation 184–5
Orchardfield 25
Outback 156
resources 298
scientific expertise 112–13

science, law and nature's backlash 133–5
single species saviours 119, 122
soil erosion 112
vermin control 112, 129–34, 184–5
weasels and stoats 128
weed control 112–14

**irrigation schemes** 38, 40, 93, 108, 137, 140–7, 153

**Irving, Helen** 36

**Jackes, Edward** 300

**Jackes family** 20–6, 260

**Jackes, Franklin** 21–3, 27, 260

**Jackes, Ronald** 23, 27

**Jackson, Andrew** 283

**Jacobs, Jane** 225

**James Hardie Industries** 272

**Japan**
aggression 137
whaling 273, 276, 278, 288

**Jennings, AV** 69–70

**Jenkins, Tiffany** 50

**Jenolan Caves, NSW** 201–2

**Johnston, Anna** 61

**Johnston, Ross** 5

**Jones, Wood** 195

**Joyce, Barnaby** 140

**Kaleski, Robert** 190

**Kalgoorlie, mining in** 260–1

**Kangaroo Island** 190

**kangaroos**
agriculture 130, 133
atomic weapons testing 171
banknotes 54
emblems/coats of arms 50, 52, 54
export of skins 180, 187, 192–3
military mascots, as 30, 54
museums 180
open season 24
population growth 307
rabbits, poisoning of 128
relocations 196
restoration 307
slaughter and persecution 24, 133, 134, 177, 180, 187, 192–3
stamps 52
vermin control 130, 133, 134, 177

**Katz, Frederick** 41–2

**Kawaja, Marie** 274–5

**Kaye, Stuart** 284

**Kelly, Petra** 71

**Kelly, William** 235

**Kelly's Bush** *see* **Sydney, Kelly's Bush dispute in**

**Kennedy, Elizabeth** 27

**Kercher, Bruce** 35, 38

**Kerguelen Islands, Antarctica** 288

**Kessell, Stephen Lackey (Kim)** 252–3

**Kings Park** *see* **Perth, Western Australia, campaign to save Kings Park in**

**Kirby, Michael** 47

**Knight, Allan** 71–2, 154

**koalas**
emblems 52
exports, ban on 187–8
habitat loss 195
Kangaroo Island 195
museums 180
national heritage 61
nationalism 17
open season in Queensland 187
public opinion 176, 187
slaughter for fur 58, 176, 180, 187–8, 195
stamps 53
tourism 61
translocation programmes 183, 195

**kookaburras** 53, 196

**Kosciusko State Park, NSW** 141, 145–7, 263

**Krieger, Leonard** 10

**La Niña** 303

**Ladd, Harry** 80

**Lake Bonney, South Australia** 45

**Lake Burley Griffin** 237, 244

**Lake Pedder hydropower project** *see* **Tasmania, Lake Pedder hydropower project in**

**land clearing** 29–30, 32, 90–1, 103–7 *see also* **ring-barking**
aesthetics 30
agriculture 91, 103–7, 304
bush, taming the 32, 90–1, 99–100, 103–7
closer settlement schemes 99–100
colonisation 103, 304
degradation of landscape 67, 103, 107
fire 103–4
forestry governance 105, 252
habitats, protection of 185
prickly pear, obligation to clear 117
soldier settlement schemes 102
technical innovations 103
vermin control 129

**land rights of Aboriginal people** 82, 84–5, 93–8
- activism 66
- atomic weapons testing 15, 162–3, 165, 167–72, 313
- biodiversity conservation 85, 303
- bush, taming the 32, 89–90, 92
- Canberra 231, 244
- climate change 109
- closer settlement schemes 99
- colonisation 14–15, 93–6
- compensation 98
- compulsory purchase, no prohibition on 98
- Constitution 47, 66, 98
- Crown land, territories treated as 96
- culture 89, 313
- customary land rights 50
- dispossession 4, 11, 13, 14–15, 44, 81–2, 92–6
  - Canberra, planning 231
  - closer settlement schemes 99
  - habitat destruction 303
  - Gurindji people 84
  - Ngunnawal people 231
  - Outback 156
  - second dispossession in early- and mid-20th century 96
  - Snowy Mountains Scheme 141
- employment 264–5
- English law 47, 49–50
- fire, use of 66, 90, 253
- forestry governance 253
- franchise 12
- Gadigal people 95–6
- *Gove* case 96–7, 265
- governance 12, 13, 14–15, 253
- Gurindji people, confiscation of lands of 84
- Healthy Country Planning 313
- Indigenous Land Use Agreements (ILUAs) 79, 85
- Indigenous Protected Areas (IPAs) network 85, 313
- Jari Aboriginal Land Council's restoration of Ngunya Jargoon IPA 313
- knowledge and custom 67, 92, 247, 313
- Little Desert by Wotjobaluk people, stewardship of 77–8
- *Mabo* ruling 50, 67, 84–5, 97–8
- Maralinga 161, 162–3, 165, 170–1
- Maralinga Tjarutja people, eviction of 163
- mining 85, 96–7, 264–5, 313
- missions and fringe camps, moves to 44
- Murray Island, customary land rights on 50
- national parks 15, 85, 204, 217
- Native Title Act 1993 15, 19, 67, 84–5, 97–8, 265, 313
- nature reserves 313
- Ngunnawal people, dispossession of 231
- Northern Territory (NT) 84–5, 96–7, 265
- Outback 155–6
- overlapping tenures 94
- pastoral leases 94
- places, renaming 305
- property tenure 93–8
- proprietary control, amount of land under Aboriginal 313
- public participation 12
- Queensland, bauxite mining in 264
- recognition of land title 96–8
- reserves 15, 44, 82, 96
- restoration of land 15, 168–70, 312–13
- revival of ownership, prohibition on 98
- self-determination 66, 312–13
- Snowy Mountains Scheme 141
- soldier settlement schemes 96
- sovereignty 50, 96
- states 43–4
- stewardship 66, 77–9, 82, 85–6, 92, 97, 313
- *terra nullius*, notion of 14–15, 49–50, 81–2, 199, 273
- trespass 260
- unpeopled places narrative 198, 199
- urban communities seeking to manage and restore land 313
- Yolngu people of Eastern Arnhem Land 96–7, 265

**land use planning** *see* **town and land use planning**
**Langton, Marcia** 159
**lantana** 114
**Latham, John** 279
**Law of the Sea Convention 1982 (UNCLOS)** 275, 283
**law reform** 175, 182–6, 189, 224–9, 254, 269–70
**law schools in 1970s, teaching of environmental law in** 314
**Lawson, Henry** 59, 137
**lawyers** 7, 13, 50, 211, 314
**Lazarus, Richard** 3
**leasing**
- Blue Gum Forest, NSW, campaign to save the 208–10
- conditional purchase leases 99, 106
- Crown land 94, 254–5

grazing leases 141
improvement leases 99
mining 261–2
pastoral leases 93–6, 99, 104
prickly pear 117–18
**legal personality of nature** 95
**Legg, Stephen** 247
**legislation**
Aboriginal people 19, 32, 82, 84–6
administrative laws 43
air pollution 270
common law, supplementation of 5
cruelty to animals 177
effectiveness and enforcement of legislation 192–4
grandfathering 307–8
habitats, protection of 185
incremental reform 175, 182–6, 189, 254
indenture legislation 44–5
law reform 175, 182–6, 189, 254, 269–70
lowered expectations 306
manipulation 68
mining 262–4
planning 220
political control 31–2
pollution control 268–71
precedents 315
prestige projects, bespoke legislation for 46
procedural laws 43
Snowy Mountains 144–6
soil erosion 257
standing to challenge 228–9
Statute of Westminster Act 1931 48–9
strata-title legislation 225
sustainability concept in legislation 306
Tasmania, hydropower in 46, 152–3
vermin control 6–7, 129–31
window-dressing, as 68
**leisure time, increase in** 175, 200–1
**Lemmon, Nelson** 142
**Leopold, Aldo** 58, 198
**licensing**
best practicable means (BPMs) 45
dilute and disperse solution 46
fisheries 53
hunting 25, 183, 187, 191, 193, 288
logging 43, 249
mining 43, 261–2
nature conservation 183
pollution control 270
states 43, 45–6
whaling 288
**Lindenmayer, David** 253
**Lines, William** 33, 209
**Lipton, Phillip** 15–16
**litigation** *see also* **standing**
access to courts 12–13
negligence claims 271–2
protests 67
public interest 65, 314
**Little Desert, Victoria, protests against agriculture in** 76–9, 103, 146
forestry governance 246
Little Desert National Park 76, 79
Little Desert Settlement Scheme 78
mallee scrub 65, 66, 76
malleefowl, protection of 76
Save Our Bushlands Action Committee 78
media 78
soldier settlement schemes 78
Wotjobaluk people, stewardship by 77–8
**Lloyd, Alan** 78
***locus standi*** *see* **standing**
**logging** 28, 249
**Lord, Clive** 191
**Lowe, Miranda** 178
**Lucke, Horst** 48
**Lupton, Roger** 149
**Lyons, Joseph** 82, 123
**lyrebirds** 17–18, 53, 61, 176, 183, 186, 195–6

***Mabo*** **case** 50, 67, 84–5, 97–8
**Mabo, Eddie** 50
**McAulay, Alexander** 149
**McAuslan, Patrick** 227
**McCann, Joy** 274
**McClelland Royal Commission** 161, 163–6, 168–72
**Macdonald, Donald** 61–2
**MacDonald Island** 291, 294
**McDonald, William** 78, 294
**McDonald, Monica** 263
**McGrath, Ann** 155
**McGuire, Paul** 92, 244
**Machin, Rebecca** 178
**McHugh, Siobhán** 145
**Macintyre, Greg** 50
**Macintyre, Stuart** 11
**McKell, William** 142, 256
**Mackellar, Dorothea** 23, 59, 248
**McKernan, Michael** 108
**McLachlan, Noel** 58
**Macquarie Island** 291–3

**Macquarie University, Centre for Environmental Law established at** 314
**Madsen, Otto** 125
**magazines** 63, 75, 180, 240, 248
**malleefowl, protection of** 76
**Maralinga, South Australia, atomic weapons tests in** 160–3, 165–71, 309
**Marika, Milirrpum** 97
**marine environment**, *see also* **Southern Ocean and Antarctica**
  acidification of coastal waters 304
  Antarctica 289–90
  climate change 304
  constitutional jurisdiction 189
  Great Barrier Reef, protests against mining in 19, 79–81
  oil pollution 270
  seabed, minerals on the 262
**market mechanisms** 4, 7–8, 14–16, 225, 297, 315
**Marsh, George Perkins** 248–9
**Marshall, Jock** 28
**Marston, Hedley** 166
**Martin, Laura** 309
**Martin, Paul** 94
**Martin, Steve** 155
**Mawson, Douglas** 56, 275, 277, 279, 285, 287, 293
**media and publicity** 13, 61, 70, 75, 78, 110–11, 163, 166, 186, 206, 210, 259, 267
  birds, protection of 186–7
  Blue Gum Forest, NSW, campaign to save the 210
  Canberra 219, 229, 237, 239–40
  Colong Caves, protests against mining in 75–6
  dust storms 254
  engineering mania 137, 140
  forestry governance 211–12, 247, 252
  Great Barrier Reef, protests against mining in 65, 66
  insecticides 258
  Kings Park in Perth, campaign to save 214–15
  Little Desert, Victoria, protests against agriculture in 78
  lyrebirds 195
  magazines 63, 75, 180, 240, 248
  national parks 206
  nature conservation 175, 184–7, 190, 193
  photographers 203
  pollution control 266–7
  rabbits 126–7
  radio broadcasts 181
  ring-barking 105–6
  Snowy Mountains Scheme (SMS) 140
  vermin control 133
  whaling 276
  zoos 181
**Melbourne, Victoria**
  Canberra, planning 229
  Dandenong Ranges 192, 202, 271
  Melbourne Zoo 180–1
  neighbourhoods, creation of well-serviced 44
  regional plans 44
  transport networks 44, 68
  Transportation Plan 1969, protests against 68
  urban amenities 44
  urban sprawl 192
  Yarra River, protection of 268
**Menzies, Robert** 11, 159, 162, 167
**Mercer, David** 299
**Meredith, GPW** 132
**military** *see* **soldier settlement schemes**
  atomic weapons testing, risks faced from 165, 170–2
  mascots 30, 54
**Milne, Christine** 312
**Minard, Pete** 112, 113
**mining regulation** 260–6
  Aboriginal land rights 85, 260, 264–5, 313
  accountability 264
  agriculture 261
  Antarctica 283–4, 287, 288
  Broken Hill
    Barrier Fields Naturalists' Club 265
    Broken Hill Council 265
    Broken Hill Proprietary (BHP) 260
    Hunter River Remediation Project, BHP leadership of 312
    regeneration 312, 265
    soil erosion projects 265
  Bureau of Mineral Resources, Geology and Geophysics 262
  Cape York Peninsula, Rio Tinto mines in 313
  Carmichael coal mine, approval of 315
  climate change 260
  Colong Caves, NSW, protests against limestone mining in 19, 74–6

colonisation 260, 262
Commonwealth 262
conditional approvals 262
conflicts of interest 262
Constitution 262
corporations 15–16
corruption 262
Crown, reservation of minerals for the 14, 94, 262
cultural significance 260, 266
degradation of landscape 260, 265
economic significance 260
employment 260–1
  Aboriginal people 264–5
  death of workers 261
environmental impact assessments, lack of 263
environmental standards 262
Federation 262
forests, effect on 206, 261
gold 22, 28, 54, 260, 262–3, 266
Great Barrier Reef, protests against mining in 19, 79–81
Indigenous Land Use Agreements (ILUAs) 85
Kalgoorlie 260–1
leases 96
legacy issues 265
legislation 262–4
leases 261–2
licences 43, 96, 261–2
Mining Acts 262–4
mining warden's courts 264
Mount Kembla coal mine explosion, NSW 261
Mount Mulligan mine disaster, Queensland 261
national parks 206
nature reserves, mining in 263
New South Wales (NSW) 45, 262–5
Northern Territory (NT) 262
offset 309
open cut mines 260–1
Outback 155–6
political influence 6, 260–1
pollution 260–8
population growth 260
property tenure 93–4, 96
public opinion 264
regulation 262–3
rehabilitation/restoration of sites 262, 265–6, 312–13
royalties 262
sand dunes, mining 182, 261
silver deposits 262
sludge, pollution from 263
South Australia 265
states
  legislation 262–3
  mining departments 262
  property tenure 93, 96
Tasmania 262–4
Victoria 261, 263
water management 262
waterways, dredging 261
Western Australia 262–3
Wollongong, fast-track approval of coal loading facility at 45
**Mitchell, Elyne** 58, 67, 110, 198, 256
**Mitchell, James** 91
**mobile poaching gangs** 193–4
**Molonglo River, Canberra** 231, 233–4, 236, 244
**monarchy** 31, 49, 54
**Monte Bello Islands, Western Australia, atomic weapons testing on** 159–62, 163, 169
**Moore, Charles** 103
**Moran, Albert** 56
**Morgan, Ruth** 140
**Morris, Albert** 265
**Morris, Margaret** 265
**moths, importation of *Cactoblastis*** 119–20, 121–2, 124
**motor vehicles, rise in use of** 200, 225, 226
**Mount Ainslie** 233, 239
**Mount Kembla coal mine explosion, NSW** 261
**Mount Lyell copper mine, pollution from** 263
**Mount Mulligan mine disaster, Queensland** 261
**Mount Majura** 240
**Mount Stromlo** 240
**Mount Wellington/Kunanyi, Tasmania** 202, 305
**mountaineering** 200
**Muir, John** 198, 249
**Mulligan, Martin** 57, 297
**Mulligans Flat's reserve, fencing of** 310
**Mundey, Jack** 70
**Mungomery, Reginald** 122–4
**Murray-Darling basin** 17, 37–8, 41, 95, 107, 141, 143, 148, 304

**Murray Island, customary land rights on** 50
**Murray, Simon** 301–2
**museums** *see* **nature museums**
**mythology of era before environmental law** 3–4, 314–15
Aboriginal rights and history 315
academic writings 3–4, 314
Environmental and Planning Law Journal, launch of 314
Environmental Defenders Office (EDO), NSW, launch of 314
Land and Environmental Court in NSW, establishment of 314
law schools in 1970s, teaching of environmental law in 314
legislation, precedents for 315
Macquarie University, Centre for Environmental Law established at 314
National Environmental Law Association, launching of 314
public interest litigation and advocacy 314
**myxomatosis, introduction of** 128–9

**Namadgi National Park, Canberra** 189, 241
**Namatjira, Albert** 156
**nation-building** 41, 55, 141–3, 159, 172, 236
**National Environmental Law Association, launching of** 314
**national heritage** 50–4, 61, 143, 284, 366
**national identity** 4, 18, 29–30, 63, 219–20, 202, 229, 231
**national parks** 201–7 *see also* **Tasmania's Mount Field, campaign to stop logging in; nature conservation**
Aboriginal people 15, 85, 204, 217
Adelaide, Belair foothills near 202
aesthetics and scenery 59–60, 201–7, 214–18
artists 202
associations and groups 60, 79, 202
biodiversity 217
Blue Gum Forest, NSW, campaign to save the 74, 197, 207–11
Blue Mountains National Park 207, 211
Bouddi Natural Park 13, 66
bushfires 218, 302–3
climate change 218
Colong Caves, protests against mining in 76
colonisation 202–3, 207
economic interests 12, 59, 74, 76, 206–11, 217
forestry governance 249, 252
Greater Blue Mountains National Park 210
Hastings Caves State Reserve and Mount Field National Park 195–6
Hattah-Kulkyne National Park 103
Hobart, Mount Wellington/Kunanyi in 202
joint management with Aboriginal people 85
Kings Park in Perth, campaign to save 214–16, 217
Kosciusko State Park 141, 145–7, 263
Lake Pedder, Tasmania 71
Little Desert National Park, Victoria 76, 79
management and funding 207, 214, 217–18
Melbourne's Dandenong Ranges 202
Namadgi National Park, Canberra 189, 241
national identity and patriotism 202
National Parks and Wildlife Act 1967 141
New South Wales (NSW) 14, 141, 145–7, 201–2, 206–7, 217–18, 263
Outback 155–7
photographers 156–7, 202–4
property tenure 94
Queensland 6, 194, 217
Royal National Park, NSW 74, 201, 206
scenery and landscapes 201–6
specialist management agencies 207
stealing plants 194
stewardship 201
Tasmania 12, 56, 71, 195–6, 202, 203–5, 207, 213, 264
tourism 202–3, 217
Victoria 63, 76, 79, 202, 205–7
visitation facilities, lack of 207
water catchment 202
wilderness 197–8
worthless land, located on 217, 297
Yellowstone National Park, United States 202
**national security** 137
**national significance, identification and protection of built and natural items of** 71
**national trusts, establishment of** 226–7
**nationalism** 17–19, 50–7, 255–6, 275
**native title** *see* **land rights of Aboriginal people**
**natural history museums** 57, 59, 175, 177–82
**natural history societies** 57, 59–60, 102, 178, 241
**natural science writing** 61–3
**naturalists** 57, 59–60

**nature conservation** 17–18, 20, 32, 175–96
*see also* **biodiversity conservation; soil erosion**
Aboriginal people 175–6, 183, 188
advocacy 175
aesthetic turn 175
agriculture 177, 189–90, 191–2
Antarctica 273, 284–5, 287–91, 293–4
artists 175–6
beauty 175, 183, 185
birds 60, 176–7, 181–91, 194–5, 214
Canberra, greening 241
celebrating nature 57–63
charismatic/iconic flora and fauna 175, 176, 183, 187–8
coats of arms, flags, coinage and stamps 176
colonisation 298
common law rights, restrictions on 183
Commonwealth 186–9
community groups 12, 60, 64–7, 78–9, 141, 178, 193, 210–16, 293
covenants 95
Crown land 130, 185–6, 190
cruelty to animals 175, 177
diminishing returns 298, 300
economic factors 183
effectiveness and enforcement of legislation 192–4
Federation 176, 177
flora, protection of 185–6, 189
habitats, protection of 185, 192
hunting 176–7, 183–4, 188
international trade 186–7
invasive species, threats from 184–5
koalas 176, 187
law reforms 175, 182–6, 189
leisure time, increase in 175
licensing 183
long and short arm of the law 192–4
media 175, 184–7, 190
national parks 297
natural resources 20
nature museums, zoos and botanic gardens 175, 177–82
New South Wales (NSW) 183–4, 189–90, 191–2
open seasons 24, 119, 184, 188, 192–3
partly protected species 183
path dependency 298, 300
pest control 176–7, 182, 192
public opinion 176–7, 186–7, 192
Queensland 192
restoration of degraded environments 183
rural issues 20
science 183–4
Snowy Mountains 141
soil erosion 254–60
South Australia 190
Tasmania 190–1
threatened fauna 183, 194–6
translocation programmes 183, 196
transport, improvements in 175
unprotected species 183–4, 188, 189–90, 192
vermin 177, 184–5
wilderness 197
wildlife
conservation 189–92
valuing 175–7
wholly protected species 175, 183, 189
writers/literature 175–6
**nature for nation (1901)** 35–63
English law, shadow of 47–50
federalism 35–43
nationalism 50–7
nature, celebrating 57–63
states 43–7
**nature for nature (1967)** 64–86
Aboriginal people, recognising 32, 81–6
Colong Caves 74–6
community activists 32, 64–8
Great Barrier Reef 79–81
Kelly's bush 68–71
Lake Pedder 71–4
Little Desert 76–9
protesting for better environmental laws 32, 64–8
**nature museums** 175, 177–82
Aboriginal people, remains and relics of 178, 179
Australian Museum 178, 180
colonisation 178–80
cultural shift 178
dioramas 178–9
governance 177–8
hunting 180
magazines 180
natural history organisations 178
public engagement 178
radio broadcasts 181
revisionist narratives 178
scientific community 177–8
scientific racism 178

Tasmanian Museum and Art Gallery 132
trophy hunting 178–9
universities, scientists in 178
**nature repair mechanism, proposal for** 309
**nature reserves and wildlife sanctuaries** 192
Aboriginal people 313
Antarctica 288
Earth Sanctuaries 309–10
Hastings Caves State Reserve and Mount Field National Park 195–6
Kangaroo Island 190
Kerguelen Islands, establishment of a conservation reserve on 288
Kings Park in Perth, campaign to save 214
mining 263–4
public advocacy 14
subantarctic islands 288, 293
Two People's Bay, Western Australia 216
**nature writing** 57, 61–2, 67
**Neale, Timothy** 66
**negligence claims** 271–2
**neo-liberalism** 8
**New Farm Power House, Brisbane, pollution from** 267
**New South Wales (NSW)** *see also* **Orchardfield, NSW; Snowy Mountains Scheme; Sydney**
Aboriginal people 82, 96, 313
acclimatisation societies 113
agriculture 189–90, 191
Air Pollution Control Branch, Department of Public Health 270
Alkali, &C Works Regulation Act 1906 (UK), legislation based on 270
Australian Museum 178
bank notes and coins, waterfalls featured on 54
birds, protection of 60, 189–90
Blue Gum Forest, campaign to save 74, 197, 207–11
Broken Hill, regeneration of 265
bushfires 218, 222
Catchment Areas Protection Board 257
Clean Air Act 1961 45, 269–70
Clutha Development Pty Ltd Agreement Act 1970, public opposition to 45
closer settlement schemes 99
Colong Caves, NSW, protests against limestone mining in 19, 74–6
Conservation Authority, establishment of 43
Conservation Society 258
Crown lands 99, 254–5
cruelty to animals 177
disaster relief 108
drought proofing irrigation schemes 108
emblem, kookaburra as the state 197
Environmental Defenders Office (EDO), launch of 314
Fauna Protection Act 1948 191–2
fencing 127
flooding 109, 222
forestry governance 22, 26, 29, 104–5, 222, 247
Great Dividing Range 207
habitat conservation 190, 191–2
Hunter River Remediation Project, BHP leadership of 312
hunting 176
improvement leases 99
indenture legislation 45
Jari Aboriginal Land Council's restoration of Ngunya Jargoon IPA 313
Jenolan Caves 201–2
Kosciusko State Park 141, 145–7, 263
Land and Environmental Court, establishment of 314
licensing regime for major industrial plants 270
litigation 271
Local Government Act 1919 268
media 206
mining 191, 206, 261–7
Mount Kembla coal mine explosion, NSW 261
Murray-Darling basin 37–8
Murrumbidgee Irrigation Area 137
myxomatosis, introduction of 129
national parks 14, 74, 201–2, 206–7, 217–18
nature conservation 183–6, 189–90, 191–2
noxious plants and animals, control of 189–90, 222
NSW National Parks and Primitive Areas Council 206–7
pastoral leases 99, 104
planning 44, 221–3, 228–9
platypus as state animal emblem 52
pollution control 222, 268–70
prickly pear 116, 117–20
Public Health Act of NSW 1896 222
Public Health Act 1928 268
rabbits 127, 129
research stations, establishment of 258

residential areas, industrial uses near 268–9
ring-barking 104–5
riparian rights 94
river catchments 257
Royal National Park 74, 201, 206, 217
Smoke Nuisance Abatement Act 1902, difficulties in enforcement of 269
Snowy Mountains 145–6
soil erosion 43, 254–8, 265, 302
soldier settlement schemes 100
standing 228–9
Tallowa Primitive Reserve 207
unprotected species 183–4, 189–90, 192
vermin control 130–1
Wagga Wagga, pollution of water supply by mining operations in 266–7
waratah as state floral emblem 52
water 94, 222, 266–7, 269
Wild Life Preservation Society 189, 206
Wilderness Act 1987 198

**New Zealand**
Antarctica
Auckland Islands, reserve established on the 288
governance preference 282
support for UK's and Australia's claims to 279, 284
Lake Manapouri from inundation by a dam, campaign to save 65
penguins, slaughter of 292–3
pests 128
rights of nature 95
Soil Conservation and Rivers Control Act 1941 256–7
translocation of species 194–5
wallabies, translocation of 194–5
weasels and stoats, introduction of 128
whaling 277, 278
Wildlife Act 1953 191

**Ngunnawal people, dispossession of** 231
**Nixon, Francis** 204
**Noble, John** 83
**noisy scrub bird, re-discovery of** 216
**Noongar People** 106, 214
**Northern Territory (NT)**
Aboriginal people 84, 96, 97, 156, 265
birds, protection of 188
Commonwealth control 17, 40, 84, 188, 262
crocodiles, hunting 189
land rights of Aboriginal people 84–5
mining 262
Newhaven Property for threatened species, exclosure of 310
restoration 310
South Australia, separation from 17, 188
Top End 62, 188
Uluru (Ayers Rock), photographs of 156–7

**novel ecosystems** 307
**noxious species,** *see also* **pest control; vermin control**
insects 120
snakes 130, 248
weeds 26, 100, 112–13, 117, 120, 129–30, 222, 232, 237
wildlife 25, 99, 112–13, 129, 189–90, 222, 237

**nuisance**
abate, power to 222, 242
common law 221
mining 263
Nuisance Removal and Disease Prevention Act 1846 220
private 221, 223, 268, 271
public 221, 223, 242, 271
smoke 242, 269
vermin 114, 124–6

**official secrecy** 167, 169, 172
**oil exploration** 50, 65, 79–81
**oil pollution** 38, 80, 270
**O'Malley, King** 229, 232–3, 235–6
**Onus, Eric** 168
**oolacunta (desert rat-kangaroos), extinction of** 158
**open seasons** 24, 119, 184, 188, 192–3
**Orchardfield, NSW** 20–8, 260
Aboriginal people 22, 27–8
aerodrome, proximity to Armidale 300–1
Armidale 21–3, 25–6, 114, 230, 300–2
capital, siting of the 230
change of ownership 300
chemical pollution from pesticides and herbicides 110
climate change 302
colonisation 22, 26, 302
cropping 22–3
deforestation 22, 26, 302
degradation of landscape 28, 301–2
destruction of the orchard 300
drought 302–3
Dumaresq Shire (Armidale Regional Council), acquisition by 300
England, emulation of 26–7, 28, 114–15
foreign species introduced by settlers 25

founding 21–2
homestead, destruction of the 300
livestock grazing 22
native animals, destruction of 23–5
rabbits, control of 26
restoration 32–3, 300–5
soil erosion 25–6, 259, 302
vanishing continent 20–8, 32–3, 300–5
**Ord River, damming of** 137
**O'Regan, Tom** 56
**Outback** *see also* **atomic weapons testing in the Outback; bush, taming the; wilderness**
Aboriginal people 92, 155–6
aesthetic and spiritual appreciation 156
cattle, introduction of 156–7
colonisation 90, 93, 155–6, 159, 247
documentary film 155
environmental degradation 156–7, 172
iconic, Outback as 155
intergenerational equity 157
land use 155
mining 155–6
national parks 59, 155–7
tourism 155
Uluru (Ayers Rock), photographs of 156–7
writers 156, 200, 247
**Oxley, John** 22

**Page, Earle** 197
**Papua New Guinea** 56, 188
**Parkinson, Alan** 170–1
**parks** *see* **national parks**
**partly protected species** 183
**Pascoe, Bruce** 28, 109, 253
**pastoral leases** 93–6, 99, 104
**Paterson, Andrew Barton 'Banjo'** 141, 266
**Paton, Alistair** 112
**patriotism** 29, 36, 176, 202, 209
**Pauly, Daniel** 306
**peace activism** 166, 167
**Pearce, Noah** 169
**penguins** 292–3, 294, 308
**periodisation** 1901-1967 17–20
**Perth, Western Australia** 70, 132, 196, 291 *see also* **Perth, Western Australia, campaign to save Kings Park in**
**Perth, Western Australia, campaign to save Kings Park in** 214–16, 217
bushland reserve, as a 214
Commonwealth Games in 1962, aquatic centre for 214–15, 217
media 214–15
modernist town planning, effect on 216
Noongar People 214
Parks and Reserves Act 1895 214
Permanent Reserves Act 1899 214
public figures, recruitment of 215–16
public opinion 215
Society for the Preservation of Kings Park and Swan River 214–15
women's lobby groups 215–16
**pest control** *see also* **vermin control**
birds 24–5, 111–13, 119, 130, 176–7, 190, 194
nature conservation 176–7, 182, 192
pest fauna, language of 192
pesticides 10, 23, 25, 110–11
**pet industry** 186
**Philip, Prince, Duke of Edinburgh** 19, 182, 216
**Phillip, Arthur** 95–6
**Phillip Island, Victoria** 195
**Phillips, Marie (Betty)** 145
**Phillips, Ruth** 178
**photography** 56–7, 73, 156–7, 197, 202–4
**Piguenit, William** 207–8
**Pinchot, Gifford** 248–50
**piping shrike** 53
**place names** 305
**planning** *see* **town and land use planning**
**plants** *see* **forestry, trees and plants**
**plastic pollution** 266, 298, 315
**Plater, Zygmunt** 3
**platypuses** 52, 181, 182
**Plumwood, Val** 66, 198
**poetry** 23, 27, 33, 50, 59, 73, 79, 137, 202, 248, 266
**police** 22, 25, 83, 177, 190–1
**Pollard, James** 106–7
**pollution control** 266–72
air pollution 222, 261, 269–70
all practicable means 45
law reform 269–70
Senate Select Committee reports 19
UK legislation 269–70
all practicable means 45
burdens on businesses 270
chemical pollution from pesticides and herbicides 110–11
cities 266–7
colonial era 268
common law mechanisms 268, 271
conflicts of interest 262–3

corporate structuring to avoid accountability, use of 272
employment, provision of 266
enforcement machinery, lack of 269
forestry governance 246–54
injunctions 271
legislation 268–71
licensing 270
litigation 271–2
media 266–7
mining 260–8
negligence claims 45, 271–2
New South Wales (NSW) 266–71
all practicable means 45
Clean Air Act 1961 269–70
licensing regime for major industrial plants 270
planning 222
private litigation 271
Public Health Act 1928 268
residential areas, industrial uses near 268–9
Smoke Nuisance Abatement Act 1902, difficulties in enforcement of 269
Wagga Wagga, pollution of water supply by mining operations in 266–7
Water Act 1912 269
nuisance 268, 271
oil pollution 38, 80, 270
Orchardfield 110
pesticides and herbicides 110
planning legislation 268–9, 271
plastic 266, 298, 315
public health 266, 268–9
public interest standing 271–2
Queensland
Clean Air Act 1963 269–70
Commonwealth's Senate Select Committee on Air Pollution, review by 270
Public Interest Group's 1973 report *'Legalized Pollution'* 271
water pollution 269
radioactive waste 70, 161, 168–72
regulation 269–72
residential areas, industrial uses near 268–9
rural areas 266
sewage management 268
sludge 263
soil erosion 254–60
standards, lack of 269–70
standing 271–2
Sydney 266, 268–9
Tasmania 268
trespass claims 271
Victoria 269–71
waste management 268
water 19, 45–6, 222, 261–2, 268–71
Western Australia 268–9
zoning 268–9
**polyarchy** 4, 7–8, 11–12, 14, 67–8, 172, 216, 225, 258, 297, 315
**Pontin, Ben** 4, 221, 268
**Poole, Charles Lane** 252–3
**population, human**
Aboriginal 82–3, 162, 231
cities 29, 89, 224–6, 239
colonisation 28
environmental constraints 90
gold rushes 260
immigration control policy 41, 226, 260
populate or perish slogan 41
**Powell, Joseph** 9, 17, 57
**precedents, following English** 31, 44, 47–8, 177, 228, 269
**prestige projects, bespoke legislation for** 46
**Preston, Brian** 33
**Prevost, Jean** 288
**prickly pear** 112, 114–20, 184
biological control 119–20, 134–5
Commonwealth Prickly Pear Board (CPPB) 120
financial rewards 118–19
leases, forfeiture of 117–18
moths, importation of *Cactoblastis* 119–20, 121–2, 124
scientific knowledge 31
statutory obligations to clear 117
**primitive areas** 32, 90, 146–7, 197–218
**Privy Council** 35, 47–9, 96
**professional groups** 60, 252
**property tenure and rights** 7, 93–8 *see also* **land rights of Aboriginal people; solider settlement schemes**
adverse possession 95
bush, taming the 32, 93–8
Canberra, greening 239
colonisation 14–15, 93–6
conservation covenants 95
corporations 15–16
Crown immunity 11
Crown ownership 11, 94–6
economic interests 95
English system 5, 32, 93, 94–5
Federation 93, 96

franchise 12
freehold, percentage held as private 94
leasehold of Crown land, private management as 94
market mechanisms 14–16
mining 14, 93–4, 96
national parks 94
overlapping tenures 94
pastoral leases 93–6
planning 227–8
prickly pear 116
rivers, diversion of 95
scarce resources, conflict over 11
sedentism 95
states 43, 93, 96
water rights, allocation of 14
**protests** *see* **advocacy groups, activism, campaigns and protests**
**public awareness of nature** 60–1, 63, 175, 247
**public engagement** *see* **public participation and engagement**
**public inquiries**
Canberra, construction of 236, 238–9
drought 255
federalism 42–3
forestry governance 250, 252
legal profession 13
McClelland Royal Commission 161, 163–6, 168–72
Snowy Water Inquiry 147
Tasmania, Lake Pedder hydropower project in 42–3, 71–2, 74, 311–12
**public interest**
**administration of law** 66
litigation 65, 314
major resources and industrial projects 46, 253
soil erosion 255
standing 228, 271–2
**public opinion**
atomic weapons testing 163, 166–8, 170
cruelty to animals 177
degradation of land 110
Great Barrier Reef, protests against mining in 80–1
habitats, protection of 192
historic buildings and intimate neighbourhoods, threats to 226
international trade 186
Kings Park in Perth, campaign to save 215
koalas 176, 187
nature conservation 176–7, 186–7, 192
planning 226
Royal National Park, NSW 206
scenery, loss of 192
zoos 182
**public participation and engagement**
Aboriginal people 12
Canberra 242, 244
ecological restoration 306
forestry governance 248
governance 12–14, 67–8, 248
institutionalisation 64–5
museums 178
planning 227–8
polyarchy 12
Snowy Mountains 147
town and land use planning 12–13
zoos 181–2
**public transport**
Canberra 233–4, 236–7
logging for railways 11
protected species, trade in 175
railways 11, 234, 236
**publicity** *see* **media and publicity**
**Pyne, Stephen** 246

**Queensland**
Aboriginal land rights 264
agriculture 192
badge, arms and emblem 50–1
bauxite mining 264
Bradfield scheme 138
Brigalow Belt 106
Brisbane 123, 187, 266–7, 270
Bureau of Land Conservation 257
canal estates 182
cane toads 10, 120–5
Clean Air Act 1963 269–70
coral reefs, effect of climate change on 304
Fauna Protection Act 1952 192
fencing 127
flooding 109
forestry governance 248–9, 250–1
Fraser Island beaches, protection of 39
Great Barrier Reef, protests against mining in 19, 79–81
habitats, protection of 185, 192
Heron Island, wallabies on 186
hunting 184, 187, 192
Innisfail warden court 79, 264
koala as state emblem 52
Lake Eyre Basin 137–8

Land and Water Resources Development Act 1943 257
mining 264, 266
Mount Mulligan mine disaster, Queensland 261
national parks 6, 194, 217
natural history societies 60
nature conservation 182, 185–6, 192
North Queensland Naturalists' Club 248–9
open seasons 187, 192
pastoral leases 94–5, 99
perpetual leasehold 100
pest control 176–7, 182
pest fauna, language of 192
pollution control 269–71
prickly pear 106, 116–20
Public Interest Group's 1973 report '*Legalized Pollution*' 271
rabbits 127
ring-barking 105–6
Royal Commission on the Development of North Queensland 250–1
sand-mining 50, 182
soil erosion 357
Sunshine Coast, vandalism on 194
Tamborine Mountains 217
travel writing 58–9
water pollution 45–6, 269
Wildlife Preservation Society of Queensland 79, 80, 182
zoos 181

**quolls** 26, 121, 128, 130, 180, 184, 189, 305

**rabbits** 25, 112, 114, 116, 125–9, 239
agriculture 125
biological control 128–9, 134
cats into the wild, release of 128
collateral damage 128
colonisation 114–15, 125–6
Commonwealth Institute of Science and Technology (CISI) 128–9
Crown lands 127
droughts 127
European rabbit, British sub-species of the 126
fencing 127
food and fur, as a source of 125–6
immunity to myxomatosis 129, 135
inspectors 127
myxomatosis, introduction of 128–9
native predators, elimination of 128
New South Wales (NSW) 26, 127, 129
Orchardfield 26
Outback 156, 158
poisoning 127–9, 239
Queensland, fencing in 127
quolls, extermination of 128
scientific knowledge 31
soil erosion 126, 254, 255
South Australia 126, 127
sports hunters, introduction by 124–6
subantarctic islands 293
vermin control 26, 184, 255
Victoria 78, 125–7
Western Australia, building a fence in 127
writers 126–7

**racism** 178, 183
**radio** 13, 61, 63, 181
**rainbow lorikeet** 196
**rainfall records** 107–8, 254
**rainforest** 6, 59, 246
**Ratcliffe, Francis** 105, 126–7, 256
**Red Hill, Canberra** 239
**Red List of the IUCN** 303
**Reece, Eric** 72
**regulatory capture** 12, 68
**remaking the land** 89–93
**reserves** *see* **nature reserves and wildlife sanctuaries; reserves for Aboriginal people**
**reserves for Aboriginal people** 15, 44, 82, 96
**residential associations** 226–7
**resource users and polluters** 32, 246–72
forestry governance 246–54
mining regulation 260–6
pollution control 266–72
soil conservation 254–60
wise use 297
**restoration of a continent** 297–315
Aboriginal people 15, 168–70, 312–13
atomic weapons testing 164, 168–71, 309, 313
biodiversity 33, 306, 309
climate change 298, 307–8
colonisation 307
community groups 309–10
community opposition 307–8
complexities and costs 307–10, 312
corporate sector initiatives 312
Decade of Ecosystem Restoration 2021–30 (UN) 33, 74, 306, 312
ecological reconciliation 308
enlightened despotism 312

Environment Protection and Biodiversity Conservation Act 1999 (Cth) 304, 308–9
environmental restoration 33, 305–13
existing and proposed restoration 308–13
government and non-government institutions, collaboration between 33
UN Decade on Ecosystem Restoration 2021–30 33
existing restorations 308–13
fencing/enclave model 309–10
governance 305–7, 311–12
grandfathering 307–8
historical baselines 307–8
improving the status quo, importance of 306
international law 306
lowered expectations 306
mining 260, 262, 265–6, 312–13
nature conservation 193
nature repair mechanism, proposal for 309
new agenda 297–300
novel ecosystems 307
Orchardfield and the vanishing continent 32–3, 300–5
place names 305
private sector initiatives 309
proposed restorations 308–13
reforestation 234, 308
renaming places with original Aboriginal names 305
renewal ecology 308
restoration, definition of 308
Society for Ecological Restoration Australasia (SERA) 307–8
stewardship of Aboriginal people 313
sustainability concept in legislation 306
Tasmania, Lake Pedder hydropower project in 74, 311–12
threatened species 304
UN Decade on Ecosystem Restoration 2021–2030 74
wildlife corridors 310
**revisionist narratives** 178
**Reynolds, Henry** 82
**Richardson, Margaret (née Jackes)** 20–1, 24
**ring-barking** 23, 30, 103–6, 240
agriculture 25–6, 92
forestry governance 248
media 105–6
nature conservation 190, 248
prosecutions 99
soil erosion 104, 254
tax on unimproved land 104–5
**riparian rights** 94
**Rischbieth, Bessie** 215
**rivers, rerouting or harnessing** 93, 137–8
**roads and freeways** 44, 78, 141, 144–7, 197, 216, 222–3, 225–9, 234, 306
**Roberts, Brian** 288
**Roberts, Mary** 180
**Roberts, Stephen** 98
**Robin, Libby** 33, 66, 79, 247
**Rolls, Eric** 114, 184
**Rolls, Mitchell** 61
**Roosevelt, Franklin D** 256
**Rose, Deborah Bird** 198
**Rosenzweig, Michael** 308
**Rothwell, Donald** 283
**rural land** 93–5 *see also* **bush, taming the; Outback; wilderness**
Canberra, planning 219
gerrymandering 12
hunting by magistrates 193
land degradation 110
nature conservation 20
pastoral leases 94–5
planning 219, 224
pollution control 260, 266
reactionary and outdated, rural White people as 89
reverence for rural life 89–90, 107, 176
science 9, 106
vermin control 130–1
**Russell, Bertrand** 167
**Russian's Mirny Station** 287

**salinisation** 107
**sanctuaries** *see* **nature reserves and wildlife sanctuaries**
**sand drifts** 265
**sand-mining** 182, 261
**Sawer, Geoffrey** 43
**scenery** *see* **aesthetics and scenery**
**Schorr, David** 4
**scientific expertise** 5, 9, 305
Antarctica 31, 281–90
bases and stations 275, 282, 284–8
conferences and scientific groups 288–9
expeditions 274–5, 278–9, 282, 284–5, 289
International Geophysical Year (IGY) 281, 282, 288, 290
Scientific Committee on Antarctic Research (SCAR) 290

atomic weapons testing 31, 159, 172
authoritarianism 9–10
biodiversity 192
cane toads 122, 134–5
degradation of landscape 31
depoliticisation 9–10
elitist decision-making 10
engineering mania 136, 140
forestry governance 10, 246–7
governance 4, 7–10, 13, 246–7, 297, 315
government agencies 9–10
International Geophysical Year (IGY) 281, 282, 288, 290
International Science Council 290
invasive species 112–13, 133–5
modernisation 9–10
museums 177–8
national parks 31
nature conservation 183–4
official secrecy 172
Outback 156
pedology 31
pesticides 10
racism 178
Scientific Committee on Antarctic Research (SCAR) 290
Snowy Mountains 146
soil erosion 256
subantarctic islands 294
universities, scientists in 178
vermin control 134
whaling 278
writing 61–2
zoos 181
**Scott, James** 10
**Scott, James C** 137
**Scrivener, Charles** 220, 231, 237
**seals, fur and elephant** 292–3, 294
**Seddon, George** 141
**separation of powers** 35
**Serventy, Vincent** 64
**sewage management** 268
**Sexton, John** 50
**Shackleton, Ernest** 285
**sharks** 130
**Sheets-Pyenson, Susan** 178
**Sherratt, Tim** 140
**Shevelow, Kathryn** 177
**Shine, Richard** 124
***Siege of the South* film** 285
**slums** 89, 216, 219, 222, 226–7
**Smiles, Samuel** 259
**Smith, Charles Throsby** 231
**smogs in London, UK, response to** 269
**snakes** 125, 130, 183, 196, 248
**Snowy Mountains Scheme** 30–1, 139–49
Aboriginal people, dispossession of 141
agriculture 141
alpine summit, protection of 146–7
climate change 148–9
cloud seeding 148–9
Commonwealth 11, 41–2, 142–6
Commonwealth and State Snowy River Committee 144
Constitution 11, 142
dams 141, 144, 147
defence, Commonwealth's power over 41–2, 143
economic security 143
employees, number of 139
environmental impact assessment, lack of 143–4
environmental issues 143–9
federalism 18
grazing leases 141
High Tops, dispute over use of 146–7
historic landmarks, inclusion in American Society of Civil Engineer's list of 143
Hydro Authority 141
Kosciusko State Park 141, 145–7
Murray and Murrumbidgee waterways 141, 143, 148
legislation 144–6
media 140
nation-building, as 141–3
National Heritage List 143
national pride 136
NSW, Victoria and the Commonwealth, supplemental agreement between 145–6
planning 141–3
public participation 147
rainfall 148–9
renewable energy 148–9
Riverina district 141, 147–8
safety practices 148
salinity in Riverina district 147–8
Snowy 2.0 140
Snowy Hydro's Discovery Centre 148
Snowy Mountains Hydro-electric Authority 143–7
Snowy Mountains Hydro-electric Power Act 1949 144–5

Snowy-Murray Development 141
Snowy River 141
Snowy-Tumut Development 141
Snowy Water Inquiry 147
soil erosion 141, 145–6
Soil Conservation Service 141, 145
water conservation 144–5
**Society for Ecological Restoration Australasia (SERA)** 307–8
**Soeterboek, Chris** 9
**soil erosion** 30, 254–60
agriculture 257–60
bush, taming the 110
common law 43
Commonwealth 257–8
conservation 254–60
Constitution 11
DDT, use of 259
drought 254–6
dust storms 31, 107, 110, 254, 256, 265
incremental reforms 254
institutional capacity 257
invasive species 112
legislation 257
mining 265
nationalism 255–6
New South Wales (NSW) 26, 31, 43, 104, 254–8, 265
New Zealand 256–7
Orchardfield 25–6, 259, 302
pastoralists 254
professionalization 8–9
public interest 255
Queensland 257
rabbits 126, 254, 255
ring-barking 104, 254
science 112, 256
Snowy Mountains 141, 145–6
South Australia 255, 257
Victoria 257
water, soil and forestry management, coordination of 43
Western Australia 254, 257
**soldier settlement schemes** 17, 30, 78, 100–3, 258
Aboriginal people 96
agricultural banks, state-run 102
agriculture 92, 102
clearing land 102
colonisation 14
World War One 100–2
World War Two 102
**South Australia** *see also* **Adelaide, South Australia**
Animals and Birds Protection Act 1919, inadequacies of 190
Apcel, exemption from liability of 45
Arid Recovery 309
atomic weapons testing 15, 159–71
birds, shooting 176
closer settlement schemes 99–100
Crown land 190
flag, piping shrike featured on 53
Fauna and Flora Reserve Act 1919 190
Forest Trees Act 1873 249
forestry governance 249
indenture legislation for major resources and industrial projects 45
Kangaroo Island, reserve on 190
Lake Bonney 45
Lake Eyre Basin 137–8
Maralinga, South Australia, atomic weapons tests in 160–3, 165–71, 309
Murray-Darling basin 37–8
natural history societies 60
nature conservation 182, 186, 190
Northern Territory (NT), separation from 17, 188
planning 224
rabbits 126, 127
restoration 310
River Murray Waters Agreement 40–1
Sand Drift Act 1923 255
soil erosion 255, 257
sulphur mine, lack of rehabilitation of a 265
threatened species 309
travel writing 59
wind erosion, duty to control 255
Woomera, South Australia, rocket testing in 159–60
**Southern Ocean and Antarctica** 273–94
aesthetic values 289
Agreed Measures for the Conservation of Antarctic Fauna and Flora 1964 290–1
Antarctic Treaty 1959 40, 281–4, 294
accessions, number of 283
achievements 281–2
background 281–2
consensus decision-making 282–3
conservation 289–90
Consultative Meetings 283, 289–91
Consultative Parties 283, 289–90
Madrid Protocol 1991 273, 291

negotiations 282, 289
territorial claims, freezing of 282–3
Auckland Islands 288
Australian Antarctic Division (AAD) 275, 291
Australian Antarctic Exploration Committee 274
Australian Antarctic Territory (AAT) 275, 280, 284, 286
Australian Antarctic Territory Acceptance Act 1933 280, 284, 286
Australian Capital Territory (ACT) to AAT, application of laws of 40, 284
BANZARE 279, 285–6
bases and stations 31, 275, 282, 284–8
biodiversity 289
birds, protection of 289
British Antarctic Expedition 274
Casey Station 275
climate change 304–5
colonisation 273, 285
common heritage of mankind 273, 289–90
Commonwealth 17, 273, 275, 284, 286
conservation 273, 284–5, 287–91
Convention on the Conservation of Antarctic Marine Living Resources 1980 284
CSIRO's Wildlife Division 289
Davis Station 275
effective control or occupation 281
Exclusive Economic Zone (EEZ), declaration of 283
expeditions 274–5, 278–9, 282, 284–5, 289
exploitation 273–8, 281, 287
final frontier 273–5
first landings 274
fish and cetaceans, exploitation of 275, 283, 287
geopolitical rivalries 273, 281, 283–4
global commons 273
governance 273, 282, 284–91
Heroic Age of Antarctic exploration 274
International Geophysical Year (IGY) 281, 282, 288, 290
international law 275, 285, 289
invasive species 293–4, 304
krill populations, decline in 305
mapping 278
maritime zones, enlargement of 275
Mawson Station 275, 282, 284, 286
melting snow packs and ice-sheets 305
mining 283–4, 287, 288
national heritage 284
nationalism 275
New Zealand 279, 288
preservation and conservation of living resources 289–90
reserves, establishment of 288
Russia's Mirny Station 287
scientific research
Australian Antarctic Division 275
Australian Antarctic Exploration Committee 274
bases and stations 31, 275, 282, 284–8
conferences and scientific groups 288–9
conservation 289
cooperation 274, 281–2
disturbances to flora and fauna from expeditions 289
expeditions 274–5, 278–9, 282, 284–5, 289
International Geophysical Year (IGY) 281, 282, 288, 290
International Science Council 290
Scientific Committee on Antarctic Research (SCAR) 290
scramble for Antarctica 278–81
size of territory 40, 274
sovereignty/territorial claims 277, 278–80
Antarctica Treaty 287–91
Australia's claims 273, 275, 277, 279–80, 287, 289, 291
France, rival claims from 279–80, 281
freezing claims 282–3
Norway, rival claims from 279–80, 282
overlapping claims 281–2
recognition of Australia's claims 284
UK claims 17, 278–9, 285, 287
Special Conservation Area (SRA), designation as 290–1
Specially Protected Areas, designation of 291
Specially Protected Species, designation of 291
stamps 286
subantarctic islands of Australia 291–4
symbolic possession for territorial annexation for uninhabitable land, sufficiency of 279
temperature rise 304
*terra nullius* doctrine 273
tourist visitations 291
treaty on conservation of living resources, proposal for 290
UN Law of the Sea Convention 1982 (UNCLOS) 275, 283

United Kingdom 273–9
conservation 290
sovereignty claims 278–9, 285
transfer of UK claim to Australia 17, 279, 287
waste management 288
whaling, rise and fall of 275, 276–8, 279, 287, 288
wilderness, as 274
**sovereignty**
Aboriginal people 50, 85
Antarctica 40, 273, 275, 277–85, 287, 289, 291
colonisation 97
national identity 29–30
**Special Conservation Area (SRA), designation of Antarctica as** 290–1
**Specially Protected Areas (SPAs), designation of** 291
**Specially Protected Species (SPSs), designation of** 291
**spiritual values** 29, 58, 110, 146, 156, 197–8, 249
**stamps** 52–3, 176, 203, 286
**standing**
accountability, lack of 228
common law 228
legislation, effectiveness and enforcement of 193, 228–9
person aggrieved test 228–9
public interest 271–2
Tasmania, Lake Pedder hydropower project in 228
town and land use planning 12–13
**states and territories** 43–7 *see also* **Australian Capital Territory (ACT); New South Wales (NSW); Northern Territory (NT); Queensland, South Australia; Southern Ocean and Antarctica;** Tasmania, **Victoria; Western Australia**
Aboriginal people 36, 43–4
agriculture 108
Australian Forest League chapters 249–50
best practicable means (BPMs) 45
Commonwealth 38–40, 189
coordination 43, 44
Crown immunity 46
economic development 43
English common law, problems with application of 43
enlightened despotism 11, 44–5
film units 56
financial assistance from Commonwealth 39–40
forestry governance 249–50
indenture legislation for major resources and industrial projects 44–5
legislation 36, 262–3
licensing of pollution 45–6
major resources and industrial projects 44–6
management of natural resources 36
mining 96, 262–3
municipal authorities, creation of 43
nature conservation 185, 189
pastoral leases 93
planning 43, 44–5
prestige projects, bespoke legislation for 46
property tenure 43, 93, 96
resource licences, allocation of 43
social settlement schemes 17
statutory law 43
town and land use planning 43, 44–5
wise use standard 43
**Statute of Westminster Act 1931** 35, 48–9
**Stead, David** 206
**Steiner, Rudolf** 258
**Stevens, Donald** 165
**stewardship**
Aboriginal people 66, 77–9, 82, 85–6, 92, 97, 313
federalism 46
legislation 108
national parks 201
whaling 275
wilderness 200
**Streeton, Arthur** 176
**Strickland, Shirley** 215
**subantarctic islands of Australia** 291–4
Australian Antarctic Division (AAD), administration by 291
campaigns and activism against slaughter 293
conservation 291, 293–4
exclusive economic zone (EEZ) 291, 294
exploitation 291–4
fur and elephant seals, slaughter of 292–3, 294
Heard and McDonald Island group 291, 294
Macquarie Island 291–3
penguins, slaughter of 292–3, 294
sanctuary for wildlife, designation as 293

science and research 294
sovereignty 291
Tasmania 291–4
World Heritage status 291–4
**suburbs, naming of** 243
**sugarcane plantations, protection of** 10, 120–5, 134–5, 177
**Summerfield, Victoria, compulsory acquisition and closure of town of** 308
**sustainability** 14, 299, 306
**Sutherland, Jane** 176
**Swain, Edward** 10, 250–1
**swamp gums** 211, 213, 250
**Sydney, New South Wales** *see also* **Sydney, Kelly's Bush dispute in**
Canberra, planning 229, 230
Castlecrag 243–4
Cumberland plan of 1948 225–6, 268–9
flat-roofed houses 243
Georges River area, developments around 226, 313
Green Bans on residential development 19, 65, 70–1, 225
Green Belt 225
Harbour Scenic Protection Areas 225
historic buildings and intimate neighbourhoods, threats to 226
housing, demands for new 226
immigration, increase in 226
national trusts, establishment of 226
planning 44, 222, 225–6
Green Bans 19, 65, 70–1, 225
State Planning Authority 226
*Sydney Region Outline Plan* 226
vertical expansion 44, 225
pollution control 266, 268–9
population growth 29
regional plans 44
remodelling, inquiry into 44
Royal Commission 1908 44
strata-title legislation 225
Sydney Harbour Trust Act 1900 223
Taronga Zoo, opening of 180
vertical expansion 44, 225
walking/hiking groups 200
Woolloomooloo, name of suburb 305
zoning 268–9
**Sydney, Kelly's Bush dispute in** 68–71
Battlers for Kelly's Bush 70
Builders Labourers Federation (BLF), alliance between community groups and 68, 70
community groups 68, 70
environmental assessments 70
foreshore bushland remnant 65, 69
Green Bans on residential development 19, 65, 70–1
housing, plans for 69
Hunters Hill Trust 69
planning 68–9
protests 65, 68–71
public opinion/participation 68–70
State Heritage Register, entry on 70
Wallumedegal people, remnants of 69

**Tainter, Joseph** 298
**Taronga Zoo, Sydney, opening of** 180
**Tasmania** *see also* **Hobart, Tasmania; Tasmania, hydropower in; Tasmania, Lake Pedder hydropower project in; Tasmania's Mount Field, campaign to stop logging in**
Aboriginal people in Oyster Cove 204
activism 71
Animals and Birds Protection Act 1919 190–1
Animals and Birds Protection Board, creation of 191
bank notes and coins, timber-cutting featured on 54
botanic gardens 182
community groups 46, 74, 213
Cradle Mountain, protection of 204–5, 213, 264
Crown Lands Act 1903 250
dam-building 16, 19, 137, 139
Emu Bay, name of 305
exemption of liability 45
film unit 56
flooding 109
forestry governance 45, 211, 250, 252–3
Hastings Caves State Reserve and Mount Field National Park 195–6
kelp forests, effect of climate change on 304
kookaburras 196
licence fees and royalties 191
Local Government Act 1906 268
lyrebirds 195
media 203
mining 204–5, 213, 261–4
Mount Lyell copper mine, pollution from 261, 263
mountaineering 200
national parks 12, 56, 203–5, 207, 213

natural history societies 60
nature conservation 182, 190–1
nature reserves, mining in 263–4
photographers 56–7, 203–4
pollution control 268
scenery preservation zone along Gordon River 203
Scenery Protection Act 1915 205, 213, 263–4
Scenery Preservation Board 205, 207
soldier settlement schemes 102
stamps 203
subantarctic islands 291–4
Tarkine rainforests 246
Tasmanian Midlands wildlife corridor 310–11
thylacine featured on coat of arms, persecution of 52
tourism 203
United Tasmania Group 6, 72
Van Diemen's Land Company 15
walking/hiking groups 200
Waste Lands Act 1885 211
water pollution 268
wilderness 71, 203
wildlife corridor 310–11
World Heritage listings 137, 205

**Tasmania, hydropower in** 149–54 *see also* **Tasmania, Lake Pedder hydropower project in**
1950s, expansion in 153–4
Central Highlands 149–51
dams 16, 19, 137, 139, 152, 154, 203
dispersal or neutralisation of pollution 152
enlightened despotism 152
film unit 56
Franklin River, damming of 71, 136–7, 154, 197, 213, 246
Gordon River, damming of 154
government, involvement of the 150
Great Lake Power Scheme 149–51
Hydro-Electric Commission (HEC) 16, 46, 68, 71–4, 136–7, 150–4
industrialisation 152, 154
irrigation schemes 153
legislation 152–3
Mount Field National Park, forestry concession in 152
Rivers and Water Supply Commission 153
Scenery Preservation Board 153
Waddamana power station 149–52
Waratah, electrification of 149

**Tasmania, Lake Pedder hydropower project in** 19, 42–3, 71–4, 146
art 73
Attorney-General, overruling of decision to grant a fiat by 228
bespoke legislation 46
Commonwealth 71, 73–4
Constitution 136
damming 154, 213
environmental impact assessment, lack of 72
global importance of Lake Pedder 72
Hydro-Electric Commission 46, 71–2, 74, 139
iconography of wilderness 197
Lake Pedder National Park 71
national park status, revocation of 217
National Parks and Wildlife Act 1970, breach of 46, 65
photographers 73
protests and activism 65, 71–4, 197, 213
public inquiry 42–3, 71–2, 74, 311–12
restoration 74, 311–12
Restore Lake Pedder group 74, 312
retrospective legalisation 74
Scenery Preservation Act 1915 205
South West Tasmanian Action Committee 72
standing 228
Tasmanian Greens 72
Tasmanian Wilderness World Heritage Area 311
UNESCO 72
United Tasmania Group 6, 72
World Heritage Committee 311

**Tasmania's Mount Field, campaign to stop logging in** 197, 207, 211–13, 250
Animals and Birds Protection Board 213
Australian Newsprint Mills (ANM) 211–12, 252
Flora and Fauna Conservation Committee 213
Florentine Valley Wood Pulp and Paper Industry Act 1932 211–12, 252
hydropower 152
National Park and Florentine Valley Act 1950 213
national park at Mount Field, creation of 207
old growth forests, loss of 207
political interests 212–13
pulp and paper industry 211–12, 250, 252

Scenery Preservation Act 1915 211
Scenery Preservation Board 212
swamp gums 211, 213, 250
timber concessions 211–12

**Tasmanian devils** 54, 130, 180
**Tasmanian tiger/wolf** *see* **thylacines**
**tax**
Commonwealth and states, concurrent power of 39–40
unimproved land 99–100, 104–5

**taxidermy trophies** 132, 178, 186
**Taylor, Thomas Griffith** 90–1
***terra nullius* doctrine** 14–15, 49–50, 81–2, 199, 273
**territorial sea** 81
**territories** *see* **states and territories**
**textbooks** 48
**threatened fauna** 28–9, 183, 194–6, 303
Biodiversity Convention 306
birds 59, 107–8, 176, 195–6, 216, 302–3
desert rat-kangaroos (oolacunta), extinction of 158
Earth Sanctuaries 309–10
Environment Protection and Biodiversity Conservation Act 1999 (Cth) 304
legislation, effectiveness and enforcement of 192
Newhaven Property, NT, for threatened species, exclosure of 310
Red List of the IUCN 303
renewal ecology 308
Threatened Species Day 132
Threatened Species Recovery Hub 304
translocation 183, 194–6

**Throsby, Charles** 231
**thrushes, introduction of** 241
**thylacines**
agriculture 133–4
Beaumaris Zoo 132, 180–1
bounties 132
extermination 132, 180–1, 305
sheep killing 132
stamps 53
Tasmania's coat of arms 52, 133
Tasmanian Museum and Art Gallery 132
Threatened Species Day 132
vermin control 131–4

**Titterton, Ernest** 164
**toads** *see* **cane toads**
**Toohey, Brian** 168, 170
**torts, exemption of liability from** 45; *see also* **common law**
**tourism** 61, 155, 200–3, 206, 217, 242, 291
**town and land use planning** 32, 219–45 *see also* **Canberra, planning of the; town and land use planning in United Kingdom**
Aboriginal people 44
amenity, concept of 5, 221, 223, 297
back gardens and community gardens, food production in 259–60
city beautiful movement 44, 222, 232, 233
colonisation 219
consultation, right of 228
coordination 44
democracy 223
discretionary powers, exercise of 223
elected representatives, lack of involvement of 223
enlightened despotism 225
experts, culture of 225, 227–8
freeways, backlash against building of 44
garden city movement 44, 221, 232, 233, 236, 239–40, 244
Green Belt 225
greening 222
historic buildings and intimate neighbourhoods, threats to 226
Hobart 226–7
housing, demand for new 226
immigration, increase in 226
indenture legislation for major resources and industrial projects 44–5
Kings Park in Perth, campaign to save 216
law reform 221–9
layouts 221
legislation 220
market 225
mining 262
modernist planning 44, 216, 219–24
motor vehicles, rise in use of 225, 226
New South Wales (NSW) 44, 222–3, 228–9
notification, public's right to 228
Outback 155
pollution control 268–9, 271
population booms in cities 224–5
post-war construction boom 44
post-war planning shifts 224–9
precedents, use of foreign 44
private property, protection of 227–8
procedural obstacles, lack of 68
professionalization of town planning 225
public opinion 226

public participation 227–8
residential associations 226–7
sedentism 95
Snowy Mountains scheme 141–3
South Australia 224
standing 12–13, 228–9
states 43, 44–5
Sydney 68–9, 225–6
United States 44, 221
vertical expansion 44, 225
Victoria 228
Western Australia 224
zoning 44, 223–5, 239, 268–9
**town and land use planning in United Kingdom** 220–1, 223–4
Barlow inquiry 223
cholera 220
common law, role of 221, 223
drains 221
housing legislation 221
Housing Town Planning etc Act 1909 221
injunctions to stop nuisances, use of 221
law reforms 221
mandatory planning to curb loss of agricultural land 223
nuisance, torts of private and public 223
precedents for colonies 220–1
Public Health Act 1848 220–1
sanitation reforms 44
standing 228
street paving 221
Town and Country Planning Act 1932 223
Town and Country Planning Act 1947 223
Town Planning Institute 221
water supplies 221
zoning 223–4
**trade unions** 7, 68, 70, 80, 167
**tragedy of the commons** 93
**translocation programmes** 183, 194–6
**transport** *see* **public transport**
**travel writing** 58–9, 200–1
**treaties and conventions** 38
**trees and plants** *see* **forestry, trees and plants**
**Truchanas, Olegas** 73, 203
**Turnbull, Paul** 179
**Tynan, Elizabeth** 159, 163, 166

**Uluru (Ayers Rock), photographs of** 156–7
**UN Decade of Ecosystem Restoration 2021–30** 33, 74, 306, 312
**UN Law of the Sea Convention 1982 (UNCLOS)** 275, 283
**United Kingdom** *see also* **English landscape, emulation of; English law; town and land use planning in United Kingdom**
air pollution 269–70
Antarctica 273–9
atomic weapons testing 159–72
governance 31
Heard and McDonald Island group 294
industrial pollution 268
nostalgia for UK 113
nuclear programme 159–72
smogs in London, response to 269
South Pole, expedition to the 285
standing 228
symbols of UK, use of 51–2
Westminster system of responsible government 353
whaling industry, end of 277
**United States**
American Planning Association 221
Antarctica 281, 289
birds, protection of 187
city beautiful movement 31, 221
Dust Bowl crisis 31, 110, 256
environmental law history 3
Forest Service, primitive area as a land designation of 90
forestry governance 10, 248, 250
Japanese whaling industry, support for 278
Migratory Bird Act 1913 187
national parks 202
national security of Australia as assured by US 35
planning 221, 224
primitive area language, in forests or parks governance 90, 210
public trust doctrine 31
restoration projects 309
separation of powers 35–6
soil erosion
Dust Bowl crisis 31, 110, 256
soil fertility 107
Soil Conservation and Domestic Allotment Act 1936 256
Soil Erosion Control Act 1935 256
Wilderness Act 1964 198
Yellowstone National Park 202
zoning, town planning 224
**unpeopled places narrative** 198, 199, 202
**unprotected species** 183–4, 188, 189–90, 192
**Upton, Sydney** 248

**urban areas** *see also* **particular urban areas (eg Sydney, NSW)**
Aboriginal people 67, 313
amenities 6, 44
back gardens and community gardens, food production in 259–60
city beautiful movement 44, 222, 232–3
community groups 19, 68, 227, 243
garden city movement 44, 221, 232, 233, 236, 239–40, 244
historic buildings and intimate neighbourhoods, threats to 226–7
planning 17, 44, 216, 220, 223–5
pollution control 266–7
population 29, 89, 224–6, 239
restoration and management of land 89, 313
slums 89, 216, 219, 222, 226–7
sprawl 41, 192–3, 225, 234, 237
urbanisation 29, 68, 89, 195, 220, 223
**Ussher, Kathleen** 245

**vanishing continent** 20–33, 63, 247, 297, 303, 305–6, 300–5, 315 *see also* **restoration of a continent**
**Verbeck, Miriam** 94
**vermin control** 112, 129–34, 225 *see also* **pest control**
agriculture 130–3
bounties 119, 129, 132, 185
classification 177
clearing 129
collateral damage 133
colonisation 6–7, 129, 134
Crown conservation reserves 130
cruelty 177
fencing 129, 131, 132–4
inspectors 127, 131, 135, 193–94
invasive species 112, 129–34, 184–5
legislation 6–7, 129–31
media 133
native species, persecution of 129
nature conservation 177, 184–5
New South Wales 130–1
prickly pear 184
property control 134–5
regulation 135
rural land governance 130–1
scientific underpinnings, lack of 134
**Victoria** *see also* **Melbourne, Victoria**
air pollution 270
bank notes and coins, waterfalls featured on 54
best practicable means standards 270
bushfires 218, 253
Clean Air Act 1958 45, 269
Conservation Council of Victoria (Environment Victoria) 79
Conservator of Forests, appointment of 249
Crown timber reserves to farmers, opposition to alienation of 261
Cultivation Advances Act 1927 108
Dandenong Ranges 102, 192, 202, 271
drought 108
exemption of liability for pollution 45
fencing 127
flooding 109
forestry governance 246–7, 249, 253, 261
Forests Act 1876 249
Forests Protection League 261
Grampians 202
Hattah-Kulkyne National Park 103
Heytesbury Settlement Scheme 102
indenture legislation 45
Little Desert, Victoria, protests against agriculture in 19, 46, 76–9, 103, 146
Little Desert mallee scrub to wheat and livestock farms, opening 65, 66
litigation 271
media 247
mining 261, 263, 268
Murray-Darling basin 37–8
myxomatosis, introduction of 129
national parks 63, 202, 205–7
nature conservation 182, 184–5
penguins, safeguarding and restoration of population of 308
Port Phillip Bay, restoration of coastal teatree forests alongside 309
property tenure 127
rabbits 125–7
River Murray Waters Agreement 40–1
Sludge Act 1885 263
Snowy Mountains 145–6
Soil Conservation Board 257
soldier settlement schemes 100–3
standing, public rights 12–13
Summerfield, compulsory acquisition and closure of town of 308
Town and Country Planning Act 1961 12–13, 228
Victorian Fisheries and Game Department 193–4

walking/hiking groups 200
zoos, restrictions on private 181–2
**Victoria, Queen** 35, 53

**Wadham, Samuel** 92–3
***Walkabout* magazine** 61, 102
**Walker, Kenneth** 266
**walking groups/clubs** 13–14, 175, 199–201, 206–7, 212–13, 217
**wallabies** 25, 54, 128, 184, 187, 189, 194–6
**Wallumedegal people** 69
**Walsh, Peter** 162–3
**waratah** 52
**Waratah, Tasmania, electrification of** 149
**Ward, Edward** 167
**Wardlaw, Henry** 168
**waste management** 268, 288, *see also* **pollution control**
**water** *see* **dams, drought; irrigation schemes; water management**
**water management,**
allocation of rights 5, 14, 17
**Aboriginal people** 95
Australian Water Resources Council 41
Canberra, greening 234, 241
Commonwealth 17, 37–8, 42, 81
Constitution 37–8, 41
Crown control 11, 93–94
dredging 261
droughts 107–9
irrigation schemes 40, 108, 137, 140–7, 153
Lake Pedder 71–74
marine 4, 37, 80, 189, 275, 283, 288, 291, 294
mining, pollution from 261–3
national parks 202
planning 221–2
pollution control 19, 45–6, 222, 261–2, 266–71
salinisation 107
sewage management 268
soil, water and forestry management, coordination of 43
Senate Select Committee reports 19
Snowy Mountains 144–5
standards, lack of 269
Water Conservation and Irrigation Commission 145
**Watson, Don** 28
**Webber, Horace** 265
**Weber, Max** 139
**wedge-tailed eagles** 102, 182
**Weindorfer, Gustav** 204–5
**Western Australia (WA)**
Aboriginal Heritage Act 1972 46
agricultural banks, state-run 102
atomic weapons testing 159–62, 163, 169
botanic gardens 182
cane toads 125
Clean Air Act 1964 269
clearing, fencing and cropping 99
colonisation 106
conditional purchase leases 99, 106
Conservator of Forests 252
Crown immunity 46
Crown land, purchase of 99
dingoes and wild dogs 133
Dirk Hartog Island 307
emus, slaughter of 131–2
fencing 127
film units 56
flag, black swan featured on 53
forestry governance 29, 251–3
Gondwana Link 33, 310
Group Settlement Scheme 99
Health Act 1911 268
Kings Park 214–16
kookaburras 196
mining 262–3
Monte Bello Islands, atomic weapons testing on 159–62, 163, 169
Native Flora Protection Act 1940 194
natural history societies 60
nature conservation 185
Noongar people, devastation of culture of 106
Ord River, damming of 137
pastoral leases 94–5
Perth 70, 132, 182, 196, 214–16, 291
pollution control 268–9
public inquiries 252
rabbits 127
railways, logging for 11
restoration 307, 310
ring-barking 106–7
Sand Drift Act 1889 254
secessionist movement 18
soil erosion 265, 257
stamps, natural heritage on 53
Swan River colony 53
Town Planning and Development Act 1928 224
Two People's Bay, re-discovery of noisy scrub-bird in 216

water pollution 268
Wheatbelt 106–7
wildlife corridors 310
**Weston, Thomas Charles** 239–40, 242
**Whalan, Douglas** 6
**whaling** 276–8
Antarctica 275, 276–8, 279, 283, 287, 288
Australian Whaling Commission 276
Commonwealth 277–8, 288
Convention for the Regulation of Whaling 1931 288
governance 276–8
greed and excess 276
International Convention for the Regulation of Whaling 1946 288
International Court of Justice (ICJ) 278
International Whaling Commission (IWC) 278, 288
Japan 273, 276, 278, 288
licences 288
media 276
New Zealand 277, 278
scientific research 278
shore-based whaling 276–7
stewardship, international context to 275
United Kingdom, end of industry in 277
Whaling Act 1935 288
Whaling Industry Act1949 276
Whaling Regulation Act 1934 (UK) 276
**White, Steven** 133, 177
**Whitelock, Derek** 271
**Whitlam, Gough** 18, 19–20, 42–3, 70–1, 74, 81, 84–5, 168, 311–13
**Whittington, Don** 271
**wholly protected species** 175, 183, 189
**Wilcox, Murray** 224
**wilderness** 197–201 *see also* **bush, taming the; Outback**
Aboriginal people 198, 199–200, 202
access, increase in 200–1
aesthetic and spiritual appreciation 197–8
Antarctica 274
Blue Gum Forest, NSW, campaign to save the 211
bushwalking 199–201
car ownership, increase in 200
colonisation 66, 197–8
cult of wilderness 197–8
cultural shifts 198, 200
fear or disdain of colonists 198
iconography 197–8
leisure time, increase in 200–1
mountaineering 200
national parks 197–8, 200–1
nature conservation 197
photographs 197, 202–3
primitive area language 90, 197
protests 66
stewardship 200
*terra nullius* doctrine 199
tourism 200–1
train tours 200
travel writers 201
unpeopled places narrative 198, 199, 202
walking/hiking groups/clubs 199–201
**wildlife** *see also* **birds; invasive/foreign species; kangaroos; koalas; nature conservation; nature reserves and wildlife sanctuaries; threatened fauna; thylacines; vermin control**
army mascots, as 30, 54
bandicoots 158, 184, 189
Canberra, greening 240–3
cats 26, 54, 112, 128, 133, 184, 293, 204
charismatic species 17, 29, 175, 176, 183, 187–8, 195
conservation 189–92
corridors, habit 310
cruelty to animals 175, 177
dogs 25, 54, 125, 129, 131, 133–4, 183, 290, 307
fashion, campaigns against trade in fur and feathers for 60
flying foxes 23, 129–30, 133, 183, 192
foxes 114, 158, 184–5
importing exotic fauna 240–1
noxious species 25, 99, 112–13, 129, 189–90, 222, 237
Orchardfield 23–5
partly protected species 183
planning 222
quolls 26, 121, 128, 130, 180, 184, 189, 305
seals, fur and elephant 292–3, 294
unprotected species 183–4, 188, 189–90, 192
valuing wildlife 175–6
wholly protected species 175, 183, 189
wombats 25, 54, 127, 134, 177, 184, 189, 192
**Windeyer, WJV** 48
**Wollongong, NSW, fast-track approval of coal loading facility at** 45

**wombats** 25, 54, 127, 134, 177, 184, 189, 192
**women**
lobby groups 70, 215–16
rural life 89
vote, right to 12
wildlife, use of 186
Women's Service Guild 215
**Wooding, Robert** 140
**Woolloomooloo, name of Sydney suburb** 305
**World Heritage listings** 20, 79, 81, 137, 143, 205, 291–4, 311
**Wran, Neville** 70
**Wright, Judith** 59, 66, 79, 110
**writing**
academic writing 314
children's books 57–8
nature writers 57–9, 61–3, 175–6
Outback 156
poetry 23, 27, 33, 50, 59, 73, 79, 137, 202, 248, 266
rabbits 126–7
travel writers 58–9, 200–1
**Yarra River, Melbourne** 54, 268
**York Main, Barbara** 28
**Young, Blamire** 52
**Young, Elspeth** 213
**Young, Liz** 64

**zoning** 44, 223–5, 239, 268–9, *see also* **town and land use planning**
**zoos** 175, 177–82
Beaumaris Zoo, Tasmania 132, 180–1
breeding programmes 181–2
colonisation 178
hunting 182
media 181
Melbourne Zoo 180–1
public engagement 181–2
public opinion 182
Queensland, fauna reserve in 181
science and education 181
Taronga Zoo, Sydney, opening of 180
thylacines, extinction of 132, 180–1
Victoria, restrictions on private zoos in 181–2

www.ingramcontent.com/pod-product-compliance
Ingram Content Group UK Ltd.
Pitfield, Milton Keynes, MK11 3LW, UK
UKHW020233290926
15470UKWH00002B/526

9 781509 969029